The Poor Among Us

A History of Family Poverty and Homelessness in New York City

Ralph da Costa Nunez
and Ethan G. Sribnick

Foreword by Leonard N. Stern

White Tiger Press — New York

© 2013 The Institute for Children, Poverty, and Homelessness
44 Cooper Square, 4th Floor
New York, NY 10003
E-mail: info@ICPHusa.org

Cover image: Collection of the New-York Historical Society, 79722d
Book design: Alice Fisk MacKenzie

Note on quotations:
Every effort has been made to quote historical sources as they were written, including, in some cases, errors and irregularities in spelling and grammar.

Published by:
White Tiger Press
44 Cooper Square, 4th Floor
New York, NY 10003

Library of Congress Cataloging-in-Publication Data is available

ISBN 978-0-9825533-4-3

Printed in the United States of America

Contents

Foreword

It has been twenty-six years since I first ventured into the world of homelessness. Recognizing that homelessness was in fact a family and, more importantly, a children's issue, I helped found Homes for the Homeless, a nonprofit organization based in New York City that houses over 530 families and 1,000 children every day. We have served over 47,000 families and 65,000 children, over 112,000 people, during the last quarter-century. In 1990 we founded the Institute for Children, Poverty, and Homelessness to investigate the causes of and solutions to family homelessness, as well as to bring together experts on both the policy and practice sides. Yet in spite of all the good work of these organizations, and others like them across the country, family homelessness is still present in virtually every community.

I never thought I would be involved with the issue of homelessness for so long, but I have, and plan to continue that involvement and dedication. In a nation of such wealth, it may seem baffling that the story of family homelessness could be allowed to go on for so many years. But it has, and we should not be surprised. Homelessness has a history that reaches back to the earliest colonial settlements.

The purpose of *The Poor Among Us* is to look back at the history of family poverty and homelessness in New York City, from the early Dutch settlements on Manhattan Island to the twenty-first century and the Bloomberg administration of today. From the beginning, homelessness has taken many turns and manifested itself in unexpected ways. Solutions from the past are still being used today to meet the needs of poor families. We have gone from the almshouses and "outdoor relief" of colonial times to the welfare hotels, shelters, and income supports of the present.

Within that context, a story unfolds, one of women and children who have lived in workhouses, in orphanages, in alleyways, and even on the street. It is not a pretty picture, but it is a real one. It is a sad but important story, and one that needs to be told.

As you read through these pages, a raw poverty emerges, showing the adversity and tragedy faced by New York's destitute and homeless families. However, it is not simply a story of despair. The history of poverty and homelessness in New York City has given us over 300 years of lessons learned, and in some cases forgotten, but always containing the seeds of hope.

Today 45 percent of the American public is either poor or near poor, and many of them will at one time or another experience homelessness. Until we have wiped this scourge from the cities and towns of our nation, our job is not done. In many ways, it is still just beginning.

For me, along with so many others, the work goes on, and it is my hope that the story encompassed in the pages that follow will get others to join our mission and achieve our goal of a time when no child or parent in America will have to call a shelter a home.

— Leonard N. Stern
Founder and Chair

Institute for Children, Poverty, and Homelessness
and Homes for the Homeless

Preface

Over the last three decades in New York City, the number of families and children experiencing homelessness has exploded. What was once a small problem involving hundreds of single adults and dozens of families has grown into a great problem encompassing thousands of adults and families with young children.

For the past thirty years I have been on the front lines of the fight against family homelessness in New York City. In the early 1980s, in the office of then-Mayor Ed Koch, I witnessed thousands of families with children turning to the city for shelter. Neither I, nor anyone else at that time, had any idea that this crisis would continue into the twenty-first century. In fact, the problem is much worse today than it was then; there are now more homeless families in New York City than at any time since the Great Depression.

What we did not fully understand in the 1980s was that this rise in family homelessness was an outgrowth of a new poverty that affected families who were largely disconnected from the mainstream economy. Parents, usually young single mothers, had little education and haphazard work experience. Public social programs remained their primary source of income, but that was not enough to meet the basic human needs of food and shelter. This new poverty persisted through economic booms, but in economic downturns it swelled, with more and more families teetering on the edge of destitution and homelessness. We were witnessing the creation of a new generation of "poverty nomads" who cycled in and out of public systems but who were unable to gain access to the opportunities that would help lift them into the middle class.

In the context of the late twentieth and early twenty-first centuries, this type of family poverty is indeed new, but not historically unprecedented. The families committed to the poorhouse in eighteenth-century New York, the children sent away from their families on "orphan trains" to the Midwest in the mid-nineteenth century, the parents in the late nineteenth century forced to place some of their children in congregate institutions so that the rest of the family could survive—these were all predecessors of today's poor and homeless families.

The goal of this book is to share what we have learned about this long history of family poverty in New York City. We have described the experience of poverty in different eras in the city's history, to understand the extent of the similarity between the poor families of the past and those of the present. We have also cataloged the many efforts to end or ameliorate poverty among New York's families. From all of this we have learned that when it comes to family poverty, there are no quick fixes. Even the most ambitious and successful anti-poverty efforts — the reforms of the Progressive Era, the legislation of the New Deal, and the programs of the War on Poverty — failed to lift every family to stability.

There are, however, valuable lessons to be learned. We cannot abandon the efforts begun by our predecessors to improve the lives of poor families. This history shows that we should understand our limitations and be wary of snappy slogans and simple ideas. But it also demonstrates that, tempered by the successes and failures of the past, we can craft pragmatic policies that will truly improve the lives of poor and homeless families, both in New York and across the country.

— Ralph da Costa Nunez
New York City, March 2013

Introduction

On February 12, 1834 Bridget McPhalen and her two sons, four-year-old Patrick and one-year-old John, made the trip uptown to Twenty-first Street, then the outer limits of New York City. Here they entered Bellevue, a complex of buildings along the East River surrounded on three sides by ominous eleven-foot walls. One massive bluestone structure, the largest building in the city, dominated the campus. This was New York City's public almshouse, the destination for McPhalen and her young children, who sought shelter from the cold winter. McPhalen, a forty-year-old Irish immigrant, told the managers of the almshouse that she was married; her husband had either gone to look for work or abandoned his family. McPhalen and her children resided in the almshouse through the winter and spring before being discharged on July 24, 1834.[1]

On January 14, 2002 Jackie Fuller and her two children, sixteen-year-old Shanna and twelve-year-old Darian, made the long trek from the East New York section of Brooklyn, where they had been living with relatives in an overcrowded apartment, to the Bronx. They carried their possessions in three suitcases, their destination a nondescript single-story brick building on 151st Street. Arriving that evening, Fuller and her family entered the bright, windowless rooms of the Emergency Assistance Unit (EAU), the city's intake center for homeless families. A forty-four-year-old, black New York City native, Fuller had recently returned from Memphis, where she had lived and worked since 1994. As she explained to the workers at the EAU, Fuller's marriage had dissolved, and, unable to find work, she could not afford housing for her family. After spending that night in a facility in the Bronx, the family received temporary placement in a studio apartment in a dilapidated building on Ocean Avenue in Brooklyn. They would remain there for over a month before the city notified them that they were eligible for placement in a private, nonprofit transitional shelter.[2]

The stories of the McPhalens and the Fullers are separated by 168 years and a host of other differences. The world of modern New York City in which Jackie Fuller lived would have been unimaginable for Bridget McPhalen. The barrier of race might make it difficult for the white, Irish McPhalens to identify with the black Fullers. The terminology used to discuss these families in their own times would also be different; the McPhalens were "paupers," the Fullers a "homeless family." The roles of city, state, and local government in these two eras might also create divergent sets of expectations for the two families. Yet, for all that changed, the experiences of these families—both headed by single mothers appealing to the city for shelter, for their very survival—were strikingly similar.

This book asks why these similarities exist. Why, after all this time, are there still families, like the Fullers, unable to afford basic human necessities, including housing? The answer is to be found in the complex mix of economic, social, and structural forces responsible for the development of New York City as it exists today. Only by examining the experiences of poor families within the context of New York's growth can we come to understand what has changed and what has not. This book examines the continuity and change that define the story of New York's most destitute families—from the beginnings of the city, in the 1620s, to the present. The purpose of this examination is twofold. First, in a time when New York has some 10,000 homeless families with children, this book provides a deep investigation of how we got to this point, uncovering the series of circumstances that led to this sad state. Second, it describes the experience of family poverty in the past and in the present, explaining what has driven families into poverty, what institutions they have turned to for support, and which policies and thinkers have influenced the structure of their lives. It is at the level of the family, and the individuals who make up families, that this sense of continuity and change becomes clear.

Few have explored the dynamic of family poverty—as distinct from individual poverty—over such a long period. This book does so in a single locale, New York City.[3] Poverty has existed in New York as long as, if not longer than, it has anywhere in the United States. And today, New York confronts family poverty and homelessness in greater numbers than any other community in the country. Over its long history New York has served as a laboratory in the experimental efforts to confront the problems of poverty and homelessness. Many of the ideas for fighting family poverty either originated in New York City or reached their fullest expression in this great metropolis. This book looks to examine the history of New York City as a model for understanding urban family poverty in the United States.

The Poor Among Us examines the experiences of poor families across eight distinct eras. In each of these periods, a particular constellation of economic, intellectual, and institutional forces transformed the lives of these families. Put another way, the experience of family poverty was and is dependent upon economics—the nature of the New York economy and the cycle of expansion and contraction; ideas—conceptions of what caused poverty and how best to ameliorate it; and institutions—which public and private entities helped provide for the poor. In each of these areas, a clear pattern of continuity and change demonstrates how, in so many ways, family poverty is very different today from what it was in the past—and how, at the same time, there are experiences that are essentially the same.

Economic Forces

New York, with its deep, protected harbor, became active first in the trade economy, creating great instability for those who worked in the ports, due to the seasonal nature of the work and the varying value of goods being transported around the world. In the nineteenth century, trade gave way to manufacturing, increasing the number of jobs for unskilled workers but also creating a labor market with marked uncertainty. In good times work was plentiful, but during the many economic downturns of the nineteenth and twentieth centuries, work disappeared. Each of these recessions and depressions had deep costs for families with fewer resources. Shops and factories closed. Particular industries disappeared. The loss of work sent families spiraling into poverty. In the late twentieth century, manufacturing in New York became unprofitable and was replaced by a service economy. This transformation created widespread economic suffering for those families who could not find work at decent wages.

During these cycles of boom and bust, New York continued to grow. From a small Dutch outpost of fewer than 1,000 people on the southern tip of Manhattan, New York blossomed into a city of more than eight million, covering 301 square miles over five boroughs. A good economy in New York has frequently acted as a magnet, pulling in people from around the world. Irish and German immigrants dominated this process for much of the nineteenth century. Italians and Eastern European Jews arrived in large numbers in the late nineteenth and early twentieth centuries. Beginning in the 1920s blacks, both migrants from the American South and immigrants from the Caribbean, flowed into the city. After World War II these groups were joined by a massive influx of Puerto Ricans. Since the 1970s immigrants from Asia, Central and South America, Africa, and Eastern Europe have transformed New York's neighborhoods and places of work. When the economy has soured, these successive waves of transplants have largely remained anchored in New York, riding out the economic storm. The result has been broad shifts in the ethnicity of poor and homeless families, from Irish and German, to Italian and Jewish, to black and Puerto Rican, to an ever more diverse mix.

Intellectual Forces

The shifting interpretations among New York's public and private leaders concerning the causes of poverty have had deep implications for poor families. The dominant belief for most of the eighteenth and nineteenth centuries was that poverty stemmed from flaws in the poor themselves. These shortcomings could be religious: a lack of piety on the part of the poor family. Or they could be behavioral: a family could be the victim of its own laziness and indolence. Or they could be habitual: poverty could be based in drunkenness or other immoral tendencies. Public and private efforts to ameliorate poverty through the nineteenth century comprised attempts to reform the poor through a mix of religion and punitive measures so that they could better provide for their families.

The Depression of 1893 and the response of a new generation of reformers, in what became known as the Progressive Era, challenged this earlier perspective. Progressives observed that structural economic factors, such as economic downturns, often created poverty, and that the environments in which the poor lived and worked perpetuated their poverty, while also making these families vulnerable to physical dangers and deadly disease. These new ideas were reflected in a series of measures to assist the poor in the early twentieth century and, during the Great Depression, in the legislation that created the American welfare state. In the late twentieth century, however, the framework of this welfare state came under attack as reforms, echoing the beliefs of the nineteenth century, attempted to alter the behavior of the poor and create strong incentives for them to enter the workforce.

Changing perceptions of childhood have played a large role in shaping policies and organizations' actions on behalf of poor families. In the 1830s, with the emergence of middle-class notions of childhood as a separate stage of development in need of protection, the precarious lives of poor children first became a concern. That in turn catalyzed efforts to remove children from institutions such as the almshouse, to make institutions for children more "homelike," to find substitute homes for poor children who lacked supervision, to end child labor, and to build public playgrounds. Even today the desire to provide the best opportunity for children — especially poor children — influences the direction of social policy.

Interpretations of the causes of family poverty have also been closely related to discussions of housing. Today we would call New York's most destitute families — such as the Fullers — homeless families. In previous eras no such term existed. Concern about the homes of the poor first arose in the 1840s, when an epidemic of children working and living on the street gave great urgency to the issue. Reformers, such as Charles Loring Brace, became concerned not only about whether children had roofs over their heads, but also whether they had appropriate "homes" to provide them with an idyllic childhood. Over the late nineteenth century, however, homelessness came to refer not to children or families, but almost exclusively to single men. At the same time, reformers began to focus on the shortcomings in housing for the poor. A series of laws, culminating in the Tenement House Act of 1901, helped ameliorate the worst aspects of poor sanitation and overcrowding in poor people's housing. But such laws did little to help poor families find decent and affordable homes. Urban-renewal projects often simply pushed poor families to the edges of the city. Even public housing provided only a small number of units for the poorest New Yorkers. This dearth of housing for the city's most destitute families came to a head in the 1980s, when thousands appealed to the city each year for shelter, ushering in an era of family homelessness that continues today.

Institutional Forces

From the beginning, providing for New York's poor and homeless families was a joint public and private venture. Religious congregations, some charged with a public duty, became the first institutions to take on poverty. As a system of public municipal relief developed, churches and synagogues remained as providers for the poor. The balance between private and public efforts has shifted over time. After the construction of the first municipal almshouse, in 1736, the city came to play a more dominant role in the provision of relief for poor families, both within the poorhouse and for families within their own homes. New, private organizations that developed in the nineteenth century, such as the Society for the Relief of Poor Widows with Small Children, were motivated by a desire to keep families out of the almshouse, which they viewed as a danger to the souls of upstanding individuals. The nineteenth century saw a proliferation of nominally private institutions that often served a public function and received public support. These included, in particular, institutions for children, such as the House of Refuge and the Colored Orphans' Asylum. One of the most influential private organizations of the nineteenth century, however, was strongly anti-institutional in its approach. The Children's Aid Society worked to place children in private homes rather than institutions. Catholic and Jewish organizations took the opposite approach, setting up massive congregate institutions to help provide for the children of their coreligionists.

Meanwhile, public-assistance rolls continued to grow over most of the nineteenth century, as the city, controlled by political machines, saw the appeal to voters of a generous system of relief. In reaction, in 1876 reformers successfully cut off all cash relief in New York City. From that time until 1931, virtually all relief in New York was private, mostly under the supervision of New York's powerful Charity Organization Society. That trend was upended during the Great Depression, when the state and then national government joined with the city in a new commitment to take public responsibility for the poor. The late twentieth century saw a revival of efforts to use private organizations to provide for poor and homeless families; still, as in the past, these are largely partnerships in which the ultimate responsibility for New York's neediest lies with the public.

Much of the narrative in this book is told at a macro level, demonstrating how economic, intellectual, and institutional forces shaped the lives of poor families. But the book's ultimate focus is experiential, concerned with explaining how individuals fared amid these forces. At the heart of every family is a child or children. These children, who frequently experienced the worst suffering, most often caught the interest of reformers hoping to improve the lives of the poor. Today, with a city and nation still suffering an epidemic of childhood poverty, it is important that we better understand the history of such children and the costs of poverty in their fragile lives. The stories of children from the past — such as those in the McPhalen and Fuller families — are the ones this book proudly tells.

Settlements in Manhattan and what would become Brooklyn. Published in 1776, this map indicates the extent of development in both locations. *Lawrence H. Slaughter Collection, The Lionel Pincus and Princess Firyal Map Division, The New York Public Library, Astor, Lenox, and Tilden Foundations.*

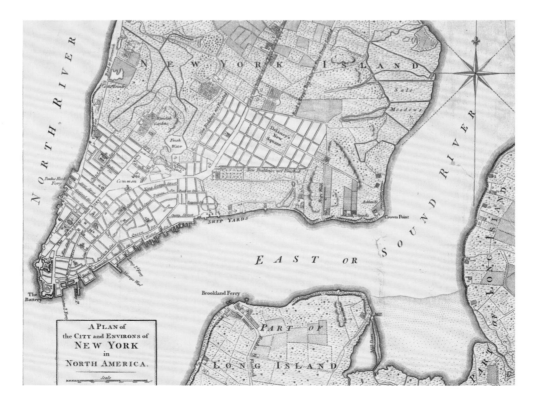

Chapter 1

Poor and Homeless Families in Colonial New York

June 1738: a Danish woman and her children were on a return voyage to Denmark, from the island of St. Thomas, when their ship caught fire and sank. Rescued and taken to the port of New York, the family entered the city with no possessions or means of support.

October 1739: Anna Maria Sneyder of New York, a single mother, went blind. The city leaders decided that her son would be sent away as an apprentice — when he was old enough; at the time he was all of five.

December 1739: Mary Green, a New York resident and mother of two, was badly burned. The city leaders instructed that the elder child be bound out — that is, contracted as a servant or apprentice — as soon as possible. In the meantime, the family could not live on its own.

November 1746: Four-year-old Pearey Phagan was found by himself, "his father and mother having left the city" of New York.[1]

In their turn these children and families headed down New York's notoriously crooked streets to a new residence. On the way they passed brick houses several stories high, built in the Old Dutch style, with gables facing the streets and balconies on many roofs.[2] At last they approached the edges of the city's developed area, at what is now Chambers Street. There, on the northern end of where City Hall Park is today, stood the place of last resort: a two-story stone structure, fifty-six feet long and twenty-four feet wide, looming large over the unimproved lands to the north as it did over the lives of poor and homeless families. This was the New York Municipal Almshouse.[3]

Colonial New York was an unstable place. The port brought a constant flow of goods and individuals in and out of the city; the seasonality of trade made work, and income, plentiful in good weather but scarce in the winter. Most families in the city seemed to live just above the level of subsistence. A bad stretch in the economy, a bout of disease, or a tragic injury could easily push a family into destitution.

As would remain true throughout New York's history, women—who struggled to provide for their children after divorces from, desertion by, or the deaths of their husbands—headed the poorest families. The city helped many women and children in need by providing fuel, food, or cash and by facilitating the practice of binding out. For the most desperate of families, and for orphaned or abandoned children, there was the almshouse, or poorhouse, given a permanent structure in 1736 after being housed in a series of rented buildings.

In theory, separate institutions would address the situations of the aged and disabled, the able-bodied poor unable to find jobs, and "vagrants" who refused to work.[4] In New York the common council, the city's ruling body, combined these different functions in the almshouse. The new institution was, therefore, intended to serve two divergent ends. On the one hand it was meant as a deterrent to the "Idle Wandering Vagrants" and "Sturdy Beggars," potentially dangerous, rootless men who entered the city. The poorhouse would either train these men in the rigors of labor and imbue them with a work ethic or serve as a punishment for their laziness. On the other hand, the poorhouse and the larger system of relief were intended to provide refuge for those families and individuals who, due to misfortune, could not be expected to work.

The decisions of the common council and other leaders of early New York, however, were grounded in misperception. The council was alarmed by those "living Idly," fearing that the "unimployed become debauched and Instructed in the Practice of Thievery and Debauchery" and viewing the single, unemployed male vagrant as a threat to society.[5] Yet women and children, many in families, rather than single men, made up the largest percentage of relief recipients during the colonial era. The response to poverty over the eighteenth and into the nineteenth centuries, then, was often driven by the image of male vagabonds unwilling to labor rather than the reality of families forced into destitution by the deaths or illnesses of wage-earning husbands and fathers, the strains of immigrating, or simple misfortune.

Poverty grew along with the city. From the Dutch settlement of New Amsterdam—later to become New York—in the 1620s to the American Revolution, the city was transformed from a trading post in the Dutch empire to a major port connecting the British colonies with the mother country. As the city's economy developed, immigrants from Europe and other colonies were drawn to the burgeoning metropolis. From a village of only 150 to 200 houses and about a thousand people in 1645, New York grew to become the third-largest city in North America by 1760 and the largest city in the newly independent United States as of 1790. One effect of this sometimes-rapid population growth, and of the variability of the trade economy, was the increasing number of people who struggled to stay fed, clothed, and housed. As city leaders confronted this growing problem,

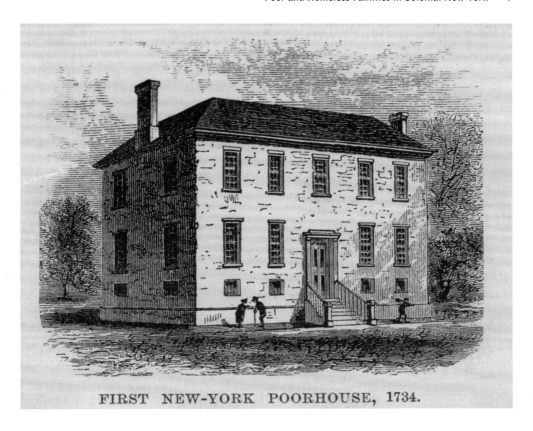

FIRST NEW-YORK POORHOUSE, 1734.

New York's first poorhouse. Opened in 1736 (misdated above) on the outskirts of town in what is today City Hall Park, the poorhouse (or "almshouse") grouped the unemployed, the homeless, and the sick under one roof. *Picture Collection, The New York Public Library, Astor, Lenox and Tilden Foundations.*

they initiated two practices that would have a long trajectory in the social policies of the city: they attempted to limit the public costs of caring for the poor, and they tried to make the receipt of public aid an unattractive option for those in need.[6] In spite of these practices, so-called poor relief was consistently the largest item in the New York City budget throughout the colonial period.[7]

Over the colonial era a series of economic transformations and acute crises — fires, war, influxes of refugees — all created instability that often undermined parents' ability to provide for their families or left the families without shelter. In response to each of these crises, the colonial leaders found various ways to deal with the poor and dislocated. The institutions and legal structures developed in the colonial era would have lasting influence on the lives of poor and homeless families over much of the nineteenth century.

The Colonial Origins of Poverty Relief

By 1626 the Dutch had established a permanent settlement on the island of Manhattan, naming it New Amsterdam. There, the settlers constructed Fort Amsterdam to protect their colonial claim and built thirty houses out of tree bark, as well as a stone counting house. Moving away from the southern tip of Manhattan, some settlers cleared and planted fields for farms, also called *bouweries*. New Amsterdam soon became the nexus of the colony of New Netherlands, connecting widespread frontier outposts engaged in the fur trade.[8] Of course, native peoples—the Lenape—already lived on Manhattan Island and amid the surrounding areas that the Dutch had settled. From the perspective of the Europeans, the Lenape appeared to be in a permanent state of poverty. Surrounded by natural resources, they were content to subsist through hunting, fishing, and basic farming. To the Dutch they were simply *wilden,* or savages.[9] From another point of view, just the opposite was true. For native communities the great inequalities of wealth that would haunt European societies were nonexistent. Power and prestige in these societies was often gained by providing for those who needed assistance. Homelessness, except among those who had been banished, was unheard of.[10]

As the English would later, Dutch settlers brought with them their own systems of social organization and transplanted their own approaches to caring for the less fortunate. In the small community that developed into New Amsterdam, the ties among neighbors and congregation members provided most relief for the poor. The Dutch Reformed Church, the primary source of social assistance in the Netherlands, administered aid to the destitute in the new colony. Ministers were in charge of collecting donations for that purpose. Most aid was provided in the recipients' homes; however, following the practice in Holland, the Reformed Church in New Netherland also established almshouses, or deacons' houses. Unlike the English institutions that would later supplant them and provide shelter for a range of individuals, the deacons' houses were reserved for the elderly impoverished. The church also helped care for the sick, with trained *sieckentroosters* (comforters of the sick) visiting the homes of the seriously ill and offering spiritual guidance. The support of the poor by the Reformed Church took on something of a public character. New Amsterdam was a heterogeneous society, with English Puritans and Quakers; Swedish, German, and Finnish Lutherans; and Jewish immigrants from Holland and Brazil. In most cases these religious communities looked after their own, but the Reformed Church was expected, if necessary, to care for all of the poor.[11]

Still, the Dutch Reformed Church provided support mostly for coreligionists, creating a congregational system that would remain in use by the Dutch community after the English conquest. Other Dutch approaches to social welfare, administered by state rather than church institutions, were forerunners of later English practice. Dutch authorities imported orphans from Holland and bound them out as servants, a practice that would be replicated in English efforts to aid poor and orphaned children. A Dutch orphan was typically bound to a master for two to four years. Once the term expired, the child could choose to renew the contract or remain free and receive up to about fifty acres of land in the Dutch colony. A girl who married was immediately released from her contract. While alleviating poverty in the mother country, this practice also populated the colony with orphans from the homeland.[12] The structure of the first "poor law," passed in 1661, anticipated an issue that would concern New York for decades after the end of Dutch rule: residency. The law limited assistance in New Amsterdam to those who were settled residents of the city, in an effort to keep vagrants from other towns or colonies from receiving aid. The struggle to limit aid to those officially settled would be a constant one for the port city, an entry point for both Europeans and those from other colonies.[13]

The fall of New Amsterdam to the English, in 1664, transformed the colony and the experience of poor families. In the short run, the terms of surrender for the Dutch colony maintained the status quo. The language, culture, and property of the Dutch remained intact, and the Reformed Church was able to collect taxes, hold religious services in Dutch, and oversee the provisions for the poor and sick that had been developed in New Netherland.[14] Still, the Duke of York, proprietor of the colony of New York and the future King

Fort Amsterdam. This 1908 etching depicts Fort Amsterdam, on the southern tip of Manhattan, in 1626. *Picture Collection, The New York Public Library, Astor, Lenox and Tilden Foundations.*

James II, quietly moved to develop English practices in his new holding. The successive governors of New York, appointed by the duke, carefully navigated between the existing Dutch structures and the desire to impose English practice. In terms of poverty relief, the English governors did not disturb the practices of the largely Dutch stronghold of what had become New York City; instead, they created a system of taxation and care for the poor that applied only to the English communities surrounding the city. For some time, this "patchwork" system was effective. New York governor Edmund Andros reported in 1678 that the colony had "noe beggars but all poore cared for."[15]

In 1683 Thomas Dongan, the newly appointed governor of New York, allowed for the first elected assembly for the colony. This new legislative body quickly began developing a code of uniform laws for New York, including a system of municipal taxation and support for the poor that displaced the Dutch practices still in place in New York City. As was the case in other English colonies, this law was patterned after the Elizabethan Poor Law of 1601. Care for the poor was to be a public responsibility, with taxes collected specifically

Old Reformed Dutch Church, Fulton Street, 1776. As the official church of the colony of New Netherlands, the Dutch Reformed Church was the city's first purveyor of social assistance. *Eno Collection, Miriam and Ira D. Wallach Division of Art, Prints and Photographs, The New York Public Library, Astor, Lenox and Tilden Foundations.*

OLD REFORMED DUTCH CHURCH 1776.
Formerly standing in Fulton St. near Smith St.
Drawn by Mrs Elizabeth Sleight in 1809.

for that purpose. This responsibility would be based at the local level; each county in the colony was given autonomy in deciding how to implement its system of relief. Accordingly, each county was responsible for providing relief only for legal residents of that county. This gave rise to many disputes over where people legally resided, and counties spent a great deal of time and energy challenging claims of residency and transporting the poor to places where they became charges of other localities. In most cases individuals were settled in the counties of their birth, unless the individual had resided in another county for two years without becoming a public charge. The law regarding settlement was also intended to be preventive. Newcomers to a locality were required to demonstrate that they would not become a drain on the public coffers. If they had no identifiable trade or skills, counties could demand that they put up security to indemnify the locality against the possible cost if they ended up on the poor rolls.[16]

The final piece of the English system of poor relief in New York was a legal structure that facilitated binding out poor and abandoned children as apprentices and servants. An indenture was a contractual agreement in which a master agreed to care for and train a child in return for his or her labor. Much of the system of poverty relief in the colony was dedicated to initiating and attempting to oversee such indentures.[17] Twelve-year-old Thomas Hill, to give one typical example, was apprenticed with the consent of his guardian, William Hollins, to Christopher Gilliard, a cordwainer—or shoemaker—in New York City. According to the indenture, Hill was not to "Committ Fornication nor Contract Matrimony" during his seven-year term; he was also barred from playing "Cards, Dice or any other unlawful Game." In addition, the agreement required that he receive permission for any absences and that he not "haunt Ale houses, Taverns or Playhouses." Gillard, for his part, was required to provide "sufficient meat drinke Apparell Lodging and washing" and to "teach his said Apprentice in seaven years to read and write English and in the Cordwainer's Trade." At the successful conclusion of this term, Gillard was to give Hill two new suits of clothing.[18]

In order to manage the affairs of the growing city, the governor granted a charter, effective as of 1684, that divided New York into wards, with an alderman and an assistant elected from each ward. The aldermen and assistants, along with a mayor and recorder appointed by the governor, constituted the common council, which was authorized to make laws and ordinances for the city. In the hierarchical society that was colonial New York, the right to vote or hold office, to be a "freeman," depended largely on status. One could be a freeman by birth, but to earn the status one had to train as an apprentice in a trade or become a merchant. No poor people, servants, slaves, apprentices, or women were, in the language of the day, "free"; they were dependent upon others and, therefore, were barred from full citizenship. Indenture, the placing of poor children in positions as servants or apprentices, could be a path, at least for boys, to becoming freemen.[19]

To oversee the system of caring for the poor, the city's freemen would, each January, elect two churchwardens. These officials evaluated the claims of those in need and, when appropriate, distributed the funds collected through the poor tax. Given the requirement that the city care only for its own poor, the churchwardens attempted, whenever possible, to transport poor families out of the city or even the colony. In 1720, for instance, the common council provided eight shillings and six pence for the transportation expenses of Ann Thorp and her three children to Woodbridge, New Jersey, where her husband resided. At times the city would even pay for transportation overseas. In 1723 the church-wardens granted fifty shillings to Christian Tobias, on the condition that "the said Chris-tian Tobias & his wife & children transport themselves … to Antegua without Delay that they be no longer a charge to the Parish."[20]

When a poor family were confirmed residents of the city, the churchwardens usually provided what was known as "outdoor relief," that is, relief provided to recipients in their own homes. The churchwardens, for instance, gave Mary Fryar Wido "thirty shillings towards the Support and Relief of her and three Small Children who are Objects of Char-ity."[21] While some families received cash, more common was relief in kind, such as fire-wood, food, or clothing. At times the city provided assistance in the form of medical care or even funeral expenses.[22] Much of this support was seasonal, corresponding to hardship brought on by the slowdown in work during the winter months. Relief rates also increased in response to economic downturns or epidemics that led to lost work and, therefore, lost wages.[23] The assistance that religious institutions, such as the Dutch Reformed Church, gave to their members kept the rates of public aid relatively low. Still, relief of the poor became an accepted function of city government in colonial New York. This did not mean, however, that receiving relief was without stigma. Beginning in 1707 the common council required recipients to wear on their right shoulders badges of red or blue cloth reading "N:Y." Without the badges they would be considered ineligible for relief. The frequency with which the officials supervising the relief system repeated this proclamation indicates the difficulty in getting recipients to comply and the concerted effort to denote the depen-dent status of so-called paupers.[24]

The alternative to "outdoor relief" was "indoor relief"—assistance to the poor re-siding in an almshouse. In the early years of English rule in New York, the government was hesitant to commit to building a structure to house the truly destitute. As a halfway measure, the city would, at times, appropriate money to board an indigent individual with a neighbor who acted as a caretaker. In 1700 the city rented a house on Broad Street as a place to care for the poor as well as "a house of Correction for the punishing of Vagabonds and Idle persons that are a nuisance and Common Grievance."[25] Between 1712 and 1735, though, less than 10 percent of relief recipients on average were placed in this rented alms-

CITY HALL AND GREAT DOCK, 1679.

City Hall, the Great Dock and the harbor, 1679. New York was first and foremost a port town. *Picture Collection, The New York Public Library, Astor, Lenox and Tilden Foundations.*

house, with most poor families receiving outdoor relief. [26] Of the 187 children on the relief rolls during those years, approximately 26 were boarded with neighbors, and at most five entered the almshouse. The evidence suggests that most, if not all, of the children relocated to private homes and the almshouse were orphans. Before 1736, then, the poorhouse remained predominantly the domain of elderly widows or men too old or too sick to work. [27]

For most of the early eighteenth century, the system of poverty relief overseen by the churchwardens adequately cared for the truly destitute of the city. Temporary crises, however, created acute social-welfare challenges for the city government. The mass immigration of Palatine Germans, in 1710, created the first crisis of family homelessness in New York City. The ranks of these Protestant Germans from the Rhine Valley had been decimated by decades of violent religious conflict in the German principalities. Most recently, the French invasion of the Rhineland, in 1707, had left an epidemic and famine in its wake, pushing the Palatines into destitution. Seeking assistance from a Protestant monarch, they appealed to Queen Anne of Britain, who agreed to settle a large number of German immigrants in New York's sparsely populated Hudson River Valley. When more than 2,800 Germans sailed for New York City, in April 1710, no one appeared to have considered how the city, with a population of fewer than 6,000, would house, even temporarily, this massive influx of immigrants. By the time the Palatines arrived, in the summer, 446 had died on the voyage and many others were too weak or sick to work.[28] With the Palatines quarantined on Nutten (now Governors) Island, the city hurriedly constructed houses and hospitals and pitched tents to provide makeshift shelter. Still, hundreds of immigrants died over the summer. To address the problem Governor Robert Hunter ordered that the children among the Germans be apprenticed. Eighty-four children were bound out, several against the will of their parents; of these, forty-one were apprenticed to masters in New York City. The Palatine crisis was finally resolved when most of the immigrants were transported to tracts of land surrounding the Hudson, although about 350 of the Germans, mostly widows and orphans, remained and settled in New York City.[29] As late as 1713 the churchwardens budgeted fifteen shillings for an "Old Palatine Man," a legitimate "object of charity," to purchase "shirts & etc."

Most families in early eighteenth-century New York lived on the cusp of destitution. Of the city's population of 8,622, according to a 1730 census, nearly three-fifths held

Robert Hunter, colonial governor of New York, 1710–20. To relieve the Palatine immigration crisis, Hunter ordered that the children of the new immigrants be apprenticed to masters in New York regardless of the families' wishes. *Print Collection, Miriam and Ira D. Wallach Division of Art, Prints and Photographs, The New York Public Library, Astor, Lenox and Tilden Foundations.*

property of £10 or less, a quite meager amount. These families lived at or near subsistence level, with women and children, largely dependent on what men earned, particularly vulnerable to falling into poverty.[30] While both single and married women worked outside the home, especially in poorer households, their incomes alone were rarely enough to support families.[31] Furthermore, English common law placed severe restrictions on the property and earnings of married women. Unless they took specific legal action, women lost control of any property they owned before marriage and became ineligible to buy or control property once they were married. Any earnings a married woman might receive automatically became the property of her husband. When a husband died without a will, the wife received a life interest in one-third of any real property he owned, but all personal property and the remaining real property automatically became the inheritance of the oldest male child. All this made it virtually impossible for a married woman to save wealth to support herself in the case of her husband's death.[32] It should be no surprise, then, that most recipients of public relief in the colonial era were women and children.

Families in the Almshouse

"The Nessessity, Number and Continual Increase of the Poor within this City is very great and Exceeding burthensome to the Inhabitants thereof," reported the common council in December 1734.[33] To confront this growth in poverty, the council appropriated funds to build, for the first time, a structure to serve as the city's permanent almshouse.[34] On the day the building opened, in 1736, twelve adults and at least seven children entered the institution. The number of residents would grow quickly; by 1772 there were 425 persons living there.[35] The total number of families who resided in the almshouse has been lost to history, but most of the residents in the early years were women and children.[36]

The opening of the permanent municipal almshouse shifted the nature and goals of relief. Before 1736 destitute widows and their children almost always received relief in their own homes; once the doors of the almshouse were opened, many poor families, if not most, were confined there.[37] However, the construction of the almshouse did not bring an end to outdoor relief. On paper the policy of the city was that all of the poor receiving aid were required "to be Relieved and Maintained" in the poorhouse; if "any such poor refust to be Maintained and supported in the said Workhouse and Poorhouse," they would become ineligible for relief.[38] Even after 1736, however, over 30 percent of recipients received aid in their own homes.[39] Still, the function of the almshouse in the city had changed; it soon became a catchall institution, providing for orphaned and abandoned children and destitute families along with the elderly, the incapacitated, and the "sturdy beggars."[40]

This change in the direction of poverty relief was motivated by a combination of factors, including increasing numbers of poor in the city and concerns about the rising costs
of relief. From 1729 to 1737 New York experienced the first extended period of recession
in its history. A precipitous decline in demand in the West Indies for goods, along with
cheaper exports from Pennsylvania, cut into New York's volume of trade and undercut the
shipping industry, which had accounted for a period of significant growth for the port city.
To make matters worse, a series of epidemics — starting with a measles outbreak in 1727
and continuing with smallpox outbreaks in 1731 and 1732 — had decimated the city. The
deaths of 549 people, almost 6 percent of the population, from these diseases threatened
the economies of many households.[41] The common council's growing attention to poverty
speaks to the effects of these economic and public-health crises.[42] Between 1726 and 1734,
as the number of relief recipients increased by 84 percent, the rate for the poor tax had

A shoemaker cuts leather
while an aproned apprentice
sews. Apprenticeships
offered job training to
children living in the
almshouse. Apprentices
typically boarded with their
masters' families for the
duration of their contracts.
*Universal History Archive/
Getty Images.*

increased by 33 percent. The rising cost of poverty relief had led to something of a revolt among New York City's residents, who attempted more and more to avoid paying the tax and reacted with hostility when forced to do so. The common council's approval of construction of the municipal almshouse, then, reflected both a desire to confront the growth in poverty and the need to develop a more economical system of caring for the poor.[43]

The almshouse operated based on pragmatic concerns rather than fully formed arguments about the nature and causes of poverty. Still, the instructions given to the institution's operators combined a desire to recoup the costs of relief with an effort to inculcate the habits of work in the poor. All those able to work were required to; residents of the almshouse, the common council ordered, "may not Eat the Bread of Sloth & Idleness, and be a Burthen to the Publick."[44] Given the high number of families in the almshouse, women and children were expected to participate in many tasks.[45] Chores included working in the garden outside the almshouse, making shoes, combing flax to be processed into linen, carding wool, and spinning cotton, as well as knitting and sewing. Residents also picked oakum — separating strands from old rope to be used in shipmaking. These occupations were, at times, profitable. The almshouse recorded selling £45 worth of oakum, £4 of yarn, and £20 of vegetables from March 1738 to January 1739. This accounted for almost 40 percent of the institution's operating expenses for 1738.[46] Besides the production of such items, almshouse residents assisted in the operation of the institution, acting as teachers, nurses, and housekeepers. Along with their chores, children were also required to be educated in the almshouse.[47] The master of the institution was charged with providing children with religious education as well as teaching them "to read write and cast account." In addition to this formal education, children learned "spinning of wool, Thread, Knitting, Sewing," or other trades that would help them land apprenticeships, their most likely path out of the poorhouse.[48]

The almshouse did more than force work and education on its residents: it also regulated their lives. The "names, ages, days of admission" of everyone who entered the institution were carefully recorded, as was the date on which each left the almshouse — or died. Doctors checked every inmate for infectious diseases and lice, and if any were found, the inmate was isolated until such conditions cleared. Two articles of clothing, shirts for men and shifts for women, were issued to each resident and marked with the first letters of their names; these were washed once a week. The meals eaten in the almshouse were monotonous: sappaan (corn porridge) appeared on the weekly bill of fare five times, pease porridge (pea soup) three times, and milk porridge twice. Bedtime was set strictly at seven p.m. in the winter and nine p.m. in the summer; after those hours all fires and candles were to be extinguished, and no tobacco was to be smoked. Prayers were read to the inmates twice a week, on Wednesdays and Fridays at nine a.m. Those who missed prayers would lose their meals for the day.[49]

Eighteenth-century New Yorkers viewed poverty as closely related to crime. This perspective shaped the experience of poor families. It is telling that the structure built in 1736 was termed a "House of Correction, Workhouse and Poorhouse."[50] The concept of the workhouse had been developed in sixteenth-century England, when the municipal government of London reopened the palace at Bridewell to house the city's vagrants. Once inside "the Bridewell," a vagrant was forced to labor, the goal being to replace the inmate's "habit of idleness" with a "habit of industry."[51] (In fact, the terms "bridewell," "workhouse," and "house of correction" would remain largely interchangeable into the nineteenth century.) The example of the workhouse was expected to deter further vagrancy. This orientation applied not only to single male vagrants but also to the women and children who made up the bulk of the poorhouse residents. Those who refused to work or disobeyed rules were subject to "fetters," "shackles," or even whipping.[52] Those methods appeared to succeed: Rather than subject their lives to such regulation, many preferred to turn to private charity or search for income in other ways. After the municipal almshouse opened, the number of people receiving public relief dropped dramatically.[53]

Manhattan, seen in 1776 from across the East River in Brooklyn. The contour of the landscape—the dramatic hills rising from the shore—is remarkably different from modern-day Manhattan, whose land has been flattened by centuries of development. *Picture Collection, The New York Public Library, Astor, Lenox and Tilden Foundations.*

The almshouse was intended to regulate the city's labor as well as care for the poor. In the decades following its opening, this labor was increasingly performed by black slaves. The Dutch had brought the first African slaves into the city in 1626 to provide the labor needed to develop the colony. There was some elasticity to the definitions of "slave" and "free" in early New York, as African slaves worked alongside European indentured servants, at times gaining their freedom or making other arrangements that provided limited autonomy. With the English takeover, these lines became more strictly enforced. By the early 1700s slavery was associated exclusively with black Africans. While white indentured servants and free blacks continued to live in the city, slaves performed a large proportion of the city's labor. Between 1698 and 1738 the slave population of the city grew faster than the white population. In 1746 African Americans made up about 20 percent of the people in New York; the city had the highest concentration of slaves north of Maryland. Slaves performed all kinds of work, including blacksmithing and carpentry, but increasingly over the eighteenth century they were laborers in the city's many docks and warehouses.[54] The masters of slaves and indentured servants

NEW YORK IN 1776.

relied more and more on the poorhouse as a tool to regulate labor. Property-owning city residents could send "all unruly and ungovernable Servants and Slaves" to the institution, where they would "be kept at hard labor."[55]

The decades following the opening of the almshouse, the 1740s and 1750s, saw wars in North America, in which the British Empire and the city of New York were largely successful. Both the importance of New York as an imperial port and the size of the city grew in this prosperous period. Still, the problem of poverty did not significantly wane. The number of expansions and renovations of the almshouse in these decades points to an institution overcrowded and in constant use. Even outside the poorhouse there were signs of poverty. The Swedish botanist Peter Kalm noted a class of people in the city who "lived all year long upon nothing but oysters and a little bread." Indeed, oysters and other shell-fish proved to be a plentiful and easily accessible source of sustenance, or even income, for many poor families. One widow complained in 1752 that the death of her husband had forced her into "the greatest poverty," with only her eldest boy, twelve years of age, supporting the family — by selling oysters.[56]

Poverty greatly increased in the 1760s, as the conclusion of the French and Indian War halted the war contracts that had subsidized the city's growth. A continued rise in the cost of living exacerbated the struggles of the poor. Furthermore, the burgeoning population of the city created a housing shortage and led to drastic increases in the cost of firewood over the winters. Families of modest means found themselves forced to double up in order to afford shelter. High levels of immigration intensified and complicated these problems; between 1760 and 1775, in excess of 137,000 Europeans immigrated to the thir-teen colonies. New York City's population jumped by at least 4,000 over this period, a 20 percent increase.[57] Finally, the escalation of the conflicts that would eventually lead to the American Revolution resulted, in the meantime, in a series of boycotts of British goods that sent the city's trade-dependent economy into turmoil.[58]

In this context of economic downturn, population explosion, and political conflict, the costs of municipal poor relief shot to unprecedented heights. From 1751 to 1760 the cost of relief averaged £667 annually; for the decade of the 1760s, that figure increased to £1,677. In the years leading up to the Revolution, the costs of relief climbed to £2,778 per year. Poor families and individuals were packed into the almshouse. In 1771, 339 persons were sheltered in the municipal structure; the next year that number rose to a high of 425. In re-sponse to this growth, the city expanded the almshouse and, by 1775, had finally opened a bridewell — or house of correction — in a separate building adjacent to the poorhouse. Such overwhelming numbers of the poor brought to an end any of the efforts from the 1730s and '40s to curb outdoor relief. At great expense, the city directly supplemented poor families' earnings with cash, dry goods, and clothing. In 1775 the cost of outdoor relief exceeded

£6,000. With the city overwhelmed, churches and private charities expanded their efforts to assist the poor. Voluntary subscriptions to aid the destitute became a common practice during the winters over this period. New benevolent organizations, such as the St. George Society for the English and the St. Andrew Society for the Scots, provided for the needy among those of their national origin.[59] Occupational associations, including the Marine Society and Society of House Carpenters, also arose to provide mutual aid to out-of-work members of these professions.[60] Finally, with those combined efforts failing to make a significant dent in the numbers of impoverished, the city moved to reduce the poverty rate by increasing the apprenticeship of children and transporting vagrants outside the city limits.[61] The outbreak of the American Revolution, then, occurred at a time of great social upheaval in New York, as the city, overwhelmed with poor families, struggled to bring about the orderly system of relief it had envisioned with the opening of the municipal almshouse.

Family Poverty and the American Revolution

When the long-simmering political dispute with Britain finally boiled over into violence at Lexington and Concord, in 1775, poverty in New York became a problem with not only social but also military implications. The disorder of the depressed city would serve only to complicate and undermine the success of any battle with the British, reasoned General George Washington and the other American officers. Therefore, in the summer of 1776, as the city prepared for an expected British invasion, the municipal authorities complied with Washington's request regarding the 400 residents of the almshouse, ordering that "women, children, and infirm persons ... be immediately removed" from the city and transported to surrounding counties.[62] The Revolution, then, created a crisis of homelessness, as families were forcibly removed from the city as the battles ensued and even after New York City fell to the British, on September 15, 1776. Most families landed upstate, in Westchester, Duchess, or Ulster counties, and a special statewide committee was charged with covering the costs and overseeing the care these families received. The families were largely incorporated into the existing poor-relief institutions of the rural counties. The committee did, however, distinguish between those evacuated occupants of the New York City almshouse and those families forced into poverty and homelessness by the war. For the former, the state claimed complete authority to bind out children, while for the latter they sought parental permission to do so. In 1780 the state consolidated its approach to assisting those displaced by the Revolution, rounding up the unsettled poor from Ulster and Westchester counties and placing them in Duchess County under the supervision of the former keeper of the New York City almshouse. In this way the state essentially created an almshouse in exile. After the evacuation of the British troops, in 1783, these "patriot" poor would triumphantly return to New York City.[63]

While the counties surrounding New York were forced to deal with an influx of poor and homeless families, privation and homelessness also plagued residents who remained in the city during the war. With Manhattan under British control, New York became a place of refuge for those who had remained loyal to Britain. These "Tory" families poured into New York from all thirteen colonies. By the time the British captured the city, the flight of families had reduced the city's population of more than 20,000 to around 5,000.[64] By 1779, however, the influx of loyalist refugees had reversed this trend, causing the population to reach a record 33,000.[65] Fearing for their lives, they had abandoned much of their property in their escape. The British military authority governing the city, therefore, was forced to accommodate more destitute persons than the city had ever seen. To make matters worse, in the aftermath of the American evacuation of the city, in September 1776, a fire engulfed Manhattan. When it was extinguished, nearly a quarter of the city had been destroyed, and 300 homeless residents were forced to seek shelter in the almshouse. A subsequent fire in August 1778 destroyed another sixty-four houses.[66] The families who had remained in New York or who had fled from other areas faced a tough lot. The shortage in housing caused rents to spike to levels four times higher than before the British occupation. Many families were forced to live in "Canvas Town," a makeshift tent city constructed in the ruins of the 1776 fire. So many people crowded into the area that conditions became unsanitary. "If any author had an inclination to write a treatise upon stinks," one British observer opined, "he never could meet with more subject matter than in New York."[67] If insufficient housing did not make matters difficult enough, shortages of food, exacerbated by profiteering, led prices to rise 800 percent. While the British authorities did their best to import foodstuffs and to fix prices, their efforts were largely unsuccessful. Many of the poor families living in Canvas Town and other parts of the city survived the war years on diets of rice and baked beans. As the war came to an end, British officials were likely relieved that the city never succumbed to the massive famine that some feared would unfold.[68]

Given the difficulties New Yorkers experienced during the Revolutionary War, both the victorious patriots in exile from the city and those who remained in Manhattan for the course of the war probably felt some relief over the conclusion of hostilities and the British evacuation, in November 1783. Still, the social dislocation created by the war continued to plague the city in the months after the Americans retook control. Even before the British left, the American provisional council created to oversee New York and the sur-rounding counties had begun making plans for governing the district. The council soon named three commissioners to temporarily manage public poverty relief.[69] Their charge was not an easy one. The British, it seems, had left the almshouse and other institutions that provided for the poor and vagrants in disrepair and had abandoned a population of "idle wicked and dissolute Persons" who were terrorizing the city. In addition, the poor who had been sent back from their exile upstate needed care.[70] The state assembly moved quickly to establish a new poor law that reinstated the colonial-era residency restrictions for relief. Newly appointed mayor James Duane and the reconstituted common council that governed the city soon attempted to take control of the system of poor relief. Duane appointed a board of commissioners and charged them with overseeing both the almshouse and the bridewell. Their orders were to provide structure for assisting the deserving poor in the "benevolent" almshouse while, at the same time, cracking down on what Duane called the "idle and profligate Banditti" by punishing them in the bridewell. In 1788 state legislation formally granted authority for poor relief to the city's commissioners, who would function as the welfare authority for the city through the first half of the nineteenth century.[71]

Importantly, the Revolution did not lead to any reevaluation of the methods of poverty relief. The provisions spelled out when the almshouse was opened, in 1736, were

Fire of 1776. The fire destroyed nearly a quarter of the city and forced 300 homeless residents to seek shelter in the poorhouse. *Picture Collection, The New York Public Library, Astor, Lenox and Tilden Foundations.*

James Duane, mayor of New York City, 1784–89. *Following the social up-heaval resulting from the British occupation and American Revolution, Duane attempted to re-form the city's system of poor relief by creating a board of commissioners to oversee the almshouse and the bridewell. Print Collection, Miriam and Ira D. Wallach Division of Art, Prints and Photographs, The New York Public Library, Astor, Lenox and Tilden Foundations.*

essentially reestablished under the new American authority. If anything, given the unrest that continued in the city, the almshouse commissioners used measures that were both more restrictive and more frugal in order to maximize the value of poor relief. While there was no census of the almshouse in the period immediately following the Revolution, it appears that the institution once again became a haven for poor families. Two years after the British evacuation, of the 301 residents of the almshouse, 133 were women, and an additional ninety-nine were children. Most poor and homeless men, it appears, were treated as vagrants and either sent to the bridewell or transported out of the city.[72]

The End of an Era

In 1790, according to the first federal census, New York was the largest city in the new nation. Over the next decade it would also become the nation's busiest port and a major manufacturing center. For most of the colonial period, the problem of poverty had been manageable. Only in moments of crisis—mass immigrations, epidemics, economic downturns, and war—did the system of poor relief seem unable to care for poor families adequately. In the next chapter of New York's history, as the nation's metropolis developed, poverty became more and more a part of the urban experience.

Yet the measures the city used to deal with the problem of family poverty remained strikingly similar. Outdoor relief, indoor relief, and indenture would remain the tools of antipoverty efforts in the period from the 1790s to the 1830s. What would change were beliefs about the causes of and the best approaches to relieving poverty. In addition, the rise of a host of private responses to the misfortunes of families in the early nineteenth century would recast the experience of poverty in New York City.

Poor families in the colonial era were often contrasted with criminals. A vagrant needed to be punished, but a widow with young children was deserving of aid. But in many cases families and "vagrants" were housed together and treated similarly in the almshouse. Nineteenth-century reformers would attempt to separate the various categories of the poor more successfully. In this context, the contrasts of deserving versus undeserving, virtuous versus immoral, and laboring versus idle would increasingly influence responses to family poverty, as private and public authorities struggled to determine on which side of these divides individual families fell and whether they were truly, in the terms of the day, "objects of charity."

New York City, 1833. Map of New York City marking important thoroughfares in Manhattan and Brooklyn. *The Lionel Pincus and Princess Firyal Map Division, The New York Public Library, Astor, Lenox and Tilden Foundations.*

Chapter 2

Child and Family Poverty
in a Manufacturing City

In the summer of 1793, the letter Abigail Dougal had long been waiting for arrived. After spending four months in New York City's municipal almshouse with her two children, Dougal had finally received word from her husband, John, requesting that his family join him in Philadelphia. Presumably John had found work in the City of Brotherly Love; the deprivation that Abigail and her children had suffered would now, it seemed, come to an end. Yet the family — "bare in clothing and destitute of money" — could not afford the cost of travel to Philadelphia. With no choice, Abigail appealed to the city's chief welfare administrators, the commissioners of the almshouse and bridewell. She begged them for assistance in paying for transportation, "promising," the commissioners recorded in their minutes, "that she would nevermore be bothersome to our City." Persuaded by her case, the board agreed to grant Abigail up to three and a half dollars to pay the passage for her and her children. A week later, however, the commissioners reconsidered. "Having become more particularly informed regarding her character," the commissioners "revoked the said order." Most likely, in an attempt to provide for her family, Abigail had engaged in prostitution. Rather than travel to Philadelphia, the children would stay in New York under the care of their paternal grandfather. Abigail, it appears, remained a resident of the almshouse.[1]

Abigail Dougal was only one of hundreds of mothers and fathers who petitioned the city between the 1790s and the 1830s for help in caring for their families, but her story was typical. Dougal faced an increasingly crowded and expensive city and the emergence of an economic system in which men — and sometimes women — were forced to rely more than ever before on wages earned outside the home. The struggles of poor families became more difficult in this new environment, as skills were devalued and wages for manual labor decreased. Men like John Dougal traveled the country looking for work; women like

Abigail looked for work they could complete at home along with their domestic duties and sometimes resorted to prostitution.

In this new environment, with escalating poverty and social unrest, leaders in both government and new, private benevolent associations attempted to create greater stability. Their efforts were driven by two impulses. The city's elite, embracing the new economy as one conducive to ameliorating poverty, emphasized the importance of work and the opportunities for all family members—men, women, and children—to bring in wages. At the same time the elite, disturbed by the prostitution, drunkenness, and illegal peddling that accompanied downturns in the economy, attempted to impose a moral and religious order on an increasingly disorderly society. These two values—work and morality— would suffuse reform efforts over the early nineteenth century. Reforms to the city's public system of poverty relief; efforts to provide alternative, private forms of charity to poor families; and, finally, efforts to care for needy, unsupervised, orphaned children were all based on a belief in the importance of labor and moral instruction.

The Transformation of Work and Home

From 1790 to 1830 the population of New York increased sixfold, from 33,000 to 202,000.[2] That growth, in part a result of high levels of immigration, transformed work and life in the city. With an influx of people looking for jobs, wages declined. This factor contributed to a reorganization of craft production in New York, a process occurring in other American cities as well. For decades craftsmen and their families had lived behind or above their workshops, with all family members contributing to the businesses. When a master craftsman hired an apprentice or journeyman, he (only men were formally trained in the crafts) often came to live in the master's household, receiving a place to sleep and meals along with his wages. Even outside the crafts this pattern was largely followed; shopkeepers lived above their shops, and when they hired help, those employees became integrated into the households. In the late eighteenth century, however, that system began to founder. With a ready supply of cheap labor, masters began hiring journeymen and other workers who did not live in their homes but simply completed tasks for set wages. By 1816 most journeymen were living apart from their masters. Masters themselves began moving away from their workshops. The most successful were able to buy homes separate from their workplaces; the less successful, squeezed out by the lower production costs in large shops, often became wage workers themselves.[3]

The economic and physical distance between the rich and poor increased over this period. From the start of the colonial era through the years immediately following the

Revolution, the wealthy, middle class, and struggling poor had lived and worked in close proximity in Lower Manhattan. After the 1790s, however, the changing nature of work in New York transformed the city's neighborhoods as well. The wealthy, buoyed by a revived merchant economy and assisted by the development of omnibuses — horse-drawn public carriages — moved to the outskirts of the city. Bond and Bleecker streets, for instance, had become particularly fashionable addresses by the 1820s. The middle classes, similarly unlikely to live in the buildings in which they worked, also established households outside the city center. This left members of the emerging working class, least able to afford the costs of transportation and no longer housed with their employers, to live in areas close to where they worked — the docks and downtown workshops. Low wages and high rents soon filled these poor communities with shared, crowded quarters. New York's first slums had begun to develop.[4]

Such changes in work had broad repercussions, but they affected different segments of society in different ways. The merchant elite and entrepreneurial artisans who managed to thrive in this new economic environment came to control a greater portion of the city's wealth, but most watched their share of it shrink.[5] For unskilled laborers on the docks or licensed cartmen who transported goods throughout the city, population growth created more competition for work and drove wages down. At times laborers like John Dougal had

Atlantic Dock in Brooklyn. The docks of Brooklyn and New York provided low-wage jobs for many residents of both cities. *Picture Collection, The New York Public Library, Astor, Lenox and Tilden Foundations.*

ATLANTIC DOCK, BROOKLYN, N. Y.

to travel to other cities to find employment. As in the colonial era, seasonal downturns, such as the slow periods that occurred each winter, or disruptions of work—created, for example, by epidemics—hit these low-paid workers and their families especially hard.[6]

The economic changes had even more drastic effects for skilled workers. Journeymen and masters of small enterprises saw their professions transformed. As the household system of production came to an end, skilled workers found themselves cast aside by their former masters. Rather than working toward the day when they would run their own shops, journeymen were now forced to search out and bargain for employment in the city's growing "manufactories." To be sure, those small workshops, employing handfuls of laborers, were a far cry from the industrial plants that would emerge in the twentieth century or even from the fabric mills taking form in the early 1800s in cities such as Lowell, Massachusetts. Still, workers in New York were experiencing the process of early industrialization first-hand. Increasingly over the nineteenth century, once-valued craftsmen struggled to generate enough income to support themselves and their families.[7]

Racial restrictions also shaped work in the city. Successive emancipation laws in 1799 and 1817 gradually ended slavery in New York; on July 4, 1827 slavery was effectively outlawed in the state. Indentured servitude, however, continued unabated, especially for African Americans. Many blacks remained legal servants of whites under either New York law or through agreements they negotiated with their former masters. Between 1790 and 1810, even as more slaveholders freed their slaves, about a third of free blacks in the city remained in white households, an indication of their continued, albeit negotiated, servitude.[8] Most free blacks in New York City, however, lived with their own families and provided for their households through wage labor. African American men struggled to find consistent work in an economy that restricted their choices. Some found jobs in the artisan trades, using skills they may have learned as slaves, either as assistants to masters or in their own shops as carpenters, coopers, cabinetmakers, butchers, and bakers. Others even became well-known as tobacconists. But the changes in the nature of work over the period fell hard on black men; the proportion of African Americans in the artisan trades actually decreased in the period during which most blacks in New York were gaining their freedom. Blacks managed to dominate certain unskilled trades; virtually all of the city's chimney sweeps and many area oystermen, for example, were African Americans.[9] But most black men could find work only as common laborers or sailors. This work was often seasonal, leaving long stretches of unemployment and, in the case of mariners, extended periods away from home and family. [10]

The cries of "hot corn, hot corn, here's your lily white hot corn" by women peddlers were common sounds on the city's streets. In order to make ends meet, both black and white working-class families needed all members of their households—men, women, and children — to work and contribute income. Along with boiled corn, women sold herbs and roots they had foraged or clams collected from local beaches. Those from slightly better-off families might sell vegetables from backyard plots. The easiest way, however, for women to earn wages and keep up with their domestic duties was to bring "outside work" into the home. For black women, this often meant bringing in wash. White women, alternatively, increasingly brought in sewing. While both peddling and "outwork" provided autonomy and flexibility, they brought in extremely low wages. Children, meanwhile, might pick rags on the street or watch younger siblings to free up time for the parents to work. Older children could find better-paying jobs in manufacturing or domestic service.[11]

The greatest difficulties for a family arose when a husband died. A minister working in the almshouse described the experience of one widow with ten children. Her husband had been a cartman with little savings, and once she had paid "the expenses for his sickness and burial," she was destitute. Four of the children were able to provide for themselves, the minister explained, "and one or two can give some assistance to the mother, by tending the four younger children, while the mother washes or sews for the necessaries of life." The work, however, would barely cover the family's expenses. "For a single room she pays twenty-five dollars, yearly rent," the minister noted, "and earns a part of this by sewing nankeen pantaloons and common shirts, *for the eighth of a dollar* for each garment."[12] While the changing pattern of work made this piecework possible for women, it also drove wages down, making it extremely difficult for single-parent households, especially female-headed households, to stay afloat. With strict sex segregation in the labor market, a woman's wages were pegged at levels sufficient to supplement the earnings of a male breadwinner but were rarely enough to support a family. Realizing how dependent women were on the wages of other household members, one New York charity of the period noted that women were "more exposed to a sudden reverse of circumstances" and therefore were more likely to fall quickly into poverty.[13]

Given these economic realities, some women, faced with long-term destitution or residence in the almshouse, chose to support their families through prostitution. In 1793 the commissioners of the almshouse noted "the great number of women of ill fame, now confined in Bridewell."[14] While the number of prostitutes in the city during that period is difficult to calculate, it seems safe to conclude that the count grew into the thousands over the opening decades of the nineteenth century. One minister estimated in 1811 that "in such a city as this" there were "not less than seven-thousand females" driven to "prostituting themselves for a piece of bread."[15] By the 1830s the number of prostitutes may have reached the tens of thousands. One historian has estimated that over the entire nineteenth century, as much as 5 to 10 percent of the female population of New York City aged fifteen to thirty engaged in prostitution at some time. The low wages available for women's work in the garment trades or as servants certainly contributed to this phenomenon; unlike other professions, prostitution provided women with a living wage. The most disturbing trend noted by the burgeoning community of philanthropists and reformers was the emergence of younger and younger women in prostitution. These were not mothers struggling to put food on the table, but older children contributing to the family economy or single girls attempting to make it on their own. At times their acts were not explicit exchanges of money for sex. Instead, they sought "treating," meals or entertainment provided by men with the implicit expectation of sex in return. Reformers saw the rise of prostitution and the lowering of sexual mores as signs of a decline in morality that was closely connected to the increasingly severe poverty in the city. The desire to institute a new social order framed their work with the poor.[16]

Work, education, and religion became a threefold prescription universally applied by reformers to the emerging social inequality. In spite of the reality that much of the city's poverty was grounded in the unfolding economic and demographic transformations, that work was becoming more uncertain, and that wages were increasingly insufficient to meet families' needs, work became the primary focus of efforts by reformers—ranging from almshouse commissioners to private philanthropists—not only to ameliorate poverty but to prevent it. If idle people could be taught to work, if jobs were found for those who were struggling to stay employed, if children could be reared with a work ethic, then poverty would be significantly reduced, so the thinking went. Through education, children could learn the habits of mind and body that would lead them to the virtue of labor rather than the vice of idleness and the depths of pauperism. For a true end to poverty, however, children, along with their parents, needed to be imbued with a spirit of piety that only religious instruction could provide. Idleness, in the mind of the irreligious, led inevitably to the sins of drink, gambling, and prostitution. God's providence was mysterious, but, reformers believed, faith was certainly necessary for economic success. This trinity of cures—work, education, religion—would structure the efforts to alleviate family poverty from the 1790s to the 1830s and would continue to influence attitudes toward poverty into the later nineteenth century.[17]

Public Poverty Relief

"Oh God! If poverty be my lot, assign me not a residence among such transgressors: let me die in some solitary hovel, where I shall not hear thy name blasphemed." Thus wrote Ezra Stiles Ely, chaplain to the almshouse, in fashioning a prayer for all good people to avoid the almshouse and its unsavory residents. Ely, born in rural Connecticut in 1796, was a deeply religious man. An ordained Presbyterian minister, he had taken his first position as the pastor of a church in Colchester, Connecticut. After two years with that congregation, driven by a desire to minister to the poor and sick, Ely moved on to New York City, where he became chaplain to the city's hospital and almshouse. Ely, a man with sharp features and a mane of tight curls, was young—in his mid-twenties—and burned with a passion to build an upright Christian nation. What Ely encountered in New York, however, tested his faith. Drunkenness, prostitution, and abject poverty ran rampant in the city. He was especially disturbed by the municipal almshouse. One entry in his diary read, "This evening I preached again in the alms-house in such atmosphere as has made me almost sick." On another occasion when he preached at the almshouse, he noted in the background "the faint cries of a sick babe, at a young female's breast, and the dying groans of an expiring prostitute."

Ely did not blame the managers of the almshouse for the wretchedness he encountered. In the last decades of the eighteenth century and the first decades of the nineteenth, the municipal almshouse, overburdened by a widening stream of inmates, had reached an irrevocable state of disorder and disrepair. "The plan of the house is radically wrong," Ely commented. Residents lived in large rooms that all connected with one another. In some

Ezra Stiles Ely, chaplain to New York's public almshouses. Ely's work with the inmates of the almshouse gave him a firsthand understanding of the troubled institution. He became particularly concerned with the evils to which children were exposed. *Print Collection, Miriam and Ira D. Wallach Division of Art, Prints and Photographs, The New York Public Library, Astor, Lenox and Tilden Foundations.*

B.Otis Pinxt.   Childs Sc.

EZRA STILES ELY D.D.

quarters whole families, "husbands and wives, with children," would "sleep together." They might share a room with an unmarried couple who met in the institution. Some residents were married in the almshouse, a practice that led observers such as Ely, who gave credence to genetic theories of poverty, to fear that those newlywed couples would "procreate a future race of paupers." Ely himself sympathized most with the few righteous poorhouse residents, who were "vexed with the filthy conversation of this second Sodom."[18]

The "second Sodom" that Ely observed in 1811 was, in fact, a relatively new institution. The first almshouse was already forty years old and had housed hundreds if not thousands of residents when it was subjected to the disorder of the Revolution. In the years following the British evacuation, the city struggled to find room for the growing number seeking residence in the poorhouse. As the almshouse ran out of space, poor families and individuals were left in abandoned barracks built by British soldiers. Rooms in the bridewell and the ground floor of the city jail were also appropriated to house the poor.[19] In 1797, in response to the overcrowding and disorder, the city opened its second almshouse behind the first, still near what is now City Hall Park. The new institution, however, could barely keep up with the continuing growth in the number of residents in the early years of the new nation. In November 1785 there had been 202 adults and 99 children residing in the almshouse; by November 1808 those figures were 597 and 244, respectively.[20] While

New York City's second almshouse. Built in 1797, the almshouse appears on the left (with the sign reading American Museum) in this etching of City Hall Park. Rising poverty rates in the city quickly caused the building to become overcrowded. In 1816 the city replaced this institution with a new almshouse at Bellevue. By 1825 the original structure had been transformed into a museum. *Picture Collection, The New York Public Library, Astor, Lenox and Tilden Foundations.*

NORTH END OF THE CITY HALL PARK, 1825.

the number of residents varied by season, the trend over the early years of the nineteenth century was of nearly uninterrupted growth in the almshouse population. The rate of growth exceeded even that of the city's population as a whole.[21]

Immigration greatly increased the resident count in both the city and almshouse. In 1796 the commissioners of the almshouse stood alarmed at the number of immigrants, especially those from Ireland, living in the facility. Between 1784 and 1796, the commissioners noted, the Irish presence there had more than tripled. In this period most Irish immigrants were Protestants—Anglicans or Presbyterians from Northern Ireland—joining those who had fled Germany, France, or England. Even before the massive immigration of Irish Catholics in the 1830s and 1840s, Irish immigrants were viewed with concern. Shiploads "landed destitute and emaciated" and could be found "hudling together in cellars and sheds, in and about the Ship-Yards."[22] During the summer many fell prey to the fever epidemics that plagued the port. In the winter significant numbers of these immigrants, unable to find work or shelter, were forced to turn to the almshouse. The presence of so many "foreign paupers" presented a vexing problem for the almshouse commissioners and New York's common council. The city was required to care for the poor within its midst or arrange for their transportation to their last places of settlement. That was difficult if the person had settled in another town in New York or another state, but the city could, if necessary, simply cover the costs of transportation. For poor immigrants, however, that solution was all but impossible. While the city, in select cases, agreed to transport paupers back to Europe, the expense of doing so for all of the growing number of foreign poor made that option untenable. Furthermore, New York law provided that until they became residents elsewhere, immigrants were considered to be settled in the cities in which they had entered the country. In most cases that meant New York. In 1796 the city appealed to the state for relief from this burden. The state legislature provided a grant the next year to help offset the cost of aiding foreign immigrants and, in 1798, implemented a tax on goods sold at auction in the city, providing a stream of revenue to support the immigrant poor.[23]

The 1798 law also allowed the city for the first time to pay the almshouse commissioners. By 1800 the oversight of poor relief had been put in the hands of three commissioners, two paid professionals and one volunteer, with the first commissioner overseeing the day-to-day operations of the almshouse. This was part of the wholesale specialization and professionalization of governance in the city. No longer were a few magistrates sufficient to enforce the desires of the mayor and the common council. Now there was a Board of Health and a Street Department, a superintendent of wells and pumps, and a superintendent of public buildings and grounds. Even with all these new specialized functions, the system of poverty relief made up the largest portion of municipal expenditure over the early 1800s, at times amounting to as much as one-fourth of the city's budget.[24]

The end of slavery placed additional pressures on the public system of poor relief. The 1799 New York State gradual-emancipation law allowed slaveholders five years to turn over elderly slaves to the overseers of the poor without any financial obligations for their support. Masters were permitted to free, and in essence abandon, any slave children over the age of one. In the six lower counties of the state, hundreds of young slaves were cast off, adding to the almshouse populations. Even those blacks who were emancipated when they were older often struggled to survive in their new lives as free people. The earning potential of black families was so low that, in some years, as many as 70 percent were on the city's outdoor-relief rolls. In 1790, before the emancipation law spurred increases in the freeing of slaves, only nine blacks were residing in municipal institutions; by 1810 that number had reached seventy-two.[25]

Spurred by the increasing burdens on the institutions of public support in the early nineteenth century, the city laid out clear directives for the provision of public relief. The almshouse itself would not be open to "persons unwilling to work;" such cases would be addressed by "the vigilance of the police" or by sentencing to the bridewell. Those willing and able to work but unemployed would not be sent to the poorhouse either; instead, the city would attempt to find jobs for them. As long as they worked, the city would provide food for their families. In most cases in which poor families required support, the city's policy was to make every effort to provide it in their own homes and not in the almshouse. Such families would be eligible for tickets entitling them to meals prepared in the almshouse kitchen. In that way the city could avoid burdening the almshouse or exposing families to its unseemly characters. The almshouse, then, was left with the most extreme cases of poverty—those brought to it by "disease and misfortune," residents made destitute by "the effects of vice and intemperance," the aged who were unable to care for themselves, and young children "thrown upon public charity for support and education." Ideally, these classes of paupers would be kept separate, with attention given to their unique needs.[26]

Children, the city declared, required the most attention. Matrons were assigned to supervise the children, keeping them separated by sex and "as much as possible from the other paupers." In order to escape a life of pauperism, children needed to be "habituated to decency, cleanliness and order, and carefully instructed in reading, writing, and arithmetic." "Girls," the city noted, "should also be taught to sew and knit." All of the children were expected to read the Bible and other religious books. For recreation, children were permitted to play "sports and pastime, as may contribute to their health" under the supervision of "some discreet and sober person."[27]

The ideal that the city spelled out for the care of children dissolved in the reality of the overburdened almshouse. Some rooms in the facility had "seventy or eighty children" sleeping together with "all their beds" touching. Other children, despite the prohibition against exposing them to adult paupers, would "ramble through" the institution and "live entirely with old people." Ely, the almshouse chaplain, became personally involved with one boy who complained that in the almshouse he "had been put into a bed which contained five boys besides himself. They considered him a stranger and kicked him out. The boys used profane language, were lousy, and he could not endure the thought of living there." Having promised the boy's deceased mother that he would look after the child, Ely took the boy home rather than subjecting him to further abuse in the almshouse.[28] Even the schooling of the children suffered as a result of the overwhelming numbers in the institution. In August 1793, with the almshouse "too much crowded" with children and several already taken ill with a seasonal fever, the commissioners adjourned the school "for one month" and decided that "the Schoolroom be occupied as more airy accommodation for the children."[29]

Overseeing the children consumed much of the almshouse commissioners' time. It was necessary to find and hire wet nurses for abandoned and illegitimate infants. The commissioners preferred that infants be cared for, when possible, outside the almshouse. In some cases they provided allowances to the children's biological mothers to care for them. "Margaret Weeks," for instance, was a "female bastard child" whose mother, "Hannah Baker," received "several shillings per week" for nursing her. In other cases the commissioners supported orphaned children in the care of relatives. For example, Sarah Peterson successfully appealed to the commissioners for six shillings a week to help care for the children of her husband's brother, who, along with his wife, had perished in an "epidemic fever."[30]

The cases of black children who arrived at the poorhouse prior to the state's 1827 emancipation of slaves were particularly vexing, since the board needed to determine if a given child was free or enslaved. One "black boy" brought to the almshouse was discovered upon investigation to be the slave of one Richard Yates, but the commissioners concluded that the boy was "a notorious thief" and that, since the master did not want him back, they should "send him away." In other cases the commissioners stepped in to protect African American children from abuse. In 1796 "a black girl by the name of Hannah Born, aged about 10 years," was sent to the almshouse by the city's magistrates "for protection from the cruelty of her Master, William Buchanan of this city." The almshouse commissioners named a committee to investigate her legal relationship "to the said Buchanan, whether that of a slave or an Apprentice, and particularly in respect to the usage she has met with in his service." This investigation would determine the extent to which the commissioners could and would intervene on behalf of the child.[31]

With indenture and apprenticeship still common for poor black and white children, the almshouse commissioners spent much of their time overseeing these systems

New York City's third almshouse, at Bellevue on the East River. Opened in 1816 to replace the older almshouse, Bellevue contained the almshouse proper, two hospitals, a workhouse, a penitentiary, a chapel, a firehouse, and buildings to house employees. The structure was later converted to a hospital for the city's poor. *Picture Collection, The New York Public Library, Astor, Lenox and Tilden Foundations.*

of substitute care. Many of the complaints they heard concerned accusations of mistreatment at the masters' hands. In 1791 "a poor child by the name of Jane Newman was bound Apprentice to John G. Gassner." Two years later Jane's sister appeared before the commissioners complaining that the "child is very ill used, being so frequently and cruelly beat and whipped and her schooling neglected." The commissioners appointed a committee to investigate this claim. After talking with Gassner's neighbors, they came to the preliminary conclusion "that the complaint was not well founded." In other cases indentures were resolved based on the mutual desires of the master and the child's family. The commissioners agreed to cancel the indenture of Nicholas Huych with a shoemaker after both the boy's mother and the master appeared, requesting an end to the contract.[32]

Even with many poor children placed with better-off families across the city, the poorhouse continued to provide shelter to a large number of families and children. In 1811, with the second almshouse overrun and in disrepair, the city began work on a replacement. Given the residential and commercial growth surrounding the site of the previous almshouses—and with the new City Hall reaching completion at the center of the park—the city chose a location farther uptown on the East River known as Bellevue. The new campus of buildings that opened in 1816 created, according to one visitor, "a very grand and beautiful appearance." Open to the shores of the river, the site was surrounded on the three other sides by an eleven-foot wall. Behind the wall, the bluestone almshouse, three stories high and 325 feet long, formed the largest structure in the city, providing enough space for separate divisions for men, women, and children. In addition to the almshouse, the complex of buildings at Bellevue included a workhouse, a penitentiary, and two hospitals, along with a chapel, firehouse, superintendent's residence, and other structures to help care for residents and maintain the facilities.[33]

The new almshouse reflected the changes occurring in the city's economy. The institutions at Bellevue, including the almshouse, would be part of "a complete system of manufactories," mimicking the industrialization that was occurring outside the walls of the complex. Given "the great improvement in labor saving machinery & the simplicity of operations lately introduced into manufactures," the overseers of the new institution expected that "even Children … could be profitably exercised in trades and the lighter Branches of manufactures." The productivity of the children would "remunerate the expences of their nurture," prepare them "to procure a livelihood," and provide advantages for their "education & morals." Industrialization of the almshouse, therefore, would both help the city pay for what was becoming the leading cost in its budget and, more importantly, help inculcate in children the discipline and habits necessary to function as laborers in the new economy.[34]

Private Responses to Poverty

On November 22, 1774 Isabella Graham's husband, a Scottish doctor in the British Army, died of a fever on the Caribbean island of Antigua. As she dressed for the first time in the black garments of mourning, Graham became determined to dedicate the remainder of her life to God. She would never remarry and would always wear the clothes of a widow. Pregnant with her fifth child at the time of her husband's death, Graham chose, after the birth of her son, to return with her family to the home of her father, in Scotland. Left almost penniless, Graham struggled to provide for her children and her elderly father. At times the family was so poor that they survived on only porridge and potatoes. Forced to find a way to care for her family, Graham opened a small school in the town of Paisley, and later, boosted by that institution's success, she established a boarding school for young ladies in Edinburgh. Having been an object of charity, Graham now began, along with her wealthy friends and benefactors, to provide charitable assistance to other families in need.[35]

Graham's ultimate desire, however, was to move to America. She had spent time in North America before the Revolution when her husband was stationed there, and hoped to return to help prepare the United States for its providential role as "the country where the Church of Christ would eventually flourish." Graham arrived in New York City in 1789 and soon opened a successful girls' school. Her connections among the elite religious and philanthropic figures in New York eventually allowed her to retire from teaching and dedicate herself entirely to charity. As a widow herself, who had once struggled to provide for her family, Graham was particularly interested in helping those families trying to survive after the deaths of husbands and fathers.[36]

When the wife of one of the officers of the St. Andrew's Society, which aided Scottish immigrants, became alarmed at the lack of assistance for poor widows, Graham went into action. In 1796 she hosted in her home a meeting of the prominent women of the city. That meeting led to the creation of the Society for the Relief of Poor Widows with Small Children (SRPW), an organization assisting the widows in New York City unable to sufficiently provide for their young children. Graham was selected as first directress, the chief officer of the society. The SRPW evolved from a tradition of assistance to people of particular national origin, such as the Scots or the English, or particular professions, such as sailors and carpenters. The 1790s saw the advent of associations, such as the SRPW, that were less interested in where a potential beneficiary was from or what work he or she did than in the person's character, behavior, and faith. These organizations were sympathetic to the plight of the poor, but they were also concerned with creating a society grounded in Christian piety, in which vices such as drinking and gambling would no longer draw the unfortunate into pauperism, begging, and prostitution.[37]

Graham approached her work with a particular austerity, often leaving home after breakfast with nothing but a few rolls of bread and not returning until eight in the evening, having spent the day and evening looking after the poor and suffering widows who required her aid.[38] The mission of Graham's society was to provide an alternative to the almshouse for upstanding, virtuous widows. Only women could serve as members of the organization, although donations were welcome from both women and men. The society's volunteers, known as managers, would visit each widow who requested aid and investigate her "character and circumstances." Managers covered different districts of the city, with Graham supervising all of their work. A widow was eligible for aid only if she had at least two children under the age of ten in need of support. If a potential beneficiary refused to place an older child out to work or in an apprenticeship, the society would deny any assistance. Any sign of "immorality" would exclude a widow from receiving aid. The society believed that poor widows' paths out of poverty would be paved with industry and piety. Therefore, managers were instructed to "create and maintain habits of industry among their applicants" and attempted to find "suitable employment" for the widows. Their visits to families often included prayer and the distribution of religious tracts. In theory, the society would not simply give cash handouts; "relief" was provided in the form of "neces-

Isabella Graham, founder of the Society for the Relief of Poor Widows with Small Children. Graham believed that cultivating piety and Christian morality was key to lifting widows out of poverty. *Print Collection, Miriam and Ira D. Wallach Division of Art, Prints and Photographs, The New York Public Library, Astor, Lenox and Tilden Foundations.*

saries, never in money." In times of great need, however, the board would vote on a cash allowance to be distributed to all the widows on their books. Even so, the SRPW celebrated its role in lifting women out of poverty and keeping them from becoming dependent on municipal relief or residency in the poorhouse. In 1798, in the midst of a yellow-fever epidemic, Graham reflected on what the new society had accomplished. "We have spent three hundred dollars this winter," she reported, "and nearly all upon worthy objects." But the need for further assistance seemed endless. "The poor increase fast," she continued, "emigrants from all quarters flock to us, and when they come they must not be allowed to die for want. There are eight hundred in the almshouse, and our society has helped along many, with their own industry, that must otherwise have been there."[39] The SRPW was not alone in its fight against poverty in New York City; organizations such as the Humane Society and the Assistance Society also reached out to those in need. But no organization remained as focused on the needs of poor families as the SRPW.

Some early-nineteenth-century organizations argued that both public and private assistance to the poor did more harm than good. The Society for the Prevention of Pauperism, most notably, argued that the poor would be better served "were they required to abandon all hope of relief from the public, and to rely solely upon their own exertions, and to abstain from the use of ardent spirits, and to forego every extravagance, and become sober, industrious, and economical." The emerging antipoverty associations of the time all agreed, however, that New Yorkers needed to become productive, efficient, and devout in order to avoid poverty. Whether charity, such as the assistance provided by the SRPW, supported or undermined New Yorkers in modifying their behavior remained a subject of debate in this period and during future economic transformations.[40]

The Rise of Institutions for Children

Providing for dislocated and destitute children created both a challenge and an opportunity for the new private benevolent associations. On the one hand, children were particularly vulnerable to destitution and required much greater care and supervision than adults. On the other hand, children could be living examples of how work, education, and religion would place potential paupers on the path to success. The best way to meet the children's needs and achieve the associations' goals, it was felt, was through institutional care. Of course, children had received care in the almshouse for decades, but the private organizations believed that that facility, which exposed its residents to immoral types, had failed to care for children appropriately. In contrast to the municipal institutions, the private asylums would focus specifically on children, providing an escape from poverty and vagrancy.[41]

New York's Orphan Asylum Society was a direct outgrowth of the Society for the Relief of Poor Widows. The work of the SRPW was largely successful in keeping widows and their children out of the almshouse, especially in those cases in which the organization was able to supplement the widows' own job earnings. The SRPW's approach broke down, however, when a widow took ill or died. The only option for the children in such cases was the poorhouse, an institution that, in the words of one reformer, left the children with "no melting heart to feel, no redeeming hand to rescue them from a situation so unpromising for mental and moral improvement."[42] Hoping to help the orphans avoid that fate, Isabella Graham and the other officers placed the children with members of the society. But as the number of children in need of care continued to grow, that proved to be a temporary solution at best. Inspired by reading of an orphanage in Germany, Joanna Bethune, Graham's daughter, suggested the formation of an orphan asylum for New York City. Run exclusively by women, like the SRPW, the Orphan Asylum Society was organized in 1806 and immediately rented a house to serve as a shelter for the first twelve orphans it took in. In 1807 the society began work on a permanent building that could house up to 200 children. The orphanage was available only to children who had lost both parents, but those who

The Orphan Asylum Society of the City of New York,
Located in Bloomingdale road, near West Seventy-third street.

The Orphan Asylum Society of the City of New York. Founded in 1806, the asylum, located near West 73rd Street, provided an alternative to the almshouse for impoverished children. Although limited to serving "full orphans"—children with no living parents—the Orphan Asylum set a precedent for the later establishment of other institutions, which offered care to children with one living parent as well as other impoverished children. *Picture Collection, The New York Public Library, Astor, Lenox and Tilden Foundations.*

were allowed to reside in the asylum would be "educated, fed and clothed." Even more importantly, they would have "religious instruction, moral example, and habits of industry inculcated in their minds," which would prepare them, once they reached the appropriate age, to be bound out for further training.[43] The orphan asylum provided the first alternative to the almshouse for institutional care of children. Its founding was soon followed by the appearance of other institutions, such as the Roman Catholic Asylum, established in 1817, which promised to care for Catholic orphans without subjecting them to the Protestant indoctrination integral to the Orphan Asylum Society.[44]

While these orphanages provided a new means of caring for children whose parents had died, many other children remained either abandoned or largely unsupervised. In

The Catholic Orphan Asylum. Elizabeth Ann Seton, co-founder of the Society for the Relief of Poor Widows with Small Children, converted to Catholicism late in life and instructed members of the Sisters of Charity to establish the Catholic Orphan Asylum in New York. *Robert N. Dennis Collection of Stereoscopic Views, Miriam and Ira D. Wallach Division of Art, Prints and Photographs, The New York Public Library, Astor, Lenox and Tilden Foundations.*

1812 John Stanford, a Baptist preacher who ministered to the almshouse and other public institutions, sounded the alarm about the "number of vagrant children and youth who day and night infest our streets." Action needed to be taken, Stanford explained, to assist children "found in our streets, and attending our docks, without any visible means of support, who can give no correct account of themselves, without parents, and whose situation[s] prompt them to indolence, depredation, and vice." Vagrancy was a crime in New York, but rather than imprison youths, Stanford suggested the creation of "A House of Refuge" that would provide the guidance, models of Christian virtue, and habits of industry that these children clearly lacked.[45] Stanford's cause caught the attention of the Society for the Prevention of Pauperism. Reforming children and youth, they reasoned, might truly alleviate the problem of pauperism. In 1824, newly reconstituted as the Society for the Reformation of Juvenile Delinquents, the association appealed to the state legislature to incorporate and provide financial support for an institution to care for vagrant and delinquent children under the age of sixteen. "It is an asylum," explained the society, in "which boys, under a certain age, who become subject to the notice of the Police, either as vagrants, or houseless, or charged with petty crimes, may be received."[46] In response, the legislature passed an act providing that all children "committed as vagrants, or convicted of criminal offences" in the city would be sent to the New York House of Refuge.[47]

When the house of refuge opened, in 1824, John Stanford, who had inspired the new institution's creation, spoke about its mission. The house of refuge, he declared, would extract "the core of pauperism." The "trade of mendacity had been carried on, principally by the children of the indolent and worthless." By removing "such children from the streets," the new asylum could end the cycle of pauperism. Bells shaped these children's lives into an industrious routine. A bell would awake them at dawn. Fifteen minutes later, another bell would denote that they were to emerge washed, dressed, and ready for the day. Subsequent bells would signal the children to report for morning prayers and an hour and a half of "literary instruction." With the following bell, children would show up for a breakfast usually consisting of bread, molasses, and a coffee substitute made from rye. A bell after breakfast meant that they were to attend the various workshops in the institution. This was followed by an hour break for lunch, then a return to work. Children who finished their tasks early, and who had exhibited exemplary behavior, were allowed time for recreation; others were required to labor until the supper bell rang, at 5:00 p.m. Following supper, another bell indicated that it was time to return to the classroom for another hour and half of instruction followed by evening prayers, and the final bell sent the children to their cells for bedtime.[48]

Work provided the principal means of reforming the children. When the institution opened, boys were drafted for such jobs as cleaning up the grounds, constructing a new building, and erecting a wall. Girls performed the domestic tasks needed to keep the institution running and planted grass. Later, the work of the children was leased to contractors who, at times, provided instruction in particular skills. Some boys, for example, were trained in tailoring, shoemaking, or coopering, and some girls worked at "making Women's Shoes and Gloves," "Knitting, and Needled Work of all Kinds." But most of the labor was made up of monotonous tasks that required little thought or training. Boys, for example, might cut corks and pegs or pick oakum; girls would wash, iron, and do general housework. One task that children of both genders and all ages completed was folding pages to be used by bookbinders.[49]

Discipline consumed most of the time of the institution's superintendent. Children accustomed to spending night and day on the streets with little adult supervision bridled at the minute-by-minute scheduling and the long hours of labor in the house of refuge. They frequently ran away, avoided their assigned tasks, and disrupted meals. In an attempt to maintain control over the inmates, the administrators combined a system of rewards with various methods of punishment. Children were grouped into four classes. Class One consisted of "the best behaved and most orderly Boys and Girls," whom the rules defined as "those who do not swear, lie, or use profane, obscene, or indecent language or conversation, who attend to their work and studies, are not quarrelsome, and have not attempted to escape." Class Four comprised "those who are vicious, bad & wicked." The other classes fell in between those extremes. Classes were fluid; every day children wore badges on their arms indicating which they were currently in. The rewards for good behavior included special treats and relief from work. Children in Class One occasionally received dessert, "a pudding or pie," after Saturday dinner. Those inmates who went at least a month with no infractions were "allowed Saturday afternoon for amusement, play, and recreation."[50]

Punishments ranged from simply barring a child from "play and exercise" to restricting movement with handcuffs, leg irons, or the ball and chain. Children who committed lesser offenses were usually required to eat meals apart from their peers or were sent to bed without supper. Those who continued to misbehave were restricted to diets of bread and water, saltless gruel, or just tea for all meals. Those who had attempted to escape or harm the staff or other children were placed in solitary confinement. Finally, the worst offenders received corporal punishment. Some boys who had disrupted mealtime were tied facedown over a barrel, and, with their pants removed, were whipped with "the six line cat." Out of frustration, residents were sometimes punished with a combination of measures. One boy managed to free himself from handcuffs with a key he had made. He was placed in confinement with his leg chained to the wall and fed only bread and water.[51]

The house of refuge was a particularly harsh environment, but its underlying values were the same as those of other organizations serving the poor: work, education, and religion. By lending structure to their lives, exposing them to hard work, training them in trades, providing them with a formal education, and, perhaps most importantly, improving their morals through religious education, the founders of the house of refuge imagined they were setting these children on a new track. Pauperism, crime, and life on the streets were no longer their destiny. The orphan asylum and the house of refuge were, therefore, both child-welfare institutions. Both intended to provide a new parental structure for those children who lacked adult oversight due to neglect or death. Their successes, while limited, provided a model for institutions across the country.[52]

"We have not been accustomed to consider this as a public institution, being we may say, wholly supported by private beneficence," wrote the officers of the orphan asylum.[53] In truth, however, both public and private sources supported the house of refuge and the orphan asylum. The orphan asylum was frequently aided by the state legislature. In 1808 the legislature authorized the city to raise $5,000 by lottery to help the Orphan Asylum Society build a permanent institution. Starting in 1811 the society received annual grants from the state legislature to assist in the operation of the asylum. Beginning in 1825 the house of refuge received an annual grant of $2,000 from the state legislature. In 1826, formally recognizing its public function, the state legislature declared that the house of refuge was the official reformatory for juveniles in the state of New York. The orphan asylum and the house of refuge were private institutions, but they provided a public service to the city and state and received funding accordingly.[54]

Although they received public support, the orphan asylum and the other, similar orphanages founded in the early nineteenth century maintained strict control over whom they admitted to their institutions. One particularly invidious restriction was based on race; no African American children were permitted to reside in the New York Orphan Asylum or the other two orphan asylums that had opened by the 1830s. Abandoned and orphaned African American children had one place to go: the almshouse. Even there, they were not accorded the same treatment as white children. While some effort was made to keep white children apart from other paupers, black children were mixed among the adults. While white children would attend classes in the schoolroom, black children received no education. To make matters worse, in 1837 the city opened Long Island Farms, a new facility for children, across the East River in Queens. All the white children were removed to this new locale, but the black children were forced to remain behind in the almshouse.[55]

For a group of white women reformers, this situation was unacceptable. After convincing the almshouse commissioners that the African American children were "in a most neglected and suffering condition," three women marched down to the almshouse

Thanksgiving dinner at the Colored Orphan Asylum. The asylum, established in 1837, cared for hundreds of African American children who would otherwise have grown up among poor adults in the public almshouse. *Picture Collection, The New York Public Library, Astor, Lenox and Tilden Foundations.*

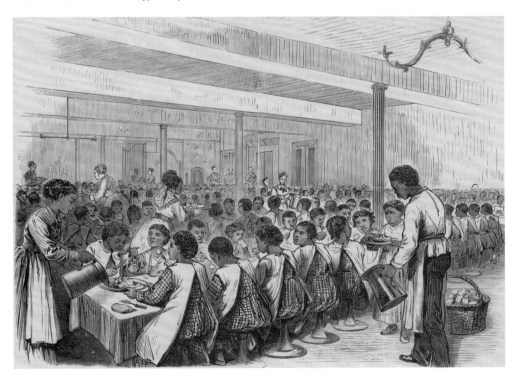

and took five children away. Since no coachmen would drive this interracial group, each woman carried a child while the other two children walked the twenty blocks, in the summer heat, to the house on West Twelfth Street they had purchased to serve as the New York Colored Orphan Asylum. After that building was consumed in a fire, in 1842, the asylum moved to a new facility on Fifth Avenue between Forty-third and Forty-fourth streets capable of housing 150 children. By 1863, 1,257 children had passed through the doors of the Colored Orphan Asylum.[56]

Most of the residents of the orphanage were not true orphans; instead, they were victims of the devaluation of black labor in New York City. Black women confronted with the deaths of their spouses, or with husbands' long absences at sea or in search of work, often faced the difficult decision of abandoning their children to the asylum, requesting outdoor relief from the city, or moving their families into the almshouse. In fact, most children were brought to the orphan asylum by relatives, neighbors, or their parents. Many single mothers placed their children in the asylum in order to take positions as domestic servants. In some instances, employers covered the cost of boarding servants' children as part of the servants' compensation. While parents maintained connections to their children in the orphanage, contact was severely restricted. Visits by parents to the institution were limited to three hours per month. Parents were expected to show deference to the institution that cared for their children; those who used "disrespectful language to the matron" were barred from seeing their children unless they apologized. Finally, children needed permission from the matron to go beyond the front door of the institution, even if their parents accompanied them. The Colored Orphan Asylum provided a service for parents unable to find child care while they worked; however, in placing children in the asylum, black parents essentially relinquished their parental role to a white-run institution.[57]

Like those who operated the "white" orphan asylum, the managers of the Colored Orphan Asylum attempted to prepare children for upstanding and productive lives. They imagined the institution to be a substitute "family" for their young charges, providing the type of care and structure they believed the children may not have received at home. Religion infused the daily schedule. Before children ate breakfast they heard a reading from the Bible, and after supper they listened to another reading and recited the Lord's Prayer. Each mealtime was also accompanied by a moment of silence for private prayer and reflection. Additionally, the orphans attended a Methodist Sunday School. Education formed the other pillar of the asylum, with the children spending most days in the classroom. When the managers determined that a child was ready to work, usually at around ten to twelve years of age, they arranged for the child to be indentured. Often, children were sent to rural areas in Westchester County, Long Island, New Jersey, or Connecticut. The distance from the city, which made contact with parents and other relatives difficult, as well

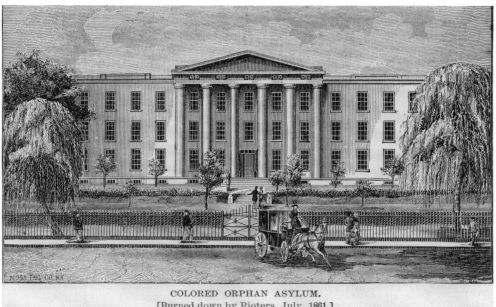

COLORED ORPHAN ASYLUM.
[Burned down by Rioters, July, 1861.]

The second home of the Colored Orphan Asylum. First established in 1837, the asylum moved to the building shown here in 1842. During the 1863 Draft Riots, a violent mob turned its fury over the Civil War on black children and burned the orphanage down. *Picture Collection, The New York Public Library, Astor, Lenox and Tilden Foundations.*

as the unfamiliar environment led many children to resist these placements. It appears that few of the orphans actually completed their indentures by remaining as apprentices until they turned twenty-one. For some children, residence at the orphan asylum was a stepping-stone to becoming skilled workers or members of the educated African American middle class. For most, given the limited work opportunities for blacks in New York City, the asylum simply prepared them for life among the city's struggling African American working class. As was its mission, the Colored Orphan Asylum assisted black families in need; it did not fundamentally reorder race relations in the city.[58]

The advent of specialized institutions for children would shape future debate over social policy in New York City and across the country. Reformers were convinced that children would have better lives if they were removed from the corrupting influences of the urban slums and, instead, exposed to the rhythms of hard work, the enlightenment of education, and the saving grace of Christianity. Some children responded well to that trifecta, found economic success, and became the examples that the institutions boasted about. Others ran away and returned to lives of poverty and vagrancy. It seems likely, however, that most emerged from these institutions and went on to live typical working-class lives, struggling to get by—and not fall into poverty—in the industrialized city.[59]

A City Transformed

The process of industrialization did not occur overnight. Gradually, masters stopped living in their workshops, stopped incorporating journeymen into their households, and stopped taking on apprentices. In the mid-1830s this process was far from complete, but its economic and social consequences were already evident. Newly poor New Yorkers seemed to be constantly searching for work. Certain areas of the city became reserved for the poor and avoided by the "respectable," upper classes. A number of tasks became associated with a particular gender or with certain racial groups, such as sewing for white women or manual labor for black men.[60] Most significant of all, the new economic structure led to increasing numbers of people living on the streets or requiring the aid of the city or private charities just to survive.

Children emerged as a special interest of the new benevolent institutions formed in this environment. Adult paupers, according to prevailing beliefs, had little chance of redemption. But in the newly democratized United States, all children had the potential to become upstanding and successful citizens. The primary means of rescuing children in this period was the residential institution. Asylums were developed to care for the orphan, the vagrant or delinquent child, and the half-orphan. By the end of the 1830s, such specialized institutions had proliferated across the cities of Brooklyn and New York.[61]

The city's emerging public and private social-welfare system soon faced its most difficult test to date. In the spring of 1837, due to a plunge in the price of cotton, hundreds

Boys in a bedroom at the Colored Orphan Asylum. The asylum was extremely strict; its goal was to provide religion-infused structure to the children's lives so as to prepare them to be "productive" members of society. Although its charges were black children, white charity workers governed the institution. *Robert N. Dennis Collection of Stereoscopic Views, Miriam and Ira D. Wallach Division of Art, Prints and Photographs, The New York Public Library, Astor, Lenox and Tilden Foundations.*

of Wall Street firms collapsed. The effects rippled throughout the economy, as the stock market and the price of real estate in the city declined precipitously. What would become known as the Panic of 1837 affected all New Yorkers, but it was particularly hard-felt by those families already teetering on the edge of poverty. By the winter, thousands were unemployed. To confront this crisis, the city would have to amass both public and private resources and build on the institutional legacy of the early nineteenth century.

Color map of Lower Manhattan and part of Brooklyn, denoting wards. *The Lionel Pincus and Princess Firyal Map Division, The New York Public Library, Astor, Lenox and Tilden Foundations.*

Chapter 3

Poor and Homeless Children in Mid–Nineteenth Century New York

In 1854 an agent from the recently formed Children's Aid Society (CAS) came upon a young girl selling wax matches and buttons on Twentieth Street. The agent quickly learned that the girl, Maggie, was an orphan living with her aunt. In order to provide assistance to the "bright little girl," he invited her to attend one of the society's industrial schools, where she could learn a trade. When Maggie failed to appear at the school the next day, the agent decided to visit the girl at the address she had provided. Arriving at the top story of a house, where the girl's family lived, the visitor was shocked. A "very respectable neatly-dressed young woman" met him at the door. "Everything in the room was as neat as good care could make it. The floors white with scrubbing, hearth swept, windows clean, and all looking like the home of an honest, cleanly, working woman. There was a nice large mirror on one side, and a mahogany case of drawers, and some pretty dishes in a closet which showed they had been once in good circumstances."[1]

As the visitor talked with the woman, Maggie's aunt, he learned that her husband was an iron molder who, because of the recent economic downturn, was out of work. The husband spent his days looking for work and picking up odd jobs. The woman had tried to find washing or sewing that she could complete at home, but she refused to work outside her house. "I cannot give up keeping a home together for him and poor Maggie there," she explained. The burden of helping the family survive, then, fell to the young Maggie. The aunt refused to let the young girl beg, but she would buy matches for "a cent and a half a box" and resell them on the street "for three cents." "Sometimes I don't make three cents a day," Maggie told the visitor, "and sometimes two shillings." This activity kept the girl occupied from seven in the morning until four-thirty in the afternoon without a break for lunch. The plight of Maggie and her family deeply touched the Children's Aid Society agent. "I could hardly keep my tears while the woman was talking," he reported. To him, the family's condition was more troubling than the abject poverty and "ignorant pauperism" he typically confronted. "The hard straits of honest industry," he concluded, "what is more pitiable?"[2]

The Children's Aid Society visitor who arrived at Maggie's dwelling focused on details. The well-kept furniture and dishes and the aunt's attention to dress, desire to stay at home, and efforts to keep the apartment clean and neat all received mention in his journal. Those features caused the visitor particular distress but also likely gave him hope that Maggie could escape from the poverty that her uncle and aunt confronted. Cleanliness, proper dress, and the idea of home—not the workplace—as the appropriate realm for women were all middle-class values of the mid-nineteenth century. Reformers believed that these values, if inculcated among the poor, would provide a path to prosperity.

In contrast with the moralism of earlier reformers, including Isabella Graham, the midcentury charity workers, such as those at the CAS, displayed a scientific pragmatism and a desire to uncover the root causes of social ills. They did not exclude consideration of character and morality from their analysis of the destitute, but they saw the social and physical environment in which the poor lived as a factor that contributed to their moral failings. At the heart of this generation's vision for reform was an ideal of the home—an ideal based in the norms of middle-class homes that had emerged by the 1830s and 1840s—and the reformers saw the city itself, with its crowded neighborhoods and temptations of vice, as a prime obstacle to poor New Yorkers' realizing this ideal.[3]

This focus on the ideal of the home gave rise to a new term in the reformers' vocabulary: "homeless." New York City philanthropists had used the word in earlier eras, though infrequently and casually, when describing the poor people and vagrants they intended to aid. By the mid-nineteenth century the word had received new life, as reformers developed language to describe the people, mostly children, they encountered on the street. Often these children were "without shelter" and slept in boxes or on the docks. When asked where they lived, the children often replied, *"Don't live nowhere!"*[4] But even those children who had places of residence, who lived *somewhere,* were, in the conception of the reformers, "homeless"—lacking the domestic arrangements that made a dwelling worthy of being called a home.[5]

The economic crashes that battered the city of New York and the United States in the middle of the nineteenth century made it especially difficult for the poorest New Yorkers to meet middle-class expectations of a home. Beginning with the Panic of 1837, the economy faced alternating periods of boom and bust. A slight recovery in 1839 was followed by a downturn that lasted until 1843; a period of growth that started in 1848 ended with the Panic of 1854; prosperity in 1856 and early 1857 dissolved in a recession that lasted another year. The Civil War years of the 1860s brought economic contraction, followed by a period of expansion; the conclusion of the war brought another series of recessions, in

1865 and 1869, ending in the economic collapse of 1873.[6]

Amid this economic roller-coaster, New York developed many of the features that would long define it as a city—high numbers of immigrants, large numbers of manu-factories, and densely constructed housing. To create order in this urban environment, reformers in both the public and private sectors systemized efforts to relieve poverty. Children became a particular focus of these middle-class reformers. As middle-class par-ents sheltered their own children from physical labor and the violence and unseemliness of the world outside their homes, they became painfully aware of young people unable to experience idyllic childhoods and absorb the values of a middle-class environment. Unlike efforts to help poor adults—some of whom spoke foreign tongues and practiced for-eign faiths—work with poor children, reformers imagined, could instill values early and therefore bridge the potentially dangerous divisions of class, ethnicity, and religion. Yet middle-class attempts to intervene in the homes of the poor would only further inflame these tensions. In the midst of the Civil War, the worst nightmare of the New York elite was realized when their city erupted into riot.

The Ideal of Home and the Reality of the City

The transformations of home and work that had reshaped the economy of New York City in the early nineteenth century also reshaped the cultural and social norms of city life. As the wealthy and the middle classes became more isolated in neighborhoods at some distance from the manufacturing districts and the port, they developed new expectations about the distinct roles of men, women, and children and a new interest in the homes in which they lived. Such changes first became evident among elite New Yorkers. With work downtown now physically separated from homes in Greek revival mansions and brown-stones above Bleecker Street, work and home became two different worlds. In eighteenth-century patriarchal households, men governed their homes, but the chores of men, wom-en, and children were intertwined. Now, men, off at work, ruled the world of business and finance, while women reigned over the newly separate domestic sphere. Guidebooks such as Lydia Maria Child's 1829 work *Frugal Housewife* began to codify the role of women in the domestic realm. Women were expected to run their households and, usually with the help of servants, maintain high standards of cleanliness, decorum, and cuisine.[7] By the 1840s and 1850s, those social norms had spread from the wealthy to an emerging middle class made up of professionals, clerical workers, and successful manufacturers. Modeling themselves on the wealthy, middle-class families came to see their homes, purchases, and behavior as emblematic of their class aspirations.[8]

The Victorian family. Eastman Johnson's depiction of an ideal family—large, prosperous, and leisurely—indicates the importance of home, childhood, and family among the newly emerging American middle class. Victorian domestic and moral conventions shaped public policy relating to poverty and homelessness for many decades. *Johnson, Eastman (1824–1906). The Hatch Family. 1870–71. Oil on canvas, 48 x 73 3/8 in. (121.9 x 186.4 cm). Gift of Frederic H. Hatch, 1926 (26.97). The Metropolitan Museum of Art, New York, NY, U.S.A. Image copyright © The Metropolitan Museum of Art. Image source: Art Resource, NY.*

As the advice literature of the period made clear, rearing children was considered to be among the most important tasks that women supervised in the home. Mothers were expected to provide children with training that would build character and imbue them with the republican virtues of American society. It was from their mothers that both boys and girls would learn standards of dress and behavior. Finally, middle-class mothers would prepare children for the formal schooling they would receive outside the home. Conspicuously absent from the training urban middle-class children received was manual labor. Only fifty years before, the sons of middle-class artisans would have been expected to serve as apprentices and learn trades. By the 1840s and 1850s, middle-class childhood was sheltered from the world of work. Children were expected to play and learn rather than prepare for their future employment.[9]

This romanticized understanding of childhood shaped the perspective of a new generation of reformers. "Every one who has ever loved the face of childhood," announced the CAS in 1854, "or whose home is brighter with the presence of merry children, will feel what it is for a boy or girl to be thrown out alone in the bleak city."[10] This vision of the ideal home, free of the stresses of work and dedicated to the rearing of children, could not have been more different from the reality experienced by the city's poor and working-class families.[11] Large-scale immigration, crowded housing conditions, and new patterns of economic production created deeply concentrated urban poverty that had detrimental effects on family structure and housing stability.

Over the 1840s and 1850s, massive numbers of immigrants, many from Ireland and Germany, settled in New York City. Economic and political refugees fleeing the Irish Potato Famine of the 1840s and German revolutions of 1848 hoped to remake their lives in the city. Between 1840 and 1859 an average of 157,000 immigrants entered the port of New York every year; for the twenty years before 1840, the average had been only 25,000 immigrants per year. The burden this placed on the city was immense. The number of immigrants who entered the port in 1854 exceeded the entire 1840 population of New York City. Not only did the immigrants' sheer numbers shatter any previous records, but their nationalities threatened America's largely Anglo-Saxon makeup. Of those who arrived in the United States between 1840 and 1859, about 40 percent were from Ireland and another 32 percent were from the German states, while only 16 percent were English.[12]

Not all of the immigrants who disembarked in New York remained in the city; most quickly departed for other parts of the country. Still, between 1840 and 1860 the population of New York City increased by more than 400,000 persons, and that of Brooklyn grew by more than 250,000; much of that growth was driven by immigration.[13] The proliferation of German along with Irish brogues, as well as sundry other languages and accents, transformed the sounds of the New York street. The immigrants concentrated in particular sections of the city. In 1855 over half of the residents in fourteen of the city's twenty-two wards were foreign-born; in two wards 70 percent of residents were of foreign birth.[14] The areas now known as the East Village and the Lower East Side contained *Kleindeutschland,* the heart of New York's German community. The Irish were found in districts across the city but were in particularly high concentration at the lower tip of Manhattan, near City Hall Park, and in the desolate section surrounding the intersection of Baxter, Park, and Worth streets, known as Five Points. Even these neighborhoods, however, were not homogeneous. A particular block in Five Points, for instance, could be mostly German-Jewish, an adjacent block Irish, and the subsequent block African American.[15]

As newcomers entered the city, the demand for housing in lower Manhattan, where most work opportunities were located, drove up rents. The result was the creation of multifamily dwellings that became known as tenements. Beginning in the 1830s, buildings that had once housed a single family as well as storefronts or workshops were each divided into two to five apartments with a shop or saloon in the front portion of the ground floor. Such wooden structures became infamous for their decrepitude. These early tenements

A depiction of Five Points as it would have appeared in 1827, published in *Valentine's Manual* in 1855. The drunken, violent atmosphere of this poor neighborhood is contrasted with the decorum of the upper-class gentlemen standing aghast in the foreground. *Museum of the City of New York /Art Resource, NY.*

were often two stories tall and only twenty to twenty-five feet wide and twenty-five to thirty feet deep, providing restricted space in the typically two-room apartments. The shortage of exterior windows allowed only limited ventilation in the summer, while drafty walls and leaks exposed residents to the elements in the colder months.[16]

In the 1840s new brick buildings constructed to serve as tenements quickly replaced much of the old, makeshift wooden housing. By 1855, in the notoriously crowded neighborhood of Five Points, brick tenements outnumbered wooden ones by a ratio of three to two. Also twenty-five feet wide, these buildings were fifty feet deep and could be as high as five stories. With the exception of a small commercial space on the first floor, each floor housed four two-room apartments. The main room of each apartment measured twelve feet by twelve feet, had two windows, and usually served as the kitchen, living room, and dining room combined. The second, windowless, eight-by-ten-foot room was known as the "sleeping closet." In total, a typical tenement apartment measured 225 square feet.[17]

The average tenement apartment of this size, at least in Five Points, housed five people. However, 46 percent of these apartments each contained six or more people, and more than 15 percent housed eight or more each.[18] With space at such a premium, finding a place for everyone to sleep was difficult. Family members often slept in a single room or even a single bed. In one family, one child was forced to sleep "under the bed, another under the table, a third by the stove, and the fourth at liberty to roll over any of her sisters."[19] Beds were often piles of rags or straw covered in "bed clothes"; these could be easily pushed aside to make room for daytime activities.[20] In one case, in an appallingly dank basement apartment, five children shared a single bed.[21]

Such overcrowding made conditions extremely unsanitary. The streets were filled with garbage and animal excrement. Pigs roamed the neighborhoods, reducing the former but increasing the latter. To deal with human waste, landlords placed outhouses behind the tenements. While the city had begun in the mid-nineteenth century to lay sewers, by 1857 only a quarter of Manhattan had access to them; most poor communities had no sewer access. In most cases, then, the outhouses connected only to cesspools, bins that had to be emptied periodically. To make matters worse, landowners, in an effort to maximize profits, frequently built smaller dwellings in the rear yards of street-facing tenements, leaving only an outhouse between the two buildings. Such crowding seriously overburdened the outdoor facilities. In one particularly outrageous case, forty-one families shared a single, unimaginably filthy privy. When it rained, the cesspools overflowed, sending human waste flooding into the streets and leaking into basement apartments. Not surprisingly, visitors to poor neighborhoods such as Five Points often commented on the stench.[22]

View from the steeple of St. Paul's Chapel, looking south toward Lower Manhattan, in 1845. The crowding in much of downtown New York is evident. *I.N. Phelps Stokes Collection, Miriam and Ira D. Wallach Division of Art, Prints and Photographs, The New York Public Library, Astor, Lenox and Tilden Foundations.*

These neighborhoods had become almost exclusively poor and working class since the middle class had moved en masse to areas farther uptown. In marked contrast to the experience of the upper class, for many workers—especially women—the social and economic changes further increased the intimacy between work and living space. Industrialization in New York did not lead to a prevalence of massive factories with production occurring on-site from beginning to end. Instead, in many cases, production combined highly skilled labor in small shops with less-skilled labor completed outside them. As ready-made garments became accepted among all classes of society, and as New York emerged as the nation's leading producer of such clothing, this industry shaped the lives of thousands of New Yorkers. At the heart of the system stood the "sweater," who received cut cloth from the manufacturer and contracted with individual laborers to make sure that the sewing was completed according to the required specifications. The incentive for such middlemen was to find workers who would complete the work for the lowest cost per piece and therefore maximize the profits of the middlemen. Given the glut of poor laborers, that was not a difficult proposition. For those who gave their sweat to the system, however, living on such low wages was difficult. The proliferation of sewing machines in

Women at work in a skirt factory. The article accompanying this image, which appeared in *Harper's Weekly,* extolls the virtues of such "healthy and lucrative" employment for women. Despite the Victorian romanticization of motherhood and domesticity, many women had to work to support their families. *HarpWeek, LLC.*

the 1850s made workers, especially women, even more dependent on the "sweating" system. Unable to afford their own machines, workers would pay a few cents of their wages to rent them from middlemen. The family system of production that had shaped the lives of colonial artisans and had continued through the early development of the garment industry broke down in the face of this industrial system.[23]

Transatlantic migration, crowded housing conditions, and transitions in the nature of work were all disruptive to family structure. Poor children were burdened with increasing responsibility for providing family income but also gained more time free from parental supervision and, therefore, increased opportunities to get into trouble. Poor women often found themselves widowed or deserted. Without the social-support networks of the old country, illegitimate infants were frequently abandoned. The number of orphans or runaways living on the streets or caring for siblings in unstable living conditions was, in the eyes of reformers, an epidemic. Both public and private organizations set out to make sense of this social crisis and to provide practical solutions that would relieve the poor and, perhaps more importantly in the eyes of the city's leaders, preserve stability in New York.

Organizing Relief

In the aftermath of the Panic of 1837, the city entered an economic depression the depths of which it had never before experienced. In January 1838, as the bitter winter unfolded, newspaper publisher Horace Greeley commented on the drastic steps many people were taking just to survive. "Some," he observed, "subsist on the scanty earnings of former days, some are aided by relatives or personal friends, and some manage to avoid starvation with the few shillings which partial and precarious employment or still more uncertain beggary afford them." But, Greeley continued, there were still thousands, "not less than ten thousand," he estimated, who were "in utter and hopeless distress, with no means of surviving the winter but those afforded by the charity of their fellow citizens."[24] Greeley's estimates were probably conservative. In 1838, 80,000 people received public relief in New York City.[25] The widespread poverty caused by the economic crisis depleted public coffers and pushed many private organizations to the brink of bankruptcy. This strain led private philanthropists and public administrators to question the structures that had developed over the early nineteenth century. Relief, these reformers observed, had been costly—fighting poverty had required raising taxes and exhausting private donations—but it had not been effective. Over the 1840s reformers in the public and private spheres attempted to systemize relief in order to provide a greater return on every dollar taxed or donated.[26]

The New York Association for Improving the Condition of the Poor (AICP) exemplified a transition from a narrow, Protestant, moralistic view of poverty as largely an outcome of individual sin to a secularized attempt to address both the causes and effects of poverty. To be sure, the AICP was grounded in the Protestant philanthropy of the age; it was created by the New York City Tract Society, one of the several Protestant missionary groups in the city, and its longtime leader, Robert M. Hartley, remained a devout Presbyterian throughout his tenure. But the work of the organization was not merely about saving souls; it was about attacking both individual moral failings and the social disorder of the city, which he believed were the root causes of poverty. Forged in an era of belief in the possibility of salvation for every soul, the AICP saw pauperism not as a permanent state, but as a temporary condition that could be relieved by individual reformation. Such reform did not necessarily require the acceptance of Protestant Christianity per se, but it did call for adopting middle-class habits and decorum. If individuals could refrain from drinking and gambling, learn to work hard, and save money, then they could, except in cases of extreme economic depression or family emergencies, lift themselves out of poverty.[27]

Hartley set out to reform private relief in New York City systematically. The traps that led the struggling poor into pauperism were many, but included, in his interpretation, the profligate distribution of aid in which many philanthropists engaged. Such reckless giving, Hartley argued, only created dependency; what was needed instead was a "scientific method" that actually worked to lift individuals out of poverty. Having abandoned a successful business career to become executive secretary of the AICP, Hartley initiated a new efficiency in the distribution of private assistance; the AICP would be able not only to provide aid to more families and individuals but to do so at less cost.[28]

Professional "visitors" — all men — formed the crux of Hartley's system of relief. In 1844, the organization's first full year of operation, the AICP divided the city below Fortieth Street into 236 sections and assigned one visitor to each. These men were required to serve several functions. First, they had to identify and visit the poor families within their sections. Second, they were to determine if these families fit the criteria necessary for assistance from the AICP and, if not, refer them to the most appropriate public or private agency or institution. The handicapped or insane were sent to city institutions; those unable or unwilling to give up lives of pauperism were sent to the almshouse. The organization's massive register of those who had already received assistance from the AICP, other private organizations, or the city helped identify abusers of charity. Finally, for those families who passed through this "vast sieve" and were deemed worthy of assistance, visitors were charged with providing limited and appropriate material aid as well as providing "friendly intercourse" in order to "reform character" and bring about moral uplift.[29]

The work of the visitors demonstrated the helpful and practical, albeit restrained, assistance provided by the AICP. When families had no place to burn coal, the association lent stoves. When families needed clothing or food, AICP workers took up collections of used clothing and leftover "cold vittles." One visitor discovered a poor immigrant family out of money with nowhere to turn. Along with "religious instruction and consolation," the AICP provided food, clothing, and medical care for the ill wife and found work for the father and the family's five children. In a similar case a visitor found an Irish family with a father too sick to work, a mother who was also ill, and two small children. The visitor arranged for a doctor to care for the family until the husband's health improved and he was able to find a job. The work of the visitors was not predetermined. Instead, they searched for the best and most economical means of assisting families so they could survive, or even thrive, without further aid.[30]

"Physical evils produce moral evils," Hartley proclaimed. "Degrade men to the condition of brutes, and they will have brutal propensities and passions."[31] The environment of

"Doing the slums." The practice of "slumming" in Manhattan—in which wealthy "tourists" visited the slums of the city in order to "appreciate" how the poor lived—dates from the first half of the nineteenth century. *Courtesy of the Library of Congress.*

the slums, Hartley suggested, was a cause of, or at least a contributing factor to, poverty. The AICP, therefore, led a number of campaigns to improve conditions for the poor. They opened dispensaries to provide medical care, created a savings bank to help establish habits of thrift, and established a bathhouse so the poor could remain clean. They pushed for legislation to secure the purity of milk and to bring about tenement reform. Following their "scientific" approach to charity and relief, they based many of these campaigns in monthlong studies and analyses of the communities of the poor. In 1855 the AICP even opened its own "model tenements" between Mott and Elizabeth streets, initially renting all the apartments to blacks, who, the association had found, had the most difficulty in finding quality housing in the city.[32]

The AICP became one of the dominant private charitable organizations in New York, but it was not alone in its desire for reform. Over the same period, in reaction to the same pressures of immigration, depression, and expanding slums, the city government attempted to reform its services to better alleviate poverty. To do so required a massive investment in and reorganization of the services overseen by what would become known as the Almshouse Department. By the end of the period, the city had developed a robust and far-reaching public social-welfare system. Reform of the unwieldy complex of institutions within the city's Almshouse Department was, by necessity, slower and less coherent than the overhaul of private charity that Hartley realized through the AICP. The institutions the department oversaw included the massive almshouse at Bellevue, which accommodated some 1,400 inmates; the City Prison and Penitentiary on Blackwell's Island (now Roosevelt Island), in the East River; and the city Lunatic Asylum, also on Blackwell's. In addition, the Almshouse Department oversaw the provision of outdoor relief to thousands of families annually in the form of fuel, food, and cash while managing the city's public hospital. To reform this complicated operation required sustained vision and leadership, a proposition made difficult by the electoral competition over control of city government.[33]

In spite of these difficulties, the city managed to develop a more rational and responsive, but no less expensive, system of public relief. The first reform initiated by the city was aimed at children. For decades, reaching back to the writing of Ezra Stiles Ely, critics of the almshouse complained that children living among the adult paupers learned habits of indolence and criminality from those who surrounded them. In 1831 the city purchased 230 acres of farmland on the East River shore of what is now Queens with the intention of building an institution to house children. The project, however, encountered numerous delays; construction of a building to serve as a nursery and schoolhouse did not begin until 1835. Two years later, when the Almshouse Department finally moved all the white children across the river to Long Island Farms (black children were barred from the new institution), the campus remained incomplete and undersupplied. For its nearly ten years in operation, however, an average of 600 children were in residence at the institution, attending school and receiving care from the matron and superintendent.[34]

Even if Long Island Farms could have met all the physical needs of the children — and records show routine shortages of food, clothing, and fuel — it was doomed to fail. Given the expectations for a loving, sheltered childhood that existed by the 1840s, middle-class visitors found the institution established by the city to be lacking.[35] Visiting the farms in 1842, the writer Lydia Maria Child described the buildings as "clean and comfortable" and believed the children appeared "happy." But she questioned whether these young public charges received all that they truly needed. The sustenance "which the spirit craves," Child explained, "the public has not to give. The young heart asks for love, yearns for love — but its own echo returns to it though empty halls, instead of answer." Child had no specific criticism of those who ran the institution, but she lamented "that there are no mothers there." Instead, everything moved "by machinery, as it always must with masses of children, never subdivided into families." The question of how to create more loving, family-like environments to care for children, both inside and outside institutions, would haunt generations of reformers.[36]

At the same time, city leaders attempted to make municipal government more efficient. The prominent lawyer and Democrat Robert H. Morris, winning his first one-year term as mayor in 1841 and subsequently elected for two more years, declared that the city "government should be so systemized as to be carried on by the least number of agents compatible with its importance."[37] To achieve these ends, and to bypass the spoils-seeking common council, Morris advocated the direct election of heads of the various city departments. In reference to public poverty relief, Morris called for the city to create specialized institutions — a workhouse for able-bodied poor and an upgraded almshouse for those deserving of aid — by moving the whole almshouse apparatus from Bellevue to new structures to be constructed on Blackwell's and Randall's islands. Morris, however, was not able to implement these reforms before a nativist candidate defeated him in the mayoral election of 1844. Morris's vision, however, would be realized in 1845, with the reorganization of the Almshouse Department under the control of a single, elected almshouse commissioner.[38]

Moses G. Leonard, the city's first elected almshouse commissioner, took it as his charge to modernize the city's system of poverty relief. A Democratic Party activist and former congressman, Leonard directed the almshouse long enough to complete its reorganization before departing for San Francisco in the midst of the gold rush. By 1848 Leonard had successfully opened a new campus of institutions on Blackwell's Island that included separate almshouses for men and women, converted the old almshouse at Bellevue into a public hospital, and established a campus of buildings on Randall's Island to serve as an improved nursery, replacing the failed experiment of Long Island Farms. Leonard also established the annual reports of the Almshouse Department, providing a clear account-ing of the number of persons receiving care and relief from the city.[39]

Those changes did little to reduce the number of aid recipients, which remained steady, or to reduce costs, since the Almshouse Department continued to represent the fastest-growing portion of the city budget into the 1850s. They did, however, transform the experience of the residents in city institutions.[40] That was especially true for the chil-dren in the almshouse nursery on Randall's Island and in the private, but partly publicly supported, Colored Orphan Asylum. The life of an abandoned child—or foundling, in the terminology of the time—was a struggle from the moment of birth. While a number of private institutions had opened to care for orphans and half-orphans in the 1830s, un-til after the Civil War the city's Almshouse Department bore sole responsibility for caring and providing for abandoned children. In addition, the city became the caretaker for all the orphans who, for various reasons, were excluded from the private orphanages. Ran-dall's Island emerged as the center of public welfare for children in New York City, but the collection of institutions that made up the almshouse nursery was unequipped to deal with infants. For newborn children, therefore, the city continued to rely on a network of nurses. Some of these women were widowed, but most claimed to be married, although their husbands may have been absent. Whatever their circumstances, nursing almshouse babies provided a significant source of income—so much so that some women would take on infants from the almshouse even before they had weaned their own children. Infants would remain with these nurses until they were two or three years old. Some were adopted at this stage; most, however, were transferred to the collection of buildings on Randall's Island.[41]

The managers of the nursery on Randall's Island saw the institution as representing a romantic, pastoral ideal, in contrast to the urban squalor from which their charges had been rescued. Commissioner Leonard emphasized that rather than overlooking increas-ingly crowded Manhattan, the buildings elevated at the center of the island afforded "a view of Flushing bay, the intervening islands and adjacent country—one of the finest prospects in the vicinity of New York."[42] The twenty-two-acre clearing on the island abut-ted the shore on one side and was surrounded on three others by "a neat picket fence." The twelve buildings contained within these fences constituted two institutions: the nursery proper, including a schoolhouse and children's residences, and the nursery hospital, in-cluding structures to care for physically ill indigent children and "the Idiots' Dwelling" for the mentally disabled.[43]

Leonard took particular pride in this new campus of buildings on Randall's Island. "Having been incommoded with miserable and unsightly hovels for many years," as he boasted soon after the nursery opened, in 1848, New York could now take satisfaction in "possessing the most thoroughly complete, convenient and elegant establishment for the rearing of young orphans of the City's care known in the world—here, true humanity can fulfill its ennobling mission." Many features of the children's dormitories had indeed been unavailable in previous institutions and were largely absent from the tenement neighborhoods. The buildings were all connected to the fresh water of the city's Croton Reservoir system and served by a sewer system that released all of the waste into the river. Innovative facilities inside the dormitories supplied warm and cold running water to a circular tub, ten feet in diameter, "used for bathing by a dozen of the children at once." A special pipe sprayed water so children could wash their hands and faces, an attempt to reduce the eye infections common in the institution.[44]

The children on Randall's Island spent most of their time in school or at work. Boys completed farm work or learned the tailoring trade by making men's clothing. Girls also sewed, producing clothing and towels for use in the various almshouse institutions.[45] Still, some of the children's time was reserved for recreation. Children played on the landscaped grounds, or, during "the inclement season," in two brick "play-houses."[46] The nursery also constructed separate bathhouses for boys and girls to allow for healthful swimming away "from the turbidness of the water and the strong currents of the river."[47] Reflecting new conceptions of childhood, the almshouse commissioners placed importance on providing

The Nursery Establishment on Randall's Island. The nursery provided a home for poor, abandoned, and orphaned children separate from the adults in the municipal almshouse. *Picture Collection, The New York Public Library, Astor, Lenox and Tilden Foundations.*

an "opportunity for the innocent recreation so pleasing to the youthful fancy." The alms-house nursery allowed children to act like children.[48]

But it was not simply physical activity that was expected to foster the children's healthy development; the very environment in which the nursery was placed, argued Leonard and the other commissioners, portended a decrease in the high illness and mortality rates that had characterized children's institutions in the past. "The health of the children has so much improved since their removal to *Randall's Island*," wrote Leonard in 1848, "that the salubrity and fitness of the place for their residence may now be consid-ered as fairly tested." Like Robert Hartley, the city's Almshouse Department subscribed to a belief in environmentalism. The twin evils of poverty and disease arose not only from individuals and their actions, but from the very areas in which they lived. By the act of re-moving orphaned and abandoned children to the bucolic environment of Randall's Island, the city had resuscitated their health and given them the possibility of a successful future.

Not all of the city's orphans and abandoned children went to live in the pastoral splendor of Randall's Island, however. By the decision of the Almshouse Department, New York's child welfare institutions remained racially segregated; African American children were barred from the institutions of Randall's Island. Still, by the late 1840s the city had realized it needed to take some responsibility for the orphaned black children within its borders, most of whom resided in the Colored Orphaned Asylum. In 1848 the city agreed to cover a portion of the asylum's expenses. After estimating the number of children in the asylum who were "*truly* paupers," the city agreed to pay for the care of two-thirds of the children, up to a limit of one hundred boys and girls at a rate of fifty cents per child each week. The remaining costs of the institution would be met through private donations, provided almost exclusively by the asylum's Quaker supporters. Thus, the city developed a public-private partnership that took responsibility for the care of African American chil-dren in need while maintaining the segregation of public institutions.[49]

Black children's need for institutional care in this period was particularly high. The influx of immigrants had displaced African Americans from their occupations and from the neighborhoods in which they lived. The percentage of black men in positions of skilled labor declined precipitously during the mid-nineteenth century. Even those un-skilled jobs that had once been dominated by blacks—those of domestic servant, waiter, and laborer—were now largely taken up by Irish immigrants. Faced with these chal-lenges, many blacks left the city.[50] The effects of these dislocations were evident in the heart-rending state in which many children arrived at the Colored Orphan Asylum. One five-year-old girl, described in the records only as "E_____ B_____," was once a mem-ber of a family with four children. Abandoned by the father, the mother soon contracted an illness "of almost inconceivable wretchedness" and died "of neglect and starvation."

The eldest child went to work for a master chimney sweep who abused him and refused to release him from service. The youngest child, an infant, ended up "in the arms of an intoxicated female" and was presumed dead. The third sibling was lucky enough to be adopted by "a worthy and compassionate colored neighbor." The five-year-old, however, arrived at the asylum "with her feet badly frozen and her whole appearance indicating extreme suffering." With so few other sources of support available, the Colored Orphan Asylum often meant the difference between life and death for such children.[51]

For both the white orphans on Randall's Island and the black orphans in the Colored Orphan Asylum, managers prescribed a program of indenturing once the children reached ten to twelve years of age. In the eighteenth century, an era when apprenticeship and indentured servitude were commonplace, binding a child out to a family was unremarkable; by the mid-nineteenth century, with these older legal agreements declining rapidly in use,

Girls in the courtyard of Home for the Friendless. The home, founded in 1848, was intended to address the growing problems of poor working women at a disadvantage in their dealings with employers. At Home for the Friendless, girls and women learned trades and received religious and moral guidance. *Collection of the New-York Historical Society, 70221.*

binding out had become almost exclusively a practice of public and private child welfare institutions. Both the Almshouse Department and the Colored Orphan Asylum made concerted efforts to indenture children outside the city. Placing children mostly on farms in rural communities was intended to accomplish several goals: it would train children to work, situate them within family structures, and expose them to the countryside, considered an antidote to the dangerous, immoral contagions of the city. Most of the children indentured by the Colored Orphan Asylum were sent to nearby farming communities in Westchester County, on Long Island, or in New Jersey or Connecticut. Some were placed as far west as Illinois and as far north as Maine. While the Randall's Island nursery continued to indenture children in and around the city, by the 1850s more children were sent to "the country towns of this and adjoining states," and some as far west as Iowa City.[52]

The focus on the countryside as the best place for children was based in two notions that gained popularity in the mid-nineteenth century. One was a pastoral romanticism that had a long tradition in American thought. According to this way of thinking, the country and the small village were somehow more democratic, more egalitarian, in other words more American, than urban areas. The other view of the countryside was as a relief valve for the increasing pressure of urban poverty. If the city's poor could be spread out across the country, they would find work more easily. In addition, from the upper-class perspective, the decrease in the urban concentration of poor and working-class people would lessen their ability to swing elections or even engage in violent revolt against political and economic elites. Given the European revolutions of 1848 (and the publication of the *Communist Manifesto*), such developments came to be seen as real possibilities that reformers worked to avoid. Indenturing children out in the countryside, therefore, was part of a larger effort to dilute the power of the poor and working class.[53]

Orphans, however, refused to fall in line with the desires of these reformers. Most of the orphans bound out by the Colored Orphan Asylum failed to complete their indentures. Some ran away; others sought new placements through the asylum; and in one case of outright rebellion, an orphan burned down the barn on the farm where she had been bound out. The records of the Almshouse Department provide little information about the outcomes for children placed in the countryside, but it is likely that they, too, resisted the placements. In spite of the desires of reformers, children were often unwilling to leave the networks of family and friends and ties to ethnic and religious communities they knew in the city for greater opportunities they might find in rural areas. Over the 1840s, this tension would take on new importance as experts described a crisis of homeless children in New York.[54]

The Children of the Street

"The child is as susceptible to surrounding influences as the rose-bush or the bird, the spring violet or the unweaned lamb," preached the Reverend Thomas L. Harris in 1850. "Nay as much more susceptible as its organism is more complicated and delicate and its capability more divinely beautiful and lasting." Harris concluded that "unless the atmosphere of the home be genial, healthful, loving and beneficent the child must grow to maturity, imperfect, unhealthful and depraved." According to middle-class reformers, mid-nineteenth-century New York City faced an explosion of children who were not growing up in homes, at least homes of the loving type Reverend Harris described. The outcome, observers feared, would be a growing population of the impoverished and dangerous.[55]

The first to sound the alarm over this problem was George W. Matsell, the chief of the city's first professional police force. In an 1850 report of the police department, Matsell attempted to describe and quantify the "constantly increasing number" of what he termed "vagrants, idle and vicious children of both sexes, who infest our public thoroughfares, hotels, and docks." These children, "growing up in ignorance and profligacy," were "destined to a life of misery, shame and crime, and ultimately to a felon's doom." Matsell sorted these street children into several categories. First were those, mostly boys, who stole "cotton, sugar, spirits, coffee, teas" from the city's piers. Second were the young girls who worked as "crossing sweepers," sweeping the streets at intersections purportedly to keep the mud off pedestrians' shoes but actually to extort tips. Third were the girls who peddled "fruits, socks, toothpicks," and other small items and who in many cases, according to Matsell, also provided sexual acts for "the miserable bribe of a few shillings." Fourth were the boys whom Matsell "termed 'Baggage Smashers.'" He described them as gathering "around steamboat landings and railroad depots," ostensibly "for the purpose of carrying parcels, for persons arriving in the city," but also willing to "steal when opportunity offers." Some of these boys lived on the streets or "occasionally in cheap lodgings." An even larger class of boys engaged in similar behavior but had families to return to at night. Finally, in addition to the more than 3,000 children Matsell estimated to be "embryo courtezans and felons," there were an additional 2,383 who did not attend school. If Matsell's figures were to be trusted, a significant number of New York's poor juveniles spent every day unsupervised and up to no good.[56]

This was not the first time New York's respectable classes had become alarmed at the problem of child vagrancy. Reverend John Stanford's letters on this issue had helped create the New York House of Refuge, an institution that by the 1850s had become the juvenile reformatory for New York State, sharing Randall's Island with the almshouse nursery. But the house of refuge's mission had become much more focused on reforming juvenile criminality than on curbing the acts of poor and homeless children that only bordered on the criminal. Some, including Reverend Thomas L. Harris, advocated the opening of a new institution, a "Home for Children," that could provide for the homeless children Matsell had described. With the support of the AICP, the New York Juvenile Asylum was chartered by the state in 1851 and charged to care for any children from the age of five to fourteen who were found in public places "in the circumstances of want and suffering, or abandonment, exposure or neglect, or of beggary." The institution opened its doors in 1853; a year later it was sheltering 200 children.[57] Like the other institutions of the day, the juvenile asylum emphasized the homelike qualities of its facility. "The government of the Institution has been strictly parental," the managers of the asylum reported. "The prominent object has been to give a home feeling and home interest to the children — to create and cultivate a family feeling."[58]

The most influential response to the problem of homeless children, however, was not the creation of more institutions but the establishment of a program grounded in an anti-institutional perspective. The program sought to place children not in homelike institutions but in actual homes. This effort was spearheaded by Charles Loring Brace and the Children's Aid Society. Born in Litchfield, Connecticut, Brace was always a high achiever. Entering Yale University at only 16 years of age, in 1842, Brace quickly befriended the brothers John and Frederick Law Olmsted, two members of a generation of reformers who

Charles Loring Brace, founder of the Children's Aid Society. Brace believed that the city had an obligation to help impoverished children become morally decent and productive individuals; otherwise the children would "poison" society. *Print Collection, Miriam and Ira D. Wallach Division of Art, Prints and Photographs, The New York Public Library, Astor, Lenox and Tilden Foundations.*

would transform New York City—the latter in part through the design of Central Park and Brooklyn's Prospect Park. After college Brace spent a year at Yale Divinity School, studying for the ministry, before transferring to the more liberal Union Theological Seminary, in New York City. The experience of living in the city, especially ministering to those in the institutions on Blackwell's Island, changed the young Brace; by 1850 he hoped to redirect his career path from the "theological" to the "practical." Before setting out on a career in social reform, Brace joined the Olmsted brothers on a European tour. In Germany Brace was particularly impressed by *Rauhes Haus,* a farm-based orphan asylum that housed children in small cottages rather than large institutions. To Brace, the rural and family-like setting was vastly superior to institutions for children he had toured back in the U.S.[59]

In 1853, after returning to New York, Brace founded the Children's Aid Society, an organization dedicated to "the training and general improvement of the conditions of the homeless and friendless children roaming the streets of New York."[60] These were not necessarily orphaned or abandoned children; instead, the society looked to assist those children who were not receiving what Brace and others viewed as acceptable supervision, even if they were living with parents or other guardians. Brace looked to fulfill this mission without relying on large institutions. Asylums, he implied, were inconsistent with American attitudes. "They breed," he later argued, "a species of character which is monastic—indolent, unused to struggle; subordinate indeed, but with little independence and manly vigor." Rather than inspiring virtue in children, asylums often led to "a hidden growth of secret and contagious vices."[61] Most importantly, the CAS explained in its first annual report, "Asylums and City Institutions" failed to "reach a vast multitude of neglected children, who were growing up in the worst habits, but who could not in any legal sense of the term be called *vagrant*." The CAS would work to reach "homeless" children— those not living in the conditions found in middle-class homes—who, under the law, would be ineligible for institutional placement.[62]

The CAS was unabashed about the class-based political motivations for its programs. "There are no dangers to the value of property or the permanency of our institutions, so great as those from the existence of such a class of vagabond, ignorant, ungoverned children," the organization declared. "This 'dangerous class' had not begun to show itself," the CAS warned, "as it will in eight or ten years, when these boys and girls are matured. Those who were too negligent or too selfish to notice them as children, will be fully aware of them as men. They will vote. They will have the same rights as we ourselves, though they have grown up ignorant of moral principle, as any savage or Indian. They will poison society. They will perhaps be embittered at the wealth, and the luxuries, they never share. Then let society beware, when the outcast, vicious, reckless multitude of New-York boys, swarming now in every foul alley and low street, come to know their power and use it!"[63]

The CAS argued for action by appealing not only to charitable instincts but also to a sense of self-preservation, presenting the wild children New Yorkers encountered on the street as more than a nuisance. In an age of political and social revolution, such children portended a threat to person, property, and the social order.

Brace and the CAS developed a two-track strategy to deal with the problem of children in the street. On one track they would build schools, lodging houses, and a staff of visitors to investigate and aid children in New York. On the second track they would form a network to funnel poor children out of the city and into the West. While Brace feared the political outcomes of a large class of homeless children, he designed his programs not to force children into a particular social mold, but instead to make the most of the children's independence and individuality. Industrial schools taught marketable trades to girls found peddling or sweeping streets. Girls would attend school for the entire day; in the mornings they would gain a basic education in English, and after "a plain cheap dinner" at noon, they would learn "sewing and light trades, [such] as straw-braiding [and] crochet-work."[64] The CAS focused on the untapped potential of the children. The girls in their schools were "children of very ignorant parents" but were "themselves quick, bright, ungoverned, and often [of] rare personal beauty."[65] The schools provided the children with a basic and practical education that would free them from the economic demands of their potentially intemperate parents and the draw of immoral acts such as prostitution.

To Charles Loring Brace and his agents, the problem of homeless boys was even more prevalent and more troubling than that of the girls on the streets. Brace realized that the boys survived with "their hand against every man's pocket," but he was impressed by their ingenuity and "their kindness to one another."[66] Brace was particularly enamored of the newsboys, with "their sturdy independence," seeing them as junior entrepreneurs struggling to get ahead in the competitive urban environment. One agent discovered, for example, a "homeless boy—a news-boy—quick, shrewd and impudent, but weakened now by hunger. Had not slept in a home *for a year;* lies down in boxes or printing-house alleys, or in the court near the press-rooms." The boy "had 'got stuck' he said; could not sell his papers, and of course had no capital for the next day; and so went on until he was in the half-starved condition."[67] To help this population Brace set up a network of Newsboy Lodging Houses. Without providing outright charity, which might lead to dependency and pauperism, Brace developed a means to take these boys off the streets. "The first thing to be aimed at in the plan was," Brace explained, "to treat the lads as independent little dealers, and give them nothing without payment, but at the same time to offer them much more for their money than they could get anywhere else. Moral, educational, and religious influences were to come afterward. Securing them through their interests, we had a permanent hold of them." Unlike the other asylums and institutions in the city, the lodging

Interior, Children's Aid Society's Newsboy Lodging House. These dormitories provided
a safe and wholesome alternative to sleeping on the streets or in makeshift lodging.
Picture Collection, The New York Public Library, Astor, Lenox and Tilden Foundations.

houses aimed not to reform and rehabilitate a boy's character, but to cultivate the positive
characteristics already present in him.[68]

While the CAS's work within the city of New York was critical to its mission, its most
influential innovations were in placing children in the countryside. Brace, of course, was
not the first to remove children from the city and place them in the homes of families.
But unlike the leaders of other organizations, such as the Randall's Island nursery and the
Colored Orphans Asylum, he rejected the use of indenture in his system of "placing-out,"
instead relying on informal verbal agreements between the CAS agent and the substitute
guardian. The agreement required the guardian to care for and educate the child while
allowing that either party could end the arrangement at no cost.[69] Brace viewed the farm
households where children were placed as both employers and substitute families. Farmers, Brace reasoned, needed laborers to complete their work. These "laborers or 'help,'
must be members of their families." Therefore, Brace expected farmers to treat these new
laborers as they would their own children.[70] Brace realized that people accepted children
based on a variety of motivations. "People who were childless came forward to adopt children," he observed after the system was put into operation. Others applied for children to

Poster soliciting homes for children arriving on an "orphan train" from New York City. *The Children's Aid Society Records, Collection of the New-York Historical Society, 82722d.*

house as a form of charity. On the other end of the continuum, those "who really wanted the children's labor pressed forward to obtain it."[71]

The society first experimented with placing out in farm communities in upstate New York, then expanded the operation to include Pennsylvania, Rhode Island, and, to a limited extent, the upper New England states. In 1854 the CAS took its first group—forty-six children—by railroad and lake boat to Dowagiac, Michigan. The states of Ohio, Indiana, Illinois, Iowa, Missouri, Kansas, and Michigan, then considered "the West," would receive 90 percent of the children who "emigrated" from New York through the society. By 1884, 60,000 children had been placed out by the CAS.[72]

Given the system established by the organization, the experience of the children who rode what came to be known as "orphan trains" was fairly uniform. "We were taken from the train to the Methodist Church," recalled one boy. "Speeches were made and folks were asked to take an orphan home for dinner. Later that afternoon we were brought back for the selection process." Adults were allowed to choose whichever of the children best fit their needs. The children, it appears, had some agency in determining if they would go home with particular families. One boy refused placement with two different farmers before being persuaded to go home with a 60-year-old couple. His selectiveness seems to have paid off. The boys eventually chosen by the farmers he had rejected "were hardly more than slaves to them," the discriminating boy recalled, but "I had the best home of all the orphans I had come with."[73] There was probably a wide range of relationships that developed between these children and their substitute caregivers. None of them were formally adopted — adoption law itself was only in its infancy, and many of these children had at least one living parent — but some appeared to develop close attachments to their new families. One agent, somewhat perversely, asked Brace to pass on the news to a set of "weeping parents" that their little Mary had "been adopted as their own" by a family in Peoria, Illinois.[74] Other children were undoubtedly exploited as cheap labor.

The programs of the CAS were not without their critics. Catholics were particularly suspicious of the organization. "Every family I visited turned out to be Roman Catholic and most of them bigoted too," Henry Friedgen, a CAS visitor, recorded one day in his journal. These families, he continued, "positively decline to have anything to do (or even take in to their hand one of our cards) with Protestants."[75] The placing-out program only

Children leaning from the window of a westbound train. "Orphan trains" were sponsored in part by the Children's Aid Society. The society sent more than 120,000 children from coastal cities to the Midwest between 1853 and the early years of the twentieth century. *The Children's Aid Society Records, Collection of the New-York Historical Society, 82697d.*

exacerbated such suspicions. Catholics claimed, with some justification, that Brace was taking their children out of the city and placing them with Protestant families.[76]

The CAS represented not only a particular religious perspective but a middle-class perspective, one defined by a culture and lifestyle increasingly different from those found in New York's slums. By the late 1850s a visit from an agent of the CAS or another, similar organization must have been a familiar experience for poor families. Some welcomed the assistance that such visitors would provide. Margaret McKenny, an Irish Catholic woman from Brooklyn, went directly to the CAS office in March 1857 to describe her desperate state. Her husband was terminally ill, and she was unable to care for her three children. She gave specific directions regarding where she could be found, and the daily record book noted her desire to "be visited as soon as possible."[77] Henry Friedgen was welcomed by many families with children who had been sent west by the CAS. He "found them thankful and glad to hear from their children." Of course, they shared "their sorrow for their separation and their anxiety" that their children were "in good places." Yet, "after being assured of this," Friedgen reported, "they feel content and happy for their children."[78]

Some families, however, put up greater resistance to such intervention. Samuel Halliday, head of the American Female Guardian Society and Home for the Friendless, described the story of Tommy Mack and the dispute with his parents. Halliday "found Tommy on the street bareheaded and barefooted, his hair standing out in sticks" as if it contained "molasses or tar." His face, also, was covered with "the tarry compound." The scant clothing the child was wearing provided little protection from the midwinter cold. "His pants," Halliday observed, "would not stay on, except by the assistance of both hands, for, in sailor phrase, they were split fore and aft — a rent more than half a yard long revealing his mottled hide." Unable to find the boy's father and learning that his mother was in prison, Halliday agreed to take the boy to his asylum. First, however, he stopped at "the photographers, where Tommy in rags, sitting on a tea-chest, had his likeness taken, making a most emphatic picture." When the mother was released from prison, Tommy's parents went to the asylum and insisted on regaining custody of their child. While the mother threatened to "burn the building down," Halliday refused to give the child up to such unfit parents. Tommy's parents took the society to court, where they had little luck. The mother and father gave "the most ardent assurances to the court of their respectability," but the case came to rest on Tommy's photograph. According to Halliday, the judge had only to examine the picture briefly before determining that the actions of the society had been legal and lecturing the parents that "they ought to be thankful that there were so good hands ready to provide for him." In the contest between the emerging social-welfare organizations and poor parents, the middle-class welfare agents clearly had the upper hand.[79]

New York's Civil War

On April 12, 1861 the rebellious southern states fired on the federal outpost of Fort Sumter, in South Carolina. The American Civil War had begun. Miles from the front lines, New York City's poor and working-class families felt the effects of the war. While the early months of the war created a demand for labor and brought high wages, those wages failed to keep pace with rampant inflation. Between 1860 and 1863 beef nearly doubled in price, the cost of coal jumped by almost a third, and rents went up between 15 and 20 percent; over the same period, wages increased by only 12 percent. The families of Union Army soldiers felt the economic effects of the war even more deeply. To help meet the needs of those families who had lost wage earners to the war effort, the city developed a system of relief for wives and children. But these funds were quickly expended. Women in need demonstrated at City Hall and outside the homes of councilmen. At one point, when such relief was suspended, 200 women protested at Tompkins Square. One mother complained, "you have got me men into the souldiers, and now you have to kepe us from starving." Community festivals raised funds to directly aid those left impoverished, widowed, or orphaned by the war, supplementing the sometimes haphazard public effort. Still, with the relative value of wages declining, workers engaged in a series of strikes throughout 1862 and 1863, demanding raises to keep pace with ballooning costs. Along with the crisis of inflation came one of shelter, as housing construction declined over the war years. Already crowded tenement districts in Lower Manhattan became more crowded and rundown; thousands of squatters settled in the rocky terrain above Fiftieth Street. This decline in the well-being of the poor and working class created simmering tensions within the city. When the federal government initiated a widespread conscription of soldiers into the Union Army, while allowing those who could afford it to get out of military service by hiring proxies, these tensions erupted into violence. The victims of this outbreak of aggression would be New York City's black residents.[80]

On July 13, 1863, the 233 children residing in the Colored Orphan Asylum were going about their normal activities. At 4 p.m. most of the children "were quietly seated in their school rooms," the younger children were "playing in the nursery," and a few ill children were "reclining on a sick bed in the hospital." It took the staff and children by surprise, then, when the institution came under attack by "an infuriated mob, consisting of several thousand men, women, and children, armed with clubs, brickbats, etc." With little warning, "four or five hundred" of these rioters entered the building "by breaking down the front door with an axe."[81] Shouting, "Burn the niggers' nest," the crowd destroyed the asylum's property and set fire to the building in a matter of twenty minutes.[82] Heroism and good fortune allowed all of the children to escape unharmed. The staff of the institution "noiselessly collect[ed] the children." "The boys were concealed under the back piazza, the

girls arranged in the dining room." With all accounted for, the staff led the children out
of the building to a police precinct house, where they found protection for the next three
days and nights, as rioting continued across the city.[83]

The destruction of the Colored Orphan Asylum was only one incident in what became known as the Draft Riots of 1863, one of the bloodiest and most destructive events
in the history of New York City. The uprising began in an effort to halt the federal draft for
the Union Army. But resistance to fighting in the war, recast since the 1863 Emancipation
Proclamation as a war to free the slaves, morphed into aggression toward abolitionists,
blacks, and the wealthy. In the view of many observers, the riot was not only a protest
against conscription, but a revolt of the poor and working class. A particularly virulent
racism animated the rioters, but for the middle-class the racial conflict was less troubling
than poor New Yorkers' demonstrated ability to shut down the city. Middle-class commentators were particularly disturbed by the fact that whole families participated in the
rioting. One writer recalled as many as "5000 men, women and children" taking part in "a
scene of wild license scarcely surpassed by any single incident of the French Revolution;

New York City Draft Riots, 1863. Rioters can be seen looting and throwing blazing
objects at the Colored Orphan Asylum. All of the children residing in the asylum
escaped unharmed. *Emmet Collection, Miriam and Ira D. Wallach Division of Art, Prints
and Photographs, The New York Public Library, Astor, Lenox and Tilden Foundations.*

women, and mothers at that, with their bare breast exposed to the winds of heaven, bran-
dishing deadly weapons and uttering foul and loathsome language."[84] Some mothers may
have simply taken advantage of the riot to loot goods that their families could not afford;
others were enraged by the draft itself, which threatened to take their income-providing
husbands and sons away from them; still other women may have been motivated by anger
at the Protestant elite and their lack of attention to the needs of poor families.[85]

By the time order was restored, on Thursday, July 17, 1863, at least 119 people had
been killed, many of them African Americans tortured and lynched by the angry mob.
In the aftermath of the riot, many blacks simply left New York City; by 1865 the city's
African American population had decreased by 20 percent.[86] Meanwhile, the white working class — mostly of Irish and German descent — began to see their prospects improve.
Employment remained plentiful, and a series of successful strikes in 1864 led to significant increases in wages. While inflation remained a serious problem, New York's poorest
classes had perhaps more money than they had ever seen before.[87] By the end of the Civil
War, New York, to all appearances, had entered a period of peace and prosperity. But just
below the surface, the tensions of race, ethnicity, religion, and class that had erupted in the
Draft Riots continued to simmer. Upper- and middle-class New Yorkers lived in fear of
another uprising, and poor New Yorkers continued to resent both the conditions in which
they lived and the interventions of the middle class into their lives.

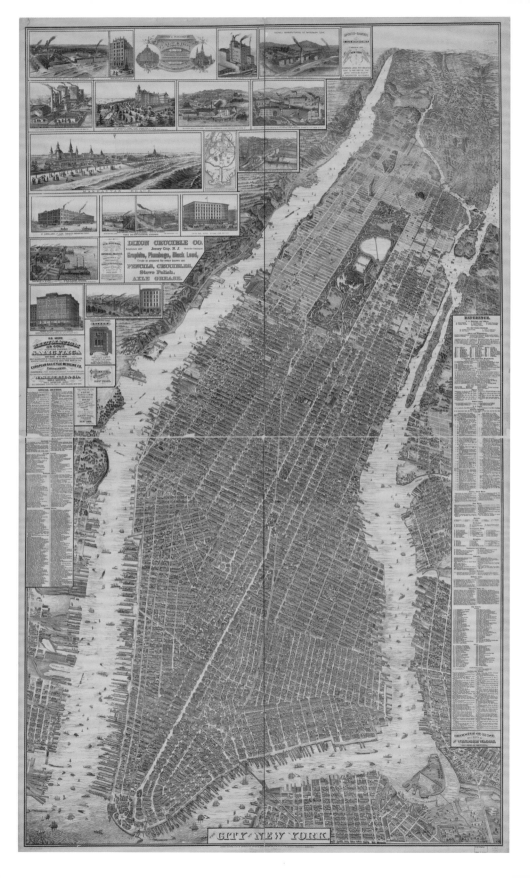

CITY OF NEW YORK.

Chapter 4

Family Poverty in the Age of Unrest

The mix of religion, ethnicity, and class that existed in late-nineteenth-century New York City created tangled lines of fear and mistrust. Natives feared immigrants. Catholics mistrusted Protestants. Blacks mistrusted whites. Jews feared Gentiles. Most importantly, the rich feared the poor. The 1863 Draft Riots revealed, for many, the class tensions simmering just below the veneer of everyday city life. The working-class uprising that briefly took control of the city of Paris in 1871, known as the Paris Commune, only heightened suspicions among New York's "respectable" classes of an imminent, worldwide revolt of workers and the poor. "There are just the same explosive social elements beneath the surface of New York as of Paris," wrote Charles Loring Brace in 1872. Evoking the memory of the Draft Riots, Brace asked, "Who will ever forget the marvelous rapidity with which the better streets were filled with a ruffianly and desperate multitude, such as in ordinary times we seldom see — creatures who seemed to have crept from their burrows and dens to join in the plunder of the city — how quickly certain houses were marked out for sacking and ruin, and what wild and brutal crimes were committed on the unoffending negroes?"[1]

These fears emerged in a period of intense urban growth. By 1870 the counties that would later become the five boroughs of Greater New York already had a population of more than one million. By the turn of the century, New York would be the second-largest city in the world. The high concentration of individuals in itself created problems in the areas of transportation, housing, and sanitation. The ethnic and religious diversity of the city complicated these already difficult issues. In 1870, 83 percent of the city's population had at least one parent born overseas.[2] While the city maintained a Protestant majority over the late nineteenth century, it has been estimated that 40 percent of the population

The City of New York, 1879. Published when the Brooklyn Bridge was nearing completion, this bird's-eye-view map testified to the city's growth. Smaller, detailed illustrations depict factories, a harbor, and other points of interest. *Courtesy of the Library of Congress.*

was Roman Catholic, and by 1890 the Jewish population had grown to 10 percent of the city.[3] The animosity among classes, ethnicities, and religious groups present in this urban crucible created what many observers believed was a potential crisis.

The economic collapse of the 1870s only exacerbated this sense of crisis. In the fall of 1873, the railroad-investment bubble that had sustained the economy in the years after the Civil War burst. The collapse of the real-estate market in the city quickly followed. A wave of bankruptcies soon engulfed investment houses and other businesses. As usual, the working poor bore the brunt of the suffering. By the winter of 1873–74, 25 percent of New York's labor force was out of work, and many of those who managed to find jobs saw their wages decline. There was no end in sight for the suffering; the economic downturn would last until the end of the decade. In later years the period would become known as "the Long Depression."[4]

While homelessness had long existed in the city, the depression of the 1870s made people living on the streets more noticeable. The word "tramp" quickly came to define the new homeless. Tramps, typically men, had no ties to particular localities or communities; they roamed the city and countryside searching for means to survive, becoming, according to middle-class observers, an army of the poor threatening respectable society. The threat created by tramps was certainly exaggerated, but the underlying problem was real. New York police stations had provided lodging for the homeless since the 1840s, but now these station houses were overrun with people looking for places to sleep. Vagrancy laws had been on the books in New York for decades, but the number of vagrancy arrests increased by 50 percent between 1874 and 1878.[5]

The rise of the tramp led to a redefinition of homelessness over the late nineteenth century. Before the Civil War Charles Loring Brace and other reformers viewed homelessness as a problem that mostly affected children. The "waifs" and "urchins" who could be found in New York were considered homeless either because they literally slept on the streets or because they lacked proper homes. By the end of the nineteenth century, however, the typical homeless person was a tramp. At times the emergence of the tramp in both the popular imagination and in the view of reformers obscured the reality of homelessness; astute observers still discovered homeless families with husband, wife and children all traveling together, and children continued to be arrested for vagrancy in New York.[6] But the growing focus on the single, male tramp increasingly reflected social trends. The number of women and children sleeping on the streets or in public lodging houses significantly declined, reaching a minuscule number by the 1890s. Organizations such as the Children's Aid Society as well as the Society for the Prevention of Cruelty to Children (founded in 1875) successfully funneled children into institutions or substitute families rather than lives of homelessness. Furthermore, as relief became increasingly privatized and organized, widowed or even deserted mothers came to be viewed as deserving of

Shantytown, probably at Park Avenue and 50th Street. Shanties housed entire families in New York during the depressions of the 1870s and 1890s. Children sit in the foreground of this undated photograph. *Collection of the New-York Historical Society, 84350d.*

assistance, allowing many families to survive without experiencing homelessness. Men, meanwhile, were largely excluded from the joint public-private social-welfare system that emerged in New York City. Instead, they were left to find work on their own or fend for themselves on the streets or in the lodging houses.[7]

In this period of economic malaise, poor families, struggling to improve their lives or simply stay afloat, faced imperfect choices. On one side was the urban machine that provided direct services to poor and working-class families in order to bolster its political strength. On the other side were middle-class and elite reformers driven by a desire to improve conditions in the city by ending corruption and waste, but also to keep political power out of the hands of recent immigrants. The ward leaders of Tammany Hall, the city's Democratic organization, were well known for providing targeted, personal aid — coal for heat, assistance with rent, jobs for the unemployed — but also for lining their own pockets. The elite reformers became known for imposing rationality and efficiency on the complex web of public and private social-assistance organizations in New York, but also for giving the appearance of a lack of sympathy for poor families.[8]

Many struggling families displayed affection both for the local political leaders who provided assistance to them and their neighbors and for the bosses of the urban machine. Even after Tammany boss William M. Tweed was arrested on charges of corruption, in 1871, he continued to find supporters among the city's poorer districts. This sentiment was certainly not shared by all New Yorkers. Critics of Tammany focused on the rampant graft that enriched its leaders, as well as the conflicts of interest that might lead ward heelers to assist individual families while, at the same time, resisting housing and sanitation reforms that would benefit the whole city. In response to the machine's approach to urban welfare, reformers embraced a scientific approach to urban problems. "The immense proportions which great cities are assuming," wrote social commentator E. L. Godkin in 1866, "make the arrangement and management of them the most important of all the problems of social science."[9] Individuals and organizations presented "scientific" housing plans, pushed for "scientific" charity, and presented "scientific" solutions to the problems of poverty and pauperism. When the investigation of Tweed revealed the depths of corruption in the Democratic machine, "scientific" reformers pushed even harder for their approach to

Dumping ground, Beach Street. "Ragpickers" like those seen here made a meager living collecting and selling usable trash. *HarpWeek, LLC.*

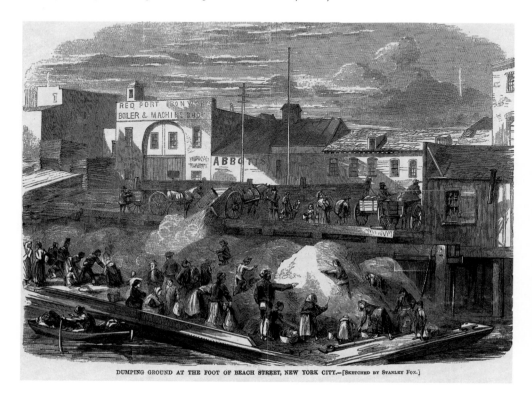

DUMPING GROUND AT THE FOOT OF BEACH STREET, NEW YORK CITY.—[Sketched by Stanley Fox.]

good government, arguing that its "honesty" and "efficiency" would benefit all residents of New York City.

New York's poor families were forced to negotiate between these conflicting approaches to poverty relief in whatever ways were necessary to survive. The scientific reformers saw themselves as secular, unbiased observers—agents of sanitation and social uplift—motivated by a desire to improve all of society. In many cases, however, as the work of such organizations as the Children's Aid Society, the Association for Improving the Condition of the Poor, and, later, the Charity Organization Society demonstrated, these reformers were perfectly willing to break up families, convert the children of Catholics to Protestantism, and otherwise control the lives of the poor. Political, ethnic, and religious leaders, on the other hand, were themselves motivated by desires for political power or for helping the poor in ways that improved the images of their own groups. With these limited options, some families turned to the burgeoning labor unions or radical political movements. Others simply made do—making use of the resources they needed, no matter the source.

The Growth of Catholic and Jewish Child Welfare

"All other institutions organized for the protection of destitute children are Protestant," wrote Levi Silliman Ives, a leading Catholic voice in New York City, "having Protestant directors, Protestant superintendents, Protestant teachers, Protestant worship, and Protestant instruction and teaching. Under such circumstances," Ives asked, "can it be thought surprising or unreasonable that poor Catholic parents should have a settled aversion to these Protestant institutions as the Christian home of their children?"[10] Over the first half of the nineteenth century, the city government and private organizations had developed an extensive array of institutions and programs for poor and homeless children. While these institutions were purportedly secular, from the perspective of Catholics like Ives and the growing number of Jews in the city, these were unquestionably Protestant organizations imbuing their charges with a Protestant worldview. The answer Ives proposed was the creation of Catholic institutions to provide an alternative to the existing, Protestant public and private institutions. Similarly, Jews developed the Hebrew Orphan Asylum to provide care for Jewish children suffering from abandonment, neglect, or poverty.

Catholic and Jewish leaders, then, had two goals in both founding new institutions in the 1860s and converting old institutions to new purposes. First, they sought an alternative plan to confront family poverty and child homelessness. Not only did they object to what they saw as Charles Loring Brace's thinly veiled efforts to convert children to

Protestant Christianity, but they also disagreed about the roots of family poverty. Where Brace saw destitute and neglectful families as the cause of their children's unsocial behavior, Jews and especially Catholics viewed the family, even the destitute family, as a bulwark against suffering. While some Catholic and Jewish institutions mimicked Brace in developing placing-out programs for poor and delinquent children, on the whole they rejected placing out as an appropriate response to family poverty. Instead, in most cases, these alternative institutions provided families with respite by temporarily taking in children during particularly desperate or trying times, then returning the children to their homes when the families regained stability. In this way, Catholic and Jewish institutions helped preserve families, rather than disassemble them in the interest of instituting moral structure, as Brace's placing out did.

The second goal of Catholic and Jewish elites was to use their charitable institutions as tools to make their poor coreligionists respectable in the eyes of New York, indeed American, society. Ives, appealing for funds for an alternative, Catholic approach to child welfare, described how for Irish youth "the allurements of vice and crime in every disgusting and debasing form" brought not only moral "ruin" but also "disgrace and obloquy on the Irish name." The mission of the institution, then, was to provide a helping hand to "these little sufferers" so they could become "instruments of good to society and an honor to their race."[11] Catholic and Jewish leaders often seemed ashamed when the actions of members of their communities did not accord with middle-class standards of behavior. One Catholic pastoral letter lamented, "Whether from poverty or neglect, … a large number of Catholic parents either appear to have no idea of the sanctity of the Christian family, and of the responsibility imposed on them of providing for the moral training of their offspring, or fulfill this duty in a very imperfect manner."[12] Similarly, a Jewish charitable organization, in an essay called "Our Poor," saved its greatest ire for "the deserters … those deprived of all honor of right and justice, without a spark of humanity, or love of human kindness, [who] basely desert their poor wives and children leaving them to the cold charities of the world in the most deplorable state of poverty, misery, and destitution."[13] Catholic and Jewish reformers saw their mission as saving the children of the poor by supporting and improving their families through direct support as well as institutional care for children. They knew they could not save every family, but they could insure the continuation of their faith while cultivating upstanding, moral citizens.

The Roman Catholic Protectory, founded by Ives in 1863, just months before the Draft Riots, was hardly the first Catholic charitable organization in the city — the Roman Catholic Orphan Asylum, for instance, had opened in 1817 — but it represented a new type of Catholic institution: one founded explicitly in response to the Children's Aid Society and to the perception that Protestant organizations were actively working to strip Catholic

Two residents of the Catholic Protectory. Catholic and Jewish orphanages strove to produce adults who embodied middle-class American ideals of morality and respectability. These photographs of two brothers, before admission to the Catholic Protectory and after five years of residence at the institution, appeared in the 1892 Annual Report of the Catholic Protectory. *Collection of the New-York Historical Society 86661d, 86663d.*

children of their faith. The institution, founded to "protect" destitute Roman Catholic children, sought out the same children of the street whom Brace hoped to save—those in "circumstances of want and suffering, of abandonment, exposure or neglect, or of beggary." These were not necessarily orphans or half-orphans, but children in need of oversight and supervision. While the protectory's charter allowed it to receive children under the age of fourteen who were being placed there by their parents "for protection and reformation," it also allowed for the magistrates of the city of New York to commit Catholic children to the institution.[14] Most of the protectory's inmates entered through the latter path, as children arrested for vagrancy or other minor crimes. In this way the population of the protectory resembled that committed to the house of refuge or the juvenile asylum, consisting mostly of juvenile delinquents or those considered to be on the path to delinquency.[15]

The protectory, therefore, served a public function in reforming children and protecting society, and the organization received public support for its work. This funding, however, was far from sufficient to cover its total operating costs, and it continued to rely on charitable contributions. In 1865, with the assistance of the state, the protectory purchased a 114-acre farm in what was then Westchester County (now the Bronx) and constructed an ornate French-gothic-style building to house boys, followed, three years later, by a similar structure for girls. The operation of the institution was placed in the hands of religious orders, with the Christian Brothers running the boys' institution and the Sisters of Charity of New York running the institution for girls. Overseeing the whole operation was a board consisting mostly of Catholic laymen, headed, at first, by Ives.[16]

Life in the protectory was rigid and regimented. Once they arose—before six in the morning—every hour of the children's day was scheduled for prayer, school, or work, with only a few minutes permitted for recreation.[17] Education was at the center of the

THE COMPOSING ROOM, PRINTING DEP'T.

Composition room at the Catholic Protectory. Training in the crafts was one aspect of a moral and practical education intended to transform child inmates of the protectory into members of the middle class. *Collection of the New-York Historical Society , 86667d, 86668d.*

institution's work. This included "the various branches of learning, as reading, writing, and arithmetic," but, as the brother who ran the boys' institution explained, encompassed even more. "Our great aim is to mould their hearts to the practice of virtue," he declared, "and, while we make them worthy citizens of our glorious Republic, to render them fit candidates for the heavenly mansions above."[18] Education also included extensive training in industrial arts. Boys learned to make shoes and hoopskirts; they were also taught the trades of printing, carpentry, and baking as well as the skills needed for work as blacksmiths, chair caners, tailors, and machinists. This instruction came in addition to the skills acquired while running the farm that provided the institution's milk and vegetables. Girls were trained mostly in dressmaking and domestic services.[19]

Like the leaders of the Roman Catholic Protectory, the founders of the Hebrew Orphan Asylum hoped, in opening their institution in 1860, to provide a Jewish alternative to the Protestant child care institutions that dominated the city. One early observer of the new institution rejoiced that some of the children "were rescued from Christian asylums, and imbibed their ideas, which have been happily effaced from their minds."[20] The managers of the Hebrew Orphan Asylum imagined the institution as a large, efficient home. "Order and mutual love," the superintendent wrote in 1868, "are the pillars which sustain the happiness and prosperity of every household."[21] Henry Bauer, an orphan who entered the asylum at age nine, still recalled, decades later, more order than love in the typical day: "Get up, say your prayers, get your breakfast, go to school, come back, study your lessons, study Hebrew, get your supper, and go to bed. Very little play, very little play!"[22] While punishments were frequent in this rigid environment, the managers attempted to find the right balance, prescribing that discipline in the asylum should "be based on mildness blended with firmness."[23] Unlike children in the Catholic institutions, where education was provided at the asylums, the Jewish orphans attended nearby public schools. This formal education was supplemented with industrial training when the Jewish asylum opened a shoemaking shop in 1869 and a print shop in 1870. The boys who worked in the "industrial school" earned wages, based on their performance, that were saved for them until their discharge.[24]

In the 1870s, because of the increasing number of poor Eastern European Jews entering New York, the Hebrew Orphan Asylum was overwhelmed with applications for admission.[25] Whereas the asylum had once admitted nearly every child sent its way, the officers now became selective in their admissions. Six-year-old Louis, for example, the youngest of five children of Russian-born Jenny Menashowitz, was denied admission to the asylum.

The Hebrew Home for Infants. Children considered too young for the orphan asylum found shelter at the home, which opened in the Bronx in 1895. *Collection of the American Jewish Historical Society.*

The Hebrew Orphan Asylum of New York. This structure, which opened in 1884 at 136th Street and Amsterdam Avenue, was home to up to 1,755 children at a time. *Collection of the American Jewish Historical Society.*

His father had died of yellow fever five years earlier in Panama, while en route to Lima, Peru. His mother had managed to pull together enough income by sending her children out to peddle nuts. But now that her older children had all married and moved away, Jenny had no source of income to care for Louis.[26] Louis may have been rejected in part because Jenny had sent her children out to work rather than laboring for income herself. In addition, applications by single parents were frequently rejected by the organization, which believed that even a single parent "should be able to support one child."[27]

In other cases the agents of the institution decided that a family would be better served by charity than by the removal of their children to the asylum. Hannah Abraham of Brooklyn asked the asylum to take her three daughters, aged five, eight, and eleven. She had been a widow for two and a half years and complained that while working as a furrier, she "hardly can earn enough to keep myself." Worse, she had no one to care for her children when she went to work, and "the eldest one has to look after them, who is only a baby herself." Rather than admit the girls, the asylum referred the case to the charity committee, a predecessor of United Hebrew Charities, so that the family could receive outdoor relief.[28]

After 1870 the vast majority of residents in the asylum were half-orphans.[29] Many of the families that placed children in the asylum expected them to remain there for only a few years while the families recovered from difficult financial straits. The contract between a family and the asylum that governed a child's placement usually provided a fixed number of years that the child would stay; in some cases families would reclaim their children even before that term had expired.[30] With so many children who had living relatives nearby, the asylum had to place restrictions on visiting. At first, visitors were permitted on the first Sunday of every month from two to four in the afternoon. Parents were barred from giving the children "confectionary or fruit," and any money was to be given not directly to the child but to the superintendent for safekeeping. Children were not permitted to leave the asylum unless they had the specific permission of the superintendent and the board of governors.[31] Later, visiting was limited further, to one day every three months.[32] While children were isolated from their families during their time in the asylum, many parents viewed the placement of their children there as a part of a strategy to insure the long-term survival of their families.[33]

This survival strategy was also seen in Catholic orphanages. The Roman Catholic Orphan Asylum of Brooklyn, founded in 1830, saw the number of children under its care expand as the city of Brooklyn — and its Catholic population — experienced significant growth in the second half of the nineteenth century. The asylum had long accepted "boarders," many of them half-orphans, whose living relatives would provide some payment for their care. In November 1863 the board of directors of the Brooklyn asylum accepted a payment of $5 per month from a Mr. McGann to care for his children.[34] Sometimes friends or relatives, rather than parents, made these payments. The orphan asylum provided a receipt in November 1873 to a Mr. Daniel Gillespie after he paid $24 for three months' board for a boy, Daniel McDermott, who resided there.[35] Unlike Protestant-directed charitable organizations, Catholic orphanages appeared willing to provide short-term assistance to poor families without undue moralizing.

Within the Catholic and Jewish institutions, the greatest tension was over the issue of placing out. The question of whether children would be better served by substitute families or by preparation for their return to their own families struck at the heart of these institutions' missions. The Hebrew Orphan Asylum struggled to find placements for children who had reached the age of fourteen or fifteen — the age at which they were deemed old enough for placement — as few Jewish families in the New York area could afford to provide for additional dependents. While the institution had some success in placing boys with Jewish farmers in the South and West, there were simply not enough eligible farmers to accommodate the number of children in the institution. Given the large number of children in the asylum who each had at least one living parent, the organization decided that the best course of action was to train the children through programs, including the industrial school, so that they could contribute income to their families or, if necessary, survive on their own earnings.[36]

The Roman Catholic Protectory's venture in placing out was more extensive and more contentious. As early as 1868 leaders at the protectory suggested creating a branch of the institution in the West (what is now considered the Midwest) to facilitate placement of children in these areas. Administrators from the asylum visited Kansas the following year and formed relationships with local Catholic clergy who might assist in the placement of children with Catholic families. The protectory was particularly sensitive to the critiques of placing out, since Catholic leaders had voiced many complaints about the same practice by the Children's Aid Society. The Catholic organization recognized that many of the children placed out west simply became "incorrigible tramp[s]" and that "the cunning little boot-black who has been two or more times 'bound out' in the West" was a common character on the streets of New York. Still, the protectory believed its program could be different. The organization made sure that its children were placed only with upstanding Catholic families by requiring recommendations from the parish priests and it committed to visiting as often as possible—"generally, twice a year"—the homes where children were placed. With these conditions in place, the protectory placed more than 1,000 children in Illinois, Iowa, and New York State between 1876 and 1879.[37]

But the program was not without critics. Mother M. Regina, who directed the protectory's institution for girls, complained in March 1879, "Our children are daily returned to the institution broken down in health and spirits, with scarcely clothes to cover them decently, and yet they have lived in families for two, three, and even five years, and during that time" no one from the protectory had come to check on them.[38] In 1881, with many of the members of the religious orders that operated the protectory complaining about the placing-out program, the institution chose to limit all future placements to New York State. Catholic child welfare organizations would not simply provide a Catholic alternative to the Children's Aid Society. Instead, they would remain local, largely institutional, and, as much as possible, devoted to returning children to their parents.[39]

The response of religious and ethnic minorities to the perceived threat of Protestant organizations would have long-lasting effects for child welfare in New York City. While Jewish and Catholic institutions continued to claim that they were creating homelike environments, by the 1880s the number of children in these asylums made a feeling of home all but impossible. The Hebrew Orphan Asylum alone housed more than 450 children in 1885; the Roman Catholic Orphan Asylum of Brooklyn cared for nearly 1,500 children in its three institutions in 1880; and in the same year the facilities of the Roman Catholic Protectory held nearly 2,000 children.[40] And these were only a small sample of the dozens of religious institutions spread across New York and Brooklyn. The total number of children in these asylums would continue to increase as a new flood of Jewish and Catholic immigrants, mostly from southern and eastern Europe, entered New York in the

late nineteenth and early twentieth centuries. For New York's mostly Protestant reformers, these "sectarian" institutions were remnants of an older approach to social welfare, a
constant reminder of the retrograde thinking that stood in their way. But for many poor
Catholic and Jewish families, these institutions provided sanctuary, a means for them to
find temporary care for their children when they faced economic crises.

At the same time that Catholic and Jewish institutions were expanding, reformers
looked for better mechanisms to alleviate the causes of poverty. In 1875 the recently created State Board of Charities published "The Causes of Pauperism," a report by Dr. Charles
S. Hoyt. Hoyt had surveyed poorhouses across the state and concluded that pauperism was caused by a combination of heredity and learned behaviors. "By far the greater
number of paupers have reached that condition by idleness, improvidence, drunkenness,
or some form of vicious indulgence," Hoyt declared. "These vices and weaknesses are very
frequently, if not universally, the result of tendencies which are to a greater or less degree
hereditary." The causes of pauperism, then, were to be found within the paupers them-

Map of Brooklyn, 1874. Even before the opening of the Brooklyn Bridge, in 1883,
urban development and poverty had spread across the then-independent city. This
map plots streetcar routes. *Courtesy of the Library of Congress.*

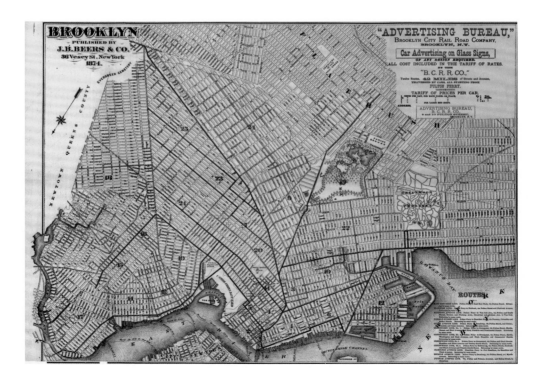

Boys receive training in a workshop at the **Hebrew Orphan Asylum.** Courses in the industrial arts were meant to prepare children for work. *Collection of the American Jewish Historical Society.*

selves. Indeed, he argued, "The number of persons in our poor-houses who have been reduced to poverty by causes outside their own acts is … surprisingly small." Given these causes, Hoyt reasoned, unless the state took action it could expect to confront generation after generation of paupers — a group he found to be "continually rearing a progeny who, both by hereditary tendencies and the associations of early life, are likely to follow in the footsteps of their parents."[41] Hoyt continued: "To keep such families together is contrary to sound policy; the sooner they can be separated and broken up, the better it will be for the children and society at large. Vigorous efforts must be instituted to break the line of pauper descent."[42] This kind of thinking angered Catholic and Jewish leaders and further motivated their own efforts at relieving family poverty.

For generations reformers had been calling for the removal of children from the poorhouse, where they were exposed to influences thought to place them on the path to pauperism and criminality. Armed with Hoyt's study, reformers finally made progress in this area. In 1875 the New York state legislature passed the Children's Law, barring the placement of any children between the ages of three and sixteen in the almshouse. This monumental act, the first law of its type in the country, permanently altered public welfare in New York City. The Almshouse Nursery on Randall's Island, which cared mostly for the children of paupers, was promptly closed, and the children were distributed to private institutions. After 1875 public institutional relief would be reserved for adults including the elderly, disabled, and mentally ill.[43] But the Children's Law had some unintended consequences. Reformers had assumed that once children were removed from the almshouse they would be received by organizations such as the Children's Aid Society, which would place them with substitute families and bring an end to any pauperizing habits. The law, however, contained a religion clause, inserted by the increasingly powerful New York City Democratic machine. The law required that each child be placed with an organization or institution "governed or controlled by officers or persons of the same religious faith as the parents of such child, as far as practicable."[44] Rather than being placed out, many poor Catholic children would be placed in the city's large sectarian institutions. Furthermore, while private organizations were barred from receiving state funds, they were allowed to receive funds from the city for providing this public service. The Children's Law, therefore, was a boon to private Jewish and Catholic institutions. By 1888 there were nearly 15,000 children in 28 private institutions at a cost to the city of over $1.5 million.[45]

Housing density on the Lower East Side, 1879. Virtually every lot in the Fifth Ward was covered with tenement housing. *From the David Rumsey Historical Map Collection.*

Improving Housing for the Poor

Even for those poor children who avoided institutional care and remained with their families, finding adequate and permanent shelter proved difficult. In many cases poor families
became refugees within their own city. The housing shortage that burdened New York was
exacerbated during the years of the Civil War, when residential construction slowed. At
the same time the downtown commercial district expanded into what was once working-
class territory, replacing existing homes with new warehouses and shops. Many displaced
families crowded into the Lower East Side of Manhattan; the city's Fourth Ward, located
along the East River, became in this period the most densely populated place in the world.
Other poor families moved into the shantytowns above Forty-second Street, where more
than 10,000 lived as squatters in the largely undeveloped territory. One shantytown,
known as Dutch Hill, was located where Forty-second Street met the East River. Here,
hundreds of shacks housed more than a thousand residents, including "untold numbers of
children, chickens, cats, dogs, and pigs," enough to warrant a branch post office.[46]

In the mid-1860s, with residential construction only beginning to pick up, the problem of overcrowding led at last to widespread public concern. A group of scientific-mind-
ed citizens, forming the Council on Hygiene and Public Health, decided that an extensive
survey was necessary to get a grasp on the problem. Dividing the city into twenty-nine
"Sanitary Inspection Districts," the Council recorded every multifamily residence within
the city. Their findings, published in 1865, were striking. A total of 486,000 persons, over
half of the city's population at the time, lived in 15,511 tenement houses. An 1867 investigation ordered by the state legislature, in Albany, found 52 percent of tenements "in a
condition detrimental to the health and dangerous to the lives of the occupants." The most
frequent deficiencies were poor ventilation, a lack of light, a shortage of fire escapes, and
slow drainage.[47]

In 1867 the New York legislature finally took action by passing a Tenement House
Law, the first effort to regulate working-class housing in the city, and empowering a
new Metropolitan Board of Health to enforce it. The law, which defined a tenement as a
building in which three or more families lived and cooked, attacked the most troubling
conditions that tenement inhabitants faced. Ventilation was required either through open-
ings between inner and outer rooms in existing tenements or, in new buildings, through
vents or windows. A fire escape was required for every tenement, and one toilet was to
be provided for every twenty residents. If a sewer was available, the privy was required
to be connected to it; however, many parts of the city, particularly areas where the poor
lived, still lacked sewers. The Board of Health was active in its enforcement of the new
code, but there were limits to what it could accomplish. The board itself explained that "a
mere technical compliance with the law of the State does not in all instances secure" truly

Squatters' colony near Central Park. Families and individuals priced out
of the housing market found shelter together in shantytowns, which became
common in mid-nineteenth-century New York City. *HarpWeek, LLC.*

Summer in the tenements. Hot weather forced the inhabitants of overcrowded, sometimes windowless tenement apartments to seek improved air circulation outside, where they slept on roofs, stoops, and fire escapes. Here, a crowd of sleeping tenement-dwellers surrounds a woman holding a sick or sleeping child. *Collection of the New-York Historical Society, 79722d.*

sanitary conditions. "As long as the massing of huge tenement-houses on limited areas of ground is allowed, and those immense structures are packed like herring with human beings, each contributing to his or her quota of poisonous gas and effete animal matter to the confined atmosphere, the bills of mortality will continue to swell, notwithstanding the small transom windows, the roof-ventilator, and the sink-trap required by law."[48] With the lax requirements of the 1867 law, new tenements continued to appear, replacing older structures. At the same time, builders started expanding into less-developed parts of the city, such as Yorkville, on the Upper East Side of Manhattan, and Harlem, on the northern end of the island, as well as moving across the East River to Brooklyn.[49]

The proliferation of new tenements brought the shortcomings of this form of housing to the attention of the public and, more importantly, social-scientific reformers. In December 1878 *Plumber and Sanitary Engineer,* a new magazine promoting urban sanitation and indoor plumbing, announced a contest for designs of a model tenement, offering a prize of $500 each for the best four entries. The response was overwhelming; 190 designs for a tenement that would fit a twenty-five-by-one hundred-square-foot lot were received, all of which were publicly exhibited to great fanfare. The winning entry, by architect James E. Ware, provided a simple solution to the problems of current tenement construction. Ware's design called for four thirty-three-foot-long units on a floor, two in the front of the building and two in the rear. The front and rear sections of the building would be connected by a narrow structure containing the staircases and the shared water closets. On each side of the passageway would be a small courtyard. The design's footprint, two wide sections connected by a slender "bar," led to the structure's colloquial name, the "dumbbell tenement."[50]

Ware's design was an improvement over those of existing tenements. The staircase, enclosed in a fireproof structure, made the means of entering and escaping from units safer; the water closets on every floor replaced privies in the yard; and the internal courtyards provided, in theory, better ventilation for the notoriously stuffy inside rooms.[51] Still, many commentators were unimpressed with the design. One periodical commented that the prizes in the model-tenement competition "were won by the most ingenious designs for dungeons."[52] And the *New York Times* observed that the contest winners "simply demonstrate that the problem is insoluble." It was virtually impossible to design humane housing with adequate light, ventilation, and toilets while at the same time maximizing the return on developers' investments by covering most of the small lot with low-cost rental units.[53]

The limitations of tenement design, underscored by the competition, inspired a movement for housing-law reform that resulted in the passage of the Tenement House Act of 1879. Most radically, the new law restricted buildings to only 65 percent of each lot. In addition, the act increased the minimum number of water closets, required all bedrooms to have windows, and stipulated that each building have a janitor. While the 1879 act provided for enforcement of the law through the Board of Health, the law also gave the board wide discretion in approving designs for new tenements. As a result, most tenements built after 1879 were based on Ware's prize-winning design. These "improved" dumbbell tenements contained larger courtyards than Ware's original design, allowing for additional ventilation. Still, the structures approved by the Board of Health usually covered 80 percent of a lot, a much larger portion than was specified by the law. These tightly packed buildings, which later became known as "old law" tenements, would typify most new housing built for the poor up until the twentieth century.[54]

Housing reform in the late nineteenth century exemplified the scientific approach to urban problems. Reformers believed that by identifying the problem, collecting data, and providing model solutions, they could overcome the challenges created by the high concentrations of poverty in New York City. But housing reform in this era also demonstrated the distance between achieving reforms on paper and improving actual conditions in the city. The 1879 Tenement House Act provided strict guidelines for the improvement of tenement buildings, but these were never fully enforced. The small internal courtyards or airshafts between buildings created by the dumbbell design often accumulated garbage and became sources of malodor and disease. "The narrow courtyard … in the middle is a damp foul-smelling place, supposed to do duty as an airshaft," one magazine reported in 1888. "Had the foul fiend designed these great barracks they could not have been more villainously arranged to avoid any chance of ventilation."[55]

The experiences of immigrants crowded into the newly built tenements further demonstrated reformers' inability to truly accommodate the needs of the poor. The three-room dumbbell tenements were quickly filled with large families, along with the boarders they took in to help pay the rent. While the shared water closets in each hall certainly represented an improvement over outdoor privies where sanitation was concerned, bathing was still a difficult task, undertaken in the kitchen or outside the home at public baths.[56] At night every surface of the apartments would be covered with people sleeping. One woman recalled, "We had ten girls sleeping on the floor."[57] During the day the rooms would turn into places of work, with men, women, and children sewing, making shoes, or rolling cigars. One Jewish immigrant recalled living in a two-room apartment with a cantor, his wife, his six children, and six boarders, including a cobbler. "The Cantor rehearses, a train passes," the man explained, re-creating the noise; "the shoemaker bangs, ten brats run about like goats, the wife putters in her 'kosher restaurant.'"[58] Those were hardly the sounds or images that housing reformers had hoped to facilitate.

Not only did the newly built tenements often fail to provide adequate housing for the number of poor families and individuals who required shelter, but they also often failed to provide permanency. Becky Brier, a Polish immigrant with a family of five, described her housing experiences: "We moved every year to better ourselves, for cheaper rent or a better apartment. But we never found more than three rooms."[59] And Brier's family was lucky. Decades later, immigrants could recall the fear of being "dispossessed," or evicted for nonpayment of rent.[60] It was not uncommon to see a woman standing outside a tenement building surrounded by a "disorderly array of household goods... the wreck of her home."[61] Confronting this problem and the poverty and destitution that caused it would become the focus of a generation of late-nineteenth-century reformers.

The Reform of Public Relief

The limited and decrepit housing available for poor families was only one area in need of reform. Public relief, both in the poorhouse and for families in their own homes, was becoming increasingly burdensome to the city in difficult economic times. Any reformer who challenged the existing forms of public relief, however, had to confront the Tammany

Children make cigars under supervision of their bedridden mother. The caption reads: "New York City—Tenement House Tobacco Strippers—Employment of children in violation of the law— Scene on East Side." Clothing and other textiles, artificial flowers, and dolls were common items produced by child labor in tenements. *Collection of the New-York Historical Society, 79720d.*

Collecting rent on the Lower East Side. A visitor, probably a landlord in search of rent, enters a family's tenement. Many families were forced to break up when a primary wage earner became too sick to work. *Collection of the New-York Historical Society, 85899d.*

machine, with its poor and working-class constituency. The system of public relief, in fact, had become one of Tammany's most effective political tools. The Democratic Party leaders of the city's poorer wards ran, in a sense, their own system of support for the poor and dislocated. George Washington Plunkitt, a Tammany activist who in 1870 simultaneously held—and collected salaries for—the positions of assemblyman, alderman, police magistrate, and county supervisor, later described his efforts to assist the poor in his district. There, he had a special corps to identify struggling families before charitable societies did. If there was a fire, for instance, he would immediately show up to see what the victim family needed. Rather than refer the family to a charitable organization, "which would investigate their case in a month or two and decide they were worthy of help about the time they are dead from starvation," Plunkitt explained, "I just get quarters for them, buy clothes for them if their clothes were burned up, and fix them up till they get things runnin' again." When a family was in danger of being evicted, Plunkitt might send a district captain to act as their counsel in court or simply pay the family's rent and provide a little extra money for food. Such actions, Plunkitt revealed, were more than altruism; they were "mighty good politics." He knew, in other words, that those families he assisted would remember on Election Day what he had done for them. "The poor are the most grateful people in the world," he maintained," and, let me tell you, they have more friends in their neighborhoods than the rich have in theirs."[62]

For New York's elite reformers, the profligate use of relief by Tammany was not only corrupt but also damaging to the long-term well-being of poor families. As part of a national movement for reevaluating relief, New York's leading citizens began a campaign to reduce or eliminate public assistance. Josephine Shaw Lowell, a descendent of the Boston-area elite, emerged as a leading voice calling for a new approach to public welfare in New York. Lowell's dedication to serving the public was formed in the struggle of the Civil War. She volunteered for the war effort, raising money for soldiers and their families, writing letters for those injured on the battlefield, attending to the dying, and teaching former slaves to read. The war also touched her life through personal tragedy: in July 1863 her brother, Colonel Robert Gould Shaw, was killed while leading African American troops in battle in South Carolina, and in October 1864 her husband of only a year, General Charles Russell Lowell, died of injuries sustained in the Shenandoah Valley of Virginia. A month later Josephine gave birth to their child, a girl she named Carlotta. A widowed mother at only twenty years of age, Josephine Shaw Lowell would never remarry, choosing to wear black for the rest of her life. A member of the New York elite, Lowell disdained high-society balls and other such events. Instead, in honor of her brother and husband, who gave their lives to end slavery, Lowell committed herself to improving society. The focus of much of her attention was the problem of poverty.[63]

Lowell's understanding of poverty was shaped by the application to human society of the recently published theories of Charles Darwin, an approach known as social Darwinism. This thinking cut in two directions. At times, to reformers including Lowell, it suggested the limitations of intervention in the lives of poor families; for example, Richard L. Dugdale's study of "the Jukes," an upstate New York family with a history of five generations of criminal and degenerate behavior, demonstrated to social observers the difficulties in overcoming "natural selection." On the other hand, Lowell also subscribed to a theory of "degeneration," which held that environmental factors such as alcoholism might cause "retrograde evolution," degrading genetic stock. This Darwin-influenced theory argued for greater intervention into the lives of poor families.[64]

The rise in poverty and homelessness during the depression of the 1870s created a new urgency among reformers to understand the problem of pauperism and to evaluate the effectiveness of public and private relief. Josephine Shaw Lowell herself, volunteering for the private State Charities Aid Association (SCAA), provided a social-scientific investigation into the problem in her 1876 report on pauperism. Lowell demonstrated the reformers' confidence in their ability to solve social problems. "Vagrancy and homelessness need not be permanent evils," she wrote; "... they can be cured and they ought to be cured."[65] She called for reforming and reducing publicly supported relief and lodging, which, according to Lowell, wasted resources by encouraging profligacy and tramping. The solution to pauperism among the able-bodied poor was to force them to work and to punish those who refused. Her answer to the social crises of poverty, then, was to actually reduce the amount of public support available to the poor. Lowell's report gained her so much attention that she was appointed to the public State Board of Charities, becoming the first woman to hold an official state position in New York.[66]

According to Lowell's writings, the misplaced generosity of public outdoor relief harmed poor families. Seth Low, a reformer working in Brooklyn and later mayor of New York City, built on Lowell's arguments suggesting that outdoor relief "(1) saps the habits of industry, (2) discourages habits of frugality, (3) encourages improvident and wretched marriages, and (4) produces discontent."[67] Outdoor relief, therefore, created paupers, the unworthy poor who lived off the public trough without giving anything back to society. Of

Josephine Shaw Lowell. Lowell changed the way charity was distributed to poor families by constructing a meticulous program of institutional collaboration. Her influence extended to almost every charitable organization in New York City. *The Schlesinger Library, Radcliffe Institute, Harvard University.*

course, Low and others admitted, there were some families that, due to death, injury, or unemployment, needed temporary assistance. Under the system of outdoor relief in place in New York and Brooklyn, however, the most deserving rarely received the most relief. Instead, outdoor relief under Tammany and other political operatives was "a vast political corruption fund." Relief dollars were distributed through the urban machines to political supporters rather than struggling families.[68] The only solution, reformers argued, was to end public relief and replace it with private charity that could directly serve those who actually needed and deserved help.

Ironically, it was the depression of the 1870s and fissures within Tammany Hall that made the suspension of relief in New York City possible. By July 1874 the budget of the city's Department of Public Charities and Correction—still recovering from the rampant corruption of the recently disgraced Boss Tweed—had been decimated by the growing demand for support. Unable to cover expenses, the city halted outdoor relief, a practice not uncommon during summers. For the first time, however, the city did not restore outdoor relief the following winter. The burden of caring for 75,000 to 105,000 people who were out of work fell to private charities.[69] The number of families on the AICP's rolls increased fivefold from 1873 to 1874.[70] While outdoor relief was briefly restored in January 1875, the city would permanently terminate cash relief in January 1876, when the Tammany machine chose reform as a way to limit the city's expenses and to keep its membership in line. Instead of public outdoor relief, the city granted funds to private organizations that in turn provided relief through charities. In addition, the city reinstituted the public provision of coal to families in need.[71] The AICP had never received public funding for its services, but in 1876 it found that "a greater burden is imposed on this Association than it can possibly bear" and agreed to accept a grant from the city.[72] The suspension of public outdoor relief in New York demonstrated that such wide-reaching reorganization of the city's charitable operations was possible. Brooklyn, led by Seth Low, followed suit and suspended all public relief in cash and kind in 1879. Public relief would not be restored in New York until 1931.[73]

Scientific Charity

Reformers including Lowell and Low did not simply want to suspend public outdoor relief; they wanted to replace it with so-called scientific charity. Public relief was impersonal, overly generous, and morally corrosive; properly organized private charity, on the other hand, provided elevation out of pauperism through, as Lowell termed it, "moral oversight for the soul."[74] Lowell believed that the moral failures and character flaws of the poor were outgrowths of the process of urbanization, which isolated them from contact with their social and moral betters. Organized contact with middle-class charity workers would provide the poor with not only material relief but models for a better life. Lowell compared charity to the flow of water. In rural towns water flowed naturally from mountain springs, and neighborly assistance created "a living stream of charity." In the city a network of reservoirs and pipes was required to bring running water, and "even our love to our neighbor must be guided through organized channels, or it will lose its life giving powers and become a source of moral disease and death."[75]

In order to provide the "organized channels" through which charity could flow, in 1882 Lowell founded the Charity Organization Society of New York City (COS), one of several American associations that formed to imitate the success of the British charity organization movement. The COS itself did not provide significant charitable assistance beyond temporary grants of food and fuel for heat. Instead, it focused on referring applicants to those organizations that could best meet their needs. The key to the COS's approach was to get all of the local private charities to participate and to track each family's usage of charitable assistance. By collecting information on every charity recipient, the COS could uncover suspicious patterns and efforts to cheat the system. An earlier effort to organize charity in the city had failed because it was unable to get full participation from the city's charities, but Lowell was persuasive. In its fifth year of operation, the organization could proudly announce that it had enlisted "nearly every important and influential relief-giving agency and nearly every self-supporting church in the city."[76] Even Catholic and Jewish organizations, suspicious of the motives of the scientific reformers, agreed to participate with the COS in some programs.[77]

At the heart of scientific charity were the "friendly visitors." The city was divided into districts, each with a committee that oversaw local work. But it was the friendly visitors — volunteers, most of them women — who actually met and formed a relationship with each family in need, made recommendations for how the family should be assisted, and followed up to check on its progress. The friendly visitor had two roles, which could conflict. First, the visitor was required to investigate requests for charity and to assess the moral quality of the family in question. She evaluated whether an applicant was "well conducted and industrious" as well as "temperate and steady" and made judgments about the family's "general moral condition." At the same time, however, the visitor was expected to form a personal bond with the family in need in order to provide the moral guidance that the COS believed was lacking in the lives of the poor. This "reunion between the classes," scientific-charity theorists proposed, would have a "civilizing and healing influence." In the end, the COS believed, it was through stubbornly developing these relationships, in "holding on with firm grip, until at last you reach the heart-strings of someone in the family," that successful moral uplift would be achieved.[78]

Mothers with children. In the 1870s an economic depression put a stable home life even further out of reach for many single mothers. This etching from *Harper's Weekly* depicts a poor mother looking into the home of a wealthy family. The poor mother bears a strong resemblance to the shrouded Virgin Mary with the infant Christ in her arms. *Collection of the New-York Historical Society, 69977.*

In spite of Lowell's frequent discussion of moral uplift, the stories that the COS recounted as evidence of its success demonstrated the robust organization and resourcefulness of the society as much as its power of moral suasion. In one case a middle-aged woman "was deserted" by her husband, "whose brain had been affected by injuries" incurred during the Civil War, and left alone to care for her eleven-year-old son and twelve-year-old daughter. The COS found work for the woman in domestic service, but her "inefficiency" cost her every job. Even worse, the COS explained, "the children were being ruined by the same untutored stupidity." A long search found that the woman had "a married and well-to-do sister in another State." The COS "induced" the sister "to care for the woman and her children in her own home, to which all were promptly emigrated." That action by the COS saved the woman from pauperism by "transferring the burden from the community to her own kith and kin."[79]

When a family demonstrated greater industriousness and moral fortitude, the COS provided more direct assistance. One German family with five children was referred to the COS by an East Side missionary. The husband was ill and unable to work, and the wife had to care for their infant. While the woman was "industrious and careful," she was also "diffident and unacquainted" with places of work. The COS "first arranged to have the infant cared for in a day-nursery," freeing up time for the mother to work. Then, "well-paid and permanent work for the mother was found in private families." Finally, the society found domestic work for the two daughters, aged fifteen and twelve. "In this way," the COS reported, "the family was made self-supporting, and continue to do well."[80]

The most impressive aspect of the society's work was the system of detailed records it developed. The COS created a card for each family with which it had contact. Every time a charitable organization provided aid to a family, a report went to the COS, which added the information to the card. Using this method, the COS could easily tell if a family was receiving aid from more than one organization. Furthermore, the society could provide detailed information about any particular family. By the mid-1890s the COS had records on 170,000 families and individuals.[81]

This sophisticated system of data collection created a largely coherent web of private charities in New York. Some families accrued decades of records of relief, with thick files of correspondence between the COS and various charitable organizations. One mother with four children, for example, applied for assistance with the COS in 1896, claiming that her husband had fled to England and abandoned her. Reports on this family dated back to 1882, when she first received relief from the AICP to help her pay for her rent, food, and fuel. Over the past decade, the COS had learned much about the family. Reports included neighbors' observations that the older children would "drink and fight" and that one daughter was "engaged" with men at night; they also noted that in 1884 the mother had refused to take work as a cleaner at the United Bank Building. The extent to which this family's need was legitimate is difficult to discern, but from the perspective of the COS, the mother was "unworthy" of additional aid.[82] Other applicants for aid were found "probably honest" but had "no faculty for getting on," as the COS described one woman in 1883. She had been married twice, and the Children's Aid Society had placed a son from her first marriage out west. Separated from her second husband—she "had heard he was dead but had no proof"—the woman was forced to provide for her young daughter, despite having little income. Reports from the Broadway Tabernacle and from All Saints' Unitarian Church revealed that she had appealed to churches for assistance "sometimes several times a year." In 1892 the mother and daughter moved out of their apartment without paying the previous month's rent. Unable to locate the family, the COS closed the case.[83]

The COS created a more thorough system of investigation and relief than the city had ever seen—more extensive than that of the private AICP or even of the system of public outdoor relief in place before the 1870s. The attitude of the society, which found the causes for poverty in the poor themselves, and the organization's extensive investigations and records certainly led to a reduction in the charity received by many families. Some critics joked that the society should be renamed the "Organization for the Prevention of Charity."[84] Others objected to the secular orientation of the society, which, in an effort to reach out to those of all religions, forbade its visitors from proselytizing. The COS, however, emphasized that it was "not irreligious" but that it worked to lead those in need "back to their own church."[85] While moralism remained at the heart of COS visiting, the secular, scientific orientation of the organization represented an effort to confront the problem of urban poverty systematically. Groups such as the COS, the SCAA, and the State Board of Charities were not content just to ameliorate poverty but sought to create changes in policy to end pauperism. This commitment to research-based efforts to improve society would prove influential for New York City's next generation of reformers.

Other Voices

The desire for greater economic stability and better living conditions—unmet by politicians and reformers—led some poor families to look for alternative outlets to make their voices heard. Many German immigrants living in the city's *Kleindeutschland*, for example, had brought with them to New York an adherence to socialism. Other members of the working class became attracted to the city's growing labor movement, associated with the broad-based Knights of Labor or the more narrowly focused trade unions of the American Federation of Labor. In 1882 unions in New York, Brooklyn, and Jersey City came together to create the Central Labor Union (CLU). On September 5 of that year, the group celebrated the nation's first Labor Day with a parade in Union Square. Included in their demands were an end to child labor and the abolition of vagrancy laws.[86]

With the many strong and competing senses of ethnic and religious identity in New York, efforts to push for better living and working conditions became clouded by other issues. The fight for home rule in Ireland, for instance, gained ardent support among the city's poor and working-class Irish families, as did a campaign to create a more democratic Catholic Church in America. On the radical side of all these issues was Father Edward McGlynn, the Soggarth Aroon, or "Priest of the People." McGlynn was particularly influenced by the work of Henry George, who argued that overcrowding among the poor and problems of class conflict in America were caused by landowners, who held onto useable tracts of land, waiting for prices to rise in order to make profits; George called for a tax on all landlords to force them to make land available to working people. McGlynn turned George's words into an attack on the elite of both America and Ireland. "Christ himself was but an evicted peasant," he preached. The priest, therefore, pushed for a close alliance between the Catholic Church and the burgeoning labor movement, an idea that proved anathema to New York's Catholic hierarchy.[87]

In 1886, with the support of the CLU, socialists, and the Knights of Labor, Henry George announced that he would run for mayor on the ticket of the newly formed United Labor Party. George showed particular ire at the condition of the tenements. "Nowhere else in the civilized world are men and women and children packed together so closely," he railed. "There is no good reason whatever why every citizen of New York should not have his own separate house and home; and the aim of this movement is to secure it." Father McGlynn became one of George's strongest supporters, often speaking on behalf of the candidate, until the archbishop of New York ordered him to be silent and suspended the priest.[88]

To oppose George in the mayoral election, the Democrats, under the influence of Tammany Hall, chose iron manufacturer Abram Hewitt. Although Hewitt had previously shown marked opposition to Tammany, the leaders of the urban machine hoped to unify the party against George. To do so, Tammany gained the assistance of the Catholic Church hierarchy and made extensive appeals to the new immigrants in the city. The Republicans named Theodore Roosevelt, a descendent of Dutch settlers and a member of the city's elite, as their candidate. Roosevelt appeared to be a new type of Republican; as a member of the state assembly, he had supported for reasons of health and safety a ban on cigar manufacturing in tenements, a bill proposed by the unions and viewed by many in his party as "socialistic." He made his name, however, as a supporter of good government and helped pass civil-service reform in 1884. He promised that as mayor he would root out corruption and run a businesslike administration.[89]

Hewitt, the Democrat, easily won the election. George came in second, followed closely by Roosevelt. While George polled well in German and Irish working-class areas, the city's poorest districts remained true to Tammany and voted Democratic. Roosevelt, it seems, was harmed in many wealthy districts by those who preferred the Democratic industrialist to the possibility of a mayor in the pocket of labor. Once in office Hewitt became an advocate of nativist policies, refusing even to watch the St. Patrick's Day parade, and lost the support of Tammany after one term. The election, however, told of a new direction in New York politics and urban reform. The Democratic machine could no longer take the votes of the poor and working class for granted; in the future they would have to appeal — if only in rhetoric — to the demands of the poor and working class. The Republican Party, at least as represented by Roosevelt, would also demonstrate a new openness to reforms that would improve urban conditions for all New Yorkers.[90]

The First Great Depression

In 1893 the U.S. economy, which had limped along after the Long Depression of the 1870s, saw another significant downturn. By the end of the year, nearly 16,000 businesses had closed. New York City, the center of American capitalism, was hit particularly hard by this economic collapse. In January 1894 the city of New York reported approximately 70,000 unemployed among its residents, about 25 percent of them women. Brooklyn reported an additional 25,000 unemployed. Across the state of New York, the unemployment rate was at least 35 percent. Among the unemployed, the city found that there were 20,000 homeless persons crowded into parks and lodging houses or sleeping on the streets. The U.S. and New York City would not see a significant recovery from this downturn, which became known as the "Great Depression," until 1897.[91]

The divisions that stymied efforts to relieve the poor over the 1870s and '80s continued in the crisis of the 1890s. While the Catholic St. Vincent de Paul Society and the United Hebrew Charities began to provide aid without in-depth investigations, the COS maintained its firm stance against indiscriminate giving, explaining that recipients' "souls must not be sacrificed in the efforts to save their bodies." One frustrated woman mocked the COS approach. "When you get to the gates of Heaven," she asked, "how will you feel when God will say go down to hell for a week until the committee meets to see if you … are worthy enough to enter Heaven."[92]

While not lowering their strict standards, the COS and other private charitable organizations were forced to innovate to meet the growing needs of the poor. The COS opened a Wayfarer's Lodge to provide accommodations for homeless men and a woodyard to provide work for unemployed breadwinners. In 1894 the COS provided men with families with the equivalent of 6,286 days worth of work chopping wood. The organization also opened workrooms where homeless women could earn money. Similarly, the AICP began a sewing project, providing work from home for thousands of needy women so that they could care for their families. The most extensive effort to aid the unemployed was the East Side Relief Committee, a joint effort of the COS, the St. Vincent de Paul Society, several churches, labor unions, and the recently opened settlement houses. Headed by Josephine Shaw Lowell, the committee provided unemployed heads of household with work cleaning streets, whitewashing buildings, making garments, sewing, knitting, and quilting. The pay was not generous—men earned $4 a week, women $3—but it provided just enough to allow families to get by without inducing what Lowell perceived as pauperism.[93]

More radical elements among the working class, including the growing labor unions and socialists, called for direct government action to deal with the depression. "When

Children at 38 Cherry Street. Neighborhood children pose for a photograph in Gotham Court, an infamous slum in New York. *Collection of the New-York Historical Society, 32332.*

the private employer cannot or will not give work," the American Federation of Labor asserted, "the municipality, state, or nation must." Anarchists such as Emma Goldman called on the unemployed to take action to meet their needs. "If you are hungry and need bread, go and get it," she reportedly declared. "The shops are plentiful and the doors are open."[94]

Partially out of fear of violent unrest, businesses began providing their own forms of relief. Yeast producer Louis Fleishman started giving a third of a loaf of bread to anyone who came to his bakery after midnight. The crowds that gathered soon popularized the term "breadline." Publisher Joseph Pulitzer began distributing bread from wagons that passed through tenement districts. Competing newspapers established their own charities, such as the Free Clothing Fund. Nathan Straus, co-owner of Macy's and a leading dry-goods dealer supplied inexpensive food, fuel, and housing to those in need.[95] Through all of this, the city made little change to its policies. It continued to give aid to the blind and coal for heat to the poor, but outdoor relief, so recently banned, did not return. Finally, in the winter of 1894, the state approved a work-relief program to be administered by the Department of Parks. This program provided 2,000 jobs for the unemployed, but, as expected, complaints arose that most jobs were distributed to those with political connections. In the spring of 1894, the public work program was dismantled; poor families would have to survive this Great Depression without help from the city or state.[96]

The widespread suffering during the Depression of 1893 made a deep impression on many New Yorkers. Even Josephine Shaw Lowell, while unwilling to change the policies of the COS, admitted that the condition of the poor families she witnessed was not due "to moral or intellectual defects on their own part, but to economic causes over which they had no control, and which were as much beyond their power to avert as if they had been natural calamities of fire, flood, or storm."[97] The perspective that poverty arose from no personal flaw among the poor themselves would animate the next generation of reformers. For Lillian Wald, a leader of that coming generation, the Depression of 1893 remained a touchstone. "Perhaps it was an advantage that we were so early exposed to the extraordinary sufferings and the variety of pain and poverty in the winter of 1893 – 94," she wrote later in life, "memorable because of the extreme economic depression." The severe want she witnessed forced to her to act without "self-analysis and consequent self-consciousness," which might have hampered her work. As Wald and her generation worked tirelessly to deal with the crisis, they dedicated themselves to preventing such large-scale suffering in the future.[98]

City of New York, 1900. Completed for the Paris Exposition, this map shows the newly formed City of Greater New York, created in 1898 through the merger of Manhattan with Brooklyn, Queens, Staten Island, and the Bronx. *The Lionel Pincus and Princess Firyal Map Division, The New York Public Library, Astor, Lenox and Tilden Foundations.*

Chapter 5

Family Poverty in the Progressive Era

To set foot in the Lower East Side in the late nineteenth or early twentieth century was to enter a world that overwhelmed the senses. "Broken roadways," "dirty mattresses," and fire escapes bulging "with household goods of every description" assaulted the eyes. The "smell of overripe fruit, hot bread and sweat-soaked clothing," of "odorous fish stands" and "uncovered garbage cans" created a "pent-in sultry atmosphere … laden with nausea." The sounds of children playing in the streets and of peddlers hawking their wares from push-carts during the day were replaced at night by the ringing of gunshots followed by silence, "then cries, and the rapid run of police."[1]

The Lower East Side, along with other crowded tenement neighborhoods, left an indelible impression on all newcomers. European immigrants, black migrants from the South, and visitors from the city's middle-class neighborhoods were all overcome by the sights, sounds, and smells of New York City's slums. The changes to these neighborhoods in the late nineteenth and early twentieth centuries were not in kind but in degree. New York's poor neighborhoods had long been crowded, but now they became even more so; New York had grown to become the world's third-most-populous city, with one of the highest levels of human density. The downtown neighborhoods displayed the most alarming overcrowding. One district in the Eleventh Ward was perhaps the most densely packed spot on Earth, comparing unfavorably with the most heavily concentrated section of Bombay.[2]

The impoverished condition of many of the new immigrants worsened the social prob-lems created by such close living arrangements. The Irish and Germans who had domi-nated immigration into the U.S. in the mid-nineteenth century were joined, as that century progressed, by immigrants from a host of nations. Those included people from Scandinavia as well as Czech, Polish, Greek, and Hungarian ethnics from the empires of Central and Eastern Europe. Large numbers of Chinese also entered the U.S. until an 1882 act of Con-gress curbed further immigration.[3] But the flood of Italians and Eastern European Jews

Orchard Street on the Lower East Side. The Lower East Side became one of the most densely populated neighborhoods in the world in the late nineteenth century. Here, litter-covered Orchard Street serves as a playground for children. *Photography Collection, Miriam and Ira D. Wallach Division of Art, Prints and Photographs, The New York Public Library, Astor, Lenox and Tilden Foundations.*

who arrived in the country over the last decade of the nineteenth century and the first decade of the twentieth dwarfed the streams of immigrants from other countries, especially in New York City.

The difficulties Italians and Jews had faced in their countries of origin shaped their lives in New York. The Italians who settled in New York came mostly from the poorest classes of southern Italy, the country's most depressed region.[4] After 1881 Jews in the Russian Empire, long victims of economic deprivation and religious persecution, faced a series of state-sponsored anti-Semitic riots, known as pogroms, that persuaded many to flee Russia for the New World.[5] While some Italians and Jews used New York as a jumping-off point to settle in other parts of the country, many remained concentrated in the city. In 1900 over 31 percent of the U.S. population of Italian immigrants and over 36 percent of the U.S. population of Russian immigrants (most of whom were Jewish) remained in New York.[6] Many of these recent arrivals crowded into the "Little Italy" of Lower Manhattan or the "Jewtown"—to use the term of one prominent observer—of the Lower East Side.[7]

After the outbreak of World War I in Europe, in 1914, the number of foreigners arriving in New York would sharply decline. The end of the war would be met with the first laws aimed at restricting the number of people from eastern and southern Europe entering the United States. But just as the spigot of immigration was turned off, a migration of blacks, mostly from the South, brought a new stream of low-wage workers into New York City. These black migrants quickly crowded into Upper Manhattan, where housing was available. By the end of the 1920s, mostly black Harlem would surpass the Lower East Side as the most densely populated and impoverished section of the city.

Middle-class observers of these new slums were, of course, disturbed by what they discovered. Jacob Riis, one of the most influential investigators of the city's slums, dramatically conveyed the living conditions in the tenements. A "flat," in most of the city's tenement districts, consisted of a "'parlor' and two pitch-dark coops called bedrooms." These rooms were filled with "piles of rags, of malodorous bones and musty paper."[8] In

Jacob Riis, journalist, social reformer, and documentary photographer. Riis emigrated from Denmark at age twenty-one and quickly found himself living on the streets without a steady job. He went on to write *How the Other Half Lives* and *The Children of the Poor,* two of the most detailed and popular accounts of poverty in New York. *Courtesy of the Library of Congress.*

addition, the foreignness of these newcomers shocked observers. Riis described how "the jargon of the street, the signs of the sidewalk … their unmistakable physiognomy," along with the "men with queer skull-caps [and] venerable beard" made it clear when one entered "Jewtown."[9] Italians, according to Riis, were cursed by "ignorance and unconquerable suspicion of strangers."[10]

In spite of the ethnic stereotypes that shaped their observations and their disgust with the unsanitary conditions in which many immigrants lived, reformers of the era demonstrated a deep sympathy for the poor. Rather than blame the poor for these conditions, investigators began to assert that the environment itself contributed to poverty. New York's poor families, Riis explained, did not choose to live in such circumstances; they simply "had no other place to live." These families were "truly poor for having no better homes; waxing poorer in purse as the exorbitant rents to which they are tied … keep rising." "The wonder," Riis declared, was not that some individuals succumbed to a pitiful and depraved lifestyle, but "that they are not all corrupted, and speedily, by their surroundings."[11]

This belief—that the environment shaped individuals—became one of dominant ideas in the period of widespread reform over the late nineteenth and early twentieth centuries, later known as the Progressive Era. The approach of previous reformers, such as Josephine Shaw Lowell, was upended; an individual's socioeconomic state was no longer viewed as a result of moral standing or faith—or lack of it—in God. In order to end poverty, crime, and poor health, reforms needed to remake the environment of the slums, not provide moral guidance. To improve the conditions in the tenement communities, progressive reformers relied to a greater extent than ever before on detailed and quantified studies of these problems. They fully believed that by finding out all they could about a problem, they could develop the best solution. Furthermore, progressives looked to combine private, voluntary efforts to better the lives of the poor with state-backed reform. Thus, the progressives imagined a broader role for the state than had previous generations. In many ways the efforts of progressives to confront the urban problems of congestion, disease, single parenthood, and child poverty in the late nineteenth and early twentieth centuries still shape the lives of poor families today.

Poverty and the New Immigrants

"*Oi Veh!*" declared one Jewish woman in a fictionalized account of her arrival and settlement in New York, "where is the sunshine in America?" Looking out her tenement window at the wall of the tenement house next door, she found her surroundings to be "like a grave so dark."[12] Recently arrived immigrants were frequently disturbed by the lack of light they encountered in New York. For both Italian and Eastern European Jewish new-comers, the two largest immigrant groups, the life they found in "the land of opportunity" did not always compare favorably with the conditions they left behind. While they had moved to escape the poverty in their native lands, they now faced a new type of poverty in the unfamiliar environment of New York.

Most Italian immigrants left from southern Italy, the Mezzogiorno, where they were part of the *contadino,* or peasant, class. They were mostly illiterate and made their living by both farming on leased land and working as agricultural laborers. Political, economic,

Outdoor "Hebrew" market, presumably on the Lower East Side. The late nineteenth and early twentieth centuries saw unprecedented immigration into New York City, including the arrival of many Eastern European Jews. *Courtesy of the Library of Congress.*

and environmental factors made life increasingly hard for the farmers of southern Italy. As the economic situation in Italy deteriorated, many young men traveled to America to find opportunities that were simply unavailable in the villages where they had been born. At first, most Italian immigrants to the U.S. planned to make money quickly before returning to Italy. Between 1907 and 1911, 73 Italians returned home for every 100 who entered the U.S. But many of those returning found that the money they had earned provided little opportunity in the still dysfunctional economy of southern Italy. While large numbers of Italian immigrants still chose to return home, more and more sent for their wives to join them or married in the United States.[13]

As more Italians committed to raising families and settling in the U.S., many made their homes in New York City. A majority (54 percent) of Italian immigrants to the U.S. listed New York City as their final destination. The heart of Italian settlement developed in the formerly Irish area between Pearl and Houston streets, east of Broadway and west of the Bowery. But Italian neighborhoods soon developed on the lower West Side, in East Harlem, and in several parts of Brooklyn and the Bronx. The Italian population in these

Old woman is shown with two small children in a tenement. The photograph's original caption reads, "Italian Ragpicker's Home." *Courtesy of the Library of Congress.*

enclaves could reach as high as 90 percent. Italians from the same region or even the same village often settled together. The Genoese and Calabrian dialects that dominated some streets on the Lower East Side were distinct from the Sicilian and Neapolitan dialects that were more prevalent on certain blocks of East Harlem.[14]

The initial areas of Eastern European Jewish settlement neighbored the Italian communities. While Italians dominated the Lower East Side west of the Bowery, Jews settled east of it, eventually filling the area bounded by Houston Street to the north and Monroe Street to the south, all the way to the East River.[15] Like their Italian neighbors, the Jews of Eastern Europe who came to the United States had fled destitution. But they had also been pushed out by religious persecution. Unlike Italians, then, Jews did not view their move to America as temporary — few ever returned to the lands where they had suffered for generations. For this reason, most Jews came to the U.S. as families; the number of male and female immigrants was almost even. Sometimes, if the family could not afford to come together, the father and older children would emigrate first, sending for the mother and younger children once they had found jobs and saved enough to pay for the others' passage. If one group was left behind it was the older generation, the parents and grandparents of the immigrants, destined to die in Russia or Eastern Europe without ever seeing their offspring again.[16]

While the Italians who settled in New York were mostly unskilled rural laborers, most Jews were skilled or semiskilled craftsmen more familiar with urban living. For generations Jews had worked as craftsman in small villages, or shtetls, producing goods and trading with the surrounding gentile peasants. More recently they had moved into Eastern European cities, taking work in mechanized factories. Given these experiences, Jews quickly adapted to peddling goods on the streets as they had in the markets of Eastern Europe. Those who came with tailoring skills quickly found work in the garment industry, often sewing pieces in their apartments.[17]

Whether Italian, Jewish, or members of another ethnic group, the new immigrants encountered similar living conditions. With tenement houses built tightly against one another, their neighborhoods were dark, loud, and smelly. The typical tenement consisted of three rooms — a kitchen, a bedroom, and a front room that served as a place of work, leisure, and, often, sleep. The quality of tenements varied. Although Ware's 1878 dumbbell tenement plan had included indoor water closets, most tenements standing in 1900 did not meet these standards. Instead, in the typical case water was provided only from an outdoor spigot and the bathroom facilities were shared privies in the backyard. Only after the reforms of the early twentieth century were bathrooms installed on every floor and some apartments equipped with sinks with running water. Even then a bathtub remained a rarity in the tenements. Twentieth-century reforms also did little to reduce the crowding in the tenements. Better-off families could afford to stay alone in three-room apartments. In these cases, typically, the parents would sleep in the back bedroom, and the children would sleep in the "living" room, rolling up their bedding in the morning to allow for work and other activities.[18] Such comparative luxury, however, was rare. A 1908 census of 250 East Side families found that about 50 percent slept three or four to a room and nearly 25 percent slept five or more to a room.[19]

Adjusting to the high costs of rent, food, and other necessities was often difficult for those new to New York. In one story recent immigrants questioned why a woman whose husband made twelve dollars a week was searching for additional work and struggling to pay the rent. The woman explained to the greenhorns that twelve dollars was a lot of money "where you used to live." There, "you had your own house and most of the food came from the garden." In America, however, "you have to pay for every potato, every grain of barley." Italian immigrants who had been tenant farmers in the old country were used to paying annual rents; the adjustment to paying rent every month was often difficult. Rent consumed a fairly significant part of the new immigrants' income. In the early twentieth century, the rent for a three-room apartment on the Lower East Side was, on average, $13.50 a month, and the average annual family income was about $600. Even when a family's annual income should have covered the cost of housing, the seasonal and irregular nature of work made it difficult to scrape the rent together each month.[20]

When a family was short on rent money, one of the easiest ways to bring in extra income was to take in boarders. Boarders were usually single men or women — often recent immigrants working to bring their families over. Taking in boarders created much tighter living conditions. Boarders were given the best accommodations, usually bedrooms to themselves; the family was left with the kitchen and an additional room for sleeping and dressing. Beyond the crowding, boarders invaded the little privacy families were able to find in the tenements. "When you have roomers in your home," one Lithuanian immigrant lamented, "it's not your home. They take it over."[21]

Judith Weissman, who spent her childhood on the Lower East Side, described living in "a fifth floor railroad flat" with two men who worked with her father. The two boarders shared the bedroom. At first Judith slept on a couch with her brother. When her father decided they were too old for that, her brother moved into the kitchen, sleeping on two chairs pushed together. Even when Judith's family moved to a better apartment, they still took in three boarders to help make ends meet.[22] Anzia Yezierska, a novelist from the Lower East Side, provided a fictionalized account of a family preparing for boarders. The narrator's family sought advice from a neighbor on how to maximize their profits. "Put the spring over four empty herring pails and you'll have a bed fit for the president," the neighbor suggested. "Now put a board over the potato barrel, and a clean newspaper over that, and you'll have a table. All you need yet is a soapbox for a chair, and you'll have a furnished room complete." Soon the family was renting their front room to three borders, and by threatening to take in a fourth, the mother was able to squeeze an extra quarter out of each of the men.[23]

Jacob Riis recounted a case in which the number of boarders and sublets approached the absurd. A tailor lived in a two-room apartment on the top floor of a tenement house on Ludlow Street with his wife, two children, and two boarders. In order to cover his costs, he squeezed his whole family and the boarders into the larger room. "The other, a bedroom eight feet square, he sublet to a second tailor and his wife; which couple, following his example as their opportunities allowed, divided the bedroom in two by hanging a curtain in the middle, took one-half for themselves and let the other half to still another tailor with a wife and child." When the sanitary police, in a surprise inspection, discovered eleven people stuffed into the single apartment, they arrested the first tailor. That such conditions could damage the property or the health of residents seemed ridiculous to the

A man and three children in their tenement apartment. The window between the kitchen and bedroom likely resulted from the Tenement House Act of 1867, which required that interior rooms have some light and ventilation. *Collection of the Community Service Society, Columbia University Rare Book and Manuscript Library.*

Large family stands in an alley. *Collection of the Community Service Society, Columbia University Rare Book and Manuscript Library.*

landlords of the Lower East Side. Riis reported that the next day, "the owner of the house, a woman," appeared at Sanitary Headquarters "with the charge against the policeman that he was robbing her of her tenants."[24]

The need to take in boarders, however, was no laughing matter. When the rent was due, those families who failed to find boarders or extra work were in danger of eviction. During the depression of the 1890s, that problem became particularly acute. Years later immigrants could remember the childhood fear of being served with a notice of "dispossess." One judge found that he had issued 5,450 dispossess notices in a year. This particular judge "rarely set the machinery of the law in motion without first making an effort to have the landlord give a little further period of grace." His hope was that an extra week might help a family get back on its feet.[25]

Not every judge, however, was sympathetic to the plight of tenants, and eviction was common on the Lower East Side. Immigrants would sometimes return home to find all their possessions on the street. One observer described the typical case. "The evicted woman" would stare at all her things, "now left in pieces on the street, a symbol of eviction and destitution." These women often had no place to turn for help. "Occasionally, she would make the last sacrifice — her pride. She brought out a china plate from the folds of her dress and placed it on one of the chairs. People would drop pennies perhaps even nickels and dimes into that plate — enough to save her from being wholly destitute."[26] For some families in such circumstances, the only place to turn was one of the "expresses" — coaches left on the streets after horses were stabled for the night — which provided temporary shelter.[27]

Resisting the power of landlords contributed to a sense of solidarity within immigrant neighborhoods. One novel gave voice to the frequent complaint of immigrant tenants. The landlord was worse than a "pawnbroker," he was a "leech" squeezing "out so much blood" each month. While his tenants lived in squalor with walls "alive with bedbugs and roaches and mice" and poorly ventilated kitchens that filled with smoke every time the stove was lit, he lived "on Riverside Drive, and his windows open out into the sunshine from the park." If the landlord wanted "another diamond on his necktie, or if his wife want[ed] a thicker fur coat," the complaints continued, all he had to do was "raise our rent."[28] Given these attitudes, "jumping the rent" was considered an acceptable practice among tenement dwellers, and it was common for families to simply move to another apartment to avoid the rent payment.[29]

When a family was evicted, neighbors did their best to help out. One resident described how his mother, herself not in the best of health, would try to secure funds for a family in danger of being evicted. "She wrapped herself in her old shawl, and went begging through the tenements for pennies," he recalled. "Puffing with bronchitis, she dragged herself up and down the steep landings of a hundred tenements, telling the sad tale with new emotion and begging for pennies." This practice was common: "Whenever a family is to be evicted, the neighborhood mothers put on their shawls and beg from door to door."[30]

At times the dormant anger at landlords would erupt into community-wide rent strikes. In 1907, for instance, 600 women organized a strike, eventually getting 2,000 names on the rent-strike rolls. The community solidarity expressed in the mass meetings and demonstrations, however, was no match for the law backed by the police. The latent anti-immigrant sentiment present in New York was expressed by Police Commissioner Stephen Bingham's reaction to the strike. "If you don't like our rents," he declared, "get out. If you are not satisfied with our system of rents, go back where you came from."[31]

In order to cover the rent and the other expenses of living in New York, families had to pool income from various sources. Most Italian men found jobs as unskilled manual laborers working on the wharves, at construction sites, in public works, or in factories. Jewish men more often became peddlers or semiskilled workers, especially in the garment industry, which they soon dominated. Women and children also contributed to household incomes. At first, much of this labor was piecework completed in the home. Jewish and Italian women often took up finishing work on clothing, and Italian wives came to dominate the artificial-flower industry. As laws restricted the labor that could be performed

A woman and children work together in a tenement making dolls.
Many poor families met basic expenses like rent and food with the
help of income earned by children. *Courtesy of the Library of Congress.*

in the tenements, and wages enticed more women into the factories, the amount of
homework declined. Still, women, mostly Italians, continued to do finishing work in their
homes until the 1920s.

Children both assisted their parents at home and were sent out to work in the factories and stores. At the turn of the century, though, the number of children in industrial
and retail work declined. Law, technology, and economics limited the work options for
children. The passage and enforcement of child-labor and truancy laws directed more
children into school over the twentieth century. At the same time, the installation of pneu-
matic tubes, cash registers, and telephones eliminated many of the "cash" boys and girls—
who would run customers' payments from salespeople to cashiers—from the operation
of the large department stores. Automation also eliminated some children's factory jobs;
others passed on to the many adult immigrants looking for work. By the early twentieth
century, children who worked did so mostly on a part-time basis, as paperboys, shoe shin-
ers, delivery boys, errand boys and girls, and peddlers.[32]

In spite of the crowded and unsanitary conditions in which these immigrants lived
and worked, most did not fall into destitution. A 1903 study found only seventeen Jewish

paupers in the almshouse on Blackwell's Island; a study from the following year discovered only sixteen Italians there. Still, in difficult times immigrants struggled to make ends meet. In addition to taking in boarders and sending children out to work, they relied on relatives and friends for assistance and, in the most desperate situations, turned to charitable or child care institutions to get through crises.

There were some differences between the Italian and Jewish immigrants who applied for charity. Italians looking for economic assistance tended not to be recent immigrants. One study of Charity Organization Society records for five blocks in an Italian neighborhood found that on average the head of the household applying for aid had lived in the U.S. for eight years and three months. By contrast, many of the Jews who applied for aid were recent immigrants. The United Hebrew Charities of New York reported that 40 percent of the new applicants for relief in 1901 had been in the country for less than a year. The reason for this difference lies in the patterns of migration. Those Italians who could not survive in America simply returned home; the families who applied for assistance, then, were those who had become established in New York and entrenched in their communities and then fallen upon hard times.[33]

A boy bootblack. Working as a bootblack, or shoe shiner, was a common form of employment for young boys in the early twentieth century. *Courtesy of the Library of Congress.*

A young girl in a tenement yard. Behind her are outdoor bathrooms, or "privies," which accommodated several families and were usually badly maintained. *Collection of the Community Service Society, Columbia University Rare Book and Manuscript Library.*

For both Italians and Jews, the most frequent reasons for seeking assistance were illness or lack of work. In many of the cases, the families had brought in additional work, sent children out to look for jobs, or received assistance from relatives before turning to charity. Usually, the family received assistance with coal, food, or rent for only a brief period before the primary breadwinner was able to return to work. The records of charitable organizations show that few cases of need were due to what were known as "moral causes," such as "drunkenness, vice, [and] idleness." However, many cases were due to familial desertion.[34] Abandonment was a frequent problem among both Italian and Jewish immigrants. The records of the United Hebrew Charities in New York from 1903 and 1904, for instance, indicate that about 10 percent of the applications for relief were from deserted women.[35] Contemporaries theorized that for both communities the anonymity of New York provided an opportunity to escape family responsibilities that the strictures of village life, church, or extended family relations made unavoidable in the old country.

The fact that men frequently entered the United States before their wives created additional temptations. Some immigrants left their families in Italy and established new families in the U.S.; when an immigrant's first wife arrived in America, he might simply abandon both.[36] The problem became so acute within the Jewish community that the *Forward,* one of the leading Yiddish newspapers, began publishing ads with photographs of men who had abandoned their wives. "Sarah Solomon," reads one such ad, "is searching for her husband who is now uptown, 38–40 years old, solid build, medium height, black eyes, black mustache, left me 2 ½ years ago. I offer $25 to anyone who will notify me of his whereabouts. … Notify me at 132 Ludlow Street, in the restaurant." Many abandoned wives took legal action against their husbands to force them to support their families. To further assist wives in such searches, Jewish charitable organizations went so far as to create a National Desertion Board in 1911.[37]

Besides charitable assistance in the form of coal, food, and cash, immigrant families also turned to child-care institutions for temporary relief during financial crises. Anti-immigrant social commentators often accused Italians of committing their children to orphan asylums in order to save money. In truth, both Italian and Jewish families usually turned to institutions to care for their children after the loss of parents due to death or desertion. These placements were frequently temporary, with parents bringing the children back home once they could afford to.[38] Immigrant children were also found in the house of refuge and the juvenile asylum, institutions intended to rehabilitate delinquents and those on the path to delinquency. A report from 1902 found more than 300 Jewish children in institutions for delinquents and pre-delinquents. Another study claimed that 28 to 30 percent of the children who appeared before the juvenile court were Jewish. The author of this later report blamed the crowded conditions and intergenerational conflict within Jewish households for this spike in delinquency; as the report summarized: "Home life is unbearable."[39]

Charitable assistance, child care institutions, and juvenile reformatories all provided ways to assist immigrant families after they had fallen into poverty or other difficult straits. For the Progressive Era reformers, however, this was not enough. Progressives looked to create preventive reforms—to change society so that the immigrants did not have to confront the problems that led to poverty. Progressives were not socialists; they did not want to further inflame class tensions. Instead, they believed that by understanding poor communities and implementing appropriate reforms they could prevent violence and unrest. The leading institution for creating this type of understanding—both getting to know the immigrants on a personal level and collecting data on their lives—was the settlement house.

The Settlement Houses

In New York's poorer neighborhoods in the early twentieth century, there was often one house that seemed out of place. It might have flower boxes and a brass plate on the door. The residents dressed differently from the rest of the community. Children might be seen entering after school, and a playground might be visible behind the house. One might even recognize leading scholars, prominent politicians, and sometimes a foreign dignitary stopping by to visit. This was a settlement house, the front line in progressives' efforts to assist poor and working-class families.[40]

The first settlement house opened in the East End of London in the 1880s, but the idea was transplanted to the U.S. when, in 1886, Stanton Coit organized the Neighborhood Guild on New York's Lower East Side. Others, mostly women, soon followed suit, opening the College Settlement in 1889, the Henry Street Settlement in 1893 (both on the Lower East Side), and Greenwich House in 1902. Settlements were intended to change both the communities and the residents' lives. Middle-class, mostly college-educated young men and women moved into these houses to assist neighborhood families and organize local communities to address their needs. But they also entered the settlements to learn from the communities and to observe as intimately as possible the experience of being poor in the city.[41]

The programs established by settlement houses were diverse, but they all aimed at expanding the horizons of poor immigrant families and helping them to build a sense of community. At first, settlements focused on providing intangible assistance to their neighbors. The settlements hosted musical concerts, lectures, and art exhibits, and organized kindergartens to prepare children for school. Soon, especially after the Depression of 1893, settlement houses attempted to assist poor families more directly. This took the form of helping with applications for private aid as well as developing plans for social reforms. Settlement workers gathered data, collected funding for private initiatives, and lobbied state and city government for legislation that would make a difference in the lives of those they worked with every day.

Men and women alike came to live in settlements, but settlement work became largely a female-dominated domain. Both Lillian Wald, founder of the Henry Street Settlement, and Mary Kingsbury Simkhovitch, founder of Greenwich House, became nodes around whom New York City's reform community coalesced. Many of those who came to live in the settlements represented the first generation of college-educated women. Having earned their degrees, they wanted to do more than manage households or take on clerical work, the opportunities typically open to women; instead they pursued work with a larger purpose. They also sought to move beyond theories and ideas and work directly on the social problems of their day. Most of the young women and men who lived in the settlement houses came from old-stock American families from the Northeast or Midwest. They were firmly in the middle class; many of their fathers were ministers, teachers, or professionals of other sorts. Most importantly, the settlement workers were idealists who saw their work as a way to make a difference in the lives of the poor while experiencing their own personal growth. For most residents living in a settlement was a temporary vocation, not a career; the average stay for a settlement worker was about three years.[42]

The typical settlement house evolved to provide various neighborhood services under one roof. In the morning young children would arrive for day care and kindergarten programs. During the day families with particular needs might come for referrals to charitable organizations for relief or medical assistance. In the afternoon school-age children would arrive to play, take part in organized recreation, or make crafts. The evening would bring meetings of various clubs, at which neighborhood residents could discuss the issues they faced and devise community solutions. Some nights, the settlement would host dances, festivals, or concerts, providing an alternative to the neighborhood saloon.[43]

The founders of the settlements sought to distance themselves from their charity-work predecessors, such as the Charity Organization Society. Charity workers, in their

Knitting class at the Henry Street Settlement. Many settlements offered courses intended to train young women to run households. *Courtesy of the Library of Congress.*

Children in University Settlement gymnasium. Founded in 1886, it was the first settlement house in the United States. *Collection of the New-York Historical Society, 84860d.*

view, emphasized individual causes of poverty and recommended top-down reforms
imposed upon the poor; settlement workers focused on the social and economic conditions that created poverty. "We had seen the charitable approach to social problems and
found it wanting," recalled Simkhovitch. "If social improvements are to be undertaken by
one class on behalf of another, no permanent changes are likely to be effected. The participation by all concerned is necessary for sound improvements." In practice, however,
traditional charitable organizations and the settlement houses often worked together.
Simkhovitch herself volunteered on a district committee of the COS and developed a
fondness for the elderly Josephine Shaw Lowell. The work of the charities also began to
change, especially after the appointment of Edward T. Devine as executive secretary of
the COS in 1896. Devine helped develop the standards for professionalized social work,
combining efforts to help individuals with a broader awareness of the social causes that
contributed to impoverishment. "Charity," he suggested, should be "a type of anticipa-
tory justice, which deals not only with individuals who suffer but with social conditions
that tend to perpetuate crime, pauperism and degeneracy." While differences certainly

remained between the established charities and the settlement houses, the two often cooperated in progressive reforms.[44]

Settlement houses played a role in nearly every social reform of the Progressive Era, but the playground movement may best exemplify how settlement workers achieved their goals. The crowded conditions within tenements and tenement neighborhoods left little space for children to play. Most children played in the streets, where they faced the dangers of foot, horse, and, later, car traffic, as well as the bad influences of neighborhood toughs and prostitutes. Settlement workers did not originate the idea of opening urban playgrounds, but they quickly latched onto it. Lillian Wald turned the backyard of the house on Henry Street into a playground, providing kindergarteners a place to run around and young adults a space to socialize and hold dances. Another East Side settlement soon followed her lead, setting up playground equipment and sandboxes on the bank of the East River. The success of these settlement developments soon led to further action. Charles Stover, a resident of the Neighborhood Guild, began pushing for development of public playgrounds on the Lower East Side in 1890. He got as far as having the city designate

Children play baseball in an alley under clotheslines. In densely populated neighborhoods with no playgrounds, children carved out space for recreation on streets and in alleyways. *Photography Collection, Miriam and Ira D. Wallach Division of Art, Prints and Photographs, The New York Public Library, Astor, Lenox and Tilden Foundations.*

and purchase a site for a playground, but after the tenements were torn down, no further progress was made. The empty lot stood as a testament to municipal inefficiency.[45]

It took several years for the settlement network to organize around this problem. In 1898 Mary K. Simkhovitch, Lillian Wald, and other prominent New Yorkers formed the Outdoor Recreation League. Wald worked to get the city to level the land designated for a playground and erect a fence around the empty lot. The league started raising money to develop the park. In 1903 the city finally agreed to oversee maintenance of Seward Park, making it one of the first urban municipal playgrounds in the country. For the progressives the benefits of social developments, such as playgrounds, were endless. As Wald explained, play and recreation provided "wholesome expression for energies which might otherwise be diverted into channels disastrous to peace and happiness"; the organized competition that parks and playgrounds provided could "replace the gang feud and even modify racial antagonisms." For these reasons Wald called for "the recognition of the child's right to play, as an integral part of his claim upon the state." Here was the essence of progressive ideology: playgrounds were good policy and therefore deserved state support.[46]

A model of Seward Park appears in a public exhibit on urban congestion. Seward Park—the first permanent, municipally funded playground in New York—set a precedent for park and recreation development in cities across the country. *Courtesy of the Library of Congress.*

While reforms, such as public playgrounds, were supported by the settlements, settlement workers did not see imposing reforms as their primary mission. According to Simkhovitch, settlement workers were not reformers. "The reformer and the settlement worker," she explained, "look at life from two different angles. The reformer, the missionary, the dogmatist of any kind, religious, political or economic, is valuable and necessary. But for the settlement the primary object is to understand the situations that arise, and by constant association so to get the slant of the neighbors that when the opportunity for change comes there will be general comprehension of what is desirable and possible."[47] Reform was a necessary outcome of settlement work, but reform had to represent the needs and desires of a settlement's neighborhood.

Even with their efforts to involve local community members, the reforms supported by the settlements faced resistance. The building of playgrounds, on its face an innocuous effort, faced subtle resistance from children, who disliked having adults structuring their playtime, and from parents, who were unable to supervise their children at playgrounds. The idea that the new playgrounds would provide an outlet for orderly play was abruptly challenged. The *New York Times* reported that at the opening of Seward Park, in 1903, the park's organizers quickly lost control, as "the crowd of 20,000 children present took matters into their own hands."[48] A force of 200 policemen was required to restore some order and allow for the ceremonial opening of the park. But the more serious form of resistance was acted out, not in raucous play, but in the daily choice of activities. In spite of the dangers of playing on the streets, a 1913 study found that both children and their mothers preferred the streets to the supervised playgrounds and settlement-house programs. On the streets children had more autonomy in their play, and mothers could peek out of their tenement windows to keep an eye on their children below.[49] Negotiating between the desires of New York City's poor communities and the desire for reform would become even more difficult as progressives turned to regulating how the poor lived and the work they could do.

Progressive Housing Reform

At the heart of the progressive understanding of poverty was a belief that the environment was a prime contributor to the problems the poor faced. Nothing shaped this environment more than the tenement housing in which they lived. As one observer asserted, "The tenement house in itself had been responsible for much of the physical and moral degradation seen in our large cities. It is, indeed, impossible to calculate how great had been the social loss and waste, how heavy the additional burden of pauperism, due to the policy of allowing landlords to hive as many human beings as possible upon a given space of land,

Child in a tenement. An unattended girl looks out from the entranceway of a tenement house. *Photography Collection, Miriam and Ira D. Wallach Division of Art, Prints and Photographs, The New York Public Library, Astor, Lenox and Tilden Foundations.*

without regard to health or decency."[50] Any attack on poverty and slum living had to begin by reforming the living conditions of poor immigrants.

The person most responsible for revealing the conditions of the tenements to the middle class and popularizing the belief that reform needed to begin with the environment was Jacob Riis. In two books, *How the Other Half Lives* and *The Children of the Poor,* Riis described a world invisible to many, one in which families crowded into tenements, exposing generations to filth, disease, and vice. Illustrated with stark photographs dramatically demonstrating the destitute conditions in which too many families lived, his books created a sensation. While Riis's analysis of the tenement neighborhoods was not the most sophisticated—he often drew upon ethnic stereotypes in his descriptions—his overarching sympathy with the struggles of poor families struck a chord with the middle class and initiated a movement for meaningful tenement reform and other improvements to the neighborhoods of the poor.[51]

Riis, a Danish immigrant who had experienced homelessness firsthand before finding success as a journalist, focused his attention on the worst living conditions in the city. The most memorable chapter of *How the Other Half Lives* examined "The Bend," a stretch of Mulberry Street not far from the old Five Points intersection. On this one square block, 155 children under the age of five died in a single year. The Bend's death rate was 48 percent higher than that of the city as a whole. Riis's examination of the apartments revealed the reason for the rampant disease there. He found one flat crammed with five adults and six children. "One, two, three, beds are there, if the old boxes and heaps of foul straw can be called by that name; a broken stove with crazy pipe from which the smoke leaks at every joint, a table of rough boards propped up on boxes, piles of rubbish in the corner. The closeness and smell are appalling."[52] In *The Children of the Poor*, Riis described an Italian family living in similarly squalid conditions. "There were three big family beds, and they nearly filled the room, leaving only patches of the mud floor visible. The walls were absolutely black with age and smoke. The plaster had fallen off in patches and there was green mould on the ceiling." Riis described the children as a "swarm of squirming youngsters that were as black as the floor they rolled upon." But, Riis emphasized, "there was evidence of a desperate, if hopeless, groping after order, even neatness. The beds were

Boy sits above a decrepit courtyard. Courtyards, intended to lend light and air circulation to tenement interiors, often became garbage receptacles instead. *Collection of the Community Service Society, Columbia University Rare Book and Manuscript Library.*

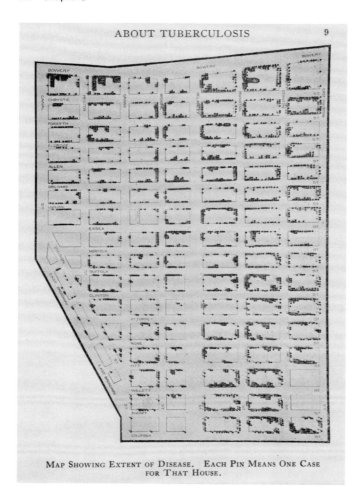

ABOUT TUBERCULOSIS   9

MAP SHOWING EXTENT OF DISEASE. EACH PIN MEANS ONE CASE
FOR THAT HOUSE.

Tuberculosis on the Lower East Side. Map showing the prevalence of tuberculosis in a Lower East Side neighborhood. TB—then known as "consumption"—was particularly widespread in poor, immigrant communities because of crowded conditions and lack of hygiene. *Collection of the Community Service Society, Columbia University, Rare Book and Manuscript Library.*

made up as nicely as they could be with the old quilts and pieces of carpet that served as covering." These were human beings, Riis made clear, striving for dignity in an undignified environment.[53]

Riis, of course, was not the first to call for tenement reform. A series of measures, most notably the Tenement House Laws of 1867 and 1879, had been taken in attempts to improve the conditions in which the poor lived. After 1879 every tenement bedroom was required to have a window opening to the outside. The result was the infamous "dumbbell tenements."[54] And these were the best of the tenements, as Jacob Riis made clear, because the law did not lead automatically to the razing of old tenements. Many families, especially those in the East Side neighborhoods where many immigrants settled, remained in the old pre-law tenements with even less access to light and air.[55]

The work of Riis and other journalists sparked a movement for meaningful housing reform. Over the late 1890s and into the first decade of the twentieth century, public and private committees and organizations strove to make the dream of housing reform a reality. The first Tenement House Committee, appointed by the governor of New York in 1894, corroborated Riis's prose and images with statistical analysis, providing a thorough examination of the sanitation shortfall in the tenements. While indoor water closets and even private toilets had become common in the middle-class housing of the late nineteenth century, they remained rarities within the tenements.[56] Of the sample of 3,984 tenement houses examined by the committee, 85 percent (3,392) had only shared water closets, located outside. On average 7.62 persons shared each commode. The risk of spreading disease was heightened by the lack of cleanliness in these outdoor toilets. One inspector witnessed a girl approach an outdoor water closet with a pail in her hands. Realizing the outhouse was already so filthy it might dirty her feet, she "threw the contents into the closet, and the excrement went all over the walls."[57] The difficulties of maintaining sanitation were further exemplified by the lack of bathing facilities in the tenements. Of the 255,033 persons living in the tenements examined by the committee, only 306 had bathtubs in their homes.[58] Given these conditions, even for the most fastidious of tenement residents the level of cleanliness remained low. The recommendations of the committee — to create public bathhouses and toilets — did little to force landlords to improve conditions within the tenements.

Into the vacuum of meaningful housing reform stepped Lawrence Veiller, a man who would lead efforts to reform housing in New York for decades. Born in 1872 in Elizabeth, New Jersey, Veiller graduated from New York's City College in 1890. A short, stocky, bearded man with a direct style that bordered on abrasive, Veiller preferred to work behind the scenes to accomplish his reform goals. For him, substance rather than appearance was what ultimately mattered; to focus on reform for the sake of publicity was an unpardonable sin. After college he went to live at University Settlement on New York's Lower East Side. Witnessing the suffering brought on by the Depression of 1893 forever changed his life and work. As he sought to provide aid during that economic crisis, he realized, "at the mature age of 20 years, that the improvement of the homes of the people was the starting point of everything."[59] Veiller soon found a job with the city's Buildings Department and began developing the extensive and detailed knowledge of tenement housing that would make him a leading reformer. In 1898 Veiller approached Robert W. De Forest, president of the COS, with a proposal to create a permanent organization focused on the problem of the tenements. De Forest agreed and joined with Veiller to form the COS Tenement House Committee, an entity that would direct the future of housing reform in New York City.[60]

There was a reason for Veiller's urgency in forming this new committee in 1898. On January 1 of that year, the city of New York (Manhattan) joined with the previously independent city of Brooklyn (King's County) as well as the Bronx, Queens, and Staten Island to form the city of Greater New York. The new charter for the expanded city allowed for a commission to develop a uniform building code across what were now New York's five boroughs. Veiller saw this as an opportunity to create serious reform for New York's tenements through the new COS Tenement House Commission. The committee recommended measures that would improve ventilation, reduce the number of fires, and limit crowding. Instead—to Veiller's great disappointment—the city commission, dominated by building interests, produced a code that allowed for taller, more crowded, and more unsafe housing. This was, Veiller commented, "a distinct step backward."[61]

The consummate political strategist, Veiller—together with the COS Tenement House Committee—responded by opening, in February 1900, an exhibition documenting life in the tenements. In the two weeks the exhibit was open in New York, it was visited by 10,000 people.[62] Photographs, charts, diagrams, and tables detailing life in New York's tenement neighborhoods surrounded the exhibit's visitors. Two maps prepared by Veiller were particularly revealing of the depth of poverty and disease in these communities. A "poverty map" reproduced the blocks of tenements in the city, demarcating each building. Black dots covered much of the map; each dot on a building represented five families at that address who had applied for charity in the past five years. Similarly, a "disease map" used a dot on a building to note each case of tuberculosis discovered there in the past five years; again, at least one dot was found on nearly every tenement house, and the worst buildings had up to twelve dots. Veiller's pièce de résistance, however, was a cardboard model of an entire tenement block. The model dramatically demonstrated what thirty-nine tenements housing 2,781 persons actually meant. It showed that the whole block shared 264 water closets, and that while residents in forty apartments were lucky enough to have hot running water, not one stationary bathtub existed in the block. The thirty-two recorded cases of tuberculosis on the block attested to the prevalence of disease; the 660 applications for charitable assistance attested to the depth of poverty.[63]

The exhibit elicited a quick and forceful response. Governor Theodore Roosevelt opened the exhibition and committed himself to winning authorization for a state commission to study the tenement problem and introduce legislation for substantive reform. When the commission was approved, Veiller was appointed as its secretary, giving official sanction to his investigations of the tenements. With this authority Veiller drafted a building code that became the Tenement House Act of 1901. Most importantly, the act prohibited any further construction of dumbbell tenements. Rather than a narrow shaft between buildings, the new law required that all future structures include true courtyards that varied in size based on each building's height. In addition, builders were required to install a private water closet in each apartment. The law made changes to existing tenements mandatory. Landlords had to replace old-style privies with more modern water closets and install windows connecting interior rooms to adjoining exterior rooms to improve ventilation. Building owners also had to provide fire escapes, add windows that supplied light to previously pitch-black hallways, and waterproof cellar floors.[64]

As important as the Tenement House Act of 1901 was, it was nearly equaled in importance by the creation of the New York City Tenement House Department. The tireless work of Veiller and his Tenement House Commission persuaded the state legislature to add this new department to the city's charter, consolidating in one agency the authority to approve new building plans, inspect completed buildings, and maintain records on all existing tenements in the city. Veiller believed this reorganization would finally provide what housing reform in New York City had long lacked: effective enforcement. Under the administration of Mayor Seth Low, a long-time reformer and ally of Josephine Shaw Lowell, De Forest was appointed as commissioner of the department, with Veiller as his deputy. The housing conditions that had horrified observers and residents of New York's slums for decades would finally be dealt with effectively. While Veiller would leave city government at the end of Low's administration, in 1903, he would remain a gadfly on housing issues, prodding future mayors to maintain the city's commitment to reasonably sanitary and safe homes.[65]

Fixing the deficiencies in housing alone, of course, would not solve the many prob-

Model tenement block, 1900. This model appeared in the Tenement House Exhibition of 1900 and showed tenement conditions on the Lower East Side. The exhibition, organized by Lawrence Veiller, highlighted the crowded, unhealthy housing conditions in low-income neighborhoods. *Collection of the Community Service Society, Columbia University Rare Book and Manuscript Library.*

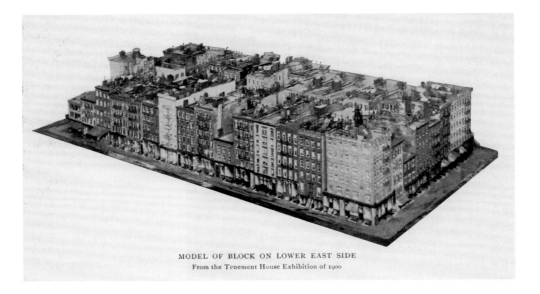

MODEL OF BLOCK ON LOWER EAST SIDE
From the Tenement House Exhibition of 1900

lems experienced in the poorer districts of New York City. Contributing to the disease, poverty, and poor sanitation was the simple problem of congestion. Florence Kelley, a resident of the Henry Street Settlement and head of the National Consumers' League, asked a question that challenged the work of housing reformers. "Instead of assenting to the belief that people who are poor must be crowded," she asked, "why did we not see years ago that people who are crowded must remain poor?"[66] This question led to a new effort to examine the social costs of the seemingly endless crowding of the slums and propose ways to curb it. In 1907 the Committee on the Congestion of Population was formed, with Mary Simkhovitch as the chair. This committee set out to demonstrate the problems created by congestion itself and to popularize the idea of planning for urban growth. In order to share its ideas with the public, the committee organized an exhibit at the Museum of

"The Tenement — A Menace to All." The illustration's original caption reads: "Not only an evil in itself, but the vice, crime and disease it breeds invade the homes of rich and poor alike." Progressive reformers maintained that improving the environments where the poor lived would result in a morally and materially improved city for all classes. *Courtesy of the Library of Congress.*

Natural History in 1908.[67] It was impossible to display the results of congestion, the *New York Times* dramatically reported , since these were found "in the cemeteries, the tuberculosis wards of hospitals, and in the penitentiaries."[68] Instead, as Simkhovitch recalled, the exhibit included "not only photographs of New York's slums, but models and interiors… bringing home the fact that the housing law had barely touched the living conditions of a large proportion of the population."[69]

Some parts of the exhibition appeared almost anti-urban; the Children's Aid Society's contribution to the exhibit contrasted photographs of sickly urban children with those showing active, ruddy-faced children in the country. But for the exhibit's primary organizers, the settlement residents living among the poor, the solution to overcrowding was not to abandon the city. "The reason the poor like to live in New York," Simkhovitch pointed out, "is because it is interesting, convenient, and meets their social needs. They live here for the reason that I do; I like it."[70] Instead, the goal of the reformers was to make the city more livable, to save the tenement dwellers from the worst excesses of congestion, and to demonstrate the need to consider the effects of future urban development. The end result of this committee's work was the creation of the national movement for urban planning. The National City Planning Conference, which formed in 1910, however, was quickly coopted by those more interested in beautifying cities than in improving living conditions for the poor.[71]

The Great Migration and Black Poverty in New York City

Poor European immigrants and their children were not the only families seeking refuge in New York City over the first third of the twentieth century. As the century unfolded, a growing number of black migrants and immigrants, fleeing destitution and discrimination, made their homes in the city. For most of the late nineteenth century, blacks had made up a relatively small proportion of the residents of New York City. While blacks began migrating to New York in greater numbers after the Civil War, in 1900 they made up only 1.8 percent of the total number of people in the five boroughs. By 1930, however, the total population of black New Yorkers had reached nearly 328,000, or almost 5 percent of the significantly larger city. While the population of the city as a whole nearly doubled, the number of blacks in New York more than tripled. Their migration was particularly concentrated in Manhattan. Over the 1920s alone, the black presence increased from 5 percent to 12 percent of Manhattan's total population.[72]

Most of these newcomers were migrants from the South. As with the European immigrants who flooded into New York over the same period, a combination of economic deprivation and persecution drove them from their former homes. Soil exhaustion and the plague of the boll weevil decimated southern agriculture in the early twentieth century, pushing black sharecroppers and farm workers further into destitution. The formalization of legal segregation and an increase in the number of lynchings made migration out of the South at times a matter of life and death. New York, with its economic opportunities for unskilled labor and its relatively moderate racial restrictions, drew blacks into the city. While black migrants would also move into other cities across the industrial Northeast and Midwest, by 1910 New York had the second-highest black population in the country after Washington, D.C.[73]

The migrants from the South were joined in New York City by black immigrants, mostly from the West Indies. Also drawn by the city's economic opportunities, these were a diverse lot from Jamaica, Bermuda, Antigua, and the Virgin Islands, along with other islands of the British West Indies. Foreign-born blacks came to make up about a third of the city's black population, by far the highest concentration of immigrant blacks in the United States. The differences among West Indian immigrants and between the immigrants and southern-born blacks created a diversity among New Yorkers of African descent that mirrored the incredible diversity among New Yorkers of European ancestry. [74]

Any differences among blacks, however, were ignored by potential employers and landlords. While southern migrants may have found more opportunity in New York than in the towns of their birth, they entered a city in which work and housing were severely restricted by race. In 1911, before the migration into New York picked up steam, settlement worker and reformer Mary White Ovington compiled a thorough investigation of black life in New York. Her findings were troubling, to say the least. No neighborhood was dominated by black residents in the early twentieth century, but Ovington found that certain sections, such as Greenwich Village and an area on the West Side known as San Juan Hill, had streets or rows of tenements that were all black. The black residents, Ovington found, usually lived in worse conditions—with "ragged paper" covering the walls or "a ceiling which scatters plaster flakes upon the floor"—and paid higher rent than their white neighbors.[75] Most blacks worked in domestic and personal service, including jobs as barbers, waiters, janitors, and laborers.[76] The low wages earned in these occupations often meant that women as well as men needed to enter the labor force; the rate of employment for married black women was over seven times higher than that for married white women.[77] Ovington argued that children bore the brunt of poor housing conditions and long hours of work. In 1908 the infant-mortality rate for blacks was 29 percent, compared with a 12.7 percent rate for whites.

At the very time that Ovington was writing, black New York was in the process of being transformed by the growth of Harlem. The arrival of the subway in Upper Manhattan, in 1904, sparked a boom in housing construction in the neighborhood. Overspeculation, however, led to a glut of housing in Harlem; as prices fell, desperate investors, who might otherwise have resisted blacks' entering the neighborhood, soon proved willing to sell or rent to blacks to recoup some of their losses. For blacks, the limited options for housing in the rest of the city made Harlem attractive. In 1905 there were fewer than 4,000 blacks north of 125th Street. By 1920 the black population of this area was 84,000. Over the next decade black Harlem grew to include the area between Park Avenue and Amsterdam Avenue from the north end of Central Park to 155th Street. This area was home to 190,000 blacks—two-thirds of the number of blacks in greater New York and 80 percent of the African American population of Manhattan.[78]

The growth of black Harlem increased segregation in the city as housing, professional services, and entertainment for blacks became concentrated there. Over the teens and into the early 1920s, Harlem was the center of elite and middle-class black culture. The author James Weldon Johnson imagined in 1920 that Harlem itself would be "the greatest Negro

Mary White Ovington. A feminist, reformer, and cofounder of the NAACP, Ovington conducted an influential study of living conditions among blacks in New York City. *Department of Special Collections and University Archives, W.E.B. Du Bois Library, University of Massachusetts, Amherst.*

city in the world." By the end of the decade, however, as housing became more crowded and fell into disrepair, the *New York Times* would comment that conditions in Harlem were "simply deplorable." Blacks from the South and the Caribbean continued to pour into New York. The result was increasing costs of housing, given that Harlem provided one of the few options for blacks in the city. Between 1919 and 1927, the typical rent in Harlem doubled. At the same time, the already restricted options for employment of blacks declined. Factory employment rates for all of New York decreased every year after 1923, cutting off an important source of income. Blacks were usually the first laid off from these plants. One sociologist divided the city's business into two types: "Those that employ Negroes in menial positions and those that employ no Negroes at all."[79]

This combination of high rents and low wages led to increased crowding into Harlem's apartments. Like the immigrants on the Lower East Side, black families packed into small living quarters, taking in boarders to help pay the rent. A 1915 study found that one in three black Harlem households contained at least seven people. As it had in other slum neighborhoods, crowding created poor living conditions and an increase in disease. Black mortality rates were 40 percent higher than in the rest of the city. The need for two in-

Two children play around a lamppost in Harlem. *Harlem had been populated mostly by Jewish and Italian immigrants in the late nineteenth century, before a large migration of African Americans began in the early twentieth century. By the 1920s Harlem was among the most densely populated and impoverished sections of the city. General Research & Reference Division, Schomburg Center for Research in Black Culture, The New York Public Library, Astor, Lenox and Tilden Foundations.*

comes frequently left children with inadequate supervision. Day nurseries cared for about 6 percent of children in Harlem who had two working parents. Another 10 percent were cared for in private homes, and about a third were watched by relatives or friends. But half of the children in need of supervision were simply left alone, which may have contributed to the high rates of delinquency in Harlem.[80]

Just as they reached out to assist new immigrants from Europe, white middle-class settlement workers and other progressive reformers attempted to improve conditions for black New Yorkers. Some settlements held back in their outreach to blacks, fearing that the presence of blacks might drive away others they hoped to help. Lillian Wald's Henry Street Settlement was open to blacks, but she also founded a separate settlement for them in the San Juan Hill neighborhood. Ovington, a veteran of the settlement-house movement, helped spark local and national action on behalf of African Americans. After reading about a 1908 race riot in Springfield, Illinois, Ovington helped organize, in collaboration with W.E.B. Du Bois's Niagara Movement, a national meeting held at the Henry Street Settlement in 1909. Here, hundreds of black and white dignitaries and experts debated the problems facing blacks in American society. Out of this meeting emerged the National Association for the Advancement of Colored People (NAACP), an organization based in New York but with a mission to improve conditions for blacks across the country.[81]

The Committee for Improving the Industrial Condition of the Negro in New York (CIICN) focused on a more local mission than the NAACP. Founded by black educator William Lewis Bulkley with the support of Ovington and other white progressive reformers, the CIICN attempted, as its name implied, to assist blacks in finding jobs and improving the industrial conditions in which they worked. The organization was divided into subcommittees, each focused on a single topic such as Legal Affairs, Trade Schools, Social Centers, and Employment. The organization's greatest accomplishments would be the formation of an employment bureau and its measured success in negotiating with unions to chip away at their policies of racial restriction.[82] In 1911 the CIICN merged with several other New York–based organizations to form the National Urban League. The New York branch of the Urban League would continue to be a leader in progressive reform over the 1920s, providing detailed studies of the growing difficulties of life in Harlem and establishing social services such as badly needed health clinics.[83]

Progressive reformers recognized that racial discrimination limited the work opportunities for African Americans. They also realized, however, that blacks in Harlem, Jews in the Lower East Side, and Italians in Little Italy all faced similar struggles based on poverty. The attack on New York's crowded and substandard housing was intended to help all New Yorkers, as were a series of campaigns intended to improve the welfare of children.

The Child and Progressive Reform

Progressive Era reformers, especially settlement workers, became increasingly focused on the particular needs of poor children. Many of their efforts looked to ways to strengthen the family and provide a better life for the children. One of the practices progressives became passionate about ending, both in New York and nationally, was child labor. Like their nineteenth-century middle-class predecessors, progressives viewed childhood as an idyllic time that should be free of the burdens of work. Instead, children often took jobs that placed them in contact with the corrupting influences of prostitutes and saloons. Children, the progressives believed, needed to be in school, developing their minds for a future as productive workers but also, and more importantly, as engaged American citizens. The reformers were sympathetic to the families forced to send their children out to work to make ends meet, but they asserted that child labor ultimately drove wages down because children accepted low pay for jobs that could be filled by adults.[84]

Settlement workers and other observers of tenement neighborhoods were shocked by the prevalence of child labor in these communities. Some of it was in the form of piece-

Unattended girls sit on a sidewalk. This photograph, likely by Jessie Tarbox Beals, exemplifies progressive efforts to use images of poor children to create the right political climate for social reforms. *Collection of the Community Service Society, Columbia University Rare Book and Manuscript Library.*

Boy carrying sticks. Children often contributed wages from odd jobs to the family income.
Collection of the Community Service Society, Columbia University Rare Book and Manuscript Library.

work that families performed together in their tenements. Lillian Wald recalled the story of one family who lived in a basement apartment with five "children engaged in making paper bags which the mother sold to the small dealers." Wald discovered the family when one of the children came to the first-aid room of the Henry Street Settlement for help. The boy's unkempt state suggested a case of neglect and betrayed the fact that he had never attended school. In fact, needing the labor of all five of the children, the family sent none of them to school and rarely allowed them outside to play.[85]

In *Bread Givers*, Anzia Yezierska's semiautobiographical novel of life on the Lower East Side, the narrator and her three sisters are required to work to support the family while their father concentrates on his Talmudic scholarship. At the tender age of ten, the narrator finds success working in a box factory and peddling herring.[86] Future labor leader Rose Schneiderman also recalled the difficulties she encountered as a young teenager working in a garment factory. "The hours were from 8 am to 6 pm," she remembered; "We stitched in the linings — golf caps, yachting caps, etc. It was piece work, and we received from 3 ½ cents to 10 cents a dozen, according to the different grades. By working hard we could make an average of about $5 a week." Their wages were reduced because they had to pay for their own sewing machines; the machine cost $45, and the girls paid $5 down and then $1 a month. If that was not bad enough, the factory burned down, and the owners, though they received an insurance settlement, resisted paying the workers for their lost machines.[87]

Children sometimes created a division of labor among themselves, separating house-work and wage-earning work. Jacob Riis described Katie, a "nine-year-old housekeeper" he met at an industrial school on Fifty-second Street. She lived with her sister and two brothers "on the top floor of a tenement in West Forty-ninth Street." The children had moved there together after their mother died and their father remarried. Katie's three siblings all worked in a hammock factory, "earning from $4.50 to $1.50 a week," while she "did the cleaning and the cooking." "I scrubs," she said in describing her daily occupation to Riis, who explained, "she scrubbed and swept and went to school." The combined family income from this arrangement "was something like $9.50 a week," which allowed them to buy some furniture on installment.[88]

Reformers did not rely on anecdotal evidence alone to make their case; in addition, they collected comprehensive statistics on the problem of child labor in New York City. They gathered data on the number of children working as newsboys and in factories; investigated the sweatshops inside tenements; and collaborated to publicize their find-ings and lobby the legislature for stricter laws. In 1902 settlement workers from around the city established the New York Child Labor Committee to formalize these efforts. Their work led the state legislature to pass a law in 1903 that significantly reduced the number of children in factories and required newsboys to be licensed by the state. Joining forces with the movement to end child labor in the southern states, Lillian Wald, Florence Kelley, and Chicago settlement leader Jane Addams established the National Child Labor Committee in 1904 opening an office in New York.[89]

The 1903 child-labor law served as a national model, but it still had shortcomings. The story of "Bessie," a girl in Lillian Wald's Lower East Side neighborhood, pointed to both the strengths and weaknesses of the law. "Bessie has had eight 'jobs' in six months," explained Wald. Her father was suffering from tuberculosis, and her mother was "the chief wage-earner." Wald continued, "The girl has been a fairly good student and duti-ful in the home, where for several years she had scrubbed the floors and 'looked after' the children in her mother's absence." But it was not surprising to settlement workers that Bessie chose to look for work to help her family. The process that she had to com-plete demonstrated the success of the child-labor law. "Bessie had had to prove by birth certificate or other documentary evidence that she is really fourteen, had had to submit to a simple test in English and arithmetic, present proof of at least 130 days' school atten-dance in the year before leaving, and, after examination by a medical officer, had had to be declared physically fit to enter shop or factory." In spite of these standards, Wald empha-

Photograph of a mother and girls in a tenement, sewing. *Courtesy of the Library of Congress.*

sized, "We are far from satisfied. Bessie, though she meets the requirements of the law, goes out wholly unprepared for self-support; she is of no industrial value, and is easily demoralized by the conviction of her unimportance to her 'boss,' certain that her casual employment and dismissal have hardly been noted, save as she herself has been affected by the pay envelope." Child labor, asserted Wald, provided little benefit to either industry or the child. To keep children out of the workplace between age fourteen, when they were first eligible for part-time employment, and sixteen, when they could leave school, Henry Street Settlement established scholarships of three dollars a week to keep kids at home, in school, or under the supervision of the settlement. These "scholarships" were directed to children of "widows" or "disabled fathers"—those, like Bessie, who were most tempted to enter the workplace.[90]

As their attitude toward child labor made clear, progressive reformers were proponents of a family wage—that is, they believed in the ideal of a single male breadwinner who could earn enough to care for his entire family. However, settlement workers, given their desire to respond to the needs of the local community, did not always organize services that strictly adhered to this ideal. Most settlements in New York, for instance, opened day nurseries—the day care centers of the time—where children of working mothers could receive care during the workday. At the same time, progressives were particularly concerned about widowed mothers who were forced into the labor market to provide for their children or, even worse, forced to give up their children to institutions or the "orphan trains."

This concern would grow into a national campaign to provide state support for poor children so they could remain with their parents. One morning in 1903, so the story goes, Florence Kelley was eating breakfast with Lillian Wald at the Henry Street Settlement, where they both resided. Perusing the morning papers, Kelley read aloud an article about an investigation by the Department of Agriculture on the effects of the boll weevil on the cotton crop. Wald remarked, "If the Government can have a department to take such an interest in what is happening to the cotton crop, why can't it have a bureau to look after the nation's child crop?"[91] Kelley and Wald soon joined Edward T. Devine, head of the Charity Organization Society, to convince President Theodore Roosevelt of the need for a new national focus on child welfare. The result was the 1909 White House Conference on Depen-

Girl sits by the bed of her sick father. In densely populated tenements with substandard sanitation, sickness and disease were rampant. The illness of a wage-earning family member could result in the unraveling of the entire home. *Photography Collection, Miriam and Ira D. Wallach Division of Art, Prints and Photographs, The New York Public Library, Astor, Lenox and Tilden Foundations.*

dent Children, which famously declared that the home was the best place for child care and that poverty alone was not enough reason to separate a child from his or her parents.[92]

The White House conference sparked two changes in public policy. It laid the groundwork for the creation of the U.S. Children's Bureau, which was a toehold for the settlement movement in the federal government. It also energized the national campaign for widows' pensions. These programs, also called mothers' pensions, provided state aid to widowed mothers who could not afford to care for their children. Such aid helped parents keep their children in the home rather than giving them up to child care institutions; it also helped affirm the ideal of the family wage by allowing mothers, with state support, to stay home to care for their children. The irony is that independent, professional women were responsible for creating a program that, rather than providing work options, reinforced the paternalistic model by making poor single mothers reliant on the state.[93]

In spite of the concentration of settlement reformers in New York City and the obvious need for assistance among poor widowed mothers, New York was not among the first states to adopt such legislation. One reason for this was the continuing power of charitable organizations within the city and state. The cities of New York and Brooklyn had ended all cash relief to the poor in the 1870s, and the 1897 charter of Greater New York had further restricted outdoor relief in all five boroughs; only the blind were eligible for public aid. Still, progressive reformers remained troubled by findings in the 1890s that many of the children placed in institutions could have been raised at home but for the poverty of their parents. In 1898, the same year that the new city charter went into effect, both houses of the New York State Legislature passed a "destitute mothers bill." This legislation would allow the Society for the Prevention of Cruelty to Children to return children in institutions to their parents and provide public allowances, equal to the amount the institutions had received to care for the children. Deriding the legislation as the "shiftless fathers' bill," opponents among the charitable establishment argued that the bill would simply encourage pauperism. These claims were persuasive to the governor of New York, who vetoed the bill.[94]

In response to reformers' activism, the private charitable institutions began to work to help children remain in their homes. In 1898 the COS reached an agreement with the city to investigate all applications for the commitment of dependent children and attempt to provide private relief for those children in their homes. Charities also began to provide their own private mothers' "pensions." Most notably, the United Hebrew Charities of New York City provided grants to about 500 widowed or deserted mothers in the period of 1908–09. That organization was joined in 1914 by the AICP, which quickly realized, however, that it would never be able with private funds to provide adequately for widowed mothers. In 1915 the AICP abruptly ended its opposition to public widows' pensions.[95]

Young children seated on a sidewalk near a street merchant. Older siblings frequently watched younger ones while both parents worked. *Collection of the Community Service Society, Columbia University Rare Book and Manuscript Library.*

Following the suggestion of the state-appointed Commission for Relief of Widowed Mothers, the New York State legislature finally passed the Child Welfare Act of 1915, a statewide system for the provision of mothers' pensions. Rather than strengthening the existing public-welfare establishment, these pensions were administered by independent county boards made up of unpaid members, an effort to avoid both the stigma of poor relief and the corruption of machine politics. The boards were authorized to provide grants for any widowed mother with at least one child under the age of sixteen in the home. While New York restricted these grants to widows, this program would become a model for the Aid to Dependent Children program, which would be incorporated into the federal Social Security Act of 1935.[96]

The Legacy of the Progressive Era

The reforms of the Progressive Era built on previous efforts to improve the lives of poor New Yorkers. Like their predecessors, progressives assisted poor families for varied and complex reasons. Some wanted to assimilate foreigners by introducing them to so-called American values. Others hoped to teach poor families to behave more like the middle-class families. Still others hoped to soothe the class tensions that, they believed, could lead to revolution and upheaval. Yet, mixed in with these various motivations were ideas that represented a distinct break with past efforts to confront family poverty. First was the progressive belief that the economy and the social environment—not individual failings—caused poverty. Second was the effort to study and listen to poor communities in developing policies and programs to meet their needs. Third was a demand for public responses—not just private charity—to attack poverty. The progressive ideology did not put an end to older ideas about poverty—that the roots of poverty lay in individual flaws or that private giving was superior to public largess—but it provided an alternative perspective, beginning a decades-long debate about public policy and the poor.

These debates would be put aside by the national economic tragedy of the Great Depression. As New York's economy began to decline in the late 1920s, progressive leaders pushed for an aggressive government response to the economic calamity. In 1930 both Lillian Wald and Mary Simkhovitch gave their support to an unsuccessful bill in Congress to create a national program that would put the unemployed to work.[97] The widespread suffering and the inadequacy of private assistance strengthened the arguments of the progressive reformers. Their ideas would prove influential in developing the local, state, and national policies that attempted to reduce unemployment and alleviate destitution among New York City's families.

Population density map showing parts of Upper Manhattan and the Bronx.
Blue regions are the mostly densely populated. *The Lionel Pincus and Princess Firyal Map Division, The New York Public Library, Astor, Lenox and Tilden Foundations.*

Chapter 6

Family Poverty in the Great Depression

The Great Depression did not begin on a single day. The nation's—and New York City's—economy contracted slowly, with production declining and unemployment increasing over several months. Many of New York City's families dated the beginning of the Depression not from national or international events, but from the moments of economic collapse in their own homes. Rose Halpern of the Lower East Side remembered when her mother lost her job and was forced to go on welfare so they would not be evicted from their tenement. Nora Mair, a Jamaican garment worker living in Harlem, recalled that her husband, trained as a draftsman, "couldn't get work in his profession" and was forced to drive a cab to make a living. Clara Ferrara in East Harlem reflected back on the time when her father went to work fixing office furniture for the Works Progress Administration. For Mollie Stiker, the Depression began when her family was evicted from the Lower East Side apartment where she had lived for her entire life.[1]

The Great Depression would last longer than any period of economic decline since the 1870s and create unprecedented suffering. It lowered the standard of living of virtually every American.[2] The downward pressure forced the well-to-do into the middle class and the middle class into a paycheck-to-paycheck existence. Many of those who belonged to the throngs of semiskilled and unskilled workers before the Depression were pushed, over the 1930s, to the level of destitution.[3] The economic crises faced by countless families were driven by the epidemic of unemployment. In 1933 more than two million nonagricultural workers across New York State were out of work.[4] In New York City, a year later, approximately 15 percent of the population was receiving public relief.[5]

Job loss had destructive effects on families and the communities in which they lived. When a breadwinner lost a job, he (or, in some cases, she) typically depleted the family's savings first, then borrowed from friends and relatives until they could lend no more. The family bought groceries on credit and pleaded with the landlord for extensions on the rent payment until, finally, all their resources were exhausted. At that point, the breadwinner was forced to turn to public or private assistance.[6] Some men, used to providing for their wives and children, could not stand to face their families when unemployed. They would wander the streets or seek out speakeasies or pool halls, returning home only at bedtime; other men would leave to find work and never return, simply abandoning their struggling families. Evictions became frequent, and families were often forced to double up. Cases in which six persons were living in one room were not unheard of. When tenants could no longer afford to pay rent, some landlords agreed to move them into previously uninhabited cellars or unheated garages.[7] Facing these struggles, New York City's families became desperate for assistance. Yet the city's limited resources for confronting such economic disaster were quickly exhausted.

New York Reacts to the Depression

As the wave of unemployment engulfed New York City, there was no unified response from the nearly 1,200 existing public and private welfare and health agencies. While these organizations normally focused on a variety of social problems, they were quickly caught up in the flood of issues emanating from the growing number of unemployed workers. A lack of food for the families of the jobless was an immediate concern. The Salvation Army soon opened six breadlines. These were joined by breadlines at the "Little Church Around the Corner," St. Vincent's Hospital, and many other institutions. By December 1930 there were fifty-three locations around the city where those in need could receive food.[8]

Other efforts focused on providing work for the unemployed. Block-aid programs recruited the unemployed to visit the neighbors on their blocks and ask for pledges of assistance. At one point nearly 200,000 workers were enrolled in such programs throughout the city. The International Apple Shippers' Association agreed to provide apples to the unemployed at wholesale prices. An impoverished person sitting next to a crate of apples, hawking the fruit, became an iconic image of the Depression. When the economic downturn was at its worst, nearly every street corner in the business district of Manhattan had at least one apple seller.[9]

Because the charter of the city of New York barred cash relief, the types of public assistance available to the city's destitute families were limited. As they had in previous economic busts, then, private charities attempted with minimal success to help those in need.[10] The AICP set up a work-relief program over the winter of 1929–30, but the $200,000 in relief wages they supplied to 1,456 heads of families made only the smallest

Shantytown on the banks of the East River. *Collection of the American Jewish Historical Society.*

dent in the growing rolls of the unemployed.[11] By the summer of 1930, the city's charities had realized that they simply did not have the funds to meet the needs of those without work. The heads of the AICP and the COS joined with those of the Jewish Social Service Association and Catholic Charities to raise additional funds to address the crisis. Seward J. Prosser, chairman of the board of the Bankers' Trust Company, was chosen to head a fund-raising committee. When the campaign ended, in December 1930, the Prosser Committee had raised well over $8 million dedicated to the Emergency Work Bureau, a city-wide work-relief program. Both men and — in a surprise to the committee — women applied to the bureau in large numbers. The Prosser Committee ruled that only "heads of families" would be eligible for aid, allowing men and women who provided for dependents to take part in the program.[12] By December 1930 the bureau was providing three days of work a week at a rate of $5 a day to more than 20,000 out-of-work heads of families. While the program was certainly a success, any sense of accomplishment was tempered by the knowledge that more than 300,000 individuals in the city remained without work.[13]

Realizing that, in spite of their herculean fund-raising efforts, they would never be able to meet the growing needs of the city, the members of the Prosser Committee turned to New York City mayor James J. Walker for further support of their relief work. Walker, interpreting the city's charter as barring public support for work relief, refused; instead, he initiated a program whereby the city's public employees voluntarily contributed one

Temporary housing in Central Park for otherwise homeless squatters, 1933. The juxtaposition of the shacks against the skyscrapers in the background illustrates the wealth disparity of the period. The colony in Central Park was known as "Hoover Valley," "Shanty Village," and "Forgotten Man's Gulch." *Nat Norman, Museum of the City of New York, Photo Archives.*

percent of their salaries to a fund for the needy and unemployed. This fund supplemented relief provided by the police, usually the first to discover the destitute, mostly in the form of food or other in-kind assistance.[14] At the same time, New York City schoolteachers established their own fund in order to provide children with free lunches, clothing, and, occasionally, cash relief. In 1930 around 50,000 children got such assistance; by 1931 more than 100,000 children had received this critical help.[15]

In April 1931 the state legislature stepped in, authorizing New York City to provide public work relief. The unemployed became eligible for part-time work at a rate of $5.50 a day. Depending on the number of days they reported, these workers earned between $44 and $71.50 a month, well under the city's average monthly income of approximately $145. The program reached its peak in November 1931, with about 17,500 persons on the rolls. For the fiscal year 1930–31, public and private sources together spent a record $38 million on relief.[16]

One of the most dramatic effects of the Great Depression in New York was the sudden growth in the homeless population. The number of homeless men requesting shelter more than doubled from 1929 to 1930; in 1934 more than two million people registered for shelter. Both the city and voluntary organizations expanded their facilities to confront this growing problem. The city's municipal shelter provided lodging for single men and women and meals to many needy people. In 1934, overwhelmed by the numbers needing shelter, the city opened two additional annexes, including one that slept 1,500 in the "largest bedroom in the world."[17] Private charities also assisted the city in providing for the homeless. The Salvation Army served 4,800 meals to the homeless and destitute at fourteen food stations across the city. Finding its men's hotel full, the organization opened additional facilities, including the S.S. *Broadway*, a reconditioned riverboat that served as a floating hotel for destitute seamen, as well as a lodging house on 124th Street exclusively for black men.[18]

These public and private facilities were dedicated almost wholly to homeless men, but homeless women and children also struggled to find shelter in the city. Travelers Aid — an organization founded in 1905 to assist unaccompanied women who arrived in New York from other states in the U.S. — opened the Guest House, a facility that provided care for twenty homeless women and their children at a time. This facility provided "a wholesome homelike atmosphere," with a separate bedroom for each family, a dining room, and a large living room. The staff included a hostess, a cook, a maid, two caseworkers, and a recreation worker. There was even a playground for the children. The Salvation Army also opened facilities directed at women and families. One was the Marjorie Post Hutton Depot, which began in 1931 to distribute free food exclusively to women. To provide shelter the Salvation Army already operated a Women's Hotel on Tenth Avenue; in March 1930 it set up the Emergency Home for Women and Children. Those who ran these facilities tried to make the surroundings "homey rather than institutional." Bedrooms slept up to four women, and meals were served in "a pleasant refreshing" dining room. The Salvation Army asked women to pay what they could but welcomed those unable to pay.[19]

While the Depression certainly made for a great number of destitute and homeless women, this population still remained largely invisible. One historian who examined images of New York City taken during the Great Depression could find only one photo, from 1930, of a woman selling apples on the street; in the many images of breadlines and shantytowns that depicted homelessness in the era, women were conspicuously absent. Just as public policy focused almost exclusively on the unemployed man, journalistic investigations tended to ignore the struggle of the destitute woman.[20]

The growing population of homeless and unattached children also remained hidden in the Depression era. As they fell further down the economic ladder, many parents found themselves simply unable to care for their children. New York's Public Welfare Law of 1929 echoed the reigning approach to child welfare: "As far as possible," the act declared, "families shall be kept together, and they shall not be separated for reasons of poverty alone."[21] Still, by December 1932 there were 23,000 children in institutional or foster-home care. The City Budget Office concluded, "The large increase in the number of children is due largely to the breaking up of homes of destitute families."[22] One Italian couple in the Bronx, in which the husband was out of work for an extended time and the wife earned little income, heard from a private agency that it might be best to temporarily give up custody of their children. The husband, however, refused. "They didn't eat a whole lot," he reasoned, "and he had to think of the whole family not just the two children."[23]

Some older children attempted to strike out on their own, with some ending up on the street. In response, the Children's Aid Society housed 250 child vagrants in its Brace Memorial Newsboys' Lodging House and also sent boys out of the city to live on its industrial farms. These boys received training in occupations such as farming, auto mechanics, painting, carpentry, and horticulture. The CAS then attempted to place these children in jobs in the city or on farms upstate.[24]

By 1931 the crisis of the Depression had drained the private and public resources of New York City. Politicians and charity leaders in the city turned to the state government, and especially to Governor Franklin Delano Roosevelt, for help. The actions that Roosevelt took in New York would provide an example to the nation of how to confront this economic quagmire—and would serve as a model for the collection of federal polices that would become known as "the New Deal."

Franklin Delano Roosevelt and the Great Depression

As the extent of the Depression became evident over 1930 and 1931, national and state leaders scurried to deal with the massing crisis of unemployment. In October 1930 President Herbert Hoover created the President's Emergency Committee for Employment, chaired by Colonel Arthur Woods. The Woods Committee, following the temperament and direction of the president, did not provide top-down direction for the economy. Rather, "the principal part of our work," Woods explained, "is co-operating with local organizations." The committee hoped to guide local communities toward successful programs to relieve the poor and unemployed, not to provide a national solution.[25]

By the summer of 1931, however, it was clear that in New York local action could not adequately confront the mounting social crisis created by widespread unemployment. In August 1931 Governor Franklin Delano Roosevelt directed the New York State Legislature to rethink the relationship between the state and those in need. "In broad terms," Roosevelt declared, "I assert that modern society, acting through its government, owes the definite obligation to prevent the starvation or the dire want of any of its fellow men and women who try to maintain themselves but cannot." He continued, "To these unfortunate citizens aid must be extended by government—not as a matter of charity but as a matter of social duty." In response to Roosevelt's request, the legislature passed the Wicks Act, providing state aid to the unemployed. Critically, the law was clear in superseding any act that was inconsistent with it. This effectively overturned the ban on home relief in place in New York City since the nineteenth century.[26]

The Wicks Act created the Temporary Emergency Relief Administration (TERA) to provide state aid for work relief and home relief directly to New York's municipalities. With the help of a 50 percent increase in the 1931 income tax, the state agreed to fund 40 percent of the expenditures of home relief. At first that was limited to in-kind aid such as shelter, food, fuel, clothing, and medicine, but subsequent revisions to the law allowed for cash grants as well. In addition, TERA would provide the wages for local work-relief programs and a portion of the salaries of administrators who would oversee such programs. Harry L. Hopkins, the "chain-smoking, hollow-eyed, pauper-thin social worker" currently running the New York Tuberculosis Association, was appointed as executive director of TERA.[27]

The expectation that this program would be temporary was reflected not only in its name but in the offices set up to assist the unemployed. The space dedicated to these makeshift facilities was frequently inadequate, creating overcrowded conditions and making any private consultation between caseworkers and clients virtually impossible. Offices often lacked necessary supplies and furniture. The staff itself was frequently overworked, undermining the quality of service that relief clients received.[28]

TERA nonetheless greatly assisted the poor families of New York City, but it did not fundamentally alter the conditions of the Depression. As New York entered the third winter of the downturn, the depths to which families had fallen proved tragic. New York City schools reported in 1932 that some 20,000 children were suffering from malnutrition. The Welfare Council tallied twenty-nine deaths from starvation in 1933. And while the election of Franklin Roosevelt as president in 1932 certainly changed the mood in the city and the nation, it did not immediately put food on the table.[29]

In his inaugural address Roosevelt promised "direct, vigorous action." And he quickly delivered. Calling Congress into emergency session, he pushed through the passage of major acts to stabilize the economy and aid the unemployed. Among the agencies created by the legislation was the Federal Emergency Relief Administration (FERA). Closely modeled on New York's TERA, this agency provided assistance to the states for relief for the unemployed. Congress also created the Public Works Administration (PWA) to establish federal funding for large-scale public projects that would help put people back to work. Both of these programs had enormous effects on poor families in New York City.

More important were the long-term social reforms initiated by the Roosevelt administration, including the landmark Social Security Act of 1935. With provisions for the aged, the unemployed, and dependent children, this act would fundamentally change the face of poverty in the United States. The creation of Old Age Assistance and the beginnings of Old Age Insurance (commonly known as Social Security) would shift the concentration of poverty from the elderly to the young. Unemployment insurance would guarantee temporary assistance during future economic downturns. Poor female-headed families received the least generous benefits under the Social Security Act. In an effort to build on the mothers' pension programs already in place in New York and forty-five other states, the Social Security Act introduced Aid to Dependent Children (ADC) as a joint federal-state program rather than a stand-alone federal program like Old Age Insurance.[30] The federal government agreed to provide a dollar for every two provided by the states, up to a maximum allotment of $18 per month for the first child and $12 for each additional child. There was no additional aid given to the mother caring for her children. Under the Old Age Assistance program, an elderly individual could receive up to $30 per month from the federal government; a single mother and her child were limited to a total of $18. Furthermore, ADC was severely restricted. The program was limited to single mothers (two-parent families were ineligible) and required that a woman have no income or other assets that would help support her family. Any additional money a woman brought in would be deducted from her monthly payment. ADC would, in some cases, provide temporary relief to single mothers as they got back on their feet following economic setbacks; in many other cases it would simply trap families at a level of subsistence.[31]

The Experience of the Depression

In spite of all the programs that made a difference in the lives of New York's families, the experience of the Great Depression remained traumatic, especially for children. "The Depression hit us very badly," recalled Rose Halpern, a teenager living on the Lower East Side when the downturn struck. "My mother lost her job." Like many others experiencing extended unemployment and destitution for the first time, Halpern's mother resisted seeking government relief. "To us," explained Halpern, "it was a terrible thing." Finally, when the family was in danger of losing their housing because they couldn't pay rent, neighbors persuaded the mother to go on welfare.[32]

Recreation for children, 1939. In these photographs, commissioned by the Charity Organization Society, children play in desolate abandoned lots. *Milstein Division of United States History, Local History & Genealogy, The New York Public Library, Astor, Lenox and Tilden Foundations.*

One of the greatest fears of children was the loss of shelter through eviction. "Have you ever gone thru a disgrace a personal shame" one child from Brooklyn wrote to First Lady Eleanor Roosevelt, after the child's family received notice that they would be evicted in ten days. With four siblings, and with her father out of work, the girl realized "the burden my father & mother have to carry." The effect on the father was particularly palpable. "Under all his jokes I can see he is suffering terrible," the girl wrote. "I'd feel ashamed to go

Two boys gather scrap metal in an alley. Children sometimes contributed income from informal labor—such as selling metal scraps—to the family economy. *Milstein Division of United States History, Local History & Genealogy, The New York Public Library, Astor, Lenox and Tilden Foundations.*

to school, " she confided. "All my friend's father's [sic] work and receive good pay except my father at times I think our name is cursed."[33]

Frank Miggs Regina, who lived on the Lower East Side, vividly remembered witnessing evictions. "They used to bring the furniture down on the sidewalk. You know what I mean? If they didn't pay their rent, they used to bring all their belongings down in front of the building. And the woman or the man or the kids used to sit there. And the neighbors then would try to help them."[34] Mollie Stiker, a child also living on the Lower East Side, had the common experience of coming home to find her apartment empty and none of her family at home. They had been evicted after falling a month behind in the rent. Luckily for the family, they were able to find new housing quickly.[35] Stiker's story, however, exemplifies the residential instability that many experienced during the Depression. Evictions became a common occurrence, and frequent moves became just a part of life for many families. The Catholic social activist Dorothy Day recalled that "in 1933, 1934, there were so many evictions on the East Side, you couldn't walk down the streets without seeing furniture on the sidewalk."[36]

Local community institutions attempted to assist those who had lost their homes. Day and her Catholic Worker movement would attempt to forestall the marshal from evicting families. When that failed, they would find available apartments and help the families move in. This work on behalf of the evicted eventually led her organization to create an entire house of refuge to provide housing for the homeless. Some organizations had more aggressive responses to evictions. The Unemployment Councils formed around the city with the support of the Communist Party would interrupt evictions in progress. Sol Rubin, a resident of the Lower East Side, recalled that the councils would "take all their belongings from the street up to their apartment to the third floor, the fifth floor … break open the seal that the marshal put on, this is very serious, and put the furniture back, put it back inside. Then the landlord had to go through the whole trouble again with courts and this and that, and finally had to throw them out again."[37]

The relief programs created by the city, the state, and, later, the federal government assisted many New Yorkers. Some unemployed breadwinners, however, simply refused to make the sacrifices required to receive public assistance. Mollie Stiker's father was an unemployed tailor. When offered work relief through the WPA, Stiker's father declined. "So they told my father we'll give you a job cleaning, being a maintenance man in a municipal building," Stiker remembered. "And my father goes, 'I can't do that kind of work. I only

A boy sits along the East River, c. 1938. Factories and industrial waste dominate the landscape behind him. *Milstein Division of United States History, Local History & Genealogy, The New York Public Library, Astor, Lenox and Tilden Foundations.*

Left and below: a squatter colony in Brooklyn, 1933. *Division of United States History, Local History & Genealogy, The New York Public Library, Astor, Lenox and Tilden Foundations.*

know how to sew. I'm willing to … if you give me a job, I'll make uniforms for mailmen or police or anything sewing.' But they didn't have that kind of job, so they said, 'either you accept this job or you don't get welfare' and we didn't get it. They didn't give it to us." Stiker's family survived the Depression through the limited piecework that her father brought in, her brother's job delivering laundry, some occasional domestic work that her mother did for neighbors, and the assistance of her aunt, who occasionally boarded with the family.[38]

The caseworkers responsible for providing home and work relief had to insure that public funds were going to those with the greatest needs. Unfortunately, this made applying for aid an invasive process. Rose Halpern acted as an interpreter when her mother went to seek aid. "They asked us a million questions," she remembered. "They asked you if you worked, how much money you had. You had to be poor all the time." Many people receiving home relief actively deceived the caseworkers by hiding additional work and income. "They paid your rent and a little more," Halpern explained, "but you couldn't exist on that little money, so my mother finally got herself a part-time job. She didn't report it." Whenever the inspectors came around, Halpern would tell them that her mother was out.[39] Josephine Baldizzi Esposito, who, like Halpern, lived on the Lower East Side, recalled the serious repercussions when an investigator discovered her mother working.[40] The discovery of new purchases or luxury items made caseworkers suspicious that relief recipients were bringing in additional money. Some people reacted violently to these investigations into their private lives. Peggy Dolan, who lived in Chelsea, clearly recalled an incident involving her neighbor, Mrs. Finnegan, who was on home relief but still was working:

"One day this welfare lady comes and she says to Mrs. Finnegan, 'Ooh, I see you got new sheets on the beds. Well, you're off relief today.'

"'Oh,' she says, 'bejeezus, is that right?'

"'Yes, that's right.'

"'Well, by God, you're gonna be off for quite a few weeks.'

"And, bingo! She knocked her down a whole flight of steps. And [the caseworker] was out of action for quite a while, for three or four months after that."[41]

These investigations kept some people from even applying for assistance. Clara Ferrara of East Harlem remembered one year during the Depression when her father, a furniture maker, could not find work. "He didn't want to go on welfare," she explained. "They came to your house and investigated. They would see if you had a radio. My father didn't want anybody in his home."[42]

Not only did caseworkers investigate home-relief recipients; they also severely restricted their autonomy. TERA initially provided relief only in-kind, limiting recipients to groceries, surplus food, used clothing, bags of coal, and rent vouchers. It restricted grocery purchases, barring items that were considered luxuries—"Cigars, cigarettes, tobacco in any form, beer, near beer, soda water, candy, pies, and cakes"—and not allowing aid recipients to get change in cash from grocers. "Voluntary shoppers" often accompanied relief recipients to insure that they were following the rules.[43]

Unemployment and poverty created and exacerbated tension and conflict within families. When Abraham Kokofsky's father lost his job, his mother quietly found work as a janitor for an apartment building. Kokofsky recalled, "My father was not a happy guy."[44] Looking back, Herman Partnow, a Jewish man from the Bronx living as a vagabond, believed his financial and emotional descent was initiated by the emasculating experience of losing his role as the family breadwinner. Once, Herman came home at three in the morning to find his kids in bed but his wife, who was working, dressed to go out on the town. Herman asked, "Sarah, what's the matter?" His wife responded, "I'm going out." He replied, "What out? … In the middle of the night, out? Go to bed, Sarah. She says: You go to bed, I'm going out." This led to the end of their relationship: "So a whole month I worried and complained and talked and finally she threw me out of the house altogether. What could I do? It was her property, I was depending on her. I was no more a man, you understand, not human, so she threw me out, twenty six years we were married."[45]

Perhaps the most vulnerable families of the Depression era were those headed by single women. Miss K., originally from Pennsylvania, raised her son, Roy, without any financial support from the boy's father. Experienced as a nanny, Miss K. found work as a live-in domestic and child's caregiver in a home where she was able to keep Roy with her. But Miss K. quickly became dissatisfied with this arrangement because her employer "drank and gave drunken parties." Once she found her own place and a day nursery for the boy, Miss K. got temporary domestic work. After losing that job she had no choice but to turn to the COS and the AICP. Those private agencies were able to find work for Miss K. in the kitchen of a luncheonette and provide a supplement that helped her pay for shelter and day care. Miss K. also took advantage of WPA courses in bookkeeping, telephone operating, and secretarial work. When her physical appearance seemed to keep her from landing an office job, the AICP helped her buy clothes and paid for a visit to a beauty parlor. While Miss K. still experienced a long stretch of poverty and unemployment, she was, by late 1941, able to secure work as a stenographer for a publishing company and care for her son on her own. This success story demonstrated the crucial nature of the public and private support that helped single mothers like Miss K. survive the Depression.[46]

New York's families experienced the Depression in diverse ways. Some managed to get by just by cutting their expenses. Others adjusted to the unemployment of a breadwinner by sending other family members out to work and pooling their wages. Still others failed to make ends meet, finding themselves evicted from their homes, forced to scramble for shelter or live makeshift lives on the street. Another subset of families simply dissolved, with husbands deserting wives or children being sent off to substitute care in institutions or foster families. Many families in all these categories looked to government — municipal, state, national — to provide financial assistance and leadership through these troubled times. In New York City, they found this leadership in the form of Mayor Fiorello H. La Guardia.

The Little Flower and the Great Depression

The problems facing New York City during the Great Depression were numerous, but for Fiorello La Guardia, mayor from 1934 to 1945, they also provided the opportunity to reshape New York City and its government. Elected with the support of Republicans and reform-oriented Democrats, La Guardia ended a line of Tammany Hall Democrats known for cronyism and corruption. In contrast to the Democratic machine, La Guardia set out to demonstrate how effective and efficient city government could be. A short, stout man with a flair for the theatrical, La Guardia, known as "the Little Flower," tried to connect

Fiorello La Guardia, known as "the Little Flower." La Guardia, mayor of New York City from 1934 to 1945, presided over numerous slum-clearance projects. *Courtesy of the Library of Congress.*

government with the common New Yorker. He would become a frequent presence on the radio, on one occasion simply reading the comics; he would arrive at fires to assess damage and talk with victims, and he would walk the streets to meet with other ordinary New Yorkers. Most importantly, during his time in office La Guardia sought to remake the city — to manage the growth occurring in the outer boroughs and to redevelop old neighborhoods. The choices made by his administration would forever change the map of New York. The arteries of transportation, the pockets of wealth and poverty that still exist today largely reflect the decisions made while La Guardia was mayor.

La Guardia followed a winding and cosmopolitan path to become mayor. The child of a lapsed-Catholic father from southern Italy and a Jewish mother from Austrian-controlled northern Italy, La Guardia was born in Greenwich Village in 1882. With his father a musician in the U.S. Army, Fiorello had a peripatetic childhood, with stops in South Dakota, Watertown, New York, and finally Prescott, Arizona. When La Guardia's father was discharged from the army due to illness, the family returned to Europe, where the elder La Guardia ran a hotel in Trieste and Fiorello found work in the American Consulate in Budapest. It was only as an adult that La Guardia settled in New York, finding a job as a translator at Ellis Island and attending New York University Law School at night. His legal practice led him to politics, and he received the Republican nomination in an ultimately unsuccessful campaign for the U.S. House of Representatives in 1914. Two years later, however, he managed the surprise upset of a Tammany-backed candidate and was elected to Congress. He resigned his congressional seat in 1919, after his election as president of New York's Board of Aldermen. In 1921 he successfully ran again for Congress, representing a district that encompassed the largely Italian neighborhood of East Harlem. La Guardia proved to be an independent voice in the House, taking on both the Democrats of Tammany Hall and national Republican leaders. In spite of his support for reform, La Guardia was defeated by a Democrat riding FDR's coattails in the election of 1932. That provided the opening for his successful mayoral run in 1933.[47]

Building on the work of his predecessors, La Guardia set out to extend relief to the thousands of impoverished people in New York. Recognizing the growing power of the federal government under FDR, La Guardia grounded the city's recovery in federal largess. The mayor sent frequent emissaries to Washington and often made the trip down to D.C. himself to lobby Congress or the president. La Guardia "is probably the most appealing person I know," FDR once commented. "He comes to Washington and tells me a sad story. The tears run down my cheeks and tears run down his cheeks and the first thing I know, he has wangled another fifty million dollars." La Guardia's success was demonstrated when huge public-works projects including the Triborough Bridge received federal funds. When the Works Projects Administration was created, in 1935, La Guardia helped direct funds to New York—at one point, one of every seven WPA dollars was being spent in the city. La Guardia made sure that this money was directed to those who needed work. When his cantankerous parks commissioner, Robert Moses, complained that he could not employ the "bums, jailbirds, and riffraff" supplied by the WPA, La Guardia grew agitated. "The purpose of federal relief projects is to give employment," the mayor shot back in a memo to all the city's commissioners. "Before arbitrarily rejecting workers and sending them back, give them a chance to make good."[48]

La Guardia's overarching desire to help those in need occasionally created errors and inefficiencies. Once he took office, the mayor attempted to quickly expand the program of relief supported by state and federal legislation. A 1935 investigation by the city's Board of Aldermen, however, uncovered suspicious funding choices, such as academic projects, meaningless survey work for white-collar relief, and, most offensively, raises for welfare-administration officials. La Guardia responded by cracking down on dubious relief programs and rescinding the raises of the administrators. In order to coordinate the many relief programs in the city, the mayor appointed a series of welfare "czars" who helped supervise policy in this difficult area. Still, La Guardia often felt trapped between the more radical Unemployment Councils—which took actions such as invading the welfare-department offices to protest a reduction in rates—and the Board of Aldermen, which attempted to place more restrictions on relief.[49]

For many New Yorkers, La Guardia became a symbol of reassurance in those troubled times. One woman from Brooklyn wrote directly to La Guardia that her husband, a WPA worker named Robert Lee, had not been paid in two weeks. He was owed at least $12, and the family had no food left in the house. "Please help me," Mrs. Lee wrote, "I have no food to feed my children. Tomorrow is Christmas and we are starving." La Guardia was so moved that he personally paid for a food package to be delivered to the family. "There is a Santa Claus," commented the Lees' oldest child.[50]

La Guardia's accomplishments went beyond delivering relief to New Yorkers. He also provided the imagination and leadership that reshaped New York, building the foundation for the city it would become. At the heart of that transformation was recognition of the need for housing reform—the fulfillment of the decades of advocacy dedicated to improving the city's slums.

Slum Clearance and Relocation of Poverty

The city that elected La Guardia mayor in 1933 had experienced a wide-reaching structural transformation over the first third of the twentieth century. Expansion of the city into the outer boroughs had quickly followed the creation of Greater New York, in 1898. For Brooklyn, the opening of the Williamsburg Bridge, in 1903, and the Manhattan Bridge, in 1909, brought additional means of crossing the East River. More importantly, the extension of two subway lines into Brooklyn provided easy access from the borough's residential neighborhoods to work and entertainment in Manhattan.[51] As the city's population climbed, more and more residents settled in outer-borough neighborhoods. Brooklyn's Coney Island, long the city's seaside entertainment district, exploded from a residential population of 33,000 in 1910 to one of 280,000 by 1930. Over the same years the Bronx neighborhood of East Tremont shot from 50,000 residents to 264,000. Even in the quiet area of Jackson Heights, in Queens, the number of people tripled. This growth in the outer boroughs greatly relieved the crowding in Lower Manhattan. By 1930, Brooklyn, with 2.5 million residents, passed Manhattan as the most populous borough.[52]

The expansion of the city across the five boroughs, however, did not bring an end to crowded conditions. Harlem, increasingly packed with people, became the most densely settled part of New York. At the same time, newly developed neighborhoods in Brooklyn and the Bronx, supposed escapes from the density of Manhattan, soon filled up with tenements; the crowded and often inadequate housing conditions had simply moved to new parts of the city. For the Brownsville neighborhood of Brooklyn, the growing avenues of transportation led to increasing speculation on property and a rush to develop. In an effort to maximize profits, developers built dwellings that could house as many tenants as possible. By 1907, then, 96 percent of all the residential units in Brownsville were tenements. To be sure, when compared with the tenements on the Lower East Side, those in Brownsville represented an improvement. Some of the Brownsville structures were built to follow the Tenement House Act of 1901 (although many buildings were small enough to avoid its regulation), and on the whole the tenements in Brownsville provided more space than was available on the Lower East Side at lower rents. These differences enticed much of the Jewish community of the East Side to move to the outer reaches of Brooklyn. By 1925 Brownsville and the adjacent neighborhood of East New York made up the largest Jewish community in the city.[53]

In the Bronx two new train lines providing access to the rest of the city opened in the early twentieth century, joining the streetcar line and the Third Avenue elevated train, which had been in operation since the late nineteenth century. The neighborhoods of the South Bronx, like the developing areas in Brooklyn, quickly came to resemble the crowded areas of Manhattan. While the housing in the Bronx varied by — and within — neighborhood and included everything from cold-water flats to modern townhouses to cottages, multifamily dwellings increasingly began to dominate. In the neighborhood of Mott Haven, for example, the majority of buildings shifted from single-family to multifamily

Apartment buildings in Queens. Despite Queensborough Realty's policies aimed at excluding Jews, Catholics, and blacks, it was nonetheless an innovator in urban architecture and development. These apartments, examples of early cooperatives, were meant to foster a sense of community. *Photography Collection, Miriam and Ira D. Wallach Division of Art, Prints and Photographs, The New York Public Library, Astor, Lenox and Tilden Foundations.*

dwellings quickly following the arrival of public transportation. Nearby Hunts Point–Crotona Park East saw the sudden development of five- and six-story apartment buildings soon after the arrival of the subway, in 1905. Densely constructed housing at times mixed with factories, giving the South Bronx an industrial character that would endure.[54]

For La Guardia this movement of population out of Manhattan, and especially Lower Manhattan, created both problems and opportunities. On the one hand, it spread the problems associated with poverty and poor housing to communities across the five boroughs; no longer could a mayor focus attention solely on Manhattan. On the other hand, the decreasing density in areas such as the Lower East Side made possible the innovations in housing that advocates had sought over the past three decades. In 1934 there were 350,000 old-law tenements still standing. Thirteen hundred still had outhouses in the yards, another 23,000 provided toilets only in the halls, and 30,000 had no bathing facilities. These buildings were not only less hygienic than more recently constructed tenements, they

Slum clearance, 1936. The city cleared twelve blocks prior to the construction of Williamsburg Houses. Seventy-eight percent of the demolished apartments had no central heating, and 67 percent had no private toilets. *New York City Housing Authority, The La Guardia and Wagner Archives, La Guardia Community College/The City University of New York.*

were also less safe. From 1918 to 1929 there were four times as many fires and eight times as many deaths in old-law tenements as there were in those structures built after passage of the 1901 law. Responding to these concerns, La Guardia forced through new legislation requiring landlords to bring old-law tenements up to minimum standards or board them up. This new housing code, combined with the economics of the Depression, led to large-scale abandonment of buildings, as owners faced tenants who could not pay and mandatory renovations they could not afford. While the city pushed landlords to make their buildings safer and more livable, some observers realized that many buildings were so old as to make the required improvements impossible. "The only ultimate cure for them," opined Tenement Commissioner Langdon Post, "is dynamite."[55]

In February 1934 the New York City Housing Authority (NYCHA) began its state-mandated mission to provide for "the clearance, replanning, and reconstruction" of the slum districts of New York. Mayor La Guardia tapped Langdon Post to head NYCHA in conjunction with his duties as tenement commissioner. Over the next four years, NYCHA demolished 1,100 tenement buildings, removing 10,000 rental units. An additional 40,000 apartments were abandoned by property owners. Those landlords who complied with the new housing code could now charge higher rents, effectively removing another 30,000 units from the low-rent category. The interborough population shifts, the city's analysis concluded, had created a housing surplus. La Guardia's and Post's policies, however, had effectively created a shortage of inexpensive housing.[56]

The solution advanced by Post and other housing experts of the time was the development of new low-rent housing for the working poor. In taking this direction, Post had the backing of the Roosevelt administration. Early New Deal legislation included federal support for a program of "construction, reconstruction, alteration, or repair under public regulation or control of low-cost housing and slum-clearance projects."[57] To oversee this program the Roosevelt administration created the Housing Division of the Public Works Administration. While the division experimented with joint public-private development, it quickly discovered the impossibility of providing suitable housing that could both return a profit and keep rents low enough for the poor to afford. Instead, the Housing

Slum clearance, c. 1934. Destruction of old, decrepit buildings created open spaces in previously crowded tenement districts. *Collection of the American Jewish Historical Society.*

Division received authorization from Congress to provide outright grants to public bodies, such as city housing authorities, covering 45 percent of the costs of development, plus low-interest loans for the remaining costs. Through this arrangement the PWA constructed fifty-one projects, including two—one being the largest PWA housing project in the country—in New York City.[58]

But Post and La Guardia were too impatient to demonstrate the benefits of slum clearance and public housing to wait for federal assistance. NYCHA, therefore, developed and built its first project—the appropriately named First Houses—on its own. Starting with existing tenements running between Avenue A and Second Avenue, NYCHA tore down every third building to increase access to light and air, then renovated the remaining structures to create 122 modern apartments with central heat. First Houses opened its doors to new tenants on January 15, 1935. The demand was overwhelming; for the 122 units, NYCHA received 3,800 applications. First Houses was a successful experiment, but

A health station in First Houses, on the Lower East Side, March 6, 1939. Here, babies are being weighed and getting checkups. *New York City Housing Authority, The La Guardia and Wagner Archives, La Guardia Community College/The City University of New York.*

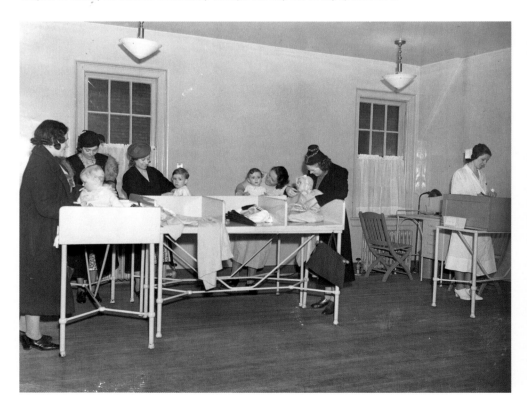

the process of creating these homes through renovation proved too expensive to copy for other public-housing projects. Still, using federally sponsored work relief to complete the construction allowed NYCHA to offer the units for $6 a room per month.[59]

The next generation of NYCHA projects in New York — built with greater involvement of the PWA Housing Division — included the Williamsburg Houses, in Brooklyn, and the Harlem River Houses, at 151st Street and Macombs Place in Manhattan. These projects were much larger than First Houses; Williamsburg Houses, for example, would eventually contain 1,622 apartments. But the demand for low-cost housing remained high; 14,000 families applied for the 574 apartments in the Harlem River complex. This demand allowed NYCHA to be selective in choosing residents. The families that moved into these two projects in 1937 had passed through a lengthy screening process. The first cut of selectivity was by race — the projects were strictly segregated, with Williamsburg open only to whites and Harlem River only for blacks. The next phase of screening, according to NYCHA, was based in both "need and merit," but in reality NYCHA refused to provide housing for the poorest New Yorkers, such as those on relief. Instead, only those with stable jobs were considered for these first projects. Every family selected for Harlem River Houses, for instance, had at least one wage earner, and one-fourth of the families had two people working. Considering that unemployment was at least 40 percent in Harlem, the population entering public housing was hardly that most in need of it. In addition to demonstrating employment, potential residents also had to prove to NYCHA administrators that they had insurance policies, bank accounts, and proper housekeeping skills. Given the residents whom NYCHA selected for these projects, it is not surprising that the administrators of Williamsburg Houses could boast in its second year of operation that "no tenant at anytime has been in arrears."[60]

These projects provided numerous services and facilities for their residents. Day care centers, nursery schools, and after-school programs offered care for residents' children. Outdoor spaces included tennis and handball courts for recreation. Meeting rooms facilitated the development of clubs and organizations such as tenant associations, community newspapers, and Boy Scout troops. The services available in these housing developments reflected a settlement house–like effort to imbue residents with a new sense of personal and civic responsibility. This mission permeated the community, from the classes for new mothers at the projects' nurseries to the weekly rent-collection visits from NYCHA administrators.[61]

Miriam Burns, who grew up in the Harlem River Houses, distinctly remembers "a white woman, I guess she was the manager," coming to her family's apartment to collect the rent. "She was not averse," Burns recalled, "to looking in the refrigerator or whatever." The NYCHA agents were instructed to chat with the families to determine if they needed help and to make sure they were properly caring for the apartments. Burns reflected that

Storytelling hour at Williamsburg Houses, August 20, 1945. The Williamsburg Houses were among the first housing projects built by Mayor La Guardia and the Public Works Administration. In addition to apartments, the housing complex included outdoor space for playgrounds, gardens, and a school. Behind this progressive design was an awareness of the need to foster community in addition to providing shelter. *New York City Housing Authority, The La Guardia and Wagner Archives, La Guardia Community College/The City University of New York.*

today such invasions into someone's home would seem "unbelievable," but as she remembers it, her mother seemed happy to show off her housekeeping skills.[62] Other public-housing residents were not so accepting of the visits of rent collectors. The Harlem River Residents Association represented the outrage of some tenants. "We demand a stop to the notorious system … giving permission to rent collectors to enter the tenant apartments in the event the tenants are not home," wrote the association. "It violates the principle of 'privacy in your home' and is ILLEGAL." Over the 1940s NYCHA phased out the visits of rent collectors, allowing residents to pay their rent at the management office.[63]

The selection of tenants and the structure of life at First Houses, Williamsburg Houses, and Harlem River Houses represented NYCHA's ideal. The city housing authority had created clean, safe, and sanitary housing for working families, either replacing or providing an alternative to tenement houses. These projects, however, were not designed to house the extremely poor. In 1940 only 5 to 8 percent of the tenants at these three projects were receiving relief through the city or the WPA. Furthermore, those overseeing the projects often failed to secure housing for the families they displaced. One thousand three hundred families were relocated to make way for the Williamsburg Houses. Of those, 439 applied to live in the project, and only 341 were accepted.[64] Over the late 1930s and early 1940s, NYCHA's desire to limit the number of truly poor families came into conflict with federal housing policy.

The federal Housing Act of 1937 created the United States Housing Authority (USHA) to replace the PWA in creating national public-housing policy. The New Yorker Nathan Straus Jr. was selected to head this new authority. Straus quickly committed his agency to a decentralized program in which the federal government would provide financing for local authorities to construct housing developments. Unlike NYCHA, however, Straus was focused on building housing for the poorest families. As NYCHA expanded into a new series of projects in the late 1930s and early 1940s, it needed to negotiate with Straus to maintain the type of residents it desired for its projects. Straus insisted on setting a maxi-

Dental clinic at Harlem River Houses. Public housing projects frequently incorporated services for the community. *New York City Housing Authority, The La Guardia and Wagner Archives, La Guardia Community College/The City University of New York.*

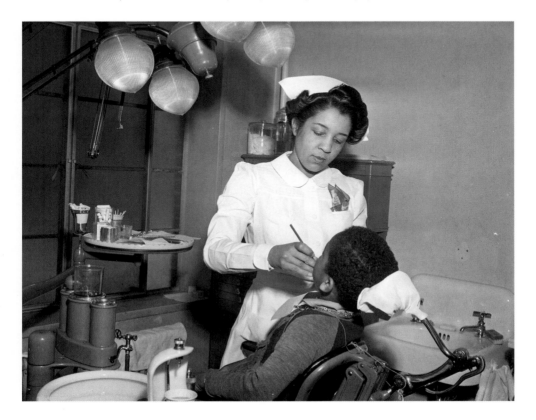

Photograph of a bedroom in the newly opened Queensbridge Houses in 1941. Queensbridge remains the largest housing project in the city. *New York City Housing Authority, The La Guardia and Wagner Archives, La Guardia Community College/The City University of New York.*

mum annual income level approximating that of the lowest third of earners across the country and ensuring that public housing would go to those most in need. From NYCHA's perspective such a limit was unacceptable. With this restriction, the city estimated that 50 percent of public-housing residents would be receiving assistance either through relief or the WPA. In the end the USHA allowed NYCHA more flexibility in selecting tenants over the income limit. That let the city set the number of assistance recipients in each project at a maximum of 30 percent. In the next set of projects, which opened in 1939 and 1940 — Red Hook, in Brooklyn; Queensbridge, in Long Island City, Queens; South Jamaica, in Queens; and Vladeck, on the Lower East Side of Manhattan — between 22 and 29 percent of tenants were on some type of government relief.[65] While this was a significantly higher percentage of such tenants than NYCHA had desired at first, it remained low compared with that in public housing in other American cities.

As it limited the number of welfare recipients in its projects, NYCHA also tried to steer residents based on race. The authority quickly abandoned the strict racial segregation it had established in the Williamsburg and Harlem River Houses. Instead, NYCHA's stated policy was that the racial makeup of a project should reflect the neighborhood in which it was built. This meant that blacks were concentrated in only a few of the city's projects. When pressed, the authority would brag that the proportion of black residents in public housing vastly exceeded the percentage of blacks in the city as a whole; in 1940 blacks occupied 12.4 percent of NYCHA's units while making up only 6 percent of the city's population. But the distribution of black families within the public-housing system demonstrated a racialized system at work. In 1941, for instance, First Houses still had no black families, Williamsburg had a single black family, Red Hook had 32 black families compared with 2,512 white families, and Queensbridge had 52 black families and 3,097 white families. Meanwhile, Harlem River housed only blacks, South Jamaica housed a combination of 312 black families and 136 white, and the recently opened Kingsborough Houses, in Brooklyn, consisted of 437 black and 729 white families.

Children rummage through trash on the street in the South Bronx in 1945. The decrepit building behind them would be torn down to build Lester Patterson Houses, home to more than 4,400 residents by 1950. *New York City Housing Authority, The La Guardia and Wagner Archives, La Guardia Community College/The City University of New York.*

At first, NYCHA leaders were open about their strategy. Settlement house leader Mary Simkhovitch, a member of NYCHA's board, explained that the "overwhelming population in New York City is white. We don't want to act in such a way and do this thing in such a way that it will deter white people from going into projects." Furthermore, one NYCHA administrator did not hide the agency's tactic of steering black families to particular projects. For projects such as Red Hook and Queensbridge, he admitted, the selection of black families "has been much more exacting than is the case with white families." Given the high demand by blacks for decent housing, NYCHA was never able to keep the proportion of blacks in public housing as low as it desired. However, through the 1940s there were instances in which units remained vacant until a white family applied, even though black families were waiting for housing. NYCHA operated on the unspoken belief that if public housing came to be viewed as minority housing, there would be less support for the program.[66]

Blacks in Depression Era New York City

On the afternoon of March 16, 1935, a sixteen-year-old Puerto Rican boy shoplifted a pen-knife from a five-and-dime store on 125th Street in Harlem. Witnessing the crime, an employee physically detained the youth, who, in struggling to free himself, bit the employee. When an ambulance arrived at the store to treat the bitten man, a rumor spread that the boy had been severely beaten; when the ambulance left empty, the word on the street was that the boy had been killed. That evening crowds gathered to protest the boy's treatment by the store's employees. Someone threw a rock, breaking the store window; soon the street erupted into a riot. The windows of stores up and down 125th Street were shattered, and extensive looting ensued. When the dust cleared the next morning, 250 shop windows had been smashed, 125 men had been arrested, more than 100 people were injured, and three blacks had died from police gunshots. "F'r all the stealin' goin' on the main thing they steal wuz food," explained one observer. "I sees a woman reach inside a busted window an' heave out two big, juicy hams, slings 'em unda her arms, an says: 'I been eatin' pig feet an' chitterlings f'r a helluva long time, but from now on I'm gonna eats ham.' An' then she traipses downa street on home. — Yeh, they been takin' plen'y a food. One a 'em says: 'Dam if I ain' gonna eat tomorrow.'" The Harlem riot of 1935 was grounded in hunger among black New Yorkers—a hunger for food, jobs, decent housing, and an end to the racial barriers that kept many blacks in a state of destitution.[67]

By the 1930s the black population of New York had exploded. At the same time, the Depression had reduced the work opportunities for all New Yorkers, but especially for blacks. In 1931 the unemployment rate was over 28 percent for black women and over 25 percent for black men. [68] By 1937 blacks, though only 5 percent of New York City's population, made up 15 percent of the unemployed.[69] Even those blacks who managed to get work found it difficult to support their families. According to one estimate, the median household earnings of Harlem's families declined by 43 percent in the first three years of the Depression.[70] The hopes for a better economic future that had motivated so many African Americans to move to New York City were now dashed by the reality of the Depression.

While whites fought for jobs as janitors and porters, blacks saw their opportunities for employment become even more limited and the jobs themselves less stable as institutional racism affected their ability to hold on to work. In unionized factories blacks were often barred from skilled or managerial positions; since those in the least skilled positions were often the first to be let go, blacks were laid off at rates higher than whites. Seniority rules also worked against blacks since, as recent migrants, they were often the last hired and the first to be laid off.[71]

Even before the Depression many black households needed at least two wage earners to make ends meet. As the Depression deepened, however, both women and men saw their wage-earning potential decline. The number of black women employed in manufacturing had fallen precipitously by 1930. Many black women looked for work as domestic servants; the pay for such jobs was so low that families pooled their resources in an effort to survive. In one family, the mother earned money as a cleaner in a shirt factory, her husband had a job as a stockman in a retail store, one son was a delivery boy, and another son unsuccessfully sought work. The family carefully budgeted their spending, paying a reasonable rent by Harlem standards and a modest amount on food. Still, by the end of the year, the family was $60 in debt.[72]

A Harlem family faced even greater difficulties when there was only one parent providing support. Mrs. S., a recent migrant from Savannah, Georgia, who came to the COS for assistance, was described by a case worker as "a pleasant-appearing, neatly-dressed, brown-skinned girl who has a somewhat restrained manner." Mrs. S. was "quite worried" because she did not know how she would care for her three girls. The children's father had abandoned the family, moving in with another woman in Jersey City, and provided no financial support for his children. Mrs. S. had worked as a live-in domestic for a family with a house in the city and a summer cottage on Long Island, cooking, cleaning, and caring for the family's three small children for $45 a month. Her own children were in the care of her mother, who had brought them up from Georgia. Three weeks before coming to the COS, however, Mrs. S. had left her job due to "acute pain in her arm and shoulder." At the same time, her mother also fell ill. The whole family had crowded into her sister's single

Left and below: children play on the street in Harlem. The lack of recreational activities and parks in Harlem led children to congregate in the streets. *Milstein Division of United States History, Local History & Genealogy, The New York Public Library, Astor, Lenox and Tilden Foundations.*

furnished room, attempting to survive on the sister's salary as a domestic. The COS agreed to help Mrs. S. find new employment.[73]

Another Harlem resident, Mrs. H., "a medium skinned colored women, with somewhat delicate features," came to the attention of the COS through the city Bureau of Child Welfare. Her husband left her after she gave birth because he did not want children. Mrs. H. wanted to keep her child, but she was having difficulty in supporting herself and the baby. She had landed a job, but, with little work experience, had lost it. Meanwhile, she was unable to find adequate child care for her five-month-old. The few day nurseries she had contacted refused to take a child so young. Her landlady would care for the child during the day, but Mrs. H. would return home to find the baby soaking wet and hungry, clearly neglected by the landlady. Mrs. H. was ineligible for state support because her husband had abandoned her so recently. The COS agreed to give her $7.50 a month. A month later, Mrs. H. returned. Still struggling to pay her bills and care for her child, she requested that the baby be placed in temporary foster care. Mrs. H. was told that the facilities for colored children were overtaxed and that if "there was any possibility of … keeping the baby with her that this would be the wisest plan." Mrs. H. was left to survive on her own with the meager COS grant.[74]

Black children had virtually nowhere to turn in New York's maze of child welfare institutions. Ideally, if a child were adjudicated by the New York City Children's Court as delinquent, neglected, or dependent — "dependent" meaning that the parents were not able to care for the child — the court would find a facility that matched the child's needs in terms of care and treatment. If the child was black, however, this system broke down. The private institutions that used public funds to provide care for dependent and neglected children could, by law, choose which children they would help. Catholic institutions, preferring to reserve space for children of their faith, often rejected Protestant black children. Meanwhile, of the city's thirty-four Protestant institutions for dependent and neglected children, only seven would accept those who were black. That left these most vulnerable children with few options. The overcrowded Colored Orphan Asylum, now located in Riverdale, in the Bronx, took in many black dependent children. In 1932 the CAS opened a cottage in Valhalla, New York, to care for black boys aged twelve to sixteen years of age. Many neglected or dependent black girls were placed in Catholic institutions or in the state reformatories for delinquents.[75]

Black families looking for even temporary child care discovered that they had limited choices. Federally supported day nurseries as well as a Catholic nursery served hundreds of children in Harlem. In addition, the CAS opened four buildings in the neighborhood that provided nursery and kindergarten care for young children of working parents. They also opened boys' and girls' clubs for older children to play and receive vocational training. Given the number of working parents in Harlem, however, these facilities failed to meet the community's needs; parents often made arrangements with family members and neighbors to care for their children.[76]

Many women found that the only way to earn wages during the Depression was to get domestic work. Unfortunately, the worsening circumstances in middle-class homes led to a decrease in the demand for domestic help. During the Depression those lucky enough to become domestics were often overburdened with chores; one worker reported "doing the work of 3 persons."[77] The glut of domestics seeking even that irregular work led to gatherings of mostly black women on street corners, groups that became known pejoratively as "slave markets." Two hundred of these markets developed across the five boroughs, but the most famous of these were the Bronx slave markets. One WPA worker investigating this phenomenon found, "seated on crates and boxes," a diverse set of women "of various ages and descriptions—youths of seventeen, and elderly women of maybe seventy." With so many women looking for work, the rates of pay were driven quite low. To negotiate the rate of 30 cents an hour was an accomplishment.[78] During the Depression years it was not uncommon to see a pay rate of ten cents per hour.[79]

Even while paying such low wages, employers continued to undercut the pay that domestic servants received. One woman, "Minnie," described how an employer reduced her pay by 5 cents for driving her home. After a full eight hours of work, Minnie expected at least two dollars in pay. Instead, she was given $1.87, an amount that supposedly included a 10 percent tip. When she left her employer's house, Minnie saw that it was already eight o'clock, two hours later than she expected; her employer had turned back the clock to cheat her out of money. For this reason, many domestics began carrying their own clocks. Another domestic discovered that her employer was stealing money out of her purse to pay her (she eventually got the employer to pay her back). In another case, a live-in domestic, Eliza Denney, was persuaded to open a bank account in her employer's name. The employer then withdrew $1,000 from Eliza's account. These, of course, were some of the worst abuses that domestic servants suffered, but they demonstrated the vulnerability of women alone in the unregulated work environment of their employers' homes.[80] In 1939 the city and state created a joint committee to investigate the "slave markets." Their only solution, however, was to open employment offices in the Bronx, bringing the negotiation for domestic work inside, away from the unseemly environment of the street. These offices made no effort to set a minimum wage or to create minimum labor protections. Instead, domestic workers were left on their own to compete for unconscionably low wages and to work at the whims of their employers.[81]

Blacks, especially in Harlem, were caught between the pressures of low incomes and high living costs. As families faced unemployment and decreasing wages during the Depression, the price of food—always higher in Harlem than in the rest of Manhattan—

actually rose. One estimate, for instance, found an 11 percent increase in the cost of food from 1934 to 1935.[82] Housing also remained especially expensive in Harlem, due simply to discrimination: the limited number of buildings in the city that accepted blacks, along with the continued influx of African American migrants, created a scarcity that drove up rents.

Two children paint at Harlem Community Art Center. The art center was intended to strengthen the community through creative activity and served a diverse group of students. Though the center lasted only 16 months, it established a precedent for similar projects in later years. *Photography Collection, Miriam and Ira D. Wallach Division of Art, Prints and Photographs, The New York Public Library, Astor, Lenox and Tilden Foundations.*

One landlord dramatically demonstrated this phenomenon in 1935, when he opened up his building to blacks and raised rents from $60 to $75 a month while reducing the building staff from seven to four. As that suggests, just because the rents were higher in Harlem did not mean that the housing quality was better. To be fair, much of the housing in Harlem was relatively new and provided amenities, such as private bathrooms, that remained rare in areas such as the Lower East Side before slum clearance. But plenty of Harlem residents were still in substandard housing. One study found people living in buildings that had been officially condemned. Thousands of other families made their homes in old-law tenements without heat, hot water, and private bathrooms. An estimated 10,000 Harlemites set up house in cellars or basements without toilets or running water. For the right to live in these decrepit conditions, blacks were often paying more than white Manhattanites.[83]

In spite of the shortage of jobs, the poor housing, and the high rents, Harlem remained the center of black life in New York City over the 1930s. Blacks did, however, begin to explore and settle in communities in the outer boroughs. By 1940 they made up 4 percent of the population of Brooklyn and 2 percent of Bronx residents. Concentration in particular neighborhoods, such as Bedford-Stuyvesant, in Brooklyn, or pockets of the South Bronx, created new black communities. In these neighborhoods residents faced problems similar to those encountered in Harlem, such as inadequate and expensive housing, as well as hostility from whites who resisted their presence. Managing the tensions that arose from expanding poverty in these parts of the city would become a major concern in the postwar era.[84]

Recovery

In December 1941 the United States declared war on both Japan and Germany, formally entering the Second World War. The industrial buildup required to fight a war pulled much of the country out of the Depression. As young men were drafted into the army and demand for labor picked up, unemployment in many cities plummeted. This was not the case in New York City. The mobilization for war took federal funding away from the programs for relief and public works that had allowed the city to limp through the 1930s. The light manufacturing that was the mainstay of New York's industry was largely unsuitable for the new War Department contracts. Amazingly, there were 50,000 more people unemployed in New York City in 1942 than there were in the Depression year of 1939.[85]

Once again, Mayor La Guardia came to the rescue. Under pressure from the persistent Little Flower, Roosevelt ordered the federal departments, agencies, and boards directing the mobilization to consult with the mayor over the available "plant and manpower facilities in New York City." This effort showed almost immediate success; between July and October 1942, 12 percent of naval contracts went to companies located in New York. An estimated 200,000 people were put to work by the end of November. By the end of 1943, New York's press would celebrate full employment in the city. New York City's Great Depression had finally come to an end.[86]

But the dawning age of prosperity would not treat all New Yorkers equally. Divisions of race and ethnicity, of neighborhood and borough, would continue to haunt the city. In August 1943 the frustrations of black New Yorkers were exposed once again, when Harlem erupted in yet another riot. The shooting of a black uniformed soldier by a white police officer initiated a night of disorder. Though La Guardia rode through the streets urging calm, 1,469 stores were vandalized, 606 people were arrested, 189 were injured, and six blacks were killed. As in any riot, the motivations of those involved were mixed. The plight of black men being sent to Europe and the Pacific to die for a country in which they were abused by white police officers certainly catalyzed the anger of Harlem residents. But the broad simmering tensions created by limited opportunity and widespread poverty provided the fuel for a riot.[87]

The challenge of the postwar era in New York City would be to uncover these festering pockets of poverty. As the nation and the city as a whole entered an era of greater economic security, the question of how to confront the entrenched and growing poverty in Brownsville, Brooklyn, or the South Bronx would focus the attention of both social reformers and those holding Gotham's reins.

Street map of Upper Manhattan and the Bronx. These areas would see economic decline over the 1960s and 1970s. *Lionel Pincus and Princess Firyal Map Division, The New York Public Library, Astor, Lenox and Tilden Foundations.*

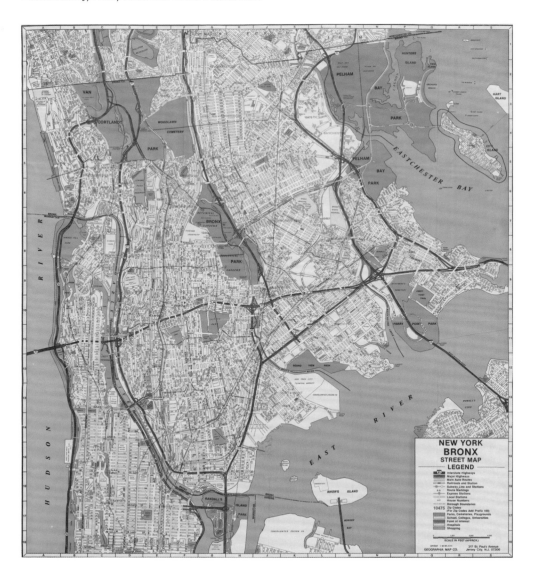

Chapter 7

Family Poverty in the Age of Deindustrialization

By 1969 Henry Harris had been working for ten years at a print shop near city hall. He earned about $190 a week before taxes; he had applied to join the printers' union, which would have significantly increased his pay, but had not been accepted. Though Harris knew that "it's pretty hard for a colored guy" to join the union, he became even more frustrated when a newer employee started receiving raises while he did not. In a fit of anger, Harris left his job. Four years later he was still out of work.[1]

In 1971 Harris, originally from New Bern, North Carolina, and his wife, Margie, who had come from Ehrhardt, South Carolina, lived with five young children in Brownsville, Brooklyn. With Henry out of work, the family turned to public assistance. Twice a month the Harrises received a welfare check for $168. Henry had worked all his life, but the decline of the printing industry, in which he had the most experience, made it very difficult for him to find a job. "I never thought I would be on welfare," Henry lamented. "They say there are no jobs 'cause you need skills. And when you have the skills they say you need something else." Under the mandatory work program for welfare recipients, Henry reported for work twice a week at the Brownsville Welfare Center, where he earned $12 every two weeks, mostly for sitting around. While he gladly participated in the program, he couldn't imagine how this supposed training would ever lead to a full-time job.[2]

The Harrises' apartment was literally falling apart. In the bathroom, which had no sink and a barely functioning toilet, one wall had collapsed, and the ceiling was about to do the same. One night Henry stepped into the bathroom to find raw sewage pouring in from a broken pipe connected to his upstairs neighbor's toilet. The rest of the apartment was in a similar state of disrepair. Henry, Margie, and the couple's infant son slept in one bedroom, while the four older children slept in the other; both rooms, like the rest of the apartment, had gaping holes in the ceiling and floor. The building next door to the

Harrises' was half torn down, but people were still living in it. With their financial situation, the Harrises were unable to move. "Only the bad places like this one take welfare," said Margie. "The other ones say they don't want kids." The Harrises had applied for public housing for almost ten years but had yet to receive a placement.[3]

The Harris family had lived through the boom and bust of the post–World War II economy in New York City. In the 1950s and early 1960s, manufacturing continued to grow in New York, attracting migrants from the South, like Henry and Margie Harris, and increasingly from Puerto Rico. Manufacturing provided many of these migrants with entry-level positions that required few skills; it also brought work for the children of European immigrants, who now made up the majority of the city's population. Not everyone thrived during these good times; some families still struggled to find adequate shelter and sustenance. However, with most of the city's working-age population employed, city government, supported by organized labor, built housing, expanded transportation, and provided other services to meet the needs of the working class.

Poor New Yorkers benefited from some of these services, but decisions about New York's future were made on the assumption that the economy would continue to grow while the number of poor families in the city would shrink. Unfortunately, not all went as planned. As manufacturing declined in New York starting in the mid-1960s, jobs, especially for low-skilled workers, began to disappear. As Henry Harris observed, industries in which it was once easy to find work — apparel, printing, shipping — now became virtually closed to new workers. In place of manufacturing, New York City would develop new service jobs over the 1970s. For workers who had once held manufacturing positions, however, low-skilled service jobs either were unavailable or brought lower pay. The result was a new class of poor New Yorkers, reliant on welfare and other government supports, with little connection to the mainstream economy.

From the 1950s to the 1970s, New York would become increasingly divided by race and ethnicity. Between 1950 and 1970 the black population of New York grew from 728,000 to more than 1.5 million, comprising nearly a fifth of the city. Over the same period the Puerto Rican population expanded from 187,000 to 847,000.[4] While the postwar economy created jobs for many whites, opportunities remained limited for blacks and Hispanics. In 1950 the unemployment rate for New York City's blacks was double that of whites.[5] By 1969 23.7 percent of blacks and 27.9 percent of Hispanics were below the poverty line, compared with only 8.4 percent of whites.[6]

At its core New York remained a global city, the home of the United Nations and the center of American finance, but surrounding the core, pocketed away in places unseen by tourists, were families — mostly black and Hispanic — struggling to get by, mired in deep poverty. This outcome was partly intentional. City planners had encouraged industry to move out of Manhattan. They had created antiseptic urban-renewal developments that forced many poor New Yorkers out of their homes and into the isolated parts of the outer boroughs, and they had planned the infrastructure that encouraged the middle class to move to suburbia. Leaders and policymakers did not foresee the urban crisis they were creating, but decisions they made produced, by accretion, vast tracks of desolate urban poverty. Efforts by poor families to fight against this desolation, encouraged by the welfare-rights movement and the War on Poverty, ended largely in failure. By the late 1970s, with the city in fiscal crisis, observers saw little hope of improvement for much of New York City. Thus did New York become a city pulled apart, with greater income disparities between upper and lower classes and between racial groups, and with middle-class flight from the city.

An Industrial City

New York was never the archetypal American industrial city. It did not have the rushing waters that powered the nation's first industrial powerhouses, such as Lowell, Massachusetts; it did it not have the connections to the hinterland that allowed cities including Cincinnati and Chicago to become the processors of much of the nation's food; it not have giant industrial plants that made Pittsburgh and Detroit symbols of American industry. But New York was, from the late nineteenth century until the middle of the twentieth century, a manufacturing city. Where other cities prospered based on their environments or their geographic locations, New York did so because of its ready supply of labor and flexible production capacity.

The limits of space in New York's crowded industrial centers led to small scale industry. In 1947 the average garment manufacturing shop in the city employed only twenty workers. A factory with more than 500 employees was rare, while thousands of shops had fewer than four employees each. These manufacturers specialized in "small batch" production of fine jewelry, specialized machinery, garments of the current fashion season, or other items that required only limited quantities. In such shops highly skilled craftsmen would work beside the less skilled and lower paid. The one industry in which New York dominated the nation was apparel. Small firms, each specializing in a particular aspect of the industry, were contracted to produce a limited number of the newest fashion item. These firms simply dipped as needed into the city's supply of low-skilled labor.[7]

In the period after World War II, New York remained a predominantly working-class city. Blue-collar workers and their dependents formed a clear majority of the city's population of eight million. In addition to manufacturing, many New Yorkers worked in con-

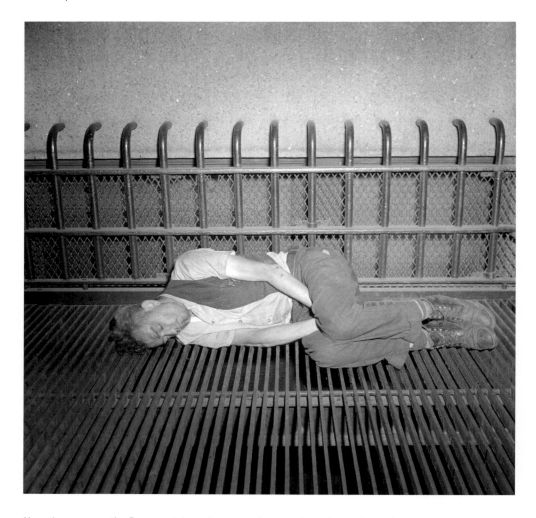

Homeless man on the Bowery. A homeless man sleeps on top of a grate on the Bowery, or Skid Row, on the Lower East Side. *Courtesy of the Library of Congress.*

struction or the ports. A smaller percentage of New Yorkers worked in service positions, such as janitors, domestic servants, and elevator operators. Most of the city's workers in this period were the children of the immigrants who had arrived in the late nineteenth and early twentieth centuries, but the promise of work continued to attract newcomers to New York City, including whites from other parts of the country, blacks predominantly from the South, and Puerto Ricans.[8]

The working-class majority and their representation through unions greatly influenced the politics and public policies of New York City. During the administration of Mayor Robert F. Wagner Jr., from 1956 to 1966, labor demonstrated its greatest power in city governance. The public policies of this period—in transit, housing, health care, and employment — provided benefits for a wide swath of New Yorkers, but they were directed at the working class and were often tied to employment. In times when most New Yorkers could access the labor market, these systems worked; industrial changes and economic contraction, however, undermined the effects of these provisions, as those at the bottom of the economic hierarchy found themselves out of work and unable to access the benefits that jobs would bring.[9]

The worst off in New York society were the homeless. The postwar economic boom had significantly reduced the widespread homelessness of the Great Depression; one historian has estimated that in the three decades following World War II, "homelessness receded to its lowest level since the mid-eighteenth century." But homelessness did not disappear entirely. Even in good economic times, some men, women and children were forced to live without permanent shelter.[10]

The type of homelessness that became dominant in the postwar era was concentrated in "skid rows," urban areas where homeless individuals congregated. In New York City the center of homelessness was the Bowery, a street that stretched diagonally from the foot of the Brooklyn Bridge in lower Manhattan up to Cooper Square, on the edge of the Lower East Side. Once a place of working-class entertainment and illicit activity, by the 1940s the Bowery had become the domain of the destitute, especially destitute men. "There are almost no women on the Bowery," wrote one investigator in 1964. He was surprised to find that there were not even female prostitutes. The hotels, lodging houses, and shelters had no women. It was rare to find women even in the area bars.[11]

For a variety of reasons the men on the Bowery could not function in New York's economy. Many of these men were older, lacking the strength to do the kind of physical labor that had supported them when they were young.[12] Rather than the structural economic causes that led these men to the Bowery, more attention was paid to the pathologies that caused homelessness — especially alcoholism. In the 1950s researchers and social workers viewed homelessness as synonymous with end-stage alcoholism. Based on the emerging conception of alcoholism as a disease, both public and private institutions began to focus on rehabilitation — helping these homeless men reenter mainstream society. Accordingly, the Salvation Army's Alcohol Rehabilitation Center provided meetings, counseling, religious services, and an employment referral service. The city also focused on treatment for alcoholism in its rehabilitation facility on Hart Island. Those who refused to participate were threatened with jail time or a loss of public-assistance benefits. At the residential center, men participated in occupational therapy and Alcoholics Anonymous meetings to prepare for a new life away from the Bowery.[13]

Though mostly hidden, some women and children experienced homelessness in this period. In 1950 the city opened a shelter exclusively for women and children in a former elementary school near the Bowery. The services for women also focused on rehabilitation and training. The shelter ran a Mother's Work Program, which required women to wash and iron their own clothes and care for their children, skills they would need to be capable mothers once they left the shelter. Compared with that of men, however, the number of women in facilities like these was low. The city's Department of Welfare provided housing for only 47 homeless women in 1963. Homelessness, both in image and reality, was largely a problem among single men.[14]

Housing the Working Class

A shortage of shelter did not affect the city's poorest residents alone; in the years after World War II, New York as a whole faced a serious housing shortage. In 1950, according to one estimate, the city had 430,000 fewer housing units than it needed. Tens of thousands of New Yorkers were forced to double up with relatives or crowd into rundown apartments.[15] City policy focused on increasing the housing available to the middle class. For example, NYCHA—technically charged with securing homes for the city's poor— broadened its mission in an effort to make middle-class housing more affordable. In the 1940s the city built a number of projects financed through the its borrowing power and tax abatements, but with no public cash subsidy. These projects were self-supporting, requiring higher rents to cover the costs of construction and maintenance. They provided decent housing for those who could not afford rent on the private housing market but who earned too much to meet the income requirements for previous NYCHA projects. The result was a public-housing system that served the working poor and the lower middle class but largely excluded the truly destitute.[16]

Housing policy outside NYCHA developed in the same direction. City and state policy, for example, encouraged the proliferation of co-op buildings by providing tax abatements for developments that accepted limited dividends and targeted low-income residents. Like other unions, the Amalgamated Clothing Workers began taking advantage of these laws as early as the 1930s, when it constructed two co-op buildings for its members, in the Bronx and on the Lower East Side. After the war the unions formed the United Housing Foundation (UHF), working closely with city planner Robert Moses to develop large-scale co-op housing for the working class. The UHF built a number of projects on the Lower East Side and in the outer boroughs, including Rochdale Village in Queens and the massive Co-op City in the Bronx. The passage of New York's Mitchell-Lama law, in 1955, provided an additional avenue for state-supported, middle-class housing. None of these developments, however, provided rents low enough for poor families.[17]

Suburbanization altered the character of the city's working class in the postwar era. Federal policies, such as affordable loans from the Federal Housing Administration and the Veterans Administration, essentially underwrote the growth of suburban housing. New highways provided easy transportation to suburban communities in New York, New Jersey, and Connecticut. Levittown, the quintessential suburban development on Long Island, for example, was completed in 1951. Many of the city's whites fled to these new communities. All told, the non-Hispanic white population of New York City decreased by nearly two million between 1940 and 1970. Still, the various state and city supports for housing allowed working people — including a large white, ethnic working class — to continue to live within the five boroughs. The city's middle-class housing projects gave working-class New Yorkers an option more affordable than suburbia. Furthermore, even as white New Yorkers departed for the suburbs, the city's population remained relatively constant as new arrivals to the city — often blacks and Puerto Ricans — took their place.[18]

The Puerto Rican Migration

In 1946 Margarita Hernández and her family found themselves in a difficult situation. Margarita's husband, a mechanic and foreman overseeing three to four hundred workers for an apparel factory in Mayaguez, Puerto Rico, had been laid off from his job. "The needle-trades industry had hit rock bottom," explained Margarita. "We did not know what to do or where to turn." The family could not pay their rent and were evicted from their home. "One day, a woman whom [her husband] had worked for, asked if he would be interested in going to work in New York," Margarita continued. "As you can imagine, we accepted, since we didn't have a chance to make a living [in Puerto Rico]." Margarita's options were particularly stark: moving to New York provided a path to survival that was unavailable at home. The choice she made was not unique; thousands of Puerto Ricans arrived at similar decisions based on the limited economic opportunities available to them on the island and the perception of plentiful work in New York.[19]

The migrants who came from Puerto Rico after World War II entered a city with an already well-established Puerto Rican population. While social scientists seemed to become aware of New York's migrant population only in the 1950s and 1960s, Puerto Ricans had been coming into New York for decades. The pathbreakers who came before the 1920s recalled a city with few connections to the island. "I remember when we had just one Puerto Rican grocery store, one Puerto Rican restaurant and one such barbershop in all of New York City," said one early migrant.[20] By 1940, however, there were more than 60,000 Puerto Ricans in New York City, concentrated mostly in East Harlem and Brooklyn. Early migrants had come on ships or, by the early 1940s, traveled on both planes and buses to reach New York. By the late 1940s direct air service had made migration relatively easy. In six hours or less, migrants could arrive in their new homes. Just as Ellis Island served as the point of entry for the hopeful immigrants of the late nineteenth and early twentieth centuries, the New York–area airports served as the gateway for Puerto Rican migrants, already American citizens, who looked for new economic opportunity in the city. [21]

The majority of Puerto Rican migrants settled in East Harlem, an area running roughly from 96th Street to 130th Street and from Fifth Avenue to the East River—at the time a Jewish and Italian neighborhood.[22] By the 1950s Puerto Ricans made up 30 percent of the neighborhood's population, while Italians remained the largest ethnic group. A decade later Puerto Ricans claimed that distinction, in an area that now became known as El Barrio or Spanish Harlem. Still, Puerto Ricans shared the neighborhood with a large black population as well as Italians and other whites.[23]

The conditions in which Puerto Ricans lived in East Harlem came to be regarded as some of the worst in the city. One study found that in 1950, 22 percent of Puerto Rican residents in New York City lived in dilapidated housing.[24] The low wages that most Puerto Ricans received, combined with the large influx of migrants looking for housing, led to crowding. In 1956, 40 percent of Puerto Rican households were overcrowded.[25] Inocencia Flores migrated in 1944 and found work in the garment industry. By 1964 she had separated from her husband and was caring for her four children through public assistance. The only place she could afford to live was a building on East 117th Street in East Harlem that was in particularly decrepit condition. The building had virtually no heat, since the landlord had stopped buying oil. To keep warm through the winter, Inocencia wrote in a diary, "All the tenants together bought the oil," but the boiler still did not provide much heat to her third-floor apartment. To make her apartment habitable, Inocencia began every day by lighting the oven for heat. The drug addicts squatting in an apartment above hers had broken the pipes, taking "the fixtures and the sink" to sell them; that caused massive leaks in her apartment, requiring her to empty a panful of water from the leak every day and sometimes to use an umbrella to get to the bathroom. Along with the lack of heat and the leaks, Inocencia had to contend with the "rats as big as cats" that had infested the building and sometimes found their way into her kitchen. She spewed her anger in her diary: "This is a terrible situation. Living that way I live in this slum house is miserable. I don't wish no body to live the way I live. Inside a house in this condition, no steam, no hot water, ceiling falling on you, running water from the ceiling, to go to the bathroom you have to use an umbrella, rats everywhere." She even looked to a higher power to improve her living conditions. "When I go to church," she wrote, "I pray for to have better house and have a decent living. I hope He's hearing." The conditions in Inocencia's building

Tenement house façades, 1966. Tenement houses line 100th Street in East Harlem; residents congregate on fire escapes and on the sidewalk below. *Bruce Davidson, Magnum Photos.*

would lead her and other tenants to join a community-wide rent strike demanding that landlords make improvements to the apartments. While Inocencia's experiences were particularly bad, these problems—lack of heat, squatters, leaks, vermin—were common in East Harlem.[26]

In spite of the poor living conditions and the tensions with other Hispanics, blacks, and whites in the area, Puerto Ricans developed a robust community in East Harlem. Markets sold Puerto Rican products, restaurants cooked food native to the island, and Spanish-language newspapers discussed matters unique to the community. Virtually everything one needed was available in this small corner of Manhattan. "I'm 23 years old, and I've been living here all my life," recounted one Puerto Rican man, "I never been out of this neighborhood." To "people who have money," he conceded, "maybe it's a dump … but this is my home."[27] The working-class camaraderie and even the noises of concentrated urban poverty became part of the identity of those from El Barrio. The author Piri Thomas recalled the excitement he felt driving through the old neighborhood after a long stretch in prison. "The ride through the Barrio was stone-great. It was like all the bright bulbs in the stores, windows, and lampposts were screaming just for me. I heard the noises I'd missed for so long—screaming broads, crying kids, hustlers, dogs yapping, and cats making holes in mountains of garbage. The stoops on 104th Street were full of people."[28]

In many ways, El Barrio resembled other lower-working-class ethnic enclaves that had formed in New York, such as Five Points, *Kleindeutschland,* the Lower East Side, and Little Italy; all contained high concentrations of poverty and substandard housing. Over the nineteenth and twentieth centuries, however, the residents of those neighborhoods, largely uneducated, unskilled laborers, were able to scrimp and save from their modest earnings or discover new economic opportunities that allowed them to move on to better living conditions. By contrast, over the 1950s and 1960s, for many of the Puerto Ricans living in East Harlem, economic opportunity was shrinking rather than growing. Puerto Ricans, along with the black migrants who had arrived during the Second World War and into the postwar period, found a New York City economy that no longer provided many low-skilled jobs and a cost of living that made it difficult to survive on the available wages. These changes would have long-term effects on family poverty in the city, as black and Hispanic New Yorkers were largely separated from sources of economic security.

The Deindustrialization of New York City

The decline in manufacturing represented another aspect of New York's unraveling. Work in New York's small-batch industries was never particularly stable. For many of the goods produced in New York—fur garments, women's clothing, toys, and cosmetics—employment was seasonal. Workers came to expect annual layoffs as part of the industry.[29] Over the 1950s and 1960s, however, competition began to undercut the profitability of industrial production in New York. Businesses began to consider permanent layoffs or relocation in order to survive. The influx of blacks and Puerto Ricans into New York in the 1950s and 1960s actually provided the low skilled and low-cost labor necessary to keep the garment industry and other New York manufacturing running, but even with these new labor sources many manufacturers were relocating outside the city limits, where lower real-estate costs could reduce the expenses of production. In 1953, 56 percent of the metropolitan region's manufacturing took place within the city limit; by 1966 a majority of these jobs had moved to suburban communities.[30]

The apparel industry provided a leading example of the movement of manufacturing out of the city and eventually overseas. The nature of the industry allowed the design and sales operations to remain in the city, while the centers of production could be moved elsewhere. The city's garment unions made concerted efforts to keep jobs in New York. They required that manufacturers give preference to local contractors, and they began organizing factory workers in surrounding states and even Puerto Rico in an attempt to create uniform labor conditions. Finally, desperate to keep production in New York, unions made concessions on wages—a move that led to a decline in the earning power of garment workers. In 1950 New York's apparel-production workers earned, on average, ten cents more per hour than other manufacturing workers in the city; by 1965 they were earning twenty-two cents an hour less than other workers. Even with these wage concessions, garment manufacturers continued to flee the city. In 1950 the industry provided 340,700 jobs in New York; by 1965 that number had dropped to 241,300, a loss of 29 percent of the garment sector's jobs.[31] Blacks' and Puerto Ricans' relative inexperience and lack of union seniority often meant that they were the first laid off. The process of deindustrialization, played out more noticeably in garment manufacturing but repeated in other industries, led directly to an increase in poverty, especially among newer arrivals to New York.

State and city officials did little to halt the march of jobs out of New York. In fact, the hemorrhaging of manufacturing plants appeared to fulfill a decades-long desire to remove industry from Manhattan and downtown Brooklyn and replace it with more aesthetically appealing and more profitable retail, residential, and commercial space. The area's first regional plan, published in 1929, painted a portrait of a Manhattan largely free of industry, with manufacturing and port facilities shifted to New Jersey and the outer boroughs. When manufacturing began to leave, in the 1950s, the actions of the city and state exemplified either ineptitude or a lack of desire to halt the process.[32]

Robert Wagner Jr.'s administration seemed unable to develop industrial policy that would keep jobs in the city. In 1959 the city announced the creation of an industrial park in the Brooklyn Flatlands, but six years later, when Wagner left office, little progress had been made on the park. Another mayoral committee recommended the creation of a "World Fashion Center" in the garment district, south of Herald Square, with four million square feet of loft space for garment production, but this plan was never developed. The city did set up a nonprofit corporation that helped to finance the construction of twenty-two plants in the city. Still, that program created or saved only 3,500 jobs. At the same time, the urban redevelopment along the East River between 1945 and 1955 — projects that included construction of the United Nations building, Stuyvesant Town, Peter Cooper Village, and the Brooklyn Civic Center — led to the loss of 18,000 manufacturing jobs, as homes and other nonbusiness structures replaced industry. By the time Wagner left office, the city had lost more than 200,000 manufacturing jobs.[33]

Urban Renewal in New York

The environmental theory of poverty, first prominent in the Progressive Era, has had a long legacy of influence. Urban renewal was the progeny of the progressive belief that changing the physical environment in which the poor lived would ameliorate the conditions of poverty. The Housing Act of 1949, part of President Harry S. Truman's Fair Deal, committed federal resources to local projects for "urban redevelopment." The federal government would cover two-thirds of the costs of purchasing sites for renewal, while localities would cover the additional third. This commitment was strengthened in 1954, when federally guaranteed loans became available to private investors who developed such sites. Urban renewal was intended to enhance the city's landscape while improving housing for the poor and responding to the needs of the communities being redeveloped. In New York City, neither of these caveats was heeded. Urban renewal became a tool used largely to clear out industry and housing for the poor, providing insufficient and isolated replacements for what was lost and all but ignoring the desires of local communities.

The man most responsible for shaping urban renewal in New York City was Robert Moses. Moses had begun his career as a reformer, working closely with Governor Al Smith and, later, Mayor Fiorello La Guardia. In his positions as chairman of the New York State Council of Parks, New York City parks commissioner, and chairman of the Triborough Bridge and Tunnel Authority — all of which he held simultaneously — Moses developed a reputation as a man who got things done. In 1946 Mayor William O'Dwyer appointed Moses city-construction coordinator in charge of all public-works projects; in 1948 he was also appointed head of the Slum Clearance Committee, which would become the primary organizer of urban renewal in New York throughout the 1950s. Moses had a grand vision for beautifying and shaping the city, but he cared little about how his plans would disrupt the lives of individuals. While the federal government technically required citizen participation in urban-renewal projects, New York had no citywide citizen advisory

Robert Moses and Robert Wagner Jr. on a housing tour. Moses, the mastermind behind numerous public-works projects over the course of close to forty years, was intent on destroying slums in favor of large developments. His efforts had an almost immeasurable effect on New York City's socioeconomic and visual landscape. *Courtesy of the Library of Congress.*

board, and Moses discouraged participation from the neighborhoods affected by the renewal projects.[34]

The renewal project Moses initiated on the West Side of Manhattan exemplified the problems created by ignoring the needs and desires of local community members. Moses had a "vision of a reborn West Side, marching north from Columbus Circle, and eventually spreading over the entire dismal and decayed West Side."[35] The crown jewel of this redevelopment, the Lincoln Center for the Performing Arts, would provide a new home for the Metropolitan Opera, the New York Philharmonic, and the Juilliard School as well as a Manhattan campus for Fordham University. In order to build Lincoln Center as a federally supported urban-renewal project, Moses had to stretch the meaning of the federal housing acts. The 1949 act restricted funding to "slums and blighted areas" that were "predominantly residential," presuming that new developments would also be of a residential nature and include at least some low-income housing to replace what was destroyed. Moses had no such plans; the housing act, he argued, provided a mechanism for slum clearance but did not mandate what replaced the demolished housing. By clearing a neighborhood designated a slum according to some measures, he claimed he was following the letter of

Making room for Lincoln Center. In 1954 Robert Moses proposed a new, centralized home for the Metropolitan Opera, the New York Philharmonic, and the Juilliard School. Over the course of the next decade, he razed entire blocks—like the one shown in this photograph—to make room for what became the largest performing arts complex in the country. *Museum of the City of New York, Wurts Bros. Collection.*

the law. Furthermore, Moses asserted that the world-class cultural center he would build would also bring desperately needed investment to the area. To make way for Lincoln Center, Moses had some 7,000 low-income units destroyed and only 4,440 new units built, with 4,000 of these being luxury apartments.[36]

Often the only warning a family received that they were required to leave their homes was a notice tacked to their front door: "DEMOLITION OF THIS BUILDING WILL BE STARTED AT ONCE. TENANTS MUST VACATE. FOR INFORMATION, CALL RELO-CATION OFFICE." But the relocation office offered little assistance in finding new housing. "When I ask them for help, they just say they can't help me," one man recalled. "Now, I don't know where else to look." Another dislocated tenant complained, "I walked from 109th Street to 23rd Street and couldn't find a thing for us. The rents are too high. There's nothing to do." When families did find places to live, their new homes were sometimes smaller and in worse condition than those they had left behind. One report recounted, "A family of two moved from a four-room standard apartment with all utilities, central heating and hot water, private bath and toilet into a three-room apartment in poor condition, with no central heating, no refrigeration, tiny bath in kitchen and a hall toilet. Another family of three moved from four standard rooms to a six-room 'railroad flat' with not a single enclosed room, holes in the floor and ceiling plaster falling."[37]

The lack of reliable information about housing options often led to frequent moves for dislocated families. Beulah Sanders, who would later become a leader in the welfare-rights movement, was forced to move with her children three times due to urban renewal. "We're just like gypsies," she said, "except we don't have a covered wagon." Even as West Side residents began in the late 1950s to organize successfully against urban renewal, they still had difficulties in finding housing. In the case of one development on the West Side, uptown from Lincoln Center, the city, faced with grassroots activism, agreed to increase the number of low-income housing units. Even then, however, the renewal project failed to replace

"Boy's Stadium." Children play catch in an abandoned lot. *Courtesy of the Library of Congress.*

Family in an East Harlem apartment,1966. Low-income housing shortages forced large families like the one pictured here into cramped, inadequate apartments. *Bruce Davidson, Magnum Photos.*

the number of low-income units destroyed. And even those apartments labeled as low-income were often too expensive for the former residents of the neighborhood. For those who could qualify, NYCHA housing was an option, but the strict requirements made it difficult—especially for those receiving public assistance. Jennette Washington, another welfare-rights leader dislocated by urban renewal, joked that for public housing "you have to pass 28 standards of behavior, and I figure I could pass about three." Washington, a single mother of five children on welfare, was, not surprisingly, rejected by NYCHA.[38]

Dislocation due to new development affected families, especially poor families, across the city. A 1953 study sponsored by the city's Board of Estimate predicted that an additional

150,000 people would be dislocated by public-works projects including urban renewal. About half of the families dislocated would be black or Puerto Rican. There is little reliable data on what happened to those relocated by urban renewal. One investigation found that a little less than one-third were accepted into NYCHA projects. Another 10 percent made the unfortunate choice of moving into other neighborhoods slated for slum clearance. An additional 11 percent found housing in neighborhoods not labeled as slums. Finally, the largest group, 42 percent, were simply unaccounted for. Moses labeled these families as "self-relocated," portraying them as people who had found their own housing. In reality, most of these families and individuals probably found marginal housing in other over-crowded poor neighborhoods.[39]

Urban renewal and public-works projects in Manhattan often moved poor families into the outer boroughs, frequently to isolated areas. Starting in the late 1940s, the De-partment of Welfare began placing "multiproblem families" that were ineligible for public housing in the old wooden bungalows of the Queens beachside community of Hammels, in the difficult-to-reach Rockaways.[40] In the 1950s and 1960s, NYCHA developed projects in the Rockaways to provide additional, and more secure, housing.

Renewal in Brownsville

Urban renewal and slum clearance did not occur only within Manhattan; government-sponsored projects also reshaped the outer boroughs. For instance, Brownsville, the working-class community in Brooklyn first developed in the early twentieth century, was in serious need of housing renovation. Even before World War II, community leaders appealed to the city to improve living conditions in the neighborhood, going so far as to publish a pamphlet entitled "Brownsville Must Have Public Housing." In one section of the neighborhood, the majority of the housing stock was more than twenty-five years old. These were, the pamphlet explained, "shacks and hovels which were flimsy, ill-designed, and badly equipped to start with, and have grown tenfold worse with age, neglect, and poor management." Many of the units lacked adequate light, air, and space; some were without heat, hot water, and bathing facilities; and a few buildings provided only outdoor toilets. Overall, the area was filled with "dirty, bad-smelling, germ-ridden structures, abut-ting upon crowded, ugly barren streets."[41]

NYCHA agreed in 1940 to tear down these decrepit structures and build a public-housing project, but the war delayed construction. Brownsville Houses, the neighborhood's first public housing, finally opened to residents in 1948. In some ways the project disap-pointed the community leaders who had pushed for its construction. Housing advocates had called for structures no taller than three stories to fit in with the neighborhood's existing buildings. Instead, NYCHA constructed seventeen six-story buildings, arguing that this was the only way to make the project economically viable and replace all the units that had been demolished. With these large structures concentrated in one section of the neighborhood, Brownsville residents' feelings toward public housing began to sour.[42]

Race would also play a role in shifting perceptions of public housing. Brownsville, together with neighboring East New York, was once the largest Jewish community in the city. Over time, however, the neighborhood had become more interracial. By 1948, when Brownsville Houses opened, blacks made up 22 percent of the neighborhood's population. Reflecting the local racial composition, Brownsville Houses was 52 percent white and 48 percent black when it opened.[43] In the unwritten racial segregation of NYCHA's developments, however, Brownsville Houses was viewed as a "colored project."[44]

Probably not coincidentally, Robert Moses and other city planners saw the neighborhood as the best place for the expansion of Brooklyn's black ghetto. This perspective would

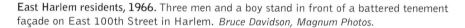

East Harlem residents, 1966. Three men and a boy stand in front of a battered tenement façade on East 100th Street in Harlem. *Bruce Davidson, Magnum Photos.*

Brownsville market. Public housing in Brownsville, Brooklyn, rapidly changed the racial and economic composition of the neighborhood in the late 1940s and 1950s. *Courtesy of the Library of Congress.*

affect future public-housing development and the long-term racial and economic composition of the neighborhood. When the first phase of the Van Dyke Houses, Brownsville's next housing project, opened in 1954, 31 percent of the families moving in were white; when the second phase of the project was completed, in 1955, 25 percent of its residents were white. In that same year, the percentage of whites in Brownsville Houses had dropped to 30 percent. The rapid influx of blacks into Brownsville, especially those entering the area's housing projects, disturbed longtime white residents. By the 1950s whites blamed public housing for destroying their community.[45]

Ironically, the residents moving into the neighborhood's new housing projects were not especially poor. Based on NYCHA's strict requirements, only a small proportion of the residents in the Brownsville projects were receiving welfare. On the other hand, poor blacks and Puerto Ricans were moving into the neighborhood's dilapidated tenements, those areas that had not been targeted for slum clearance. Moses had planned for the refugees from his urban-renewal projects to move into "soft" areas, meaning those with higher vacancy rates, such as Brownsville. One official recalled rumors that those dislocated by

West 91st Street, 1962. Two boys throw bricks amid rubble and trash in a vacant lot. *Courtesy of the Library of Congress.*

urban renewal were "dumped by the hundreds into vacant tenements in a section of Brooklyn called Brownsville." Between 1950 and 1957 the black population of Brownsville increased by nearly 50 percent.[46]

While Brownsville was still almost three-quarters white in 1957, there was a growing perception among whites there of neighborhood decline, leading a great number of them to flee the community for other city neighborhoods or the suburbs. Indications of increasing crime and social disorder propelled this flight. Youth gangs had long existed in Brownsville, but the growth in black and Puerto Rican gangs frightened longtime residents. A 1960 study of the area found 11 different gangs active in the neighborhood. According to 1961 statistics, the neighborhood's Van Dyke Houses had the highest arrest rate among NYCHA's projects, and the Brownsville Houses had the third-highest; these were some of the most dangerous projects in the city. Moses's vision of Brownsville as a dumping ground for displaced minorities was borne out; by 1962 Brownsville was 75 percent black and Puerto Rican. The racial composition of the neighborhood had been markedly recast in only five years.[47] In 1963 NYCHA announced that it was building three more public housing projects in Brownsville. The result, ultimately, was a virtual wall of public housing, cutting through the heart of the community. By the mid-1960s, with the neighborhood dominated by housing projects, Brownsville had become a community most wanted to avoid. As of 1970 the racial transformation of the community was complete; Brownsville was now 77 percent black, 19 percent Puerto Rican, and only 4 percent white.[48]

Local activists continued to push the city to beautify Brownsville and improve conditions, but with little success. Brownsville had been designated an urban-renewal area under the Title I program in 1961, and in 1968 additional plans for urban renewal were developed under the federal Model Cities program. Rather than initiating a renaissance in the community, these plans were delayed to an extent that actually made the conditions in Brownsville worse. Some buildings marked for renewal were demolished and never replaced. Landlords abandoned buildings, allowing the city to take them over, or defaulted on mortgages held by the Federal Housing Administration, which promptly demolished the structures. "Block after block had been left vacant for years," a 1973 report recounted, "forming a wasteland of gutted carcasses of buildings and rat-filled rubble." Another 1973 study concluded that "Brownsville has never really been renewed. … Urban renewal has fostered rapid and irreversible decay in those areas which the City had intended to save."[49]

Public housing in Brownsville, Brooklyn. Public housing dominated the landscape in Brownsville. This image shows Brownsville Houses—27 six- and seven-story buildings built in 1948—in the foreground, as well as numerous housing projects that went up around it afterward. *New York City Housing Authority, The La Guardia and Wagner Archives, La Guardia Community College/The City University of New York.*

Urban renewal and slum clearance, as practiced by Robert Moses and other New York City administrators, did little to alleviate poverty. Instead, the result of these programs was to make the destitute less noticeable, as many poor families relocated to more isolated sections of New York. For much of the boom of the 1960s, poor families floundered in these hidden pockets of deprivation. But Moses and his allies did not have the only vision for fighting urban poverty and blight. From Washington came a call to arms to attack these problems head-on. The War on Poverty attempted to reverse the marginalization of the poor, especially of blacks and Hispanics, and provide a different trajectory for urban America.

The War on Poverty

When President John F. Kennedy was assassinated, on November 22, 1963, his administration had already begun plans for an initiative to attack entrenched rural and urban poverty. In Lyndon B. Johnson's State of the Union address seven weeks after Kennedy's death, the new president highlighted this program by declaring a "war on poverty." The result was the passage, in 1964, of the Economic Opportunity Act. The act created several new federal programs, including the Job Corps, Head Start, and a domestic version of the Peace Corps, known as VISTA (Volunteers in Service to America).

At the heart of this legislation were the Community Action Programs (CAP). This provision allowed the newly created Office of Economic Opportunity (OEO) to fund local organizations oriented toward empowering individuals to improve their own communities. Community-action proponents viewed participation as the path out of the marginalization created by poverty. Inspired by the work of community organizer Saul Alinsky, community-action advocates were suspicious of bureaucracy and of the established social-service providers who told the poor what to do. Rather than encourage dependence on service providers, community-action programs allowed for self-direction and independence. Many of the ideas behind community action were also worked out by Mobilization for Youth (MFY), a delinquency-prevention program based on the Lower East Side. Under the influence of sociologists Lloyd Ohlin and Richard Cloward, MFY focused on creating conflict as the best way to develop community participation. For example, MFY might organize tenants to demand improvements from landlords. The improvements were important, but so were the skills and connections residents developed in these campaigns. This notion of mobilizing the poor to connect them to broader society was written into the Economic Opportunity Act's requirement that Community Action Programs be "developed, conducted, and administered with maximum feasible participation of the residents."[50]

Community action was intended to bypass established institutions to better respond to the needs and concerns of the poor. In New York, however, Mayor Wagner moved to assert his administration's control over the distribution of these federal funds. Demanding that "local autonomy be respected," Wagner created a 100-member Council on Poverty to oversee community action in the city. With members appointed directly by the mayor, the council consisted mostly of representatives of traditional social-service providers such as the United Neighborhood Houses, Catholic Charities, and the Federation of Jewish Philanthropies — precisely the agencies that the anti-poverty warriors had hoped to circumvent. Under pressure from the federal agency overseeing CAP, Wagner finally had to allow members of the Council on Poverty to be elected by neighborhood boards, but even then he rigged the system by requiring that board members be chosen by neighborhood YMCAs, churches, block associations, and traditional social-service providers. The

Playground, Lower East Side.
A boy jumps from a platform onto a mattress on Manhattan's Lower East Side.
Allan Tannenbaum.

result was that the management of community action, both within neighborhoods and citywide, was in the hands of individuals who were mostly politically connected, middle-class professionals.[51]

The Brownsville Community Council (BCC) was one of the earliest and most successful of the Community Action Programs in New York. Formed in 1964, as the details of CAP were still being worked out, the BCC was a coalition of local Brownsville organizations such as PTAs, block associations, and churches as well as groups concerned with public housing, voting rights, and the election of black officials. The BCC leaders were mostly longtime activists and included businessmen, social workers, insurance investigators, postal clerks, and homemakers. While some members of the organization's board might be considered working-class, none could be labeled as the disenfranchised poor. One leader of the organization defended the lack of poor people in leadership positions. "There are no poor people as such on the committee at present," he explained. "But there is another side of the coin: this committee has to work, and in order for it to work there must be people on it who have proven that they know how to get things done."[52]

The BCC received one of the first CAP grants in order to plan its program. The organization soon committed to establishing four Community Action Centers to co-ordinate neighborhood services and develop new initiatives based on local needs. The BCC initially focused its attention on youth programs such as Head Start, a summer camp, recreational activities, a program in civic affairs, and outreach to troubled youth. In later years the BCC turned increasingly to adult programs. These ran the gamut from job training to campaigns intended to bolster black and Puerto Rican pride to efforts to support local block clubs. The BCC took the goal of resident empowerment—or maximum feasible participation—seriously. It organized residents to push for repairs and improvements in their housing and held public events, including fairs, parades, and festivals, that increased community involvement. The BCC, like other CAP programs, successfully connected Brownsville residents to the social-service and government sectors in new ways. The primary beneficiaries of these connections, however, were middle-class and working-class residents who developed new skills and found new opportunities through the BCC. Many of these individuals went on to have long careers in city government or social services. As community action drew many of the most talented residents away from the neighborhood, the truly disenfranchised poor were left behind. For them, the BCC and other Community Action Programs became just more social-service providers, the type of institutions that the War on Poverty organizers had expected community action to supplant.[53]

In Brownsville and across the city, the War on Poverty failed to reverse the forces pulling the city apart. While the anti-poverty programs provided a path for some blacks and Puerto Ricans into the halls of power, and while some programs, such as Head Start, demonstrated marked success in providing new services to the impoverished, the creation of desperately poor communities on the margins of the city continued. With these limited positive outcomes, the War on Poverty stands out as a missed opportunity to create greater improvements in the lives of New York's poor.

Lindsay's War on Poverty and the Movement for Welfare Rights

In 1965 the *New York Herald Tribune* published a series of articles entitled "A City in Crisis," suggesting that New York was "no longer the greatest place to live." Many of the statistics cited by the newspaper pointed out the struggles of poor families. "Nearly one-fifth of the city's people live in poverty conditions … many in cramped, inadequately heated, insanitary, rat-infested apartments," the first article reported. "More than 70,000 youths now roam the streets, out-of-work and out of school, untrained and uncaring." Middle-class whites, the article continued, were fleeing the city. At the same time, "half a million people" were receiving welfare. Public-housing construction had become so backlogged that, the paper reported in January 1965, "it would take someone more than 10 years to gain admission to a public-housing project if he applied today." Most tellingly, for many observers "urban renewal has come to mean Negro or human renewal, the shifting of minority groups from one slum to another." The city was not meeting the needs of the poor; in fact, city policies in many cases had harmed the poor.[54]

The city's welfare system itself, was largely dysfunctional. Welfare clients felt belittled and demeaned by the process of applying for support and by the meagerness of the benefits. Through the mid-1960s, every applicant's income and familial relationships were thoroughly investigated. "The worst thing about welfare, you don't feel like a real person by the time they get through with you," explained one recipient. "You've got to tell them where your husband was born, and where his mother and father came from. They want to know, do you have any money in the bank? If you admit you have life insurance, you got to go home and come back with it." And welfare recipients were never free from the scrutiny of the welfare department. Even after placing a client on a regular budget, said another recipient, "some workers will come into your apartment and stand with their coats on while their eyes are going all over the place."[55]

Caseworkers themselves felt overwhelmed by their caseloads and disliked having to apply patronizing and often arbitrary rules to welfare recipients. One caseworker, using the pseudonym Frank Gell, recalled that a lesson from his training was not to provide counseling meant to solve the client's strife with his or her spouse, girlfriend, or boyfriend; the role of the caseworker was only to uncover who was contributing to the household budget. Once Gell was out in the field, though, he saw that the best way he could help his client was not to be too vigorous in enforcing the rules. "Had I been a more 'efficient' caseworker," he reflected in discussing the inspection of an applicant's apartment, "I would have flung open the closets, pulled out the drawers, and searched under the bed for the father of the children, who had disappeared six months ago. But even if he were there, hiding, I didn't want to find him."[56] Cheating was rampant; one client reported that "sometimes good caseworkers will even show you how to do it."[57] The low wages, high caseloads, and discomfort of working against, rather than for, those in financial need drove some caseworkers to form a new union, the Social Services Employees Union

South Bronx. A child looks out his window at dilapidated train tracks and housing in the South Bronx. *Stephen Shames, Polaris Images.*

(SSEU). In January 1965 caseworkers went on strike. In addition to demanding higher salaries and more vacation time, they adopted as one of their mottos "Rehabilitation Not Humiliation" for welfare clients. This was another sign of the dysfunction in the city's welfare system.[58]

As idealistic caseworkers were organizing for reform, welfare recipients themselves began to do so, placing new demands on the city. The movement for welfare rights in New York emerged from several corners in the mid-1960s. Frank Espada, a Puerto Rican activist, established Welfare Recipients Leagues in several locations in Brooklyn starting in 1964. Around the same time, Mobilization for Youth, on the Lower East Side of Manhattan, had begun organizing residents over recurring complaints about public assistance. On the Upper West Side, Jennette Washington and Beulah Sanders, veterans in the fight against urban renewal, organized their own Welfare Recipients League. Across the city, Washington observed, people "were sick of conditions on welfare and were now ready to band together."[59] In April 1966 the various welfare groups in New York met and formed the City-Wide Coordinating Committee of Welfare Groups (known informally as Citywide).[60]

The welfare-rights movement was based in a demand for respect, a rejection of the humiliation poor people were subjected to when applying for and receiving aid. The organizers of this nascent movement, however, also needed a broader and more concrete strategy around which to organize their actions. Sociologists Frances Fox Piven and Richard Cloward, both of whom were involved with Mobilization for Youth, provided a theory of welfare rights and a strategy that they believed would help expand social welfare in the United States. Piven and Cloward started with a simple fact: most people in the United States who were eligible for assistance had not applied. If, they theorized, more recipients were added to the rolls, an administrative and fiscal crisis would ensue. Such a crisis would lead to the creation, they believed, of a simplified and more universal "guaranteed minimum income." To cause this crisis, activists needed to inform potential recipients of their "right" to welfare and make sure they were receiving all possible benefits. This became the strategy of the Citywide campaign in New York as well as the other groups around the country that would form the National Welfare Rights Organization in 1967.[61]

Citywide's first campaign rooted in the crisis theory focused on gaining special grants for welfare recipients. New York's welfare regulations allowed for special grants based on specific needs; for example, if there were certain items of clothing or furniture that a family lacked, a caseworker could add the cost of those items to the family's budget, providing support beyond their regular relief check. The welfare-rights activists were able to get their hands on the New York City welfare department's list of minimum standards, which guided caseworkers' decisions to provide special grants. The standards were very specific:

A family was expected to have one sofa and one drop-leaf table. A woman was to have a minimum of three pairs of underwear. Even though these standards were modest, making requests for all of the items on the list would raise the standard of living for most welfare recipients. Welfare activists focused first on children's clothing needs. A 1960s study of New York City welfare families had found that approximately 30 percent of parents had kept children out of school because they lacked clothing or shoes, and another 20 percent had done so because they were ashamed of the condition of their children's clothes. MFY first saw success by organizing recipients to request winter coats for their children, critical items during the New York City winters. The campaign expanded from there, with recipients demanding clothing and furniture and appealing the decisions of caseworkers if these requests were denied. In Brooklyn alone, the expenditures on special grants rose from $142,759 in 1963 to over $3 million in 1968.[62]

The welfare-rights movement found a sympathetic ear in the form of John V. Lindsay, the young, attractive, liberal Republican mayor. To win election in 1965 Lindsay had put together an unprecedented coalition of the traditional Republican elite, liberal Jews, and blacks, and his administration provided a new openness to minorities and recognition of the needs of the poor. Where Wagner had reluctantly implemented the War on Poverty programs, Lindsay embraced the theory of the community action programs. Wagner had hoped to control community action through city agencies and the traditional social-service providers; Lindsay supported the involvement of the poor through community action as a way to shake up the bureaucracy. To improve the provision of social services in the city, and make government more efficient and cost-effective, Lindsay ordered a widespread study of the city's programs, to be conducted by former New Haven official Mitchell Sviridoff. When Sviridoff suggested the creation of a "super agency" to oversee and coordinate the various city social-service agencies, Lindsay created the Human Resources Administration (HRA) and installed Sviridoff as commissioner in 1966.[63]

Mitchell Ginsberg, Lindsay's first welfare commissioner and later Sviridoff's successor as head of HRA, oversaw an expansion of grants in line with the demands of the welfare-rights movement. Ginsberg halted the "midnight raids" on AFDC recipients intended to discover if they were cohabiting with men. (ADC had been renamed Aid to Families with Dependent Children, or AFDC, in 1962.) He encouraged caseworkers to enroll as many eligible recipients as possible and simplified the investigation process for new recipients, allowing for self-declaration of need. And he cooperated with welfare-rights activists to monitor welfare centers. The long-term result of Ginsberg's policy changes and of the welfare-rights movement was an expansion of welfare spending. Between 1962 and 1967 the value of welfare grants increased 45 percent. The campaign by these activists to expand benefits even further in 1968 brought immediate results. Analysis by the RAND Corporation showed a 17 percent increase in welfare caseloads between February and September 1968. In February only 53 percent of eligible recipients were receiving benefits; by September that number had reached nearly 62 percent. Driven by the increase in public-assistance payouts, HRA became the largest item on the city's budget, with costs for the administration topping $1 billion in 1968.[64]

No longer able to support such expansion of benefits, the Lindsay administration worked out new welfare rules with the state. The basic welfare grant in the city would be increased by 6 percent, and each family would receive an additional $100 a year in supplemental funds, but the special grants given at the discretion of caseworkers ended. Taking a new tack, Lindsay promised "zero growth" in the welfare rolls. "I am going to force the welfare system to back up in such a fashion that they are going to hold the line," the mayor claimed. "We are going to cut services, check cases and get the cheats off the rolls—and the only way to do it is with a fine-ground filter in H.R.A."[65]

This new, restrictive approach—an about-face from Lindsay's previous policies—was met with frustration by the welfare-rights movement. Demonstrations broke out at welfare offices across the city. Overcome with anger, some recipients broke into offices and caused significant destruction. This turn toward violence alienated many previous supporters of the movement and increased the hostility of those who had rejected the idea of welfare as a right. Piven and Cloward's theory had been that creating a crisis over welfare would lead to more generous income-support programs. The result was just the opposite: The movement had created a crisis that led to further restriction on grants and, more importantly, widened the political chasm between welfare recipients and the white working class.[66]

Coretta Scott King, the widow of Martin Luther King Jr., called the welfare-rights movement "the real war on poverty."[67] The leaders of this movement asserted that poverty was not created by personal failings or the lack of participation in public life but by a shortage of income; the best way to end poverty, then, was to provide more generous transfer payments to the poor. Observers of the welfare-rights movement have debated the extent of its influence in increasing welfare uptake. If nothing else, the movement reflected a loss of stigma for receiving welfare and a sense of entitlement to government benefits. In an age of deindustrialization, with jobs for the unskilled increasingly scarce, many families now saw welfare as the only option that would allow them to survive.

The Urban Crisis

While the battle over welfare raged on, New York City was mired in a recession. From 1969 to 1977 the city lost more than 600,000 jobs, mostly in construction and manufacturing. Many of the industries that employed low-skilled workers were affected. The city lost nearly a third of its jobs in apparel and textile production, more than a quarter of its jobs in printing and publishing, and almost half the jobs in food and beverage production. The loss of manufacturing jobs was part of a broader shift to the development of a primarily service-based economy in New York. Low-skilled workers, however, often found themselves unqualified for many of these service jobs, such as those in the financial sector. Those service jobs that were available—janitor, day care worker, security guard—were poorly paid. More than ever, New York became a city pulled apart, with a robust professional-service economy for the wealthy and an unstable unskilled-service economy for the working class. The new flood of immigrants who entered New York after 1965 heightened competition for work. While many of these immigrants were professionals or technicians who moved into the city's middle class, most entered its working class. Some ethnic groups, such as the Dominicans who crowded into Upper Manhattan and the Bronx, competed with U.S.-born blacks and Puerto Ricans for low-skilled positions.[68]

New York's grim economic straits contributed to a fiscal crisis, as tax revenues declined and the city's middle-class tax base fled. Many other factors also helped bring on the financial shortfall, including the rising demand for services among the poor. The growing uptake in AFDC and other social-assistance programs in the era of the welfare-rights movement certainly added to the city's costs, but it alone did not explain the massive growth in the city's annual budget. From $2.7 billion in 1961, the budget had increased to $13.6 billion by 1976, reflecting the costs of education, heath care, housing, transit, the City University system, and the wages and pensions of municipal employees in addition to welfare. A large portion of the budget was also dedicated to servicing the city's debt, which by 1976 had reached $12.6 billion. Up until the 1970s, the city had managed to hide its excessive debt through budgetary maneuvers. By 1975, however, banks had simply refused to underwrite any further debts for the city. This forced the state to step in and work out a way to provide additional loans while at the same time guiding the city out of insolvency. The Emergency Financial Control Board (EFCB) was created with broad powers to oversee the city's revenue and spending.[69]

The cuts made by the EFCB were widespread but, once again, had particularly dire effects for the poor. Because they often lacked seniority, blacks and Hispanics, the city's poorest ethnic groups, were laid off from their jobs in higher numbers than white workers. The number of Hispanic workers on the city payroll dropped by 50 percent, and that of blacks decreased by 35 percent, while white employees saw their ranks shrink by only 22 percent. Service cuts or increased fees for some institutions—the transit system, primary and secondary schools, the City University of New York, Mitchell-Lama housing, the municipal hospital system—affected many New Yorkers. Combined with cuts to nutrition programs, job training, drug treatment, and community action, these budgetary adjustments led to a wholesale decrease in the quality of life for the city's poorest.[70]

With these cuts to services, working-class neighborhoods began to feel dirty and unsafe to longtime residents. Elmhurst, Queens, saw its sanitation pickups reduced to one day a week. "Overall our streets are filthy," reported a local paper in March 1976. Even more ominously, the paper reported that "burglaries and muggings have been on the rise." Parts of the city already in decline, among them Brownsville and East New York in Brooklyn and the neighborhoods of the South Bronx, soon became urban wastelands.[71]

The landscape of New York neighborhoods changed dramatically with the frequent abandonment of residential buildings. The concentration of poor families, many on welfare, in particular neighborhoods made it difficult for landlords to meet their tax payments and cover the expenses for upkeep. In 1966 New York State passed a law allowing tenants in buildings with housing violations to pay only a dollar a month in rent until the violations were addressed. Unable to pay taxes while collecting such low rents, owners simply abandoned buildings. By the mid-1970s, between 20,000 and 60,000 housing units were being abandoned every year; over the period from 1965 to 1975, 200,000 units were lost.

Children playing on a heap of rubble, South Bronx. The South Bronx began to decline into poverty after 1950 and by the '70s had become a focus of national concern. Today it is home to the poorest congressional district in the nation. *Allan Tannenbaum.*

In the South Bronx many of these abandoned buildings burned to the ground. Arson—fires started by landlords looking for insurance payments or tenants looking for new housing—was often the culprit.[72]

The neighborhood around Charlotte Street in the Bronx was hit particularly hard by the concentration of poverty and the frequency of abandonment. Once a densely populated middle-class neighborhood, the area saw half of its residents receiving welfare by 1970. The inability of many residents to pay their rent created a pattern of abandonment and arson. At one time fifty-one apartment buildings stood on Charlotte Street and the surrounding blocks, providing housing for 3,000 people. By the late 1970s, only nine of these buildings remained, and eight of those had been sealed up or damaged by fire. Across the South Bronx more than 2,000 blocks were devastated; observers frequently compared the area to the German city of Dresden after it was firebombed in World War II.[73]

Gang arrest, Brooklyn. Although gang violence has been a social concern in New York since the nineteenth century, it became a hot topic in the postwar era, as immigrants of different ethnicities filtered into the city's neighborhoods. Gang membership ballooned in the 1970s and '80s, as the economy faltered and still more services to poor families were cut. *Courtesy of the Library of Congress.*

In this isolated, hopeless urban wilderness, drug abuse became rampant. Over the 1960s heroin use had spread across New York's slum neighborhoods. Piri Thomas, in his memoir of growing up in East Harlem, described the process of becoming addicted to the drug. "I never figured on getting hooked," he recalled. "I was only gonna play it for a Pepsi-Cola kick. Only was gonna use it like every seven days, that is until the day I woke up and dug that I was using it seven times a day instead." To support his growing habit, Piri sold drugs around his neighborhood. When that wasn't enough to cover the costs of his heroin habit, he turned to theft.[74] The drugs were sold virtually out in the open. "On Charlotte and Minford they sold drugs like they were groceries," recalled one resident of the Bronx. "They used to carry the drugs upstairs in a baby carriage."[75]

As drugs scourged largely abandoned neighborhoods in Brooklyn and the Bronx, crime rates steadily climbed. In the precinct that included Charlotte Street, murders increased from eighteen in 1961 to 102 in 1971; over the same period burglaries jumped from 667 to 6,443. Many of these crimes were drug related. One patrolman recalled the incessant violence in the area. "I can remember two homicides in the same building, one right after another … . There were so many homicides," he lamented. "Then there was a guy shot with a shotgun and I had to hold his guts in with my bare hands." The lack of services meant that the police handled many of the community's needs. "I delivered twenty-seven babies, even one set of twins," the police officer recounted. "They sent them home from the hospitals because there was no room for them to wait."[76]

As lawlessness spread in the South Bronx, youth gangs proliferated, claiming that they provided stability to the area. "The Police department is the biggest gang out here," explained Manny, the leader of a gang called the Turbans. "So we decided to take care of business ourselves." Rather than imposing order on the community, however, gangs spent most of their time fighting other gangs. At other times they would attack buildings, terrorizing residents and pilfering appliances and anything else that could bring some cash. Like most members of these depressed communities, gang members expressed hopelessness about life. One woman, the super at one of the buildings still standing near Charlotte Street, was shocked by an encounter with a gang member. "I said to one of them, 'You're going to get killed.' He said, 'I don't care.' I said, 'Why don't you go home?' and he said, 'There's nothing at home. My mother's a drunk.' I said, 'You don't care if you die?' and he said, 'Nope.'"[77]

Through abandonment and arson the South Bronx lost 16 percent of its housing between 1970 and 1975. While not as affected by arson, the population of Brownsville fell by 35 percent over the 1970s. Those who had the greatest economic means and connections to other parts of the city left these declining neighborhoods, thus further concentrating the poverty there. In the 1970s more than 30 percent of Brownsville's residents earned incomes below the poverty line; 30 percent of the males in the area were unemployed; and

A Puerto Rican gang, the Katos, display their gang colors on the Lower East Side.
With no prospect of employment and few social services available, young residents of New
York's most impoverished neighborhoods turned to gangs for support. *Allan Tannenbaum.*

25 percent of families were on public assistance. Not everyone thought the loss of population in these neighborhoods was a bad thing. Recognizing the economic hopelessness,
Roger Starr, Mayor Lindsay's housing-development administrator, advocated "planned
shrinkage," a decrease in services in areas such as the South Bronx and Brownsville, to encourage residents in these depressed communities to move to parts of the country where
jobs were more plentiful. Negative reaction to Starr's comments forced him to retract his
plan, but the notion that the city had simply abandoned these poor communities remained in the minds of those who lived in them.[78]

The Underclass Debate

By 1975 Carmen Santana had received public assistance for fourteen years. She received
$294 twice a month. Of that, $85 was intended to pay her rent, and the remainder to
support the family. She lived on the second floor of a four-story walkup building in Williamsburg, Brooklyn, in an apartment consisting of a living room, two small bedrooms, a
bathroom, and a kitchen. She shared one bedroom with her boyfriend, Francisco Delgado,

while the other bedroom was shared by four of Carmen's children, who all slept in a single bunk bed. The floors in the apartment were covered in peeling linoleum. The windows looked out over an abandoned building and a trash-covered courtyard. Like all the New York apartments that Carmen had lived in, this one had peeling paint, cracked plaster, vermin, and intermittent heat and hot water.[79] Carmen's struggles with poverty continued for many of her children. Her adult daughter Casilda had a baby in 1972 and began receiving welfare payments. Her son Felipe and his girlfriend, both heroin addicts, lived partly off the girlfriend's welfare check. Her daughter Inocencia dropped out of the seventh grade at the age of thirteen, three months pregnant with her first child.

This was hardly the outcome Carmen expected when, in April 1959, at the age of twenty-seven, she flew from San Juan, Puerto Rico, to New York City with Inocencia, then fourteen months old. Leaving her small hometown of Cayey, where she earned only nine dollars a week as a restaurant cook, Carmen hoped that she could find a better-paying job in Nueva York. Recently separated from the father of two of her children, Carmen also came to New York to start a new life. At first she lived with relatives, but after six months she began a relationship with Vincente Santana, another recent arrival from Puerto Rico, and moved in with him.[80]

Carmen's dream of a better life for herself and her children seemed to be coming true. She found work in a leather-goods factory, where she assembled handbags and earned $43 a week. Vincente, meanwhile, operated leather-cutting machines and earned $40 a week. While the couple worked, Vincente's mother cared for Inocencia as well as Carmen's son, Felipe, who had come from Puerto Rico to join the family. Soon Carmen and Vincente had children of their own, adding, in the end, four more members to the family.

Meanwhile, in 1961 when Carmen was pregnant with the couple's second child, Vincente's mother moved back to Puerto Rico. Without affordable child care, Carmen was forced to quit her job. A few weeks later Vincente was laid off. Carmen turned to the welfare system to help provide for her growing family. The Department of Welfare reviewed the family's situation and found they were eligible for two grants to help them meet a monthly budget of $108.30. Carmen met the requirements for ADC, which would provide a grant of $11.73 twice a month to support her and her two eldest children. Together, Carmen and Vincente also qualified for New York's Home Relief program, which brought an additional $8.71 semimonthly. The family managed to survive like this for some time. When Vincente found work he would contribute his earnings to the family. Otherwise, the two welfare grants covered the family's expenses. By the late 1960s, however, Vincente was finding it difficult to hold down a job. He began drinking excessively and became involved with loan sharks. Soon the family's home-relief checks were going toward booze and loan payments. Carmen had no choice but to leave Vincente in 1969.[81] Dependent on welfare to pay for rent and her family's expenses, the dream that had drawn Carmen from Puerto Rico to New York had failed to come true.[82]

Carmen Santana and her family represented a new segment of New York society. Mostly Puerto Ricans and blacks living in neighborhoods in the South Bronx, in Harlem, in Bedford-Stuyvesant, in Brownsville and East New York, these were families that subsisted for years almost exclusively on public support. Known as "the new poor" or "the underclass," these families showed little likelihood of returning to work. Single-parent households, headed mostly by mothers, became common among these families. It was not unusual, as in Carmen Santana's case, to find a single mother raising children fathered by different men. Drug and alcohol use became rampant. Housing remained decrepit. The streets of the neighborhoods where the new poor lived became more dangerous, subject to frequent gang violence, muggings, and burglaries. Unlike the poor families of the nineteenth and most of the twentieth century, the new poor were increasingly cut off from the labor market, isolated in areas with little hope for a better future.[83]

The rise of a ghetto underclass — poor minorities living almost exclusively in single-parent households reliant on public assistance — did not occur only in New York. Across the country, in poor, isolated urban neighborhoods that became known as "the inner city," the rates of poverty and out-of-wedlock births among black and Puerto Rican families steadily increased. In 1955, 41 percent of births to black women between the ages of fifteen and twenty-four were outside marriage; by 1968 that number had reached 68 percent. And the future for these young single mothers was not particularly rosy. In 1982, 56.2 percent of black female-headed families and 55.4 percent of Hispanic female-headed families were below the poverty line.[84]

The question of what factors created this "underclass," and, therefore, what policy approaches would best reduce its population would animate decades of debate in social-science and political circles. Some suggested that poor families, in particular poor black families, were trapped in "a tangle of pathology" — a history of slavery and oppression that had given rise to unstable matriarchal families. Others argued that economic factors and racism best explained the depressed state of these poorest families. Another group of contributors to this debate would focus on welfare policies themselves as the culprit in disrupting family structure and creating long-term dependency. Finally, some looked to the continuing low level of employment among minorities and the inability of minority women to find employed men suitable for marriage. These different interpretations would lead to various suggestions for social-policy reform over the next two decades.[85] Much of this debate was reminiscent of nineteenth and early-twentieth-century disagreements about the sources of poverty; theories of environmental, structural, and individual causes of poverty would all be represented in the wide-ranging discussion of the underclass.

Two men sit against a graffitied wall in Harlem, 1984.
Ken Heyman, Collection of the International Center of Photography.

1977

On October 5, 1977 Mayor Abraham Beame received an unexpected call from President Jimmy Carter, asking if the mayor would join him on a tour of the South Bronx. The surprise visit to the depressed neighborhood had been planned months earlier in response to criticism that the president had been inattentive to the urban poor. On that Wednesday morning, as the president's motorcade weaved its way through the Bronx, bystanders—suddenly realizing who was passing—yelled, "Give us money!" and "We want jobs!" Finally, the president and mayor arrived at an almost completely abandoned block of Charlotte Street. Observing the urban blight that surrounded him, a grim-faced Carter vowed to do something about urban poverty. A few weeks later, as Howard Cosell provided play-by-play for the television broadcast of the World Series game being played at Yankee Stadium, in the Bronx, he noticed flames and smoke in the distance. "There it is, ladies and gentleman," Cosell announced in his distinctive cadence, "the Bronx is burning."[86]

President Jimmy Carter on Charlotte Street, 1977. President Carter's visit to Charlotte Street, a desolate and abandoned block in the Bronx, directed national attention toward urban poverty, adding new fuel to the "underclass" debate. *The New York Times/ Redux Pictures.*

Day care center, 1979. The Carter administration's "urban initiative" program funded day care centers in some New York City housing projects. This is the basement center at Webster Houses in the Morrisania section of the Bronx. *New York City Housing Authority, The La Guardia and Wagner Archives, La Guardia Community College/The City University of New York.*

These two events brought national attention to the crisis of urban poverty. This new awareness of "inner-city poverty," however, would not inevitably lead to a resolution. Instead, as the nation's politics took a conservative and anti-urban turn, public policy would make the lives of many poor families more difficult. A few months before Carter's visit, incumbent mayor Beame had lost the Democratic primary for mayor to Ed Koch, a tough-talking congressman from Greenwich Village. It would be up to Koch to confront the increasingly entrenched family poverty and homelessness within New York City.

Urban development in New York City, 1625–1988. This map is color-coded to indicate periods of land development in New York City, from the early colonial period to the late twentieth century. *Milstein Division of United States History, Local History & Genealogy, The New York Public Library, Astor, Lenox and Tilden Foundations.*

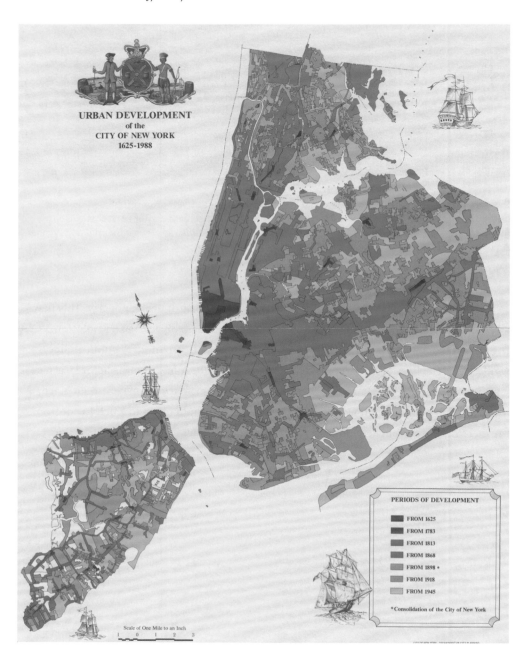

URBAN DEVELOPMENT
of the
CITY OF NEW YORK
1625-1988

PERIODS OF DEVELOPMENT

FROM 1625
FROM 1783
FROM 1813
FROM 1868
FROM 1898 *
FROM 1918
FROM 1945

*Consolidation of the City of New York

Scale of One Mile to an Inch
1   0   1   2   3

Chapter 8

Family Poverty and Homelessness in the Age of the Market

On July 4, 1982, as fireworks exploded over the East River in celebration of Independence Day, Yvonne Perez and her six-year-old son slept on the ground in Sunset Park, Brooklyn. They had spent the two previous nights on the Coney Island beach while Perez's two other children stayed with a friend. Perez and her family received Aid to Families with Dependent Children, the partially federally funded program of public assistance, but the welfare payments were no longer covering their expenses. In November of the previous year, Perez and her children had been evicted from their apartment for nonpayment of rent. For five months they stayed with a series of relatives and friends while conducting an unsuccessful search for affordable housing. In April Perez finally applied to the city for emergency shelter. She was denied and promptly applied again. On July 2, for a second time, the city rejected her request. After securing care for two of her children, Perez found the public beaches and parks, available and relatively comfortable on New York's warm summer nights, the only refuge for herself and her son.[1]

The travails experienced by the Perez family — sleeping in public, crowding in with friends and family, living in makeshift or unconventional shelters — were not new to New York. But the ways in which private organizations and public agencies understood and approached family poverty and homelessness had changed over time. In the eighteenth and early nineteenth centuries, the city's leaders would have sent families without shelter to the poorhouse. In the 1850s the Children's Aid Society sent children from such families west. Twenty years later parents often placed some or all of their children in congregate institutions while getting back on their feet and finding new housing. In the midst of the Great Depression in the 1930s, charitable organizations assisted evicted families and helped them gain access to new public supports. Child-welfare agents in the 1960s would most likely have removed any children from a homeless parent's care. By the 1980s changes in law and in practice increasingly allowed parents to hold on to their children. With housing costs in the city going up, and with the real value of welfare payments decreasing, however, more and more parents found they could not afford to keep shelter over their own heads, let alone their children's. In this decade the idea of homelessness was reshaped once again to include not only single men but families, mostly single women and their children. In 1983, when the number of these families first surpassed 2,000, policymakers began to see family homelessness as its own issue, requiring its own set of policies.

Local and national politics greatly influenced the development of new policies for poor and homeless families. The 1980 election of Ronald Reagan, the president who

Mound of trash outside a half-destroyed building. Thousands of units of low-income housing were destroyed by fire in the 1970s. *Stephen Ferry, Getty Images.*

claimed that "government is not the solution to our problem; government is the problem," marked the end of the era of liberal government that had begun with the New Deal. This, then, was an era of retrenchment in social welfare. If there is one term from this period that encapsulates the focus of social policy in New York City, indeed across the country, it is "dependency." According to a growing number of social scientists, policy makers, and politicians, poor families had become dependent on state support in ways that sapped public coffers and undermined their own self-sufficiency. The fight against dependency remade welfare across the country and in New York City.

In the view of those attacking dependency, welfare reform — both the federal acts of 1988 and 1996 and state and city initiatives to reform public assistance — was a major accomplishment. New York Mayor Rudolph Giuliani bragged in 1998 that his administration had "transformed the welfare system from one that encouraged dependency into one that increasingly enables people to take control of their own lives."[2] For the poor families that experienced welfare reform firsthand, the results were mixed. In some cases these reforms made life easier: for example, heads of families were able to find work without the fear of losing all their benefits, and child care, while still difficult to find, became more affordable with increased public subsidies. For many, however, the efforts to end dependency made desperate situations even more difficult, as families had to constantly justify their requests for aid, subject to never-ending suspicion that their cries for help were attempts to cheat the public.

In this era of social-welfare retrenchment, homelessness was the most extreme result of poverty. For the most destitute of New York families, passed over by changes in the economy and falling through the cracks of the reformed systems of public assistance — especially those families whose problems were made worse by domestic abuse, drug addiction, or a lack of friends or family to provide support — homelessness became an increasingly frequent outcome.

A New Direction for a Flagging City

On January 1, 1978 Ed Koch was inaugurated as mayor of New York. The city that Koch took over was a portrait of urban decline. Over the 1970s the city's poverty rate increased from 14.5 percent to 20.2 percent. In the same period the poverty rate of female-headed households climbed from 37.3 percent to 45.9 percent. Only a few months before Koch's election, President Jimmy Carter's surprise visit to Charlotte Street had made the Bronx a national symbol of urban desolation. Yet the city seemed powerless to reverse this trend. Once home to a thriving system of public services, New York had entered a fiscal crisis in which it could no longer service its debt. By the time of Koch's election, the city was essentially in receivership, making it difficult to imagine a path out of its dire straits.[3]

Despite all of this, Koch, in his inaugural address, provided a positive perspective on New York's past and its potential future. "I do not exaggerate when I say that New York is unique in the history of human kindness," he declared. "From its earliest days, this city has been a lifeboat for the homeless, a larder for the hungry, a living library for the intellectually starved, a refuge not only for the oppressed but also for the creative." If New York had made mistakes in the past, Koch argued, they had been mistakes "of the heart," errors on the side of generosity. New York's liberalism, Koch suggested, needed to be tempered by pragmatism. "In my administration," the new mayor announced, "I intend to bring the heart and the head together."[4]

This pragmatic approach would have direct consequences for social services for the poor. "All too often those who were charged with caring for the disadvantaged turned the generosity of New Yorkers into a form of folly," Koch observed, echoing the perspective of Josephine Shaw Lowell. In this age of austerity following the fiscal crisis, such profligacy could no longer be tolerated. New York could still be a refuge, but its generosity had to be targeted. "The money that is appropriated for the poor," the mayor asserted, "must directly benefit the poor, and in my administration a firm hand and a helping hand will be the same hand."[5]

If New York was to survive, Koch suggested, the city needed to narrow the stream of social services and welfare benefits it provided. But it also needed to invite new businesses to establish themselves in the city and encourage "urban pioneers" among the middle and upper classes to make New York their home. Koch called on all Americans to "come east" and take part in restoring "the most exciting city in the world to prime condition."[6]

The moderate, pragmatic, pro-business and pro-development stance that Koch announced at his inauguration would largely define his administration and those of his successors David Dinkins, Rudolph Giuliani, and Michael Bloomberg. It is this orientation that has made New York what it is today: a city that is safer, wealthier, more welcoming, and maybe even cleaner; but also one with pockets of abject poverty and more homeless families than ever before.

Koch and his successors did not alone shape the policies that affected the lives of the poor. The transformation to a service economy continued over the 1980s; there were 538,600 manufacturing jobs in the city in 1977 and only 360,600 in 1989. This transformation led to increased wage inequality, as wealthier New Yorkers earned more in the global economy and struggling New Yorkers took low-paying jobs in retail, security, and cleaning services. In 1977 the top 10 percent of earners had household incomes fifteen times as high as those of the lowest 10 percent. By 1986 that ratio had become twenty to one.

Burnt-out, abandoned apartment buildings surround a housing project. *Stephen Ferry, Getty Images.*

Inequality became more pronounced with the declining value of welfare benefits and the conservative political attacks on social programs. In 1985, even before welfare reform, the average AFDC payment had sunk to 63 percent of its 1968 value.[7] Decreased support for housing programs compounded the difficulties of struggling families. From 1982 to 1984, for instance, the city lost $600 million in federal assistance for low-income housing. The results of these policies became evident when recession struck the city over 1981 and 1982. In 1983 the city's unemployment rate reached 10 percent, and the poverty rate passed 25 percent. New York faced a new population of destitute families, some of whom struggled even to find shelter.[8]

Meanwhile, massive immigration—from Latin America, the Caribbean, Asia, and Eastern Europe—changed the character of poverty in New York City. The immigration reform of 1965 had finally brought an end to the restrictions on entering the U.S. put in place in the 1920s. With these barriers lowered, the economic boom of the 1980s attracted many seeking economic opportunity in the city. In 1970, 18 percent of the population of New York was foreign-born; by 1990 the official count of foreign-born individuals was 28 percent, and some observers suggested it would approach a third of the city's residents if undocumented immigrants were included. The new immigrants—in the 1980s the highest numbers came from the Dominican Republic, Jamaica, China, Guyana, and Haiti—

represented a wide variety of economic classes. Some came with high levels of wealth, education, or skill. Others, like their early-twentieth-century predecessors, came with virtually nothing. Many undocumented immigrants, often Eastern Europeans or Central and South Americans, scraped by as day laborers, gathering on street corners and parking lots hoping to find work in construction or landscaping.[9]

Dominicans formed one of the poorest groups among the new immigrants, with a median family income well below that of native-born blacks and a significantly higher poverty rate. Crowded into the Upper Manhattan neighborhoods of Washington Heights and Inwood, most Dominicans found employment in low-skilled and low-paying manufacturing jobs. The continuing transformation of the city's economy from manufacturing to service, then, hit the Dominican community particularly hard. Between 1980 and 1990 the proportion of Washington Heights residents receiving public assistance increased from 23 percent to 32 percent. By 1990, 40 percent of Dominicans in "the Heights" lived below the poverty line.[10]

From this growing poverty in Washington Heights emerged a resurgent drug trade, focusing, by the late 1980s, on crack cocaine. Crack was inexpensive, highly addictive, smokeable cocaine that quickly became popular. While politicians portrayed Washington Heights as the center of the crack epidemic, the drug trade and its concomitant violence soon spread to Harlem and poor neighborhoods in Brooklyn. The spread of the illegal drug was virtually unprecedented; city officials estimated that the number of regular users of cocaine grew from 182,000 in 1986 to 600,000 in 1988. Over the same period the number of drug-related cases of child abuse and neglect tripled. From 1987 to 1988 the city's murder rate increased by 10.4 percent, and police estimated that more than a third of the murders were related to crack. Until crack use declined, during the early 1990s, the drug and the disorder it created touched many poor families in New York.[11] In the most dire cases, these families ended up homeless.

The Crisis of Family Homelessness

For most of New York's history, homeless families were rare. Yet in moments of crisis—such as the Great Depression—families, especially single women with children, appealed to public and private resources for shelter. Even after the Depression, the city provided temporary shelter to families left homeless due to fires or other emergencies, including financial crisis. In the late 1960s, under the Lindsay administration, New York began placing such families in hotels, paying for rooms through a combination of city, state, and federal funds. The hotels willing to accept welfare clients were limited in number, and most homeless families found themselves staying in facilities with dark hallways, dingy rooms, and excessive vermin. An investigation by the *New York Times* in 1970 discovered nearly 1,000 families living in 40 different hotels, a 300 percent increase from the year before. While most had experienced emergencies that made their apartments uninhabitable, some simply could not find adequate housing for the allowance issued under welfare. Once a family was declared an "emergency case," public funding provided the total costs of the hotel stay. Still, most families looked to escape quickly from the decrepit hotels that the *Times* called a "modern horror." Unfortunately, many poor families remained in these welfare hotels for months or even years. In response to their complaints, the Lindsay administration worked tirelessly to find permanent homes for those dislocated and living in hotels. By 1972 only about 365 families were still housed in hotels. At the same time, the Henry Street Settlement, with the support of the city, opened the Urban Family Center, a shelter that provided a stable environment and extensive social services to homeless families to assist them in resettling in new homes.[12]

In the early 1980s, with poverty increasing in the city and social supports declining, the number of homeless families began to climb once again. By June 1983 the number of homeless families far exceeded the worst of the 1970s; in the next year the number

A woman and three children living in a privately run, city-funded welfare hotel.
Welfare hotels were often squalid and sometimes unsafe. *The New York Times/Redux Pictures.*

increased by nearly half, reaching 3,056 homeless families in the city. Overwhelmed by the number of families seeking housing, the city also opened its first barracks-style congregate shelter, in Roberto Clemente State Park, in the Bronx. Here, parents and children slept on cots spread across the floor of an abandoned gymnasium, awaiting placements in hotels or other shelters.[13]

The Koch administration believed the city was experiencing a temporary crisis of family homelessness. They hesitated to make long-term capital investments in shelters and other facilities; the costs of putting families up in hotels was certainly high, but they paled in comparison to the expense of building or renovating structures to be used as family shelters. The Koch administration wanted to honor its commitment to offering the poor a "firm hand" and feared making shelter too desirable. As one assistant commissioner explained in 1982, "The shelter is sometimes a much nicer place than they came from, and they are reluctant to leave."[14]

The experience of Yvonne McCain and her family belied this perspective. When she entered the room assigned to her and her three children, on the eleventh floor of the

A girl sits by a window in the Holland Hotel. Jonathan Kozol's 1988 book, *Rachel and Her Children*, made the Holland's inhumane, unsafe conditions infamous and prompted calls for shelter reform. *New York Daily News Archive/Getty Images.*

Congregate shelters housed dozens of families in shared spaces.
Here, homeless women socialize before going to sleep. © *Viviane Moos, Corbis.*

Martinique Hotel, McCain could not believe her eyes. The conditions there defied reason. The floors were soaking wet. "Both sides of the mattresses were stained all over with
urine," she later recalled. "I remember calling my mother and asking if she could bring me
newspapers to put over the mattresses." The windows overlooking Herald Square had no
bars. "I stayed up worrying that the kids didn't climb out the windows." She would never
forget how she felt when she first saw that hotel room. "I remember the feeling of despair.
I cried the whole night."[15]

McCain had come to live in the Martinique in 1982 because she and her family were
homeless. Separated from her abusive husband and with little income besides a welfare
payment, Yvonne had been evicted from her home for withholding rent from a landlord
who refused to make repairs. After applying to the city for assistance, she was assigned to
the Martinique. She and her family would spend the next four years at the hotel.[16]

McCain and her children were hardly alone. By June 1983, 2,042 families, twice the
number of the year before, were living in places such as the Martinique, the Holland, the
Prince George, or dozens of other "welfare hotels" or city shelters. Overwhelmed, the city
even resorted to placing 300 families in New Jersey hotels. This no longer appeared to be a
temporary increase in family homelessness; a crisis had overtaken New York.[17]

McCain, for one, did not become resigned to her fate. She agreed to be a named plaintiff in the Legal Aid Society's suit against the city. As *McCain v. Koch* made its way through the courts, demanding that families never be placed in conditions such as those in the Martinique, the city, in fits and starts, developed a more coherent and humane approach to family homelessness.[18]

In the 1980s the process of requesting shelter from the city was hardly inviting. All families in need of shelter had to appear at a single Emergency Assistance Unit (EAU) in Manhattan. There, they would wait for hours, sometimes days, for placements in hotels or shelters. Many families would be sent to congregate shelters before being assigned long-term placements. One man, an evicted former maintenance worker who had struggled to balance working and caring for his children, confronted the dynamics of the congregate shelter. "So I'm alone there in this place with about 200 cots packed side by side. Men and women, children," the man explained to the journalist Jonathan Kozol, "all together. No dividers. There's no curtains and no screens. I have to dress my kids with people watching. When my girls go to the toilet I can't take them and they're scared to go alone." The man eventually lost his job because he refused to leave his kids alone at the shelter when he went to work.[19]

The bureaucratic process would sometimes drive people to their wits' end. Susan, a pregnant woman, arrived at the EAU with her husband seeking shelter. While she was waiting for her placement, she noticed a sign on the wall warning that the Catherine Street Shelter was unsafe for children and pregnant women. In spite of the warning, Susan was assigned to Catherine Street, but when she arrived at the shelter she was refused admittance and returned to the EAU. After she waited a second time at the EAU, caseworkers assigned her once again to the Catherine Street Shelter. This put Susan over the edge. "I wouldn't go. They put me in handcuffs ... They said I was upset," she later recalled to Kozol. Finally, at two in the morning, the EAU found a placement for Susan and her husband at a shelter in Queens.[20]

Placement in welfare hotels, along with the rules of public assistance, had destructive effects on families. Many women receiving AFDC or other public-assistance funds chose to keep their husbands' or other partners' earnings out of their welfare budgets. This way, any earnings a man brought into the home would not count against the welfare allowance. Keeping a cohabiting man hidden from a caseworker was already difficult when a family had its own housing; in the closely observed welfare hotels, it became almost impossible. Annie, a woman with debilitating asthma who was inexplicably placed on the fourteenth floor of the elevator-less Martinique Hotel, had her husband secretly living in a room with her four children. Since her asthma was so bad, Annie could not easily go up and down the fourteen flights to sign her husband in, forcing him to sneak past the guards in

A young resident of the Holland Hotel pretends to be Superman.
New York Daily News Archive/Getty Images.

order to live with his family. Another woman, Holly, who had recently given birth to an underweight and severely compromised son, was kicked out of the Martinique because of her husband's attempt to live with her and her children. Eventually, the baby was released from the hospital and joined the family in another welfare hotel, the Mayfair; after five weeks the family was again evicted. While Holly and her family waited for days in the EAU for another placement, her newborn son contracted a virus, which led to his death. Along with strict enforcement of the rules, the stress that homelessness created also led to family dissolution. In another case at the Martinique, a mother, faced with little hope of ever providing for her family, abandoned her three children to the care of her mother and turned to prostitution to support herself.[21]

It was the destructive effect of these experiences and the physical conditions of the hotels themselves that led Legal Aid to go to court on behalf of Yvonne McCain and her children and a class of similarly situated homeless families. In June 1983 the court issued

Parks Department workers remove homeless encampments from Tompkins Square Park. The city's approach to homeless families remained distinct from their policies for homeless individuals. *New York Daily News Archive/Getty Images.*

an interim order requiring that once a family had been deemed eligible for emergency shelter, the city must "assure, insofar as practicable, that such housing meets specified minimal standards of health, safety and decency suitable for young children." Three months later the state Department of Social Services promulgated an administrative directive, 83 ADM-47, requiring that the city provide emergency shelter for homeless families or provide written notice explaining why their requests for assistance had been denied. In 1986 the court issued an injunction requiring that the city follow the state administrative directive and immediately cease holding families indefinitely in the EAU. In response to these rulings, New York City was forced to develop a more robust system for serving homeless families, one that could investigate their need for shelter, provide decent temporary shelter, and eventually transition families into permanent housing.[22]

As the state courts and legislature pushed the city to provide more extensive care for the homeless, the dimensions of family homelessness in the city were becoming evident. Between 1983 and 1987, six families entered shelter for every five that exited. By late 1986 the number of homeless families had grown to more than 4,500, and the average length of stay had increased to thirteen months. In that year the number of homeless people, including families and single adults, surpassed the level reached in 1936, in the midst of the Great Depression. While the nation's economy entered a period of prosperity, New York's homelessness problem showed no signs of ebbing.[23]

The pressure on the city to reform its homelessness policies increased from several sources. Already the state courts were ordering city officials to remove families from particularly "inhumane" welfare hotels.[24] In 1987 the Reagan administration stated that it would withhold funding for homeless shelters if the city continued to place families in welfare hotels. In early 1988 Jonathan Kozol published a series of articles in the *New Yorker,* later collected in the book *Rachel and Her Children,* depicting the inhumane conditions in the welfare hotels and the heart-wrenching experiences of hotel residents. That same year the Citizens' Committee for Children of New York focused attention on the congregate shelters, finding that 672 children still lived in these barracks-style structures, with the vast majority remaining in them for more than the legal maximum of twenty-one days. Public opinion began to demand that Koch provide acceptable care for homeless families.[25]

Advocates for the homeless were divided about the best approach to this crisis. Some saw homelessness as primarily a housing problem; if the city could provide more housing that was affordable to low-income families, they postulated, then family homelessness would decline. Other activists called for more high-quality transitional shelters, similar to Henry Street's Urban Family Center, that would offer services and training for homeless parents to help resolve the issues that had pushed them into homelessness in the first place and ensure greater economic opportunity for the future. Koch's approach split the difference in this debate, adopting elements of both approaches.[26]

In 1985, even before the state administrative directive and the McCain decision, Mayor Koch announced the most ambitious proposal of his administration: a five-year, multibillion-dollar program to build more than 100,000 units of low- and moderate-income housing. Later, this program was expanded, with plans to provide 252,000 units by 1996, 10 percent of those reserved for formerly homeless families. Many would be created by renovating the 102,000 units seized by the city through the tax-foreclosure process. In 1986 the city placed more than 2,900 homeless families in such rehabilitated apartments. The city also increased funding to the Emergency Assistance Rehousing Program (EARP), offering incentives to landlords who signed leases with homeless families. The rise in the number of units was intended to provide an affordable alternative means of keeping families out of the shelter system as well as create housing that other families could move into once they exited shelters.[27]

At the same time, Koch proposed the creation of an extensive transitional-shelter system that would quickly move families out of the congregate shelters and reduce the city's reliance on welfare hotels. These shelters, known as Tier II facilities to distinguish them

A groundbreaking ceremony in the Bronx, June 1988. The Koch administration built and renovated low-income housing. *New York Daily News Archive/Getty Images.*

from the Tier I congregate facilities, would provide a service-rich environment to prepare families to successfully transition back into permanent housing. In 1986 Koch proposed constructing fifteen Tier II shelters on city-owned land across the five boroughs. His plan quickly met with opposition from other politicians. The public was outraged by the city's earlier handling of the homelessness crisis, but few embraced the opening of new homeless shelters in their neighborhoods. After making a deal with Borough Presidents Ralph Lamberti of Staten Island and David Dinkins of Manhattan to limit the shelters in their boroughs, Koch reduced the number of new shelters to eleven, with only seven exclusively for families. Meanwhile, Koch encouraged the development of nonprofit transitional shelters funded by a combination of private donations and public money, some in buildings that had formerly housed welfare hotels.[28]

Koch's two-pronged approach—developing housing and expanding transitional shelters—met with widespread resistance. Critics on the right argued that Koch's plan was not sufficiently market oriented. Those on the left felt that the plan did not provide enough low-income housing to assist the poor and homeless. The most trenchant criticism came from a task force commissioned by Manhattan Borough President David Dinkins and led by former HRA administrator James Dumpson. *A Shelter Is Not a Home,* the task force's March 1987 report, attacked the Koch administration for the "crisis oriented framework which continues to characterize policy towards homelessness." The task force argued that family homelessness was created by escalating poverty along with a shortage of affordable places to live and could be solved only by building more permanent low-income housing. Koch's plan to build fifteen more family homeless shelters, then, was a misallocation of resources. Instead, the city should double the number of affordable housing units it planned to build from 4,000 to 8,000 and create a more generous welfare-shelter allowance that would let poor families remain in renovated apartments. This report encapsulated the "housing first" approach to homeless families, based in the belief that shelters did more harm than good and that the expansion of affordable housing would eventually end family homelessness.[29]

Koch rejected the recommendations of Dinkins's task force as simply too expensive. Meanwhile, his plan to expand the city's system of transitional shelters ran aground on

David Dinkins (right) and Ed Koch shake hands in front of a crowd. Koch served three terms as mayor of New York City before Dinkins defeated him in the 1989 Democratic Primary. Koch restored fiscal stability to the city but was perceived by many advocates as unsympathetic to the needs of the poor and minorities. *New York Daily News Archive/Getty Images.*

the rocky shores of local interests. In October 1987 the borough presidents of Brooklyn, Queens, and the Bronx wrote a scathing op-ed article in the *New York Times* attacking Koch's proposal to construct new homeless shelters. Building on the arguments developed in *A Shelter Is Not a Home,* they asked the mayor, "Why spend millions to build shelters when those funds could be used to build permanent housing?" The three politicians echoed what they heard from "community residents, advocates for the homeless, and the homeless themselves"; in effect, these elected officials were channeling a growing senti-ment among New Yorkers that supported policies to assist the homeless but opposed any programs that would bring homeless shelters into their neighborhoods.[30]

Koch's critics would have a chance to put their ideas into practice. In 1989 David Din-kins successfully challenged Koch for the Democratic nomination for mayor. Among the charges Dinkins had leveled at the sitting mayor was that he had continued to rely on the welfare hotels and that he was out of touch with the needs of the city's poor. Dinkins went on to win the general election with Koch's nominal support. The opposition to shelter con-struction within many of New York's neighborhoods, often exploited by Dinkins and other politicians, had seriously retarded the development of a coherent homelessness policy. Of the twenty transitional shelters Koch had proposed, only one had opened and six were under construction when Koch's tenure as mayor came to an end, in January 1990.[31]

In his last year in office, Koch's homelessness and housing policies finally began to pay dividends. The city placed more than 2,000 families in refurbished apartments in formerly *in rem* buildings, structures seized by the city for nonpayment of taxes. Dinkins, in keep-ing with his drive for permanent housing, continued this policy, placing an additional 1,900 families in such apartments — numbered among the 4,437 families that were moved into permanent housing in 1990. Other families in the shelter system received priority for housing subsidies and public-housing placements. In response to these policies, the shelter

A mother plays with her two boys in their room in a Tier II shelter facility. Tier II shelters meet safety and health standards and offer services to help families transition to permanent housing. *The New York Times/Redux Pictures.*

census dropped to 3,196, its lowest level since the mid-1980s. Additionally, the Dinkins administration managed to lower the number of families in welfare hotels to an average of 358 for fiscal year 1990. This was a significant reduction from the average of 1,876 in the last year of Koch's administration, evidence of a concerted effort to reduce the city's dependence on hotels.[32]

That progress, however, was short-lived. Starting in 1991 the numbers of homeless families seeking shelter in New York City began to tick upwards again, and by 1993 there were 5,500 families in shelter, including 1,159 in welfare hotels. The family homelessness problem had returned to the levels seen in the late 1980s. The reasons for this increase were several: the fact that the city made homelessness the primary path to subsidized housing enticed families in inadequate living conditions to enter the shelter system; the greater number of high-quality Tier II shelters made the family shelter system a more attractive alternative than crowded and decrepit housing; and an economic recession and the consequent rise in unemployment and poverty pushed more families into housing crises.[33]

For some women, like Coco, a young mother with two small children and pregnant with a third, entering the family shelter system appeared to provide a path to independence. Finding that living with her mother, a chronic drug addict, her abusive stepfather, her younger brother, and her children in a small apartment in the Bronx was no longer tenable, Coco appealed to the city for shelter for herself and her kids. As she explained to the journalist Adrian Nicole LeBlanc, her older brother and sister and their families had previously "gone homeless," and Coco believed that entering the shelter system would lead to subsidized housing or even a coveted spot in a public housing project. Coco arrived at the intake center with a friend to help care for her children as she explained that she had no place to live. Since she was pregnant, Coco qualified for emergency placement and was quickly sent to Thorpe House on Crotona Avenue in the Bronx. Sixteen families lived in the "4-story tawny brick building" run by Dominican nuns. Coco's apartment, with two bedrooms, a kitchen, and a living room, represented a significant improvement in her living conditions. But even with her housing and utilities taken care of by Thorpe House and with WIC (the federal food program for pregnant women, infants, and children) helping to subsidize the family's food budget, Coco's welfare payment was still stretched thin. Part of that was due to Coco's generosity — she might loan a neighbor $10 even if it meant she wouldn't have enough for busfare — and her loyalty to her original family: she gave WIC tickets to her mom.

In order to qualify for shelter, welfare, and WIC, Coco had an endless number of appointments. During weekly meetings the nuns monitored the cleanliness of her apartment, inspected the food she was providing for her family, and gave advice to prepare her for living on her own. She had to sign in twice a month to collect WIC payments and

Mayor David Dinkins and a young boy in the South Bronx. New York City's first African-American mayor, Dinkins served from 1990 to 1994. Dinkins confronted a major homelessness crisis in his time in office. *New York Daily News Archive/Getty Images.*

make periodic visits to the welfare office for recertification. Eventually Coco was scheduled to move into an apartment through the Special Initiative Program, subsidized housing where she would still receive services, but she soon realized that the providers of these apartments were even more invasive than the nuns at Thorpe. Burdened with caring for an infant, and now secretly pregnant with a fourth child, Coco instead requested a Section 8 voucher and moved into the first apartment she saw. The dirty, drug-filled, dark and dangerous building was not what Coco had in mind when she dreamed of living independently. Soon, she decided to move back into her mother's crowded apartment, the place she had hoped to escape.[34]

The increase in the number of families, like Coco's, seeking shelter outpaced the administration's efforts to move families into permanent housing. The optimism that Dinkins officials had expressed about solving the city's family homelessness problem quickly faded. "I still do not believe that hotels or congregate shelters are good for families and children," Nancy Wackstein, the head of the office of homelessness in HRA, explained, "but I have a better understanding as to why the prior administration had been forced to use these facilities." She continued, "Homelessness is a problem that has some known solutions, but very expensive solutions, and that is what will not happen."[35] Dinkins put in place some new initiatives, such as the Alternative Pathways program, that attempted to funnel poor families on public-housing waiting lists into city-renovated apartments once reserved for homeless families. The goal was to find stable housing for poor families before, not after, they entered homeless shelters. The number of apartments available under this program, however, did little to stem the tide of families seeking shelter. By September 1991 the administration had become desperate to stop the flow of families into the shelter system. In a move uncharacteristic of the liberal Dinkins, the city declared it would explore methods to investigate eligibility of families seeking shelter. The mayor also announced that he was forming a commission of experts to be headed by Andrew Cuomo, the governor's son and the leader of the transitional-housing organization HELP, to provide a new direction for the city's homelessness policy.[36]

The Cuomo Commission, as it came to be known, and its 1992 report, *The Way Home: A New Direction in Social Policy,* would establish the outline of homelessness policy in New York City for the next decade. The commission, made up of business leaders, academics, government officials, and social-service providers, conducted a thorough investigation in

An East Village housing project. *Jonathan Elderfield, Getty Images.*

order to provide coherent plans for alleviating homelessness among families and single adults. In its report, the commission rejected the notion that homelessness policy was a stark choice between more services and more permanent housing. The city needed to create more affordable housing, but it also needed to provide services that matched the specific needs of the homeless. For homeless families, this meant an improved intake process that identified a family's primary needs. While some families might be directed immediately to subsidized permanent housing, most would be directed to a "transitional program," a shelter where they could receive appropriate services that would lead to "self-sufficiency and independence." This approach would create an "intelligent continuum of care" for homeless families.[37]

The commission made specific recommendations to the city for implementing the continuum. The city should close the Tier I emergency congregate shelters and encourage the creation of a range of transitional shelters under private, not-for-profit operators. This would effectively end the city's role as a shelter provider but allow the city to oversee policy through contracts with private providers, agreements that would include performance-based incentives. The commission recommended the creation of a new city agency, independent of HRA, to oversee the homelessness-prevention system; following this suggestion, the Dinkins administration created the Department of Homeless Services (DHS). The commission also called on the city to increase its programs for homelessness prevention and develop a new rental subsidy to expand affordable housing and help move families out of the shelter system. The Cuomo Commission did not see homelessness as a temporary crisis, as the Koch administration had, or as an easily solved problem of housing shortage, as the Dinkins administration did; instead, it viewed homelessness as an ongoing urban challenge.[38] The future of homelessness policy, however, would be closely tied to public policy for poor families and attempts to develop a more streamlined and work-oriented welfare system.

Poverty and Homelessness in the Age of Welfare Reform

In 1982 the Manhattan Institute, a conservative think tank funded by a British industrialist, hired a newly minted political-science Ph.D. named Charles Murray. The Institute had recently gained renown in conservative circles for the publication of George Gilder's *Wealth and Poverty*, a wide-ranging paean to entrepreneurship that struck a chord with the new Reagan administration.[39] Murray set to work on an investigation of social policy that would be published in 1984 as *Losing Ground*. Seeing the rampant poverty across the country, Murray asked why, after billions of dollars of federal spending on welfare, the problem still existed. His answer was that welfare itself had contributed to longstanding poverty. Murray painted a compelling portrait of a fictional couple, Harold and Phyllis, working-class high-school graduates who are expecting a baby. Based on the welfare rules of 1960, Murray argued, Harold and Phyllis would get married and look for work to support their new family; in 1970, however, the welfare incentives would lead them to live together unmarried and choose welfare and other social-assistance programs over work. For Murray, then, the roots of the so-called underclass were not in cultural pathology but instead in rational choices made by people facing the perverse incentives of an irrational system.[40]

The way to reduce poverty, the libertarian Murray concluded, was — counter-intuitively — to peel back the welfare state. "It was wrong," Murray argued, "to take from the most industrious, most responsible poor — take safety, education, justice, status — so that we could cater to the least industrious, least responsible poor. It was wrong to impose rules that made it rational for adolescents to behave in ways that destroyed their futures. The changes we made were not just policy errors, not just expedient, but unjust." Removing the entire set of social-assistance programs for working-class people, including AFDC, Medicaid, food stamps, unemployment insurance, and workers' compensation, would incentivize people to find work and to marry securely. Ending welfare would be better, Murray suggested, not only for taxpayers but also for the poor themselves.[41]

Murray's book became the bible for a new conservative view of social policy. While a library's worth of books and articles were written that questioned his data, his timeline of policy history, his analysis, and his conclusions, Murray's portrait of Harold and Phyllis as rational actors in a dysfunctional welfare system would have a lasting influence.[42] The Manhattan Institute, based in liberal, social-democratic New York City, would use this book as a beachhead to launch an attack on urban social policy. In interpreting the urban crisis that had raged since the late 1970s, these conservatives rejected theories of socioeconomic causes of poverty espoused by liberals, who blamed such factors as deindustrialization, racism, and white flight. Instead, they saw a crisis of values created by Great Society liberalism, the black militancy of the 1960s, and, most importantly, a failed welfare state that perpetuated dependency.[43]

As this new, conservative view of social-welfare policies gained currency, even liberal social-welfare experts began to frame their research around the notion of dependency. In 1983 Harvard economists Mary Jo Bane and David Ellwood drafted a paper that tracked welfare dependency among low-income households. Their findings were sobering; while most welfare recipients received public assistance for only a short time, at any given time long-term welfare recipients made up the majority of the rolls. Furthermore, long-term recipients and those who frequently returned to public assistance accounted for nearly two-thirds of welfare costs. Bane and Ellwood's analysis showing that short-term welfare recipients were more likely white, divorced, and comparatively well-educated, while long-term recipients were more likely black, never-married single mothers who had dropped out of high school, added fodder to the belief in widespread dependency among the minority poor.[44]

The work of sociologist William Julius Wilson added further support to the growing view of a crisis of dependency. In his 1987 book, *The Truly Disadvantaged*, Wilson traced the dynamics of what he termed "the ghetto underclass." While Wilson blamed structural economic forces for the creation of a large, mostly black unemployed population in the nation's cities, he argued that an alternative culture among those essentially cut off from mainstream society contributed to such features as changes in family structure. Wilson, an avowed social democrat, called for broad government intervention to undo the structural elements that had created the underclass. In the political environment of the 1980s and 1990s, such policy suggestions were untenable. Instead, David Ellwood provided a centrist direction for welfare reform. First, a new non-welfare program (not, that is, AFDC) was needed to supplement the income of the working poor; in other words, to help "make work pay." Second, AFDC needed to be reformed — to become time-limited and to increase

Workfare required welfare recipients to participate in job-training programs. Here, a workfare participant works in the garment industry. *Michael L. Abramson, Time & Life Images Collection, Getty Images.*

child support from noncustodial parents. Finally, single mothers should have intensive work training to move them from the welfare rolls to the ranks of the working poor. Federal legislation, introduced by Senator Daniel Patrick Moynihan and passed in 1988, adopted many of Ellwood's suggestions by encouraging AFDC recipients to transition to work and making fathers financially responsible for their noncustodial children.[45]

In 1992 Bill Clinton, the centrist Democratic governor of Arkansas, was elected president, partly on the promise to "end welfare as we know it." Reforming social assistance in the U.S. would become one of the central goals of his administration. In 1993 Congress passed, with Clinton's urging, an expansion of the Earned Income Tax Credit. This credit, provided through the standard IRS tax filing, was originally created in 1975 to compensate workers for wages lost from Social Security taxes. It was expanded several times over the 1980s, but the 1993 revision provided nearly $15 billion a year in new cash benefits for poor and low-income workers. In essence, the Clinton administration had quietly created a negative income tax for the working poor, an alternative "non-welfare" program to support poor working families outside of AFDC — the program that reformers such as Ellwood had envisioned.[46] The next step in reshaping social welfare, reforming AFDC, proved much more contentious. Seeing Clinton's campaign pledge as an opening for wholesale recasting of the welfare system, Republicans in Congress demanded a new welfare program with strict time limits, work requirements, and incentives for marriage. Clinton vetoed welfare-reform legislation three times before finally signing the Personal Responsibility and Work Opportunity Act of 1996. Some members of his administration, including the co-author of the report on welfare dependency, Mary Jo Bane, who had served as an assistant secretary in the Department of Health and Human Services, resigned in protest over what they viewed as the draconian measures in the act.[47]

The 1996 welfare reform replaced AFDC with a new program called Temporary Assistance for Needy Families (TANF). While AFDC had been a matching grant, setting nationwide rules and minimum benefit levels, TANF was a block grant allowing states to create their own eligibility rules and set requirements for recipients as a condition of support. Still, particular features of TANF were required across all states. There was a lifetime five-year limit on receiving benefits. There was a requirement that states move progressively more recipients, eventually reaching 50 percent, to work or work activities for thirty hours a week. And there were benefit reductions as sanctions for those who refused to comply with work requirements.[48]

The experience of families living in New York City did not always match the prescriptions emerging from Washington. Rather than being wholly disconnected from the world of work, poor families often pooled resources with networks of relatives and friends, combining welfare assistance with job earnings. Kyesha was a twenty-one-year-old, African

American single mother in Harlem who earned $5 an hour working in a fast-food restaurant. This was not nearly enough to provide for herself and her son, Anthony. But Kyesha lived in public housing with her mother, Dana, an AFDC recipient with seven children of her own, who provided free child care for Kyesha. In a sense, Dana was an unofficial state-funded child care worker, while Kyesha reciprocated by contributing her earnings to the household she shared with her mother. Once welfare reform forced Dana to engage in full-time work, Kyesha would have to either cut back her work hours or pay for child care, creating a net loss in the income of the household. Reynaldo Linaro's experience as an AFDC recipient demonstrated both his continued interaction with the labor market and the shortcomings of the welfare rules. Reynaldo, a high-school student of Puerto Rican and Ecuadorian descent living in Washington Heights, worked odd jobs as a stock boy, electrician, and amateur car mechanic to contribute to his family's income. He lived with both his parents, who were technically divorced so his mom could receive AFDC payments. While his mother had once worked in a factory, she was now attending college courses and receiving only welfare payments as income. Reynaldo's father worked in the underground economy as an "off-the-books contractor," mostly for landlords who refused to pay union wages for repairs to their properties. The stories of Kyesha and Reynaldo exemplified many people's efforts to take advantage of, and sometimes bend, the welfare rules to make the system work for their families, but they did not demonstrate an avoidance of or disconnection from the world of work.[49]

Still, work became the central component of welfare reform under the administration of Mayor Rudolph Giuliani. A lawyer, Giuliani had found great success as an official in the Department of Justice under Presidents Ford and Reagan and as a U.S. attorney in New York, where he prosecuted a large number of high-profile cases. He was not a traditional Republican, having grown up a loyal Democrat, but had migrated to the Republican Party after coming to the belief that liberal views on crime and social policy lacked vigor. He was particularly attracted to the neoconservative perspective on urban policy that emerged from the Manhattan Institute. Armed with these ideas, Giuliani decided to run for mayor, losing to Democratic nominee Dinkins in 1989 before beating him four years later.[50]

At the core of Giuliani's tenure as mayor was a desire to improve the quality of life in New York City. Giuliani focused much of his attention on decreasing crime. He instated a citywide, computerized data system to keep track of local crime trends. He cracked down on petty crime, increasing arrests, and cleared panhandlers off the streets. Operating on the theory that attacking minor criminal activity would reduce the incidence of major crimes—a theory promulgated by the Manhattan Institute—Giuliani attempted to rid the city of the criminal annoyances that New Yorkers had learned to live with. By the end of his time in office, Giuliani would point to the reduction in crime as one of his greatest

accomplishments. In 1993, the last year of the Dinkins administration, there were 430,460
crimes reported; in 2000 there were only 184,111. In 1993 there were 1,927 homicides; in
2000 there were only 671. The administration credited its policies for this decrease; some
criminologists countered that the end of the crack epidemic and the booming of the economy of the 1990s also contributed, pointing to the falling crime rates in cities that did not
follow Giuliani's policies. The mayor's fiercest critics accused him of creating a police state.[51]

The economic boom of the 1990s also helped Giuliani in his efforts to remake the
city by cleaning up seedy corners, encouraging business, and subsidizing development.
Over the 1990s the city's population grew by more than 450,000, to an unprecedented size
of more than eight million people. New immigrants from China, Korea, India, Vietnam,
Guyana, Colombia, Ecuador, and Mexico joined native middle-class pioneers looking
for opportunity in the big city. This expansion of prosperity across New York, as well as
efforts to make the city more livable, had, however, unintended consequences. As service
jobs in the financial and tourism industries proliferated, poor New Yorkers with low skill
levels struggled to find work at decent wages. Gentrification, a process encouraged by the
city since the late 1970s, took root in the Giuliani years, with mostly white, middle-class

Jason Turner, 2000. Human Resources Administration Commissioner Jason Turner speaks at
the opening of the Coney Island job center. Mayor Rudolph Giuliani stands behind him.
Turner spearheaded workfare efforts in New York City. *New York Daily News Archive/Getty Images.*

residents rehabilitating large sections of previously depressed neighborhoods in Brooklyn and Manhattan. As the middle class spread across the city, more and more poor families struggled to find affordable housing. The quality of life of the poorest New Yorkers did not appear to improve under Giuliani.[52]

Even before the federal welfare reform of 1996, Giuliani was committed to pushing welfare recipients into the world of work. After he became mayor, in 1994, Giuliani—with the assistance of Governor George Pataki, elected later that year—worked to cut the city budget for social services to the poor and create stricter eligibility requirements for welfare, food stamps, and emergency shelter service. The mayor also focused his attention on Home Relief, New York State's program of public assistance, which provided for families and individuals ineligible for AFDC. In 1995 the state legislature, at Pataki's urging, passed new rules for Home Relief requiring that all able-bodied recipients participate in work programs in order to continue receiving payments. The Giuliani administration boasted that between 1995 and 1998 welfare and food-stamp caseloads declined by 30 percent.[53]

This decline, however, came at a cost to poor families. Welfare applicants were intimidated, abused, and often unjustly turned away when seeking assistance. The city looked for any excuse to eliminate someone from the welfare rolls. In July 1995, to deter fraud, the city required all potential aid recipients to be fingerprinted. That continued even after the city found that 99.7 percent of recipients were making legitimate claims for assistance. In one particularly striking case, the city rejected a homeless man's request for Medicaid because the address he provided—part of an arrangement he had worked out since he had no permanent address—was not his place of residence. In cases like this, potential recipients had to go through a lengthy appeal process, often with the aid of a nonprofit social-service agency, to receive the benefits to which they were entitled.[54]

Considering the rhetoric used by both Giuliani and Pataki, the welfare legislation passed in New York in 1997 to implement TANF was relatively moderate. Some states instituted family sanctions, an approach Pataki favored, which denied benefits to an entire family if the mother did not meet her work requirement. This feature was not passed by the New York legislature. Other states imposed family caps, creating a maximum welfare benefit no matter the size of the household. This was also rejected in New York. Nonetheless, the 1997 law spelled the end of New York State's long-standing Home Relief program, replacing it with the Safety Net program, which provided cash assistance for up to two years and non-cash vouchers, with no time limit, for food, shelter, and other needs.[55]

Empowered by the new state and federal laws, Giuliani made the bold pledge "to end welfare by the end of this century completely." Technically, the mayor made no promise to truly end public assistance, a policy change outside his authority. Instead, he was suggesting that the entire population of adult welfare recipients be required to enter the workforce. To implement this plan, Giuliani hired Jason Turner, one of the architects of Wisconsin's revolutionary welfare reforms, to lead the Human Resources Administration. Turner was deeply committed to transforming welfare to workfare — he had designed his first workfare plan while in junior high school — and saw work as much more than a source of income. Work, according to Turner, provided structure that ordered people's lives and had the rehabilitative power to solve whatever problems welfare recipients faced. For an individual with little work experience, Turner postulated, "the best preparation for work is working." For the welfare recipient who could not speak English, Turner suggested, "the best way to learn English is to interact with English-speaking people in a work-place." And for the recipient struggling with substance abuse, Turner asserted, "treatment is not a substitute for work." For Giuliani the commitment to work had multiple benefits: it would overturn the "perverted social philosophy" that began in the 1960s and had created generations of welfare dependents, and it would also reduce the welfare rolls and the enormous cost of public assistance for the city.[56]

Reorienting the massive bureaucracy of HRA toward a new, work-focused approach was no easy task. The agency was notoriously disorganized. A quarter of its case records were simply missing. In one of its offices, files were piled six feet high. To signal the transformation the city renamed its thirty-one welfare offices — formerly "income maintenance centers" — "job centers." Turner then went about remaking the entire procedure of applying for aid. A person could not apply for assistance upon arriving at the job center. Instead he or she had to wait, sometimes for up to five or six hours, to meet with a "financial planner," who looked for alternatives — such as seeking support from family — to requesting public aid. Then, the applicant had to return to the job center a second day to begin the official application process. For at least the next month, the applicant had to participate in a supervised job search. Any missed appointment without an approved excuse could void the entire application. While the applicant completed that process, a strengthened fraud-detection office screened the application and made a home visit. Forty percent of those applying failed the screening, mostly due to minor infractions or missed appointments with investigators. That, along with the work-focused culture of the job centers, had created a significant decline in the welfare rolls. Under Mayor Dinkins about three-quarters of the applicants for welfare received assistance. With the new job centers, Giuliani had reduced that fraction to one-quarter.[57]

Pushing welfare applicants into work created some success stories. Carmen Espinosa, for example, had spent 14 years on welfare, suffering with a bad back that prevented her from working. With so little experience, Espinosa had feared applying for any job, even an entry-level position at a fast-food restaurant. The city's workfare program decided she was well enough to work and assigned her to volunteer in the kitchen of a day care

Workfare programs sometimes failed to prepare people for living-wage jobs. Here, workfare participants clean streets for the Department of Sanitation in 1997. *©Najlah Feanny/Corbis SABA.*

center. Espinosa was shocked when, a few months later, the day care center hired her for a $9-an-hour position. Turner's determination to reject most excuses, including physical and mental illness, to avoid work requirements seemed to pay off in this case. In other instances, applicants spent months arguing with caseworkers over whether they were fit to work and what types of tasks they could perform. The diagnosis of the city's doctors usually trumped the evaluations of the patients' own physicians.[58]

The new, work-oriented policy placed high expectations on relief recipients. For some, these expectations bordered on unreasonable. According to workfare rules, even individuals going to school were required to participate in twenty hours of work activity per week. HRA was particularly suspicious when it found that of the 12,000 recipients taking classes, 5,000 had claimed they were unable to work due to illness. The agency called each of those applicants in to screen them for workfare. For forty-three-year-old Maureen Scott, work—for all its supposedly redemptive power—became a hindrance in her efforts to improve her earning potential. Scott, who had worked for nearly twenty years as a beautician and a nursing aide, left her husband in early 1998, after he physically assaulted her, breaking the bones around her right eye. On her own with two children to support, Scott realized that her $7.50-an-hour part-time job would no longer cover her expenses. She decided she had to earn a high-school equivalency degree if she was ever to make ends meet. Still wearing bandages from her injuries, Scott entered a GED program. "I couldn't even see," she recalled. "I was that determined to help myself." When the city's twenty-hour work requirement forced her to drop out of her all-day class, Scott was despondent. "How am I going to face my children, working in the streets?" she wondered. "Might as well call my husband, take the beating and let him pay the rent—they're doing the same thing to me."[59]

While the rules of welfare reform seemed to work against some people's efforts to improve themselves, they also failed to rehabilitate all those who were dependent on welfare. Lester Collins, a twenty-five-year-old man living in his mother's apartment in a Coney Island public housing project, was one of the first to enter the new Greenwood Job Center in Brooklyn. In less than a year, Collins had applied for welfare on nine occasions, not including the times he didn't get far enough to submit an official application, but had failed to remain on the rolls. Once, when he was actually placed in a workfare program, he quit after being assigned to clean a public bathroom. Collins demonstrated that the liberal critics may have overstated the case in claiming that those diverted from welfare might starve. He survived on odd jobs, government support in the form of food stamps and public housing, and the generosity of his mother, herself scraping by on workfare. But Collins also showed that the loss of welfare did not automatically lead former recipients to reform their ways.[60]

While welfare reform convinced many applicants it was not worth their while to apply, those who did enter the program often found the work opportunities provided by the city severely limited. Among the adults who came off the welfare rolls between July 1996 and March 1997, only 29 percent found full- or part-time jobs.[61] Those placed in the city's Work Experience Program (WEP) would often stay in the same positions for years, even asking case workers if they could keep their jobs permanently. In one crew raking leaves in Prospect Park, four of the nine members had been at the same job for three years. "I like it out here," said one of the men. "If I was sitting at home, I wouldn't be doing nothing but looking at the four walls." But the man was not making an effort to find another job. "Work is hard to find," he explained.[62]

The limited opportunities through the Work Experience Program and the low wages for workfare recipients led to the creation of Workfairness, an organization dedicated to improving these conditions. Unions, fearing competition from publicly subsidized workers, also expressed unease with the program. In April 1997 Workfairness staged a massive rally demanding that WEP participants be given permanent jobs at union wages. "They want to work," explained one organizer. "They only really want to have real jobs at a living wage." Along with several unions, Workfairness went so far as to sue the city to demand that it unionize WEP workers, a demand to which Giuliani refused to acquiesce. Many

Girl waits for shelter inside the EAU. Under Mayor Giuliani, the city pursued a policy of discouraging entrance into the shelter system. The Emergency Assistance Unit, or EAU—the first step to shelter placement—was a notoriously unwelcoming environment for both children and adults. *The New York Times/Redux Pictures.*

economists feared that as workfare recipients "graduated," and were moved out of the program, this new supply of low-wage workers would have a deflationary effect on wages, decreasing the earnings for all of the working poor.[63]

Giuliani's approach to families too poor to find housing followed his general approach to social welfare; he discouraged families, as much as was allowed by law, from entering the city's shelter system. At the same time, the Giuliani administration worked to implement one of the major recommendations of the Cuomo Commission, placing more of those families who were found eligible for assistance in service-rich transitional shelters run by nonprofit organizations. By 1996, 72 percent of homeless families were living in such facilities. The mayor struggled to free the city from the requirements created by the state and the courts. Limited resources, reasoned Giuliani, should be reserved for those truly in need. Requests for shelter had to be thoroughly investigated, and the city needed to be able to turn away unqualified applicants for shelter. Slowly, the city gained greater control over the shelter system. In 1994 the state revised its rules to allow the city forty-eight hours to make eligibility evaluations. Two years later the courts gave the city the authority to reject families' requests for shelter if they could not prove their need. Armed with these new powers, the city routinely turned families away; the number of families denied entry increased from 894 in 1996 to 7,747 in 1997. In 1998, 14,401 families were rejected for placement in transitional shelters. These efforts appeared to reduce the number of families in shelter, from an average of 5,692 in 1996 to 4,558 in 1998. However, this decline proved temporary, as the numbers increased again from 1999 to 2001, the last three years of Giuliani's administration.[64]

The efforts to discourage the poor from seeking public assistance made life particularly difficult for those families suffering from real, acute crises. Brenda Lee Fields and her two children, Ty, aged three, and Loreal, seventeen, found themselves homeless after fleeing the Bronx apartment they shared with Brenda's abusive boyfriend. Following a brief stay with her brother on Long Island, Brenda turned to the city for shelter. Brenda had to run the medieval gauntlets of DHS to secure shelter and HRA to receive financial assistance. After convincing the city of her family's need for at least temporary shelter, Brenda was sent from the Emergency Assistance Unit in the Bronx, the city's sole intake center, to the Auburn Assessment Center, a temporary shelter in Fort Greene, Brooklyn, while DHS fraud investigators followed up on her case. The Auburn center was a former hospital turned into a makeshift shelter for homeless families. The large room in which

Mayor Michael Bloomberg with homeless children at an annual Christmas Eve lunch for homeless families. *Corbis Images.*

they placed Brenda was unpainted and smelled of mold. The bathroom, used by both men and women, lacked shower curtains but was complete with roaches that fell from the ceiling on those showering. Brenda made three more trips to the EAU before she was placed in transitional housing at the Jackson Avenue Family Center, back in the Bronx. She made another dozen trips to the welfare office prior to receiving cash benefits and food stamps. Ultimately, Brenda would find work and move into her own apartment, with the help of a Section 8 subsidy. It is hard to say whether her eventual success was due to the reforms in welfare and homeless services or came in spite of these reforms. Struggles like those faced by Brenda and her family became typical in the era of welfare reform.[65]

The Data-Driven City

On the last day of 2001, only months after the tragedy of September 11 scarred the Manhattan skyline, Rudy Giuliani's tenure as mayor of New York came to an end. His successor, financial-industry guru Michael Bloomberg, had received Giuliani's endorsement, promising to keep many of his policies in place. Data had made Michael Bloomberg a billionaire. In 1979 Bloomberg discovered the power of computers when he was assigned to the information-systems department at Salomon Brothers, the Wall Street firm where he had worked since 1966. Two years later, no longer a rising star at Salomon, he was let go; but with a $10 million severance package and new knowledge of how to use technology to analyze data in the financial industry, he had everything he needed. The company he founded, eventually named Bloomberg L.P., provided detailed financial information on proprietary terminals. Known as Bloomberg Boxes, they would become the standard source of data for the industry. With his election as mayor, Bloomberg planned to apply his data-driven pragmatism to public policy.[66]

In confronting poverty and homelessness, however, Bloomberg found his faith in the power of data and social science seriously tested. The Bloomberg administration saw every problem as solvable; however, due to the fiscal conservatism of the administration, the resources for social-policy initiatives remained capped, and the patience for allowing new programs to run their course was limited. Bloomberg maintained the basic structure of welfare provision put in place under Giuliani, but he attempted to use the city as a laboratory for experiments that would relieve or reduce poverty. This gave something of a schizophrenic character to Bloomberg's anti-poverty policies. The city's major welfare programs continued to deter applicants and force recipients into jobs with low wages and little opportunity for advancement. At the same time, the city's experiments looked to increase opportunities and create conditions that would lead to a better life for the children of the poor.

Bloomberg's rhetoric about welfare and poverty was softer than Giuliani's. "I will not walk away from my fundamental belief that there are those among us who desperately need help," Bloomberg declared soon after taking office. "That sometimes, through discrimination, happenstance or just plain indifference, some people are left out of the great opportunities that this country, state and city provide." Still, Bloomberg gave only lukewarm support to reforms such as replacing work requirements with education. It seemed that Bloomberg feared altering the approach that had successfully kept welfare rolls small.[67]

In limited experimental efforts, Bloomberg showed a greater willingness than Giuliani to investigate ways to create upward mobility for poor New Yorkers. In 2006 the mayor appointed a Commission on Economic Opportunity, chaired by social reformer Geoffrey Canada and businessman Richard Parsons. Drawing on a business perspective, they called for building human capital among the children of the poor, expanding efforts to "make work pay," and targeting the subsets of the poor from whom the city would see the most return on its investment.[68]

To implement the commission's recommendations, the mayor created the Center for Economic Opportunity. The hallmark of the center's programs was the conditional cash transfer program known as Opportunity NYC. Based on programs in Mexico and other countries with many poor and middle-income residents, Opportunity NYC provided financial incentives to parents, and in some cases to young people themselves, for actions that were thought to increase the children's human capital and future work opportunities. For example, the program gave payments to parents whose elementary-school-aged children attended 95 percent of scheduled school days, high-school students who passed the Regents exams, family members who had medical checkups, and parents who maintained full-time employment. In the program's first evaluation, in 2010, the results were decidedly mixed. The injection of cash into families' budgets certainly reduced their current hardships, and the incentives showed "substantial" increases in the numbers of poor families receiving preventive dental care. But the program did not improve the educational performance of elementary- or middle-school students. Somewhat abruptly after seeing these results, Bloomberg decided to pull the plug on the experiment. "If you never fail, I can tell you, you've never tried new, innovative things," the mayor explained. "And I don't know that this is a failure. I think … some things worked, and some things didn't, and some things the jury's still out on." Bloomberg would not wait to hear the finding of the jury; instead, as was his style, he would move on to another approach in hopes of seeing greater return on both public and philanthropic investment.[69]

With regard to policies for homeless families, the Bloomberg administration was similarly attracted to those programs that promised better results—more families in permanent housing—at lower costs. Dennis Culhane, a professor at the University of Pennsylvania, supplied the intellectual fuel for that policy shift. Culhane and his colleague Randall Kuhn studied the use of shelter by homeless individuals in Philadelphia and New York. Their conclusion was that 10 percent of the population, those they termed the chronic homeless, were taking up about half of the shelter capacity. The implication for policy, worked out by Culhane in his later writing, was that the chronically homeless should receive subsidized permanent housing with indefinite supportive services. As for other homeless individuals, efforts should be made to move them rapidly into affordable housing. Such a policy should reduce the total use of shelters and provide savings to the public.[70]

Bloomberg, supported by the George W. Bush administration, looked to implement this "housing first" approach not only for individuals, but for homeless families as well. According to members of the Bloomberg administration, transitional shelters had become providers of a wide range of services that needlessly duplicated other city services. "The overarching context of the 1990's was to have a decent and service-enriched shelter system," explained Mary Anne Schretzman, a DHS deputy commissioner. "As a consequence, shelters became safety nets for mainstream system failures, primary providers of addiction treatment and job rehabilitation, rather than an answer to emergency housing crises."[71] DHS commissioner Linda Gibbs put it more bluntly. The shelters, she asserted, "served [the] homeless, they didn't solve homelessness." Rather than continue the robust system of nonprofit transitional housing that had provided shelter and services for homeless families since the implementation of the Cuomo Commission plan, Gibbs and other Bloomberg officials looked to strengthen homelessness prevention while working to rapidly move homeless families into permanent housing with community-based social services. From Gibbs's perspective, up until the Bloomberg administration the city had simply been managing individual and family homelessness; her approach would end homelessness as a major problem in New York.[72]

Before Gibbs and Bloomberg could revolutionize the city's approach to family homelessness, they had to confront rapid growth in the number of families sheltered by the city. When Bloomberg took office, in January 2002, there were an unprecedented 6,992 families in city-provided shelter. By April 2003 that number had risen to 9,482. The first thing Commissioner Gibbs had to do was simply find space for all these families. Parents and children were forced to sleep on the floors and benches of the EAU, in open violation of court orders, as the city looked for temporary shelter. While the city continued to rely on the network of nonprofit transitional shelters, they also moved families into "scatter-site" apartments and hotels. These facilities had no standing contracts with the city, allowing the administration to quickly expand or contract shelter capacity, but without the guarantees for the quality of housing conditions and services that contracts with nonprofit shelters required. DHS also attempted to move families into permanent housing, especially by increasing the number of federal Section 8 vouchers available to homeless families. The number of sheltered families that moved into permanent housing went from 3,521 in fiscal year 2002, Bloomberg's first year in office, to 7,090 in fiscal year 2004, with Section 8 and NYCHA placements accounting for more than 80 percent of those moves. These policies, along with improvements in the economy, allowed the shelter census to decrease in 2004.[73]

With the city finally getting a handle on the homelessness issue, Bloomberg saw the opening for reform in this area. The task force he appointed in 2004 produced *Uniting for Solutions Beyond Shelter: The Action Plan for New York City.* Echoing the many ten-year plans to end homelessness developed by states and localities across the country, Bloom-

PATH Center, the Bronx, 2012. Mayor Michael Bloomberg's administration reformed the intake process for families seeking shelter, replacing the EAU with the Prevention Assistance and Temporary Housing (PATH) center, shown here. *Kate Slininger, ICPH Photo Archive.*

berg set his sights on the ambitious goal of reducing homelessness by two-thirds in five years. The report focused on preventing homelessness by increasing affordable housing and intervention to allow families to remain in their existing homes, minimizing housing disruptions through efficient intake evaluations, coordinating services, making informed decisions about shelter placements, and rapidly moving families out of shelter and into subsidized permanent housing. With an eye toward prevention, Bloomberg initiated a program called Homebase, which funded community-based nonprofit efforts to identify families at risk for homelessness and work with families and landlords to forestall eviction. While the city claimed that prevention was central to reducing homelessness — Bloomberg called Homebase "perhaps the most important element of our plan" — the funding for the program remained paltry, with prevention making up only 2.5 percent of the Department of Homeless Services' budget. Reforming the intake process seemed to take on more importance, at least symbolically, as the city closed the long-despised EAU and replaced it with the Prevention Assistance and Temporary Housing (PATH) office, also in the Bronx. As its name implied, this new facility was intended to help divert families from city-provided shelter or provide them with brief stays in shelter facilities before they were rehoused.[74]

Developing a program for assisting homeless families as they exited the shelter system would prove the most difficult task for the Bloomberg administration. Although in Bloomberg's first years in office the administration had seen success in reducing the number of families in shelter through the provision of federal Section 8 vouchers and public housing slots, DHS feared that these generous subsidies were actually drawing families into the shelter system. Commissioner Gibbs explained, "We wanted to free up the Section 8 and Housing Authority units in order to reward and encourage people to solve their housing problems without moving through the shelter system."[75] Gibbs hoped to divert families from entering the shelter system except under the most dire circumstances; unfortunately, each of the housing subsidies the city developed for that purpose was too little to move large numbers of homeless families to stable, permanent housing.

Housing Stability Plus (HSP), Bloomberg's first locally based housing subsidy, introduced in December 2004, suffered from numerous flaws. It was measly, 23 percent less than the federal Section 8 voucher, and it was tied to TANF, so if families lost their welfare payments they also lost their housing subsidies. While HSP contributed to a decrease in the number of families applying for shelter, it also led to a drop in the number successfully placed in permanent housing.[76] In April 2007 the city replaced HSP with the multipronged Advantage NY program. One part of this program, Work Advantage, provided a limited housing subsidy for families entering the workforce. This subsidy was more generous than HSP and was not tied to welfare eligibility. However, it had a time limit of only two years, shorter than that of HSP, and had an income ceiling so low that a family ran the risk of losing the subsidy if a parent found a full-time job. In 2010 the city scaled back its housing subsidy even further, and the number of families eligible for the program plummeted. When Governor Andrew Cuomo cut the funding source for the Advantage program, in 2011, the city made no effort to find another funding source or to develop an additional housing subsidy.[77]

During this succession of policies, the number of applications for shelter rose, as did the number of families in the system, despite efforts to limit eligibility. At the same time, the limitations of the subsidy programs made it difficult to move people out of transitional shelter. While the city did decrease the average length of stay for a family in shelter, the shelter census — which topped 10,000 by 2009 — spoke of a return to shelter for many families who had neither the economic nor the social supports to remain in permanent housing. More than five years after Bloomberg promised to reduce the homeless population, the number of homeless families had exploded due to the creeping recession that began in late 2007 and the failure of the administration's policies.[78]

Family Poverty in the Post–Welfare Reform Era

The 1996 welfare reform has been, in the eyes of some, a resounding success. By 2008 national participation in TANF for single mothers aged eighteen to fifty-four with a high-school education or less and no other adult earners in their households had dropped to 14 percent. At the same time, 68 percent of these single mothers were working. If welfare reform was intended to get women off public assistance and into the labor market, it seemed to have worked.[79] However, many of the single mothers at work remained in or near poverty, with few prospects for economic advancement. In New York City over 40 percent of female-headed single-parent households with at least one child under eighteen were below the poverty line. For married-couple families with a child under eighteen, by contrast, the poverty rate was below 15 percent. Many of these single mothers worked nonstandard schedules that made child care difficult and unreliable. Overall, the transition from welfare to work had not made their lives or the lives of their children any easier or more rewarding.[80] Furthermore, these families still relied on other public programs. While food-stamp applications decreased in the immediate aftermath of welfare reform, they rose again after the recession of 2001. In 2008 there were twenty-eight million nationwide enrolled in the food-stamp program — recently renamed SNAP (Supplemental Nutrition Assistance Program) — and only 3.8 million TANF recipients.[81]

While most single mothers appeared to at least get by in the post–welfare reform era, a certain segment of the population failed to thrive. Economist Rebecca M. Blank calculated that at least one-fifth of single mothers with incomes below 200 percent of the official poverty level received virtually no income from either work or welfare. Blank termed these most vulnerable of the poor "disconnected women." These women's families somehow made do with the support of some public programs, including Medicaid and food stamps; private support, such as food banks; and unreported gifts and other assistance from family members, boyfriends, and the fathers of their children. For most of these women, periods of disconnectedness from both work and welfare lasted for eight months or less. One of Blank's articles on this group of women, written with Brian Kovak, noted, "This is perhaps not surprising in a post–welfare-reform world. When welfare is less available to single mothers, their economic fortunes rise and fall with their labor market opportunities."[82]

As New York City struggles to recover from the damage of the Great Recession, the question of whether a reduced social-welfare system can truly provide for the most destitute families has yet to be resolved. The rising number of homeless families, the increasing reliance on food stamps, and the empty shelves in city food pantries all speak to growing needs unmet by both the public and private sectors.

Social critics often point to history—or at least a mythologized history—in their arguments about public policy. Some point to a nineteenth century in which neighbors cared for one another without public assistance. Others idealize the New Deal as a moment when the state finally took an interest in the well-being of its citizens. Still others cite the 1960s as a time when demands for public assistance became unreasonable. In New York City, none of these moments were quite so simple. Today, just as when the first almshouse opened, in 1736, a mix of institutions, some public and some private, attempt to ameliorate the suffering of those New Yorkers who lack the basic necessities of food, clothing, and shelter. Just as the economic transformations of the past created personal dislocations in the lives of the poor, so today, in an uncertain economic environment, poor parents struggle to find housing, to provide for their children, and to navigate the maze of institutions that have been developed ostensibly to help them.

Epilogue

Poverty and Homelessness in New York City after the Great Recession

Since the earliest settlement in what is now New York, the city has confronted family poverty and homelessness. The number of poor and homeless families, however, has waxed and waned in relation to economic growth and contraction. As this book has demonstrated, homelessness often rises to crisis levels during bad economic times. We see this today, as New York continues to face the effects of the so-called Great Recession.

In March 2011 there were 46.2 million people living in poverty nationwide — the highest number in the 52 years the Census Bureau has been keeping such records. In New York City the poverty rate reached 20.9 percent, one of the highest in the city's recent history.[1]

With poverty rampant, the numbers of homeless families in New York City climbed to new heights. By the end of 2012, there were some 10,000 families in transitional shelters, and it is estimated that this number will grow in 2013.

Over New York City's history, periods of economic downturn have often driven innovative public and private efforts to reduce poverty. Growing numbers of poor and homeless resulted in the building of the first almshouse, in 1736. The rising number of boys and girls on the street in the 1840s inspired the founding of the Children's Aid Society. Economic depressions led to the creation of the Charity Organization Society, in the 1870s, and the reforms of the Progressive Era, in the 1890s. The Great Depression led to a host of national, state, and local policies that provided the basis for the modern welfare state.

Not all of these changes necessarily improved conditions for the poor. Leaders from Josephine Shaw Lowell to Mayor Michael Bloomberg have advocated policies meant to shape the behavior of poor families, and private and public interventions have often hindered as many impoverished men, women, and children as they helped. But these were attempts, however misguided, to improve society by reducing the extent of poverty.

No similar innovation seems forthcoming in reaction to the Great Recession and its aftermath. At some point the economy will recover, and the employment picture, even for the extremely poor, will improve. But the lack of action on behalf of the poor today speaks to the current direction in public policy for poor and homeless families.

The Barriers to Work

If there is a single belief that runs through the entire history of poverty in New York City, it is a belief in the value of work. New York's first poorhouse acted from the start partially as a workhouse, forcing the homeless to labor in order to compensate the city for providing them with shelter. Throughout the nineteenth century, charitable organizations encouraged or required families to work as the path out of poverty. Government programs during the Great Depression of the 1930s put breadwinners to work as a way of providing relief to families. With national welfare reform in 1996, the restorative power of work became part of the mantra of city officials and the focus of city policies.

Yet, there is a limit to the potential of work for ameliorating poverty. The number of poor families that can improve their circumstances through work is restricted by the number of available jobs. In June 2012, nearly three years after the official end of the Great Recession, the unemployment rate in New York City remained at 10 percent. When those who had stopped seeking work and those who could find only part-time jobs were included, the rate increased to 15.6 percent. With a heavily employment-focused welfare system and a shortage of opportunities for work, there are few good options for poor New Yorkers.[2]

For many families, gainful employment remains the most feasible means of creating and maintaining stable households over the long term. We should not downplay the importance of work for developing independence and self-esteem, nor should we abandon efforts to increase employment among the poor and to provide public supports to help "make work pay." Yet, we should recognize the limits of work as a wholesale solution to poverty. Over New York's history low-wage workers have confronted moments when structural change has led to a decrease in the number of positions for which they were qualified.

Both in the past and today, the single-minded focus on work has led to blaming the poor for their poverty. In the eighteenth and nineteenth centuries, the language of morality was often used to discuss the failures of the poor. The Society for the Relief of Poor Widows with Small Children investigated potential recipients for signs of "immorality" and attempted to develop "habits of industry" among its poor widows.[3] The Charity Organization Society evaluated applicants' "general moral condition" and the extent to which they were "well conducted and industrious."[4] Some clients, they found, were too "inefficient" to work or simply "unworthy" of support.[5] By the 1980s explicit references to morality were no longer part of discussions about the poor, but the notion of "dependency"—of families' living off public largesse rather than their own labor—nonetheless represented a judgment of those in poverty. In all of these periods, such loaded language was used to describe families who found themselves desperate for assistance because of economic downturns or personal crises, causes largely out of their control. Today, policies based on a belief in the value of work continue to place the onus of escaping poverty almost exclusively on the poor themselves.

The Poorest in the Age of the Market

Proponents of the American version of a welfare state celebrate the nation's entrepreneurship, the relative lack of government bureaucracy, and the relatively low tax burden. They rejoice in a system that purportedly rewards individuals for their talents rather than their connections. Yet, for all the upsides a market-based system provides, there are also clear downsides. Americans, in their commitment to a market-based welfare state, appear to have accepted that a certain portion of the population lives and will continue to live in destitution.

New York City, especially under mayors Giuliani and Bloomberg, has embraced this market approach to social policy. Whenever possible the city has applied free-market principles to urban social problems. But there is a limit to the effectiveness of free-market solutions, a point at which markets fail to provide the goods and services needed. Markets fail when there are no jobs available for those seeking work. Markets fail when families cannot find safe, affordable housing.

In spite of decades of rhetoric and "cutting-edge" policies, in spite of wars on poverty and five-year plans to end homelessness, the number of New York families among the poorest of the poor continues to grow. As long as the city and the country continue to adopt only market-based solutions to problems that are resistant to the market, the ebb and flow of poverty and homelessness will follow the booms and busts of the economy. As long as this mentality persists, all the proposals and plans will be window dressing, covering over the festering problem of destitution and homelessness, pushing the poor to places where they remain unseen by the wealthy and middle class who dominate New York today. Families, especially, will remain the hidden homeless, with children becoming the silent victims.

The Future of Family Poverty and Homelessness

New York will soon have a new mayor and a new administration shaping policy for the poor and homeless. As the city continues to recover from the economic downturn, this mayor will have an opportunity to help determine the future for desperately struggling families. One option is to continue the policy status quo, to ignore the deep historical connections between poverty and homelessness, to remain committed to market-based social policies that benefit some but force others deeper into destitution. The other option is to acknowledge the shortcomings of the current systems for education, health care, and child care and examine how these shortcomings present barriers to work for poor families; to stop viewing homelessness as a housing issue and see it for what it has always been, a poverty issue; to recognize the limits of the job market and develop creative solutions that invest in the poorest New Yorkers; and to realize the potential of the current shelter system to directly and effectively address many of the problems that poor families face.

To choose the first option, to maintain the status quo, would be to return much of public policy to the nineteenth century, when the poor were blamed for their own poverty. We can excuse the shortcomings of our ancestors as ignorance. To maintain their course today, in light of what we now know and the resources at our command, would mean consciously sacrificing another generation to a lifetime of poverty and perpetuating a cycle of homelessness for children who deserve, at the very least, the opportunity to do better.

Endnotes

Introduction

[1] "Almshouse Records," 1834, vol. 164, roll 21, New York City Municipal Archive; Raymond A. Mohl, *Poverty in New York, 1783–1825* (New York: Oxford University Press, 1971), 85; Edwin G. Burrows and Mike Wallace, *Gotham: A History of New York City to 1898* (New York: Oxford University Press, 2000), 503.

[2] Jennifer Egan, "To Be Young and Homeless," The *New York Times,* March 24, 2002, sec. Magazine, http://www.nytimes.com/2002/03/24/magazine/to-be-young-and-homeless.html?scp=1&sq=Jackei%20Fuller%20Homeless&st=cse.

[3] Before 1874 New York City was synonymous with Manhattan. In that year parts of Westchester County were incorporated into the city (later becoming part of the Bronx). In 1898 Brooklyn, Queens, the Bronx, and Staten Island were consolidated into Greater New York, forming the five boroughs, and the city boundaries, that continue today. This book examines the history of the area that would become New York in 1898. Kenneth T. Jackson, ed., *The Encyclopedia of New York City* (New Haven: Yale University Press, 1995), 277–78.

Chapter 1

[1] Meeting Minutes of the Justices, Church Wardens, and Vestrymen of the City of New York, Charged with the Care of the Poor, 1694–1747, June 13, 1738, October 2, 1739, December 18, 1739, November 1746, Manuscript and Archives Division, New York Public Library, Astor, Lenox, and Tilden Foundations.

[2] Peter Kalm, *Travels into North America,* trans. John Reinhold Forster, vol. I, 2nd ed. (London: T. Lowndes, 1773), 193–94, www.americanjourneys.org/aj-117a/.

[3] *Minutes of the Common Council of the City of New York, 1675–1776* (New York: Dodd, Mead, 1905), vol. IV, 240–41; Edwin G. Burrows and Mike Wallace, *Gotham: A History of New York City to 1898* (New York: Oxford University Press, 2000), 156; Raymond A. Mohl, *Poverty in New York, 1783–1825* (Oxford University Press, 1971), 44; Robert E. Cray, *Paupers and Poor Relief in New York City and Its Rural Environs, 1700–1830* (Philadelphia: Temple University Press, 1988), 45; David M. Schneider, *The History of Public Welfare in New York State, 1609–1866* (Chicago: University of Chicago Press, 1938).

[4] Schneider, *The History of Public Welfare in New York State, 1609–1866,* 71.

[5] *Minutes of the Common Council of the City of New York, 1675–1776,* vol. IV, 240.

[6] Michael Kammen, *Colonial New York : A History* (New York: Oxford University Press, 1996), 46; Kenneth T. Jackson, ed., *The Encyclopedia of New York City* (New Haven: Yale University Press, 1995), 351, 921.

[7] Kammen, *Colonial New York,* 287.

[8] Ibid., 29–30.

[9] Burrows and Wallace, *Gotham,* 9–11.

[10] James Axtell, *The Invasion Within: The Contest of Cultures in Colonial North America* (New York: Oxford University Press, 1986); Nancy Shoemaker, *A Strange Likeness: Becoming Red and White in Eighteenth-Century North America* (New York: Oxford University Press, 2006); Herbert C. Kraft, *The Lenape: Archaeology, History, and Ethnography* (Newark: New Jersey Historical Society, 1987).

[11] Schneider, *The History of Public Welfare in New York State, 1609–1866,* 9–16; Burrows and Wallace, *Gotham,* 59–61.

[12] Schneider, *The History of Public Welfare in New York State, 1609–1866,* 18–19.

[13] Ibid., 23–25.

[14] Burrows and Wallace, *Gotham,* 77–78; Schneider, *The History of Public Welfare in New York State, 1609–1866,* 38–39.

[15] *Documentary History of the State of New York,* ed. E. B. O'Callaghan (Albany: Charles Van Benthuysen, 1850), I, 62, as cited in Schneider, *The History of Public Welfare in New York State, 1609–1866,* 35; we borrow the term "patchwork" from Schneider. See Chapter IV, "The Patchwork of Provincial Relief."

[16] Mohl, *Poverty in New York, 1783–1825,* 38–42; Cray, *Paupers and Poor Relief in New York City and Its Rural Environs, 1700–1830,* 36–37; see also Schneider, *The History of Public Welfare in New York State, 1609–1866,* 35–37; Michael B. Katz, *In the Shadow of the Poorhouse: A Social History of Welfare in America, rev. ed.* (New York: Basic Books, 1987), 14; Kammen, *Colonial New York,* 103–5.

[17] Mohl, *Poverty in New York, 1783–1825,* 71.

[18] Robert F. Seybolt, *Apprenticeship & Apprenticeship Education in Colonial New England & New York* (New York: Teachers College, Columbia University, 1917), 88–89 as quoted in Kammen, *Colonial New York,* 253.

[19] Ibid., 106, 132.

[20] Ibid., 287; Schneider, *The History of Public Welfare in New York State, 1609–1866,* 52.

[21] Meeting Minutes of the Justices, Church Wardens, and Vestrymen of the City of New York, Charged with the Care of the Poor, 1694–1747, May 23, 1735/6.

[22] Mohl, *Poverty in New York, 1783–1825,* 41–42.

[23] Schneider, *The History of Public Welfare in New York State, 1609–1866,* 67–70; Cray, *Paupers and Poor Relief in New York City and Its Rural Environs, 1700–1830,* 44.

[24] Schneider, *The History of Public Welfare in New York State, 1609–1866,* 64; Mohl, *Poverty in New York, 1783–1825,* 42.

[25] Meeting Minutes of the Justices, Church Wardens, and Vestrymen, 1694–1747," notes February 15, 1699/1700, New York Public Library; Cray, *Paupers and Poor Relief in New York City and Its Rural Environs, 1700–1830,* 40–41; Mohl, *Poverty in New York, 1783–1825,* 43.

[26] Calculated from Steven J. Ross, "'Objects of Charity': Poor Relief, Poverty, and the Rise of the Almshouse in Early Eighteenth-Century New York City," in *Authority and Resistance in Early New York,* ed. Conrad Edick Wright and William Pencak (New York: New-York Historical Society, 1988), 167, Table 6.9.

[27] Calculated from ibid., 164–166, tables 6.4, 6.5, 6.6, and 6.8, see also p. 146; Stephen Edward Wiberly Jr., "Four Cities: Public Poor Relief in Urban America, 1700–1775" (PhD, Yale University, 1975), 69–70; Burrows and Wallace, *Gotham,* 145.

[28] Walter Allen Knittle, *Early Eighteenth Century Palatine Emigration* (Baltimore: Genealogical Publishing Company, 1965), 146–49.

[29] Cray, *Paupers and Poor Relief in New York City and Its Rural Environs, 1700–1830,* 42–43; Burrows and Wallace, *Gotham,* 130.

[30] Burrows and Wallace, *Gotham,* 144.

[31] Mary Beth Norton, "The Evolution of White Women's Experience in Early America," *The American Historical Review* 89, no. 3 (June 1984): 604–6.

[32] Karin Wulf, *Not All Wives: Women of Colonial Philadelphia* (Ithaca: Cornell University Press, 2000), 2–6; Marylynn Salmon, *Women and the Law of Property in Early America* (Chapel Hill: University of North Carolina Press, 1989).

[33] *Minutes of the Common Council of the City of New York, 1675–1776*), vol. IV, 240–41.

[34] Ibid., vol. IV, 241; Schneider, *The History of Public Welfare in New York State, 1609–1866,* 73; Burrows and Wallace, *Gotham,* 156.

[35] Mohl, *Poverty in New York, 1783–1825,* 45.

[36] Cray, *Paupers and Poor Relief in New York City and Its Rural Environs, 1700–1830,* 47; Between 1736 and 1740, 29 children resided in the almshouse. It is unknown how many children entered as part of families, but for the same period there is a record of only 11 orphans; Ross, "'Objects of Charity': Poor Relief, Poverty, and the Rise of the Almshouse in Early Eighteenth-Century New York City," 163, Table 6.2, 164, Table 6.5.

[37] Wiberly claims, "After May 1736 … over 80 percent of families relieved went to the poorhouse." The evidence for this is scant, but that which exists demonstrates a concerted effort to move all recipients, including families, into the almshouse. Wiberly, "Four Cities: Public Poor Relief in Urban America, 1700–1775," 70.

[38] Meeting Minutes of the Justices, Church Wardens, and Vestrymen of the City of New York, Charged with the Care of the Poor, May 4, 1736.

[39] Ross, "'Objects of Charity': Poor Relief, Poverty, and the Rise of the Almshouse in Early Eighteenth-Century New York City," 167, Table 6.9 According to Ross 38.4 percent of the relief recipients between 1736 and 1740 and 30. 5 percent of recipients between 1741 and 1748 received "outrelief."

[40] Cray, *Paupers and Poor Relief in New York City and Its Rural Environs, 1700–1830,* 48–49; Mohl, *Poverty in New York, 1783–1825,* 44–45.

[41] Ross, "'Objects of Charity': Poor Relief, Poverty, and the Rise of the Almshouse in Early Eighteenth-Century New York City," 149; Burrows and Wallace, *Gotham,* 150–51.

[42] Ross, "'Objects of Charity': Poor Relief, Poverty, and the Rise of the Almshouse in Early Eighteenth-Century New York City," 151–52.

[43] Ibid., 149.

[44] *Minutes of the Common Council of the City of New York, 1675–1776,* vol. IV, 305.

[45] For more on women and poor relief in colonial North America see Wulf, *Not All Wives: Women of Colonial Philadelphia,* 153–79.

[46] Ross, "'Objects of Charity': Poor Relief, Poverty, and the Rise of the Almshouse in Early Eighteenth-Century New York City," 159.

[47] Wiberly, "Four Cities: Public Poor Relief in Urban America, 1700–1775," 194.

[48] *Minutes of the Common Council of the City of New York, 1675–1776,* vol. IV, 310.

[49] "Minutes of the Justices, Church Wardens, and Vestrymen of the City of New York, Charged with the Care of the Poor," June 3, 1736.

[50] *Minutes of the Common Council of the City of New York, 1675–1776,* vol. IV, 305.

[51] Adam J. Hirsch, *The Rise of the Penitentiary: Prisons and Punishment in Early America* (New Haven: Yale University Press, 1992), 13–14.

[52] *Minutes of the Common Council of the City of New York, 1675–1776,* vol. IV, 310.

[53] According to Ross the total number of relief recipients from 1731–36, before the opening of the municipal almshouse, was 398, and for the period 1736–40 that figure dropped to 172; Ross, "'Objects of Charity':

Poor Relief, Poverty, and the Rise of the Almshouse in Early Eighteenth-Century New York City," 167, Table 6.9.

54 Burrows and Wallace, *Gotham,* 126–29; Leslie M. Harris, *In the Shadow of Slavery: African Americans in New York City, 1626–1863* (Chicago: University Of Chicago Press, 2003), 14–34.

55 *Minutes of the Common Council of the City of New York, 1675–1776,* vol. IV, 310.

56 Burrows and Wallace, *Gotham,* 187; Cray, *Paupers and Poor Relief in New York City and Its Rural Environs, 1700–1830,* 68–70.

57 Burrows and Wallace, *Gotham,* 193–95.

58 Mohl, *Poverty in New York, 1783–1825,* 47.

59 Cray, *Paupers and Poor Relief in New York City and Its Rural Environs, 1700–1830,* 74–75.

60 Mohl, *Poverty in New York, 1783–1825,* 49–50.

61 Ibid., 47–48.

62 Burrows and Wallace, *Gotham,* 229–30.

63 Schneider, *The History of Public Welfare in New York State, 1609–1866,* 100–3.

64 Ibid., 107.

65 Burrows and Wallace, *Gotham, ,* 245.

66 Schneider, *The History of Public Welfare in New York State, 1609–1866,* 107.

67 Burrows and Wallace, *Gotham,* 251.

68 Schneider, *The History of Public Welfare in New York State, 1609–1866,* 108–9; Burrows and Wallace, *Gotham,* 249–51.

69 Mohl, *Poverty in New York, 1783–1825,* 53.

70 Ibid., 82; *Minutes of the Common Council of the City of New York, 1784–1831* (New York: M. B. Brown, 1917), vol. I, 35–36.

71 Schneider, *The History of Public Welfare in New York State, 1609–1866,* 111–13; Mohl, *Poverty in New York, 1783–1825,* 52–55; *Minutes of the Common Council of the City of New York, 1784–1831,* vol. I, 48–51.

72 *Minutes of the Common Council of the City of New York, 1784–1831,* 185.

Chapter 2

1 New York Almshouse and Bridewell Commissioners Records, 1791–1855, August 19, 1793, August 26, 1793, Manuscripts and Archives Division, New York Public Library. Astor, Lenox, and Tilden Foundations.

2 Paul Boyer, *Urban Masses and Moral Order in America, 1820–1920* (Cambridge: Harvard University Press, 1992), 4; Kenneth T. Jackson, ed., *The Encyclopedia of New York City* (New Haven: Yale University Press, 1995), 923.

3 Evidence collected by Sean Wilentz demonstrates that by 1816 it was unlikely in most crafts for masters and journeymen to live in the same wards; Sean Wilentz, *Chants Democratic: New York City and the Rise of the American Working Class, 1788–1850* (New York: Oxford University Press, 1986), 400, Table 4, see also pp. 42–60; Betsy Blackmar, "Re-walking the 'Walking City': Housing and Property Relations in New York City, 1780–1840," *Radical History Review* 1979, no. 21 (October 1, 1979): 131–48; Diana diZerega Wall, *The Archaeology of Gender: Separating the Spheres in Urban America* (New York: Plenum Press, 1994), 17–35.

4 Edwin G. Burrows and Mike Wallace, *Gotham: A History of New York City to 1898* (New York: Oxford University Press, 2000), 387–95, 457–60; Blackmar, "Re-walking the 'Walking City': Housing and Property Relations in New York City, 1780–1840."

5 Wilentz, *Chants Democratic,* 25–26.

6 Raymond A. Mohl, *Poverty in New York, 1783–1825* (New York: Oxford University Press, 1971), 17–19.

7 Wilentz, *Chants Democratic,* 23–60.

8 Edwin G. Burrows and Mike Wallace, *Gotham: A History of New York City to 1898* (New York: Oxford University Press, 2000), 349–52; Shane White, *Somewhat More Independent: The End of Slavery in New York City, 1770–1810* (Athens: University of Georgia Press, 1991), 154–57.

9 Paul A. Gilje and Howard B. Rock, "'Sweep O! Sweep O!': African-American Chimney Sweeps and Citizenship in the New Nation," *The William and Mary* Quarterly 51, no. 3, Third Series (July 1994): 507–38.

10 White, *Somewhat More Independent,* 153–62.

11 Christine Stansell, *City of Women: Sex and Class in New York, 1789–1860* (Urbana: University of Illinois Press, 1987), 11–18, 52–54; Burrows and Wallace, *Gotham,* 476–78.

12 Ezra Stiles Ely, *Visits of Mercy; or The Journals of the Rev. Ezra Stiles Ely, D.D.: Written While He Was Stated Preacher to the Hospital and Almshouse, in the City of New York* (Philadelphia: Samuel F. Bradford, 1829), 40.

13 Society for the Prevention of Pauperism, Report of a Committee on the Subject of Pauperism (New York, 1818), p. 14 as quoted in Christine Stansell, *City of Women: Sex and Class in New York, 1789–1860* (Urbana: University of Illinois Press, 1987), 12.

14 New York Almshouse Records, August 12, 1793.

15 Ely, *Visits of Mercy,* 65.

16 Timothy J. Gilfoyle, *City of Eros: New York City, Prostitution, and the Commercialization of Sex, 1790–1920* (New York: W.W. Norton, 1992), 19, 58–69; Stansell, *City of Women,* 175–80.

17 Mohl, *Poverty in New York, 1783–1825.* See Part IV, "Poverty Cures."

[18] Ely, *Visits of Mercy,* 89.

[19] Mohl, *Poverty in New York, 1783–1825,* 83.

[20] These figures are drawn from annual reports from the Commissioners of the Almshouse to the Common Council, *Minutes of the Common Council of the City of New York, 1784–1831* (New York: M. B. Brown, 1917), vols. I, 184; V, 316.

[21] Jackson, *The Encyclopedia of New York City,* 923; *Minutes of the Common Council of the City of New York, 1784–1831,* vols. V, 396, X, 398.

[22] *Minutes of the Common Council of the City of New York, 1784–1831,* vol. II, 213.

[23] Ibid., II, 213; David M. Schneider, *The History of Public Welfare in New York State, 1609–1866* (Chicago: University of Chicago Press, 1938), 134; Robert E. Cray, *Paupers and Poor Relief in New York City and Its Rural Environs, 1700–1830* (Philadelphia: Temple University Press), 168–80.

[24] Edward K. Spann, *The New Metropolis: New York City, 1840–1857* (New York: Columbia University Press, 1981), 62–63; Robert E. Cray, *Paupers and Poor Relief in New York City and Its Rural Environs, 1700–1830,* 106–7; Burrows and Wallace, *Gotham,* 364, 357–58; Raymond A. Mohl, *Poverty in New York, 1783–1825,* 91.

[25] Burrows and Wallace, *Gotham,* 350.

[26] *Minutes of the Common Council of the City of New York, 1784–1831,* vols. II, 661–62.

[27] Ibid., vols. II, 662–63, 671.

[28] Ely, *Visits of Mercy,* 89, 191.

[29] New York Commissioners of the Almshouse, Bridewell, and Penitentiary, "New York Almshouse Records," August 12, 1793.

[30] Ibid., November 18, 1793, February 15, 1796.

[31] Ibid., January 11, 1796.

[32] Ibid., August 19, 1793, August 26, 1793, February 15, 1796; *Minutes of the Common Council of the City of New York, 1675–1776* (New York: Dodd, Mead, 1905), vol. II, 671; Schneider, T*he History of Public Welfare in New York State, 1609–1866,* 186–87.

[33] Mohl, *Poverty in New York, 1783–1825,* 85; Burrows and Wallace, *Gotham,* 503.

[34] *Minutes of the Common Council of the City of New York, 1784–1831,* vol. VII, 660–62.

[35] Mary S. Benson, "Graham, Isabella Marshall," *Notable American Women, A Biographical Dictionary: 1607–1950,* 1971, Biography Reference Center; Joanna Bethune, *The Life of Mrs. Isabella Graham* (New York: John S. Taylor, 1839), 17.

[36] Benson, "Graham, Isabella Marshall"; Bethune, *The Life of Mrs. Isabella Graham,* 41–42.

[37] Mohl, *Poverty in New York, 1783–1825,* 137–38; Carroll Smith Rosenberg, *Religion and the Rise of the American City* (Ithaca: Cornell University Press, 1972), 26; Bethune, *The Life of Mrs. Isabella Graham,* 51–53.

[38] Bethune, *The Life of Mrs. Isabella Graham,* 55; Burrows and Wallace, *Gotham,* 382.

[39] Isabella Graham, Joanna Bethune, and Divie Bethune, *The Power of Faith* (New York: American Tract Society, 1843), 145; "By-Laws and Regulations of the Society for the Relief of Poor Widows with Small Children," 1813, Society for the Relief of Poor Widows with Small Children, MS 2426 Misc. Microfilm 48, New-York Historical Society; "Society for the Relief of Poor Widows with Small Children, Minutes, Vol. I," 1807, Society for the Relief of Poor Widows with Small Children, MS 2426, Misc. Microfilm 48, New-York Historical Society.

[40] Society for the Prevention of Pauperism in the City of New York, "Annual Report of the Managers," 1818, Fifth Annual Report, December 17, 1821, Mohl, *Poverty in New York, 1783–1825,* 137–58.

[41] New York Orphan Asylum Society, *The Constitution and Laws of the Orphan Asylum [Society] of the City of New-York* (New York: David Longworth, 1808).

[42] Bethune, *The Life of Mrs. Isabella Graham,* 64.

[43] New York Orphan Asylum Society, *The Constitution and Laws of the Orphan Asylum [Society] of the City of New-York.*

[44] Schneider, *The History of Public Welfare in New York State, 1609–1866,* 190–91.

[45] John Stanford, "Letter to the Mayor and Corporation of the City of New York," 1812, John Stanford Papers, 1768–1862, MS 2448, New-York Historical Society.

[46] Robert S. Pickett, *House of Refuge; Origins of Juvenile Reform in New York State, 1815–1857,* (Syracuse: Syracuse University Press, 1969), 55, 65–66.

[47] "An Act to Incorporate the Society for the Reformation of Juvenile Delinquents, in the City of New York", March 29, 1824, Act of incorporation and laws relative to the New York House of Refuge, Society for the Reformation of Juvenile Delinquents, MS 2425, New-York Historical Society.

[48] Joseph M. Hawes, *Children in Urban Society; Juvenile Delinquency in Nineteenth-Century America* (New York: Oxford University Press, 1971), 41; Society for the Reformation of Juvenile Delinquents in the City of New-York, "Rules and Regulations for the Government of the House of Refuge," June 3, 1825, MS 2425, New-York Historical Society.

[49] Society for the Reformation of Juvenile Delinquents in the City of New-York, "Rules and Regulations for the Government of the House of Refuge," 9; Hawes, *Children in Urban Society; Juvenile Delinquency in Nineteenth-Century America,* 49–50.

[50] Society for the Reformation of Juvenile Delinquents in the City of New-York, "Rules and Regulations for the Government of the House of Refuge," 16, 17; Pickett, *House of Refuge; Origins of Juvenile Reform in New York State, 1815–1857*, 73–74.

[51] Society for the Reformation of Juvenile Delinquents in the City of New-York, "Rules and Regulations for the Government of the House of Refuge," 12–13; Hawes, *Children in Urban Society; Juvenile Delinquency in Nineteenth-Century America*, 42–43; Pickett, *House of Refuge; Origins of Juvenile Reform in New York State, 1815–1857*, 72–73.

[52] Pickett, *House of Refuge; Origins of Juvenile Reform in New York State, 1815–1857*, 183; Hawes, *Children in Urban Society; Juvenile Delinquency in Nineteenth-Century America*, 60; LeRoy Ashby, *Endangered Children: Dependency, Neglect, and Abuse in American History* (New York: Twayne, 1997), 31–32.

[53] New York Orphan Asylum Society, *Annual Report of the Orphan Asylum Society of the City of New York, 1865*, 14.

[54] Schneider, *The History of Public Welfare in New York State, 1609–1866*, 190; Pickett, *House of Refuge; Origins of Juvenile Reform in New York State, 1815–1857*, 63–66.

[55] Leslie M. Harris, *In the Shadow of Slavery: African Americans in New York City, 1626–1863* (Chicago: University of Chicago Press, 2003), 147–48.

[56] Ibid.

[57] Ibid., 159–61.

[58] Ibid., 162–69.

[59] Ibid., 168.

[60] Stansell, *City of Women*, 45.

[61] For more on the founding of various asylums see William Pryor Letchworth, *Homes of Homeless Children*. (1903; Reprint, New York: Arno Press, 1974).

Chapter 3

[1] Children's Aid Society, *Second Annual Report* (New York, 1855), 38–39.

[2] Ibid.

[3] Christine Stansell, *City of Women: Sex and Class in New York, 1789–1860* (Urbana: University of Illinois Press, 1987), 197.

[4] Charles Loring Brace, *The Dangerous Classes of New York, and Twenty Years' Work Among Them*. (New York: Wynkoop & Hallenbeck, 1872; Reprint, Chestnut Hill, MA: Adamant Media Corporation, 2001), 88–89, emphasis in original; Children's Aid Society, *First Annual Report* (New York, 1854), 17.

[5] Stansell, *City of Women*, 204–7; Brace, *The Dangerous Classes of New York, and Twenty Years' Work Among Them*; "Homeless," *Oxford English Dictionary Online* (New York: Oxford University Press, 2009).

[6] David M. Schneider, *The History of Public Welfare in New York State, 1609–1866* (Chicago: University of Chicago Press, 1938), 254–294; National Bureau of Economic Research, "Business Cycle Expansions and Contractions," October 22, 2009, http://www.nber.org/cycles.html.

[7] Edwin G. Burrows and Mike Wallace, *Gotham: A History of New York City to 1898* (New York: Oxford University Press, 2000), 460–61.

[8] Ibid., 726–734; Mary P. Ryan, *The Empire of the Mother: American Writing About Domesticity, 1830 to 1860* (New York: Institute for Research in History and the Haworth Press, 1982), 1–18; see also Carl N. Degler, *At Odds: Women and the Family in America from the Revolution to the Present* (New York: Oxford University Press, 1980); Nancy F. Cott, *The Bonds of Womanhood: "Woman's Sphere" in New England, 1780–1835*, 2nd ed. with a new preface (New Haven: Yale University Press, 1997); Mary P. Ryan, *Cradle of the Middle Class: The Family in Oneida County, New York, 1790–1865* (Cambridge, UK: Cambridge University Press, 1981); Barbara Welter, "The Cult of True Womanhood, 1820–1860," *American Quarterly* 18 (1966): 151–74.

[9] Burrows and Wallace, *Gotham*, 732; see also Steven Mintz, *Huck's Raft: A History of American Childhood* (Cambridge: Belknap Press of Harvard University Press, 2004).

[10] Children's Aid Society, *First Annual Report*, 13.

[11] Stansell, *City of Women*, 193–216.

[12] Burrows and Wallace, *Gotham*, 236.

[13] Ibid., 736; Robert Ernst, *Immigrant Life in New York City, 1825–1863* (Port Washington: I.J. Friedman, 1965), 187; Schneider, *The History of Public Welfare in New York State, 1609–1866*, 300–1.

[14] Ernst, *Immigrant Life in New York City, 1825–1863*, 193.

[15] Kenneth Scherzer, *The Unbounded Community: Neighborhood Life and Social Structure in New York City, 1830–1875* (Durham: Duke University Press, 1992), 49–65; Tyler Anbinder, *Five Points: The 19th-Century New York City Neighborhood That Invented Tap Dance, Stole Elections, and Became the World's Most Notorious Slum* (New York: Free Press, 2001), 42–50; Ernst, *Immigrant Life in New York City, 1825–1863*, 43; Stanley Nadel, *Little Germany: Ethnicity, Religion, and Class in New York City, 1845–80* (Urbana: University of Illinois Press, 1990), 29–36.

[16] Anbinder, *Five Points*, 72–74.

[17] Ibid., 81, 72–74; Elizabeth Blackmar, *Manhattan for Rent, 1785–1850* (Ithaca: Cornell University Press, 1989), 204–05; Burrows and Wallace, *Gotham*, 587–88.

[18] Anbinder, *Five Points,* 75; See also Ernst, *Immigrant Life in New York City, 1825–1863,* 197.

[19] Anbinder, *Five Points,* 75.

[20] Ibid.

[21] Children's Aid Society, *First Annual Report,* 21–22.

[22] Anbinder, *Five Points,* 80–87; Burrows and Wallace, *Gotham,* 588–89.

[23] Sean Wilentz, *Chants Democratic: New York City and the Rise of the American Working Class, 1788–1850* (New York: Oxford University Press, 1986), 111–29; Stansell, *City of Women,* 118.

[24] Horace Greeley, *New Yorker,* January 20, 1838, as cited in Schneider, *The History of Public Welfare in New York State, 1609–1866,* 262.

[25] Schneider, *The History of Public Welfare in New York State, 1609–1866,* 264.

[26] Paul Boyer, *Urban Masses and Moral Order in America, 1820–1920* (Cambridge: Harvard University Press, 1992), 84–86; Burrows and Wallace, *Gotham,* 619–20.

[27] Carroll Smith Rosenberg, *Religion and the Rise of the American City* (Ithaca: Cornell University Press, 1972), 245–273; Boyer, *Urban Masses and Moral Order in America, 1820–1920,* 88–90; Edward K. Spann, *The New Metropolis: New York City, 1840–1857* (New York: Columbia University Press, 1981), 83–91.

[28] Spann, *The New Metropolis,* 84–85.

[29] Ibid., 86–87; Rosenberg, *Religion and the Rise of the American City,* 248–51; Boyer, *Urban Masses and Moral Order in America, 1820–1920,* 90–91.

[30] Rosenberg, *Religion and the Rise of the American City,* 249; Spann, *The New Metropolis,* 87–88.

[31] Boyer, *Urban Masses and Moral Order in America, 1820–1920,* 93.

[32] Spann, *The New Metropolis,* 88; Boyer, *Urban Masses and Moral Order in America, 1820–1920,* 93; Rosenberg, *Religion and the Rise of the American City,* 268–70.

[33] Spann, *The New Metropolis,* 74–77.

[34] Julie Miller, *Abandoned: Foundlings in Nineteenth-Century New York City* (New York: New York University Press, 2008), 71.

[35] Ibid., 72–73.

[36] Lydia Maria Child, *Letters from New-York* (London: Richard Bentley, 1843), 220–21.

[37] New York City Board of Alderman, Documents, vol. 8 (1841–1842), 4–5, as cited in Spann, *The New Metropolis,* 54.

[38] Spann, *The New Metropolis,* 54–57, 77.

[39] Ibid., 80–82; "Leonard, Moses Gage," *Biographical Dictionary of the United States Congress,* http://bioguide.congress.gov/scripts/biodisplay.pl?index=L000248; New York Commissioners of the Almshouse, Bridewell, and Penitentiary, *Annual report of the Governors of the Alms House, New-York, for the year 1848,* 1849.

[40] New York Commissioners of the Almshouse, *Annual Report 1848,* 3–4; Spann, *The New Metropolis,* 81.

[41] Miller, *Abandoned,* 63–69.

[42] New York Commissioners of the Almshouse, *Annual Report 1848,* 17.

[43] Ibid., 17–21; Miller, *Abandoned,* 74–76.

[44] New York Commissioners of the Almshouse, *Annual Report 1848,* 19; Miller, *Abandoned,* 75–76.

[45] Miller, *Abandoned,* 77.

[46] New York Commissioners of the Almshouse, *Annual Report 1848,* 23.

[47] New York Commissioners of the Almshouse, *Annual Report 1850,* 158; *1851,* 138 as cited in Miller, *Abandoned,* 76–77.

[48] New York Commissioners of the Almshouse, *Annual Report 1848,* 23.

[49] Ibid., 1848, 39; Leslie M. Harris, *In the Shadow of Slavery: African Americans in New York City, 1626–1863* (Chicago: University of Chicago Press, 2003), 148.

[50] Harris, *In the Shadow of Slavery,* 251, 264–65, 267, 275.

[51] Colored Orphan Asylum (New York, N.Y.), *Second Annual Report of the Colored Orphan Asylum and Association for the Benefit of Colored Children* (New York, 1838), 3.

[52] New York Commissioners of the Almshouse, *Annual Report 1853,* 102; *Annual Report 1856,* 281 as cited in Miller, *Abandoned,* 82, see also pp. 80–84; Harris, *In the Shadow of Slavery,* 163–67.

[53] Miller, *Abandoned,* 82–83; Boyer, *Urban Masses and Moral Order in America, 1820–1920,* 70.

[54] Harris, *In the Shadow of Slavery,* 165–66; Miller, *Abandoned,* 82–83.

[55] Thomas Lake Harris, *Juvenile Depravity and Crime in Our City: A Sermon* (New York: C.B. Norton, 1850), 6.

[56] New York Board of Alderman, *Semi-Annual Report of the Chief of Police* (New York, 1850). Matsell's figures for "vicious" youth are over 1 percent of the population of New York City in 1850; Charles Loring Brace later estimated the number of "homeless and vagrant youth in New York" as "between 20,000 and 30,000;" Brace, *The Dangerous Classes of New York, and Twenty Years' Work Among Them,* 31.

[57] Schneider, *The History of Public Welfare in New York State, 1609–1866,* 330.

[58] New York Juvenile Asylum, *Second Annual Report* (New York, 1854), 7, quoted in David J. Rothman, *The Discovery of the Asylum; Social Order and Disorder in the New Republic* (Glenview, IL: Scott, Foresman and Co., 1971), 235.

[59] Stephen O'Connor, *Orphan Trains: The Story of Charles Loring Brace and the Children He Saved and Failed* (Boston: Houghton Mifflin Harcourt, 2001), 23–63; Joseph M. Hawes, *Children in Urban Society; Juvenile Delinquency in Nineteenth-Century America* (New York: Oxford University Press, 1971), 99.

[60] Schneider, *The History of Public Welfare in New York State, 1609–1866,* 331.

61 Brace, *The Dangerous Classes of New York, and Twenty Years' Work Among Them,* 76–77.
62 Children's Aid Society, *First Annual Report,* 7.
63 Ibid., 12.
64 Ibid., 9.
65 Ibid., 10.
66 Brace, *The Dangerous Classes of New York, and Twenty Years' Work Among Them,* 97–99.
67 Children's Aid Society, *First Annual Report,* 30–31.
68 Brace, *The Dangerous Classes of New York, and Twenty Years' Work Among Them,* 100–101.
69 Marilyn Irvin Holt, *The Orphan Trains: Placing Out in America* (Lincoln, NE: Bison Books, 1994), 62.
70 Brace, *The Dangerous Classes of New York, and Twenty Years' Work Among Them,* 225.
71 Ibid., 232.
72 Holt, *The Orphan Trains,* 47–48; Hawes, *Children in Urban Society; Juvenile Delinquency in Nineteenth-Century America,* 100–1; Boyer, *Urban Masses and Moral Order in America, 1820–1920,* 99–100.
73 Holt, *The Orphan Trains,* 49.
74 Ibid., 62.
75 Henry Friedgen, "Dayley Journal of Henry Friedgen, 1 January 1858 – 7 December 1859," October 12, 1858, Children's Aid Society Records, MS 111, New-York Historical Society.
76 Holt, *The Orphan Trains,* 106–7; Hawes, *Children in Urban Society; Juvenile Delinquency in Nineteenth-Century America,* 103–4.
77 "Children's Aid Society Astor Place Office, Record Book No. 2, Narrative Daily Record, July 1856- September 1857," March 3, 1857, p. 207, Children's Aid Society Records, MS 111, New-York Historical Society.
78 Friedgen, "Dayley Journal of Henry Friedgen, 1 January 1858–7 December 1859," May 6, 1858.
79 Samuel B. Halliday, *The Lost and Found, or, Life Among the Poor* (New York: Blakeman & Mason, 1859), 47.
80 Schneider, *The History of Public Welfare in New York State, 1609–1866,* 281–83; Burrows and Wallace, *Gotham,* 883; *New York Times,* November 3, 10, 1861; *New York Weekly Caucasian,* December 21, 1861; New York City Board of Councilmen, Proceedings 87 (1862–63): 106–9, 370–1; as cited in *The New York Irish* (Baltimore: Johns Hopkins University Press, 1996), 197.
81 Colored Orphan Asylum (New York, NY), *Twenty-Seventh Annual Report of the Colored Orphan Asylum and Association for the Benefit of Colored Children* (New York, 1864).
82 Burrows and Wallace, *Gotham,* 890; Colored Orphan Asylum (New York), *Twenty-Seventh Annual Report of the Colored Orphan Asylum and Association for the Benefit of Colored Children.*
83 Colored Orphan Asylum, *Twenty-Seventh Annual Report of the Colored Orphan Asylum and Association for the Benefit of Colored Children.*
84 S. Humphreys Gurteen, *A Handbook of Charity Organization* (Buffalo, 1882), 45, as cited in Boyer, *Urban Masses and Moral Order in America, 1820–1920,* 145.
85 Mary P. Ryan, *Women in Public Between Banners and Ballots, 1825–1880* (Baltimore: Johns Hopkins University Press, 1992), 149–52.
86 Burrows and Wallace, *Gotham,* 895–97; Ryan, *Women in Public Between Banners and Ballots, 1825–1880,* 150–52.
87 Burrows and Wallace, *Gotham,* 883–84, 900–1.

Chapter 4

1 Charles Loring Brace, T*he Dangerous Classes of New York, and Twenty Years' Work Among Them.* (New York: Wynkoop & Hallenbeck, 1872. Reprint, Adamant Media Corporation, 2001), 30.
2 Ira Rosenwaike, *Population History of New York City* (Syracuse, NY: Syracuse University Press, 1972), 71–72.
3 Ibid., 85–87.
4 Edwin G. Burrows and Mike Wallace, *Gotham: A History of New York City to 1898* (New York: Oxford University Press, 2000), 1022–23.
5 Kenneth L. Kusmer, *Down & Out, on the Road: The Homeless in American History* (New York: Oxford University Press, 2002), 24, 35–37, 39.
6 Ibid., 25, 35–56; Surveys from 1875 and 1876 for all of New York State reveal that 1.8 percent of tramps were under the age of fourteen, a small but not insignificant proportion; see Michael B. Katz, *Poverty and Policy in American History* (New York: Academic Press, 1983), 157, 166–69, 275–76, table A.46.
7 Kusmer, *Down & Out, on the Road,* 111–13.
8 William L. Riordon and Terrence J. McDonald, *Plunkitt of Tammany Hall: A Series of Very Plain Talks on Very Practical Politics* (Boston: Bedford Books of St. Martin's Press, 1994); Paul Boyer, *Urban Masses and Moral Order in America, 1820–1920* (Cambridge: Harvard University Press, 1992), 147–48.
9 E.L. Godkin, "The Future of Great Cities," *The Nation,* February 22, 1866.
10 New York Catholic Protectory, *Second Annual Report (1865)* (West Chester, NY, 1876), 61–62.
11 "Appeal," in New York Catholic Protectory, *First Annual Report (1864)* (West Chester, NY, 1876), 15–17.
12 Peter Guilday, *The National Pastorals of the American Hierarchy, 1792–1919* (Westminster, MD: Newman Press, 1954), 216–17, as cited in Maureen Fitzgerald, *Habits of Compassion: Irish Catholic Nuns and the Origins of New York's Welfare System, 1830–1920* (Urbana: University of Illinois Press, 2006), 125.

13 Hebrew Benevolent Society and Orphan Asylum of the City of New York, *Forty-Eighth Annual Report (1870)* (New York, 1870), 29–30.

14 Section 5, Charter of the Roman Catholic Protectory (1863) as cited in George Paul Jacoby, *Catholic Child Care in Nineteenth Century New York* (New York: Arno Press, 1974), 126.

15 Ibid., 126–27; Fitzgerald, *Habits of Compassion,* 105–06.

16 Jacoby, *Catholic Child Care in Nineteenth Century New York,* 129–31.

17 New York Catholic Protectory, *Seventh Annual Report (1870)* (West Chester, NY, 1876), 201.

18 New York Catholic Protectory, *Fifth Annual Report (1868)* (West Chester, NY, 1876), 134.

19 Jacoby, *Catholic Child Care in Nineteenth Century New York,* 143–45; New York Catholic Protectory, *Fifth Annual Report (1868),* 136–37; William Pryor Letchworth, *Homes of Homeless Children.* (1903; New York: Arno Press, 1974), 268–69; J. F. Richmond, *New York and Its Institutions, 1609–1872. A Library of Information, Pertaining to the Great Metropolis, Past and Present* (New York: E. B. Treat, 1872), 349–53.

20 "The Orphan Asylum," *Jewish Messenger,* 19 Oct. 1960, as cited in Hyman Bogen, *The Luckiest Orphans: A History of the Hebrew Orphan Asylum of New York* (Urbana: University of Illinois Press, 1992), 20.

21 Hebrew Benevolent Society and Orphan Asylum of the City of New York, *Forty-Sixth Annual Report (1868)* (New York, 1868), 15.

22 "An Orphan 50 Years Ago," *American Hebrew,* 8 Apr. 1910, as cited in Bogen, *The Luckiest Orphans,* 19–20.

23 Hebrew Benevolent Society and Orphan Asylum of the City of New York, *Forty-Sixth Annual Report (1868),* 18–19.

24 Bogen, *The Luckiest Orphans,* 48–49.

25 Ibid., 95–96.

26 Hebrew Benevolent Society and Orphan Asylum of the City of New York, "Applications for Admission, 1871–1875", box 12, folder 1, Records of the Hebrew Orphan Asylum of the City of New York, American Jewish Historical Society, New York, NY.

27 Hebrew Benevolent Society and Orphan Asylum of the City of New York, "Applications for Admission, 1887–1893," box 13, folder 1, Records of the Hebrew Orphan Asylum of the City of New York, American Jewish Historical Society, New York, NY.

28 Hebrew Benevolent Society and Orphan Asylum of the City of New York, "Applications for Admission, 1871–1875."

29 Bogen, *The Luckiest Orphans,* 48.

30 Hebrew Benevolent Society and Orphan Asylum of the City of New York, "Admissions and Discharges, 1862–1884," box 18, folder 1, Records of the Hebrew Orphan Asylum of the City of New York, American Jewish Historical Society, New York, NY.

31 Hebrew Benevolent Society and Orphan Asylum of the City of New York, *Forty-Sixth Annual Report (1868),* 18.

32 Bogen, *The Luckiest Orphans,* 110–11.

33 Sarah Mulhall Adelman, "Treated as a Child Should Be? New York City Orphan Asylums and Nineteenth-Century Conceptions of Childhood" (PhD diss., Johns Hopkins University, 2010).

34 Roman Catholic Orphan Asylum of Brooklyn, "Board of Directors Meetings Minutes, April 1, 1860–July 1st, 1868," Archive of the Roman Catholic Diocese of Brooklyn.

35 Roman Catholic Orphan Asylum of Brooklyn, "Roman Catholic Orphan Asylum Society Minutes, 1859–1894," Archive of the Roman Catholic Diocese of Brooklyn.

36 Bogen, *The Luckiest Orphans,* 47–48.

37 New York Catholic Protectory, *Seventeenth Annual Report (1880)* (West Chester, NY, 1880), 29, 32; Jacoby, *Catholic Child Care in Nineteenth Century New York,* 154–55.

38 Letter of Mother M. Regina to Mr. Dooley, March 1879 (Mt. St. Vincent Archives), as quoted in Jacoby, *Catholic Child Care in Nineteenth Century New York,* 153–54.

39 Ibid., 153–55; Fitzgerald, *Habits of Compassion,* 136–41.

40 Bogen, *The Luckiest Orphans,* 100–01; Roman Catholic Orphan Asylum of Brooklyn, "Roman Catholic Orphan Asylum Society Minutes, 1859–1894," March 14, 1880; New York Catholic Protectory, *Eighteenth Annual Report (1881)* (West Chester, NY, 1881), 31.

41 Charles S. Hoyt, Pauperism: *Extract From the 10th Annual Report of the State Board of Charities of the State of New York Relating to The Causes of Pauperism* (New York State Board of Charities, 1877), 195–96; see Katz, *Poverty and Policy in American History,* 103, 106–07.

42 Hoyt, *Pauperism: Extract From the 10th Annual Report of the State Board of Charities of the State of New York Relating to The Causes of Pauperism,* 196; See David Moses Schneider and Albert Deutsch, *The History of Public Welfare in New York State, 1867–1940* (Montclair, NJ: Patterson Smith, 1969), vols. II, 27–28.

43 David M. Schneider, *The History of Public Welfare in New York State, 1609–1866* (Chicago: University of Chicago Press, 1938), 89–106.

44 New York State, Laws of 1876, chap. 266; Laws of 1878, chap. 404, as cited in Schneider and Deutsch, *The History of Public Welfare in New York State, 1867–1940,* vol. II, 63.

45 Ibid., 63–65.

46 Charles Lockwood, *Manhattan Moves Uptown: An Illustrated History* (Boston: Houghton Mifflin, 1976), 236–37; Burrows and Wallace, *Gotham,* 883.

47 Burrows and Wallace, *Gotham,* 921–22; Anthony Jackson, *A Place Called Home: A History of Low-Cost*

Housing in Manhattan (Cambridge: MIT Press, 1976), 25; Citizens' Association of New York. Council of Hygiene and Public Health, *Report of the Council of Hygiene and Public Health of the Citizens' Association of New York Upon the Sanitary Condition of the City* (New York: D. Appleton and Co., 1865), 349; Richard Plunz, *A History of Housing in New York City: Dwelling Type and Social Change in the American Metropolis* (New York: Columbia University Press, 1990), 22.

48 New York City, Health Department, 3rd Report (1872–1873), pp. 43–44, quoted in Jackson, *A Place Called Home,* 34.

49 Burrows and Wallace, *Gotham,* 921–22, 991; Jackson, *A Place Called Home,* 32–37; Plunz, *A History of Housing in New York City,* 22.

50 Jackson, *A Place Called Home,* 45–54; Plunz, *A History of Housing in New York City,* 24–27.

51 Jackson, *A Place Called Home,* 53–54.

52 *The Sanitarian,* 7 (May 1879): 226, as cited in Jackson, *A Place Called Home,* 54.

53 "Prize Tenements," *New York Times,* March 16, 1879, as cited in Plunz, *A History of Housing in New York City,* 27.

54 Ibid., 24–33; Jackson, *A Place Called Home,* 61–63, 72–74.

55 Alan Forman, "Some Adopted Americans," *The American Magazine,* 9:51–52 (November 1888), as quoted in Moses Rischin, *The Promised City; New York's Jews, 1870–1914* (Cambridge: Harvard University Press, 1962), 82.

56 Elizabeth Ewen, *Immigrant Women in the Land of Dollars: Life and Culture on the Lower East Side, 1890–1925* (New York: Monthly Review Press, 1985), 150–51.

57 Interview with Yeatta Adelman as cited in ibid., 151.

58 Irving Howe, *World of Our Fathers* (New York: Simon and Schuster, 1976), 88.

59 Interview with Becky Brier (tape 108) as cited in Ewen, *Immigrant Women in the Land of Dollars,* 151.

60 Howe, *World of Our Fathers,* 89.

61 Maria Ganz, *Rebels: Into Anarchy and Out Again* (New York, 1970), pp. 77–78 as cited in Ewen, *Immigrant Women in the Land of Dollars,* 118.

62 Riordon and McDonald, *Plunkitt of Tammany Hall.*

63 Joan Waugh, *Unsentimental Reformer: The Life of Josephine Shaw Lowell* (Cambridge: Harvard University Press, 1997), 75–86.

64 Ibid., 116–19.

65 Ibid., 118.

66 Ibid., 115–18.

67 Seth Low, "Out-Door Relief in the United States," in *Proceedings of the Eighth Annual Conference of Charities and Correction (1881)* (Boston: Conference of Charities and Correction, 1881), 146; see also Barry Jerome Kaplan, "Reformers and Charity: The Abolition of Public Outdoor Relief in New York City, 1870–1898," *Social Services Review* 52 (1978): 206.

68 Conference of Charities, *Proceedings of the Sixth Annual Conference of Charities Held at Chicago, June, 1879* (Boston, 1879), 206.

69 Kaplan, "Reformers and Charity: The Abolition of Public Outdoor Relief in New York City, 1870–1898," 203–04.

70 Adonica Yen-Mui Lui, "Party Machines, State Structure, and Social Policies: The Abolition of Public Outdoor Relief in New York City, 1874–1898," PhD diss., Harvard University, 1993, 137–38.

71 Kaplan, "Reformers and Charity: The Abolition of Public Outdoor Relief in New York City, 1870–1898," 203–07; Lui, "Party Machines, State Structure, and Social Policies."

72 Robert Hartley, "Special Circulars to Visitors of the AICP," dated January 15, 1876, in AICP Notes and Correspondence to and from Robert Hartley, vol. III, 1872–76. Community Service Society Collection, Columbia University, Box 86, as cited in Lui, "Party Machines, State Structure, and Social Policies," 140.

73 Schneider and Deutsch, *The History of Public Welfare in New York State, 1867–1940,* vols. II, 47–48; Kaplan, "Reformers and Charity: The Abolition of Public Outdoor Relief in New York City, 1870–1898," 212.

74 Boyer, *Urban Masses and Moral Order in America, 1820–1920,* 146–47.

75 Josephine Shaw Lowell, *Public Relief and Private Charity* (New York and London: G. P. Putnam's Sons, 1884), 100.

76 Waugh, *Unsentimental Reformer,* 166.

77 Ibid.

78 Boyer, *Urban Masses and Moral Order in America, 1820–1920,* 150–55.

79 Charity Organization Society of the City of New York, *Second Annual Report* (1884) (New York, 1884).

80 Ibid.

81 Boyer, *Urban Masses and Moral Order in America, 1820–1920,* 149–50; Charity Organization Society of the City of New York, *First Annual Report (1883)* (New York, 1883).

82 Charity Organization Society, "Casework Files," folder R4, box 239, Community Service Society Papers, Columbia Rare Book and Manuscript Library. Based on the restrictions on the collection of the Community Service Society, we have not identified clients by name.

83 Ibid., folder R8.

84 "Mr. Peters Attacks Charity: He Sees No Merit in the Work of Prominent Citizens, " *New York Times,* 19 September 1893, as quoted in Waugh, *Unsentimental Reformer,* 163.

[85] Charity Organization Society of the City of New York, *Third Annual Report (1885)* (New York, 1885).

[86] Burrows and Wallace, *Gotham,* 1089–92.

[87] Ibid., 1094–95.

[88] Ibid., 1092–93, 1098–1101, 1105–06.

[89] Ibid., 1101–04.

[90] Ibid., 1106–10.

[91] Ibid., 1186; Charles Hoffmann, *The Depression of the Nineties; An Economic History.* (Westport, CT: Greenwood, 1970), 106.

[92] Burrows and Wallace, *Gotham,* 1188.

[93] Ibid.; Schneider and Deutsch, *The History of Public Welfare in New York State, 1867–1940,* 50–51.

[94] Burrows and Wallace, *Gotham,* 1186–87.

[95] Ibid., 1188–90; Schneider and Deutsch, *The History of Public Welfare in New York State, 1867–1940,* 52.

[96] Burrows and Wallace, *Gotham,* 1187, 1190; Schneider and Deutsch, *The History of Public Welfare in New York State, 1867–1940,* 53–54.

[97] Albert Shaw and William Thomas Stead, "Relief for the Unemployed," *The Review of Reviews,* 1894, 319.

[98] Lillian D. Wald, *The House on Henry Street.* New York: Henry Holt, 1915. Reprint, (New Brunswick, NJ: Transaction Publishers, 1991), 17.

Chapter 5

[1] Lillian D. Wald, *The House on Henry Street* (New York: Henry Holt and Company, 1915), Reprint (New Brunswick, NJ: Transaction Publishers, 1991), 4–5; Mary K. Simkhovitch, *Neighborhood; My Story of Greenwich House* (New York: Norton, 1938), 60; Abraham Cahan, *Yekl: a Tale of the New York Ghetto* (New York: Appleton, 1896), 27; Irving Howe, *World of Our Fathers* (New York: Simon and Schuster, 1976), 67–69.

[2] In 1894 New York, at that time consisting of Manhattan and part of what is now the Bronx, was the world's third-largest city, after Paris and London. Five European cities had a higher population density, but Manhattan Island alone had the highest population density in the world. Roy Lubove, *The Progressives and the Slums: Tenement House Reform in New York City, 1890-1917* (Pittsburgh: University of Pittsburgh Press, 1962), 43, 94.

[3] Roger Daniels, *Coming to America: A History of Immigration and Ethnicity in American Life,* 2nd ed. (New York: Perennial, 2002), 121–64.

[4] George E. Pozzetta, "The Italians of New York City, 1890–1914," PhD. diss., University of North Carolina, 1971, 1–39.

[5] Howe, *World of Our Fathers,* 26–30.

[6] Ira Rosenwaike, *Population History of New York City,* (Syracuse, NY: Syracuse University Press, 1972), 79 (Table 31).

[7] Jacob A. Riis, *How the Other Half Lives: Studies Among the Tenements of New York* (New York: Charles Scribner's Sons), 1890. Reprint (Cambridge: Belknap Press of Harvard University Press, 2010), 82; Donna R. Gabaccia, "Inventing 'Little Italy,'" *The Journal of the Gilded Age and Progressive Era* 6 (November 8, 2010): 7–41.

[8] Riis, *How the Other Half Lives,* 63.

[9] Ibid., 101.

[10] Ibid., 49.

[11] Ibid., 24.

[12] Anzia Yezierska, *Hungry Hearts* (New York, 1920), 264, as quoted in Elizabeth Ewen, *Immigrant Women in the Land of Dollars: Life and Culture on the Lower East Side, 1890-1925* (New York: Monthly Review Press, 1985), 60–61.

[13] Pozzetta, "The Italians of New York City, 1890–1914," 1–39; Ewen, *Immigrant Women in the Land of Dollars,* 30–36; Thomas Kessner, *The Golden Door: Italian and Jewish Immigrant Mobility in New York City, 1880-1915* (New York: Oxford University Press, 1977), 28; Donna R. Gabaccia, *From Sicily to Elizabeth Street: Housing and Social Change Among Italian Immigrants, 1880-1930* (Albany: State University of New York Press, 1984), 54–61.

[14] Pozzetta, "The Italians of New York City, 1890–1914," 71–121; Kessner, *The Golden Door,* 127–60.

[15] Howe, *World of Our Fathers,* 69–70; Ewen, *Immigrant Women in the Land of Dollars,* 63.

[16] Howe, *World of Our Fathers,* 57–63; Kessner, *The Golden Door,* 29; Ewen, *Immigrant Women in the Land of Dollars,* 52–53.

[17] Kessner, *The Golden Door,* 59–65; Howe, *World of Our Fathers,* 59–60.

[18] Howe, *World of Our Fathers,* 87–90.

[19] Ibid., 148.

[20] Ewen, *Immigrant Women in the Land of Dollars,* 116.

[21] Ibid., 120; Howe, *World of Our Fathers,* 88.

[22] Ewen, *Immigrant Women in the Land of Dollars,* 120.

[23] Anzia Yezierska, *Bread Givers: A Novel* (Garden City, NY: Doubleday & Co., Inc., 1925), rev. ed. (New York: Persea Books, 1999), 14–15, 28.

24 Jacob A. Riis, *The Children of the Poor* (New York: Charles Scribner's Sons, 1908), Reprint (New York: Arno Press, 1971), 36.

25 Howe, *World of Our Fathers*, 89–90.

26 Ewen, *Immigrant Women in the Land of Dollars,* 118.

27 Howe, *World of Our Fathers*, 89.

28 Yezierska, *Bread Givers,* 27.

29 Ewen, *Immigrant Women in the Land of Dollars,* 116–17.

30 Mike Gold, Jews Without Money (New York, 1930), 94, as quoted in Ewen, *Immigrant Women in the Land of Dollars,* 118–19.

31 Ibid., 126–27.

32 Kessner, *The Golden Door,* 44–103; Ewen, *Immigrant Women in the Land of Dollars,* 122; Howe, *World of Our Fathers,* 154–59; David Nasaw, *Children of the City: At Work and at Play,* (Garden City, NY: Anchor Press/Doubleday, 1985), 43–61.

33 Kate Holladay Claghorn, "Immigration in Its Relation to Pauperism," *Annals of the American Academy of Political and Social Science* 24 (July 1904): 196–97.

34 Ibid., 192.

35 Howe, *World of Our Fathers*, 179.

36 Claghorn, "Immigration in Its Relation to Pauperism," 192–93.

37 Howe, *World of Our Fathers*, 179.

38 Claghorn, "Immigration in Its Relation to Pauperism," 193.

39 Howe, *World of Our Fathers*, 263.

40 Allen Freeman Davis, *Spearheads for Reform; the Social Settlements and the Progressive Movement, 1890–1914* (New York: Oxford University Press, 1967), 26.

41 John Louis Recchiuti, *Civic Engagement: Social Science and Progressive-era Reform in New York City* (Philadelphia: University of Pennsylvania Press, 2007), 66; Davis, *Spearheads for Reform,* 8–11.

42 Davis, *Spearheads for Reform,* 31–38.

43 Davis, *Spearheads for Reform*; Wald, *The House on Henry Street*; Simkhovitch, *Neighborhood; My Story of Greenwich House.*

44 Davis, *Spearheads for Reform,* 18; Simkhovitch, *Neighborhood; My Story of Greenwich House,* 93; Edward T. Devine, *When Social Work Was Young* (New York: Macmillan, 1939), 114, as quoted in Recchiuti, *Civic Engagement,* 58.

45 Davis, *Spearheads for Reform,* 63–65; Wald, *The House on Henry Street,* 81–83.

46 Wald, *The House on Henry Street,* 96; Davis, *Spearheads for Reform,* 63–65.

47 Simkhovitch, *Neighborhood; My Story of Greenwich House,* 101.

48 Cary Goodman, *Choosing Sides: Playground and Street Life on the Lower East Side* (New York: Schocken Books, 1979), 45.

49 Nasaw, *Children of the City,* 35–37.

50 Claghorn, "Immigration in Its Relation to Pauperism," 203.

51 Riis, *How the Other Half Lives*; Riis, *The Children of the Poor*; Lubove, *The Progressives and the Slums,* 49–80.

52 Riis, *How the Other Half Lives,* 63.

53 Riis, *The Children of the Poor,* 11–12.

54 Lubove, *The Progressives and the Slums,* 31.

55 Riis, *How the Other Half Lives,* 19.

56 Elizabeth C. Cromley, *Alone Together: A History of New York's Early Apartments* (Ithaca: Cornell University Press, 1990), 95.

57 Lubove, *The Progressives and the Slums,* 92.

58 Ibid., 91.

59 Lawrence Veiller, Reminiscences, Columbia Oral History Project, 3 as quoted in ibid., 127.

60 Ibid., 118–20, 127–28.

61 Ibid., 118–21.

62 Anthony Jackson, *A Place Called Home: A History of Low-Cost Housing in Manhattan* (Cambridge: MIT Press, 1976), 116.

63 Lubove, *The Progressives and the Slums,* 122–23.

64 Ibid., 134–35.

65 Ibid., 152–66; Jackson, *A Place Called Home,* 122–25.

66 Florence Kelley, "The Settlements: Their Lost Opportunity," *Charities and the Commons* 16 (1906): 81.

67 Davis, *Spearheads for Reform,* 70–71.

68 Allan L. Benson, "The New Idea in the Building of Cities," *New York Times,* February 21, 1909.

69 Simkhovitch, *Neighborhood; My Story of Greenwich House,* 160–61.

70 Davis, *Spearheads for Reform,* 72–73.

71 Lubove, *The Progressives and the Slums,* 234; Davis, *Spearheads for Reform,* 72–74.

72 Ira Rosenwaike, *Population History of New York City* (Syracuse, NY: Syracuse University Press, 1972), 76, 141; Cheryl Lynn Greenberg, *"Or Does It Explode?": Black Harlem in the Great Depression* (New York: Oxford University Press, 1991), 13–16.

73 Greenberg, *"Or Does It Explode?",* 16; Gilbert Osofsky, *Harlem: The Making of a Ghetto; Negro New York,*

1890–1930, 2d ed. (New York: Harper & Row, 1971), 21–24.

74 Osofsky, *Harlem,* 131–35; Greenberg, *"Or Does It Explode?",* 17.

75 Mary White Ovington, *Half a Man: The Status of the Negro in New York* (Longmans, Green, and Co., 1911), 36.

76 Ibid., 79–82.

77 Ibid., 144.

78 Greenberg, *"Or Does It Explode?",* 15; Osofsky, *Harlem,* 108–10.

79 Osofsky, *Harlem,* 127–137; Greenberg, *"Or Does It Explode?",* 39.

80 Greenberg, *"Or Does It Explode?",* 28–39.

81 Recchiuti, *Civic Engagement,* 194–201; Osofsky, *Harlem,* 58–62; Davis, *Spearheads for Reform,* 94–95.

82 Osofsky, *Harlem,* 62–67.

83 Greenberg, *"Or Does It Explode?",* 28–41.

84 Robert Hunter, *Poverty* (New York: Macmillan, 1904), 229–31.

85 Wald, *The House on Henry Street,* 155–56.

86 Yezierska, *Bread Givers.*

87 Howe, *World of Our Fathers,* 265.

88 Riis, *The Children of the Poor,* 60–61.

89 Davis, *Spearheads for Reform,* 128–31.

90 Wald, *The House on Henry Street,* 135–38.

91 Robyn Muncy, *Creating a Female Dominion in American Reform, 1890–1935* (New York: Oxford University Press, 1994), 39.

92 Ibid., 39–40; Recchiuti, *Civic Engagement,* 125–26.

93 Linda Gordon, *Pitied But Not Entitled: Single Mothers and the History of Welfare* (Cambridge: Harvard University Press, 1998); Theda Skocpol, *Protecting Soldiers and Mothers: The Political Origins of Social Policy in the United States* (Cambridge: Belknap Press of Harvard University Press, 1995).

94 David Moses Schneider and Albert Deutsch, *The History of Public Welfare in New York State, 1867–1940* (Montclair, New Jersey: Patterson Smith, 1969), 181–83.

95 Ibid., 185–86.

96 Ibid., 187–91.

97 Murray Newton Rothbard, *America's Great Depression* (Auburn, AL: Ludwig von Mises Institute, 2000), 251.

Chapter 6

1 Jeff Kisseloff, *You Must Remember This: An Oral History of Manhattan from the 1890s to World War II* (San Diego: Harcourt Brace Jovanovich, 1989), 73, 326, 361; Mollie Stiker, "Interview with Mollie Stiker," audio cassette, 1992, Lower East Side Tenement Museum.

2 David Moses Schneider and Albert Deutsch, *The History of Public Welfare in New York State, 1867–1940* (Montclair, NJ: Patterson Smith, 1969), 294–95; National Bureau of Economic Research, "Business Cycle Expansions and Contractions," October 22, 2009, http://www.nber.org/cycles.html.

3 Lilian Brandt, *An Impressionistic View of the Winter of 1930–31 in New York City, Based on Statements from Some 900 Social Workers and Public-Health Nurses* (New York: Welfare Council of New York City, 1932), 14.

4 Schneider and Deutsch, *The History of Public Welfare in New York State, 1867–1940,* 295.

5 States United, *Urban Workers on Relief* (New York: Da Capo Press, 1971), vol. II, 3.

6 U.S., Congress, Senate, Subcommittee of the Committee on Manufacturers, *Hearings on S. 174 and S. 262, Unemployment Relief,* 72nd Cong., 1st Sess., December 1931–January 1932, p. 12–13, as cited in Albert U. Romasco, *The Poverty of Abundance: Hoover, the Nation, the Depression* (New York: Oxford University Press, 1965), 155.

7 Brandt, *An Impressionistic View of the Winter of 1930–31 in New York City, Based on Statements from Some 900 Social Workers and Public-Health Nurses,* 9.

8 Romasco, *The Poverty of Abundance: Hoover, the Nation, the Depression,* 150.

9 Schneider and Deutsch, *The History of Public Welfare in New York State, 1867–1940,* 297.

10 Andrew J. F. Morris, *The Limits of Voluntarism: Charity and Welfare from the New Deal Through the Great Society* (New York: Cambridge University Press, 2009), 3.

11 Schneider and Deutsch, *The History of Public Welfare in New York State, 1867–1940,* 299.

12 Elaine S. Abelson, "The Times That Tried Only Men's Souls: Women, Work, and Public Policy in the Great Depression," in *Women on Their Own: Interdisciplinary Perspectives on Being Single,* ed. Rudolph M. Bell and Virginia Yans-McLaughlin (New Brunswick, NJ: Rutgers University Press, 2008), 226–27.

13 Romasco, *The Poverty of Abundance: Hoover, the Nation, the Depression,* 151–52; Schneider and Deutsch, *The History of Public Welfare in New York State, 1867–1940,* 299.

14 Schneider and Deutsch, *The History of Public Welfare in New York State, 1867–1940,* 299–300; Romasco, *The Poverty of Abundance: Hoover, the Nation, the Depression,* 152–53.

15 Romasco, *The Poverty of Abundance: Hoover, the Nation, the Depression,* 153.

16 Schneider and Deutsch, *The History of Public Welfare in New York State, 1867–1940,* 301; Bureau of Labor Statistics, U.S. Department of Labor, *100 Years of U.S. Consumer Spending: Data for the Nation, New York City, and Boston* (May 2006), 17, http://www.bls.gov/opub/uscs/.

17 Joan M. Crouse, *The Homeless Transient in the Great Depression: New York State, 1929–1941* (Albany: State University of New York Press, 1986), 70.

18 Ibid., 80.

19 Ibid., 83–85.

20 Elaine S. Abelson, "'Women Who Have No Men to Work for Them': Gender and Homelessness in the Great Depression, 1930–1934," Feminist Studies 29, no. 1 (Spring 2003): 114.

21 Crouse, *The Homeless Transient in the Great Depression*.

22 Cheryl Lynn Greenberg, *"Or Does It Explode?": Black Harlem in the Great Depression* (New York: Oxford University Press, 1991), 43.

23 Charity Organization Society, "Casework Files," Box 288, Community Service Society Papers, Columbia University Rare Book and Manuscript Library.

24 Crouse, *The Homeless Transient in the Great Depression*, 77.

25 Romasco, *The Poverty of Abundance: Hoover, the Nation, the Depression,* 143–45.

26 Schneider and Deutsch, *The History of Public Welfare in New York State, 1867–1940,* 307.

27 Ibid., 308–10; David M. Kennedy, *Freedom from Fear: The American People in Depression and War, 1929–1945,* (New York: Oxford University Press, 1999), 145–46.

28 Schneider and Deutsch, *The History of Public Welfare in New York State, 1867–1940,* 332.

29 Kennedy, *Freedom from Fear,* 86; Caroline Bird, *The Invisible Scar* (New York, D. McKay, 1966), 35.

30 Theda Skocpol, *Protecting Soldiers and Mothers: The Political Origins of Social Policy in the United States* (Cambridge: Belknap Press of Harvard University Press, 1995), 457; Linda Gordon, *Pitied but Not Entitled: Single Mothers and the History of Welfare, 1890–1935* (New York: Free Press, 1994), 235–65; Michael B. Katz, *In the Shadow of the Poorhouse: A Social History of Welfare in America,* rev. ed. (New York: Basic Books, 1987), 246–47.

31 James T. Patterson, *America's Struggle Against Poverty, 1900–1994* (Cambridge: Harvard University Press, 2000), 67–69; Gordon, *Pitied but Not Entitled,* 297–98.

32 Kisseloff, *You Must Remember This,* 73.

33 Robert Cohen, ed., *Dear Mrs. Roosevelt: Letters from Children of the Great Depression* (Chapel Hill: University of North Carolina Press, 2002), 73–74.

34 Frank Miggs Regina, "Interview with Frank Miggs Regina," audio cassette, May 13, 1993, Lower East Side Tenement Museum.

35 Stiker, "Interview with Mollie Stiker."

36 Kisseloff, *You Must Remember This,* 73; Studs Terkel, *Hard Times; An Oral History of the Great Depression* (New York: Pantheon Books, 1970), 303.

37 Terkel, *Hard Times; an Oral History of the Great Depression,* 303–5; Sol Rubin, "Interview with Sol Rubin," audio cassette, May 10, 1993, Lower East Side Tenement Museum.

38 Stiker, "Interview with Mollie Stiker."

39 Kisseloff, *You Must Remember This,* 73.

40 Josephine Baldizzi Esposito and Rita Bonfiglio, "Recording of Josephine Baldizzi Esposito and Rita Bonfiglio at 97 Orchard Street and Surroundings," audio cassette.

41 Kisseloff, *You Must Remember This,* 515.

42 Ibid., 361.

43 William W. Bremer, *Depression Winters: New York Social Workers and the New Deal* (Philadelphia: Temple University Press, 1984), 55; Schneider and Deutsch, *The History of Public Welfare in New York State, 1867–1940,* 309.

44 Abraham Kokofsky, "Interview with Abraham Kokofsky," audio cassette, June 8, 1993, Lower East Side Tenement Museum.

45 Herman Partnow, "I Got an American Spine With a Heart from the Old World," May 10, 1939, American Life Histories: Manuscripts from the Federal Writers Projects, 1936–1940, Library of Congress, http://memory.loc.gov/ammem/wpaintro/wpahome.html.

46 Charity Organization Society, "Casework Files," Box 289. Based on the restrictions on the collection of the Community Service Society, we have not identified clients by name.

47 Thomas Kessner, *Fiorello H. La Guardia and the Making of Modern New York* (New York: McGraw-Hill, 1989).

48 Ibid., 336, 40.

49 Ibid., 382–87.

50 Ibid., 421.

51 Alter F. Landesman, *Brownsville: The Birth, Development, and Passing of a Jewish Community in New York* (New York: Bloch, 1969), 82–83.

52 Kessner, *Fiorello H. La Guardia and the Making of Modern New York,* 202.

53 Wendell E. Pritchett, *Brownsville, Brooklyn: Blacks, Jews, and the Changing Face of the Ghetto* (Chicago: University of Chicago Press, 2002), 14–16; Landesman, *Brownsville,* 96.

54 Evelyn Diaz Gonzalez, *The Bronx* (New York: Columbia University Press, 2004), 52–57, 59–62, 67–70.

55 Kessner, *Fiorello H. La Guardia and the Making of Modern New York,* 322–23.

56 Ibid., 323; Nicholas Dagen Bloom, *Public Housing That Worked: New York in the Twentieth Century* (Philadelphia: University of Pennsylvania Press, 2009), 28.

57 Gail Radford, *Modern Housing for America: Policy Struggles in the New Deal Era* (Chicago: University of Chicago Press, 1996), 89.
58 Ibid., 92–101.
59 Kessner, *Fiorello H. La Guardia and the Making of Modern New York,* 327–30; Bloom, *Public Housing That Worked,* 28–30.
60 Kessner, *Fiorello H. La Guardia and the Making of Modern New York,* 331–36; Radford, *Modern Housing for America,* 165–67.
61 Radford, *Modern Housing for America,* 168–70.
62 Ibid., 170; Kessner, *Fiorello H. La Guardia and the Making of Modern New York,* 332.
63 Bloom, *Public Housing That Worked,* 96–97.
64 Ibid., 80.
65 Ibid., 81–84.
66 Ibid., 86–89.
67 Greenberg, *"Or Does It Explode?"*, 3–4; Kessner, *Fiorello H. La Guardia and the Making of Modern New York,* 368–70; *"Harlem* Riot," July 7th, 1939, American Life Histories: Manuscripts from the Federal Writers Projects, 1936–1940, Library of Congress, http://memory.loc.gov/ammem/wpaintro/wpahome.html. The WPA worker who recorded this oral history transcribed this interview in dialect. As we have done throughout the book, we chose to remain true to the quote as written.
68 Greenberg, *"Or Does It Explode?"*, 44.
69 Ibid., 66.
70 Ibid., 45.
71 Ibid., 75–77.
72 Ibid., 44, 68.
73 Charity Organization Society, "Casework Files," box 287, Community Service Society Papers, Columbia Rare Book and Manuscript Library.
74 Charity Organization Society, "Casework Files," box 289.
75 Greenberg, *"Or Does It Explode?"*, 170–71.
76 Ibid., 168–69.
77 Vanessa May, *Unprotected Labor: Household Workers, Politics, and Middle-Class Reform in New York, 1870–1940* (Chapel Hill: The University of North Carolina Press, 2011), 159–60.
78 Minnie Marshall "Bronx Slave Market," December 6, 1938, American Life Histories: Manuscripts from the Federal Writers Projects, 1936–1940, Library of Congress, http://memory.loc.gov/ammem/wpaintro/wpa-home.html.
79 Brenda Clegg Gray, *Black Female Domestics During the Great Depression in New York City, 1930–1940,* PhD diss., University of Michigan, 1983. 5.
80 Marshall "Bronx Slave Market"; Gray, *Black Female Domestics During the Great Depression in New York City, 1930–1940,* 61, 79–80.
81 May, *Unprotected Labor,* 165–66.
82 Greenberg, *"Or Does It Explode?"*, 179.
83 Ibid., 184–185.
84 Harold X. Connolly, *A Ghetto Grows in Brooklyn* (New York: New York University Press, 1977), 52–55, 75 n. 1; Gonzalez, *The Bronx,* 99–100.
85 Kessner, *Fiorello H. La Guardia and the Making of Modern New York,* 539.
86 *Ibid.,* 539–540.
87 Greenberg, *"Or Does It Explode?"*, 211–13; Kessner, *Fiorello H. La Guardia and the Making of Modern New York,* 531–32.

Chapter 7

1 Josh Friedman and Frank Emerson, "Ghetto Portrait: A Family in Brownsville, Article I: Check Day," *New York Post,* August 13, 1973.
2 Ibid.
3 Josh Friedman and Frank Emerson, "Ghetto Portrait: A Family in Brownsville, Article V: Just a Place with a Roof," *New York Post,* August 17, 1973.
4 Kenneth T. Jackson, ed., *The Encyclopedia of New York City* (New Haven: Yale University Press, 1995), 920–21.
5 Ibid., 114.
6 Mark K. Levitan and Susan S. Wieler, "Poverty in New York City, 1966–99: The Influence of Demographic Change, Income Growth, and Income Inequality," *Federal Reserve Bank of New York Economic Policy Review* 14, no. 1 (July 2008): 13–30.
7 Joshua Benjamin Freeman, *Working-Class New York: Life and Labor Since World War II* (New York: New Press, 2000), 10–16.
8 Ibid., 6–20, 28.
9 Ibid., 99, 103–4.
10 Kenneth L. Kusmer, *Down & Out, on the Road: The Homeless in American History* (New York: Oxford

University Press, 2002), 6.

11 Ella Howard, *Skid Row: Homelessness on the Bowery in the Twentieth Century* (PhD diss., Boston University, 2007), 16; Kusmer, *Down & Out, on the Road,* 225–26.

12 Howard, *Skid Row,* 23; Kusmer, *Down & Out, on the Road,* 229.

13 Howard, *Skid Row,* 163–70; Kusmer, *Down & Out, on the Road,* 226.

14 Howard, *Skid Row,* 157.

15 Freeman, *Working-Class New York,* 105.

16 Nicholas Dagen Bloom, *Public Housing That Worked: New York in the Twentieth Century* (Philadelphia: University of Pennsylvania Press, 2009); Freeman, *Working-Class New York,* 109–10.

17 Freeman, *Working-Class New York,* 110–24.

18 Ibid., 28, 107.

19 Virginia Sánchez Korrol, *From Colonia to Community: The History of Puerto Ricans in New York City* (Berkeley: University of California Press, 1994), 44.

20 Lorrin Thomas, *Puerto Rican Citizen: History and Political Identity in Twentieth-Century New York City* (Chicago: University of Chicago Press, 2010), 23–24.

21 Sánchez Korrol, *From Colonia to Community,* 28, 44–46; Thomas, *Puerto Rican Citizen,* 23–29.

22 Sánchez Korrol, *From Colonia to Community,* 58; Patricia Cayo Sexton, *Spanish Harlem: An Anatomy of Poverty* (New York: Harper & Row, 1965), 7.

23 Sexton, *Spanish Harlem: An Anatomy of Poverty,* 9.

24 José Ramón Sanchez, "Housing Puerto Ricans in New York City, 1945 to 1984: A Study in Class Powerlessness"(PhD diss., New York University, 1990), 97.

25 "Overcrowded" was defined as more than 1.01 persons per room. Ibid., 96.

26 Sexton, *Spanish Harlem: An Anatomy of Poverty,* 26–30.

27 Ibid., 23.

28 Piri Thomas, *Down These Mean Streets* (New York: Knopf, 1967), 313.

29 Freeman, *Working-Class New York,* 16.

30 Ibid., 143.

31 Ibid., 146–147.

32 Robert Fitch, *The Assassination of New York* (New York: Verso, 1996), 59–87.

33 Freeman, *Working-Class New York,* 149–50; Fitch, *Assassination of New York;* Joel Schwartz, *The New York Approach: Robert Moses, Urban Liberals, and Redevelopment of the Inner City* (Columbus: Ohio State University Press, 1993), 239.

34 J. Clarence Davies, *Neighborhood Groups and Urban Renewal* (New York: Columbia University Press, 1966), 17.

35 Robert A. Caro, *The Power Broker: Robert Moses and the Fall of New York* (New York: Vintage, 1975), 1013.

36 Samuel Zipp, *Manhattan Projects: The Rise and Fall of Urban Renewal in Cold War New York* (New York: Oxford University Press, 2010), 163; Caro, *The Power Broker,* 1013–14.

37 Caro, *The Power Broker,* 973–75.

38 Felicia Kornbluh, *The Battle for Welfare Rights: Politics and Poverty in Modern America* (Philadelphia: University of Pennsylvania Press, 2007), 22.

39 Zipp, *Manhattan Projects,* 211–12.

40 Davies, *Neighborhood Groups and Urban Renewal,* 33; Caro, *The Power Broker,* 965.

41 Wendell E. Pritchett, *Brownsville, Brooklyn: Blacks, Jews, and the Changing Face of the Ghetto* (Chicago: University of Chicago Press, 2002), 64–65.

42 Ibid., 97–98.

43 Ibid., 97–99.

44 Ibid., 99.

45 Ibid., 99, 115.

46 Ibid., 121, 148; Caro, *The Power Broker,* 965.

47 Pritchett, *Brownsville, Brooklyn,* 148–56.

48 Ibid., 149, 158, 162.

49 Ibid., 243–45.

50 James T. Patterson, *America's Struggle Against Poverty, 1900–1994* (Cambridge: Harvard University Press, 1994), 138–40; Michael B. Katz, *In the Shadow of the Poorhouse: A Social History of Welfare in America,* rev. ed. (New York: Basic Books, 1987), 263–64, 267.

51 Pritchett, *Brownsville, Brooklyn,* 196; Bertram M. Beck, "Organizing Community Action," *Proceedings of the Academy of Political Science* 29, no. 4 (January 1, 1969): 162–78.

52 Pritchett, *Brownsville, Brooklyn,* 194–98.

53 Ibid., 200–209.

54 *New York Herald Tribune,* January 25 1965 in Sam Roberts, *America's Mayor: John V. Lindsay and the Reinvention of New York* (New York: Columbia University Press, 2010), 14–15.

55 James J. Graham, *The Enemies of the Poor.* (New York: Random House, 1970), 24–25.

56 Frank Gell, The Black Badge; *Confessions of a Caseworker.* (New York: Harper & Row, 1969), 20, 32–34.

57 Graham, *The Enemies of the Poor,* 27.

58 Kornbluh, *The Battle for Welfare Rights,* 26–27.

[59] Ibid., 25.

[60] Ibid., 24–26.

[61] Ibid., 36–38.

[62] Ibid., 41–55.

[63] Beck, "Organizing Community Action"; Vincent Cannato, *The Ungovernable City: John Lindsay and His Struggle to Save New York* (New York: Basic Books, 2002), 108–10.

[64] Cannato, *The Ungovernable City,* 541–42; Kornbluh, *The Battle for Welfare Rights,* 93–94.

[65] Sol Stern, "The Screws Are on the Welfare System: Down and Out in New York," *New York Times,* October 22, 1972, http://select.nytimes.com/gst/abstract.html?res=F40F12F93F5A137A93C0AB178BD95F468785 F9&scp=2&sq=Sol%20Stern%20The%20screws%20are%20on&st=cse.

[66] Kornbluh, *The Battle for Welfare Rights,* 107–8; Cannato, *The Ungovernable City,* 541.

[67] Kornbluh, *The Battle for Welfare Rights,* 105.

[68] Freeman, *Working-Class New York,* 273, 294, 301.

[69] Ken Auletta, *The Streets Were Paved with Gold* (New York: Vintage Books, 1980), 31; Freeman, *Working-Class New York,* 265–70.

[70] Martin Shefter, *Political Crisis, Fiscal Crisis: The Collapse and Revival of New York City,* Morningside ed. (New York: Columbia University Press, 1992), 135; Seymour P. Lachman and Robert Polner, *The Man Who Saved New York: Hugh Carey and the Great Fiscal Crisis of 1975* (Albany: State University of New York Press, 2010), 139; Auletta, *The Streets Were Paved with Gold* , 278; Freeman, *Working-Class New York,* 270.

[71] Freeman, *Working-Class New York,* 274.

[72] Ibid., 274–76; Jill Jonnes, *South Bronx Rising: The Rise, Fall, and Resurrection of an American City,* 2nd ed. (New York: Fordham University Press, 2002), 201–2.

[73] Jonnes, *South Bronx Rising,* 229; Auletta, *The Streets Were Paved with Gold* , 9.

[74] Thomas, *Down These Mean Streets,* 200–2.

[75] Jonnes, *South Bronx Rising,* 225.

[76] Ibid., 227–28.

[77] Ibid., 245–47.

[78] Pritchett, *Brownsville, Brooklyn,* 250–51; Auletta, *The Streets Were Paved with Gold* , 9.

[79] Susan Sheehan, *A Welfare Mother* (Boston: Houghton Mifflin, 1976), 3–5.

[80] Ibid., 11–13. Sheehan created pseudonyms for the people she wrote about.

[81] Ibid., 13–16, 24–27.

[82] Ibid., 23, 43, 56.

[83] Michael B. Katz, *The"Underclass" Debate* (Princeton: Princeton University Press, 1992).

[84] William Julius Wilson, *The Truly Disadvantaged: The Inner City, the Underclass, and Public Policy* (Chicago: University of Chicago Press, 1990), 66, 71.

[85] Lee Rainwater, *The Moynihan Report and the Politics of Controversy : a Trans-action Social Science and Public Policy Report* (Cambridge: MIT Press, 1967); Charles A. Murray, *Losing Ground : American Social Policy, 1950–1980* (New York: Basic Books, 1984); Wilson, *The Truly Disadvantaged.*

[86] Jonnes, *South Bronx Rising,* 311–17; Jonathan Mahler, *Ladies and Gentlemen, the Bronx Is Burning: 1977, Baseball, Politics, and the Battle for the Soul of a City* (New York: Macmillan, 2006), 330.

Chapter 8

[1] *McCain v. Koch,* 117 AD 2d 198 (Appellate Div., 1st Dept. 1986).

[2] Rudolph W. Giuliani, "Turning Welfare Centers into Job Centers to Build a More Independent New York," March 29, 1998, Giuliani Archives, New York City Department of Records, http://www.nyc.gov/html/records/rwg/html/98a/me980329.html.

[3] Mark K. Levitan and Susan S. Wieler, "Poverty in New York City, 1966–99: The Influence of Demographic Change, Income Growth, and Income Inequality," *Federal Reserve Bank of New York Economic Policy Review* 14, no. 1 (July 2008): 15, 20.

[4] Ed Koch, "Text of Address Delivered by Koch at His Inauguration as Mayor of New York City," *New York Times,* January 2, 1978; Jonathan M. Soffer, *Ed Koch and the Rebuilding of New York City* (New York: Columbia University Press, 2010), 146–47.

[5] Koch, "Text of Address Delivered by Koch at His Inauguration."

[6] Ibid.

[7] Peter H. Rossi, *Down and Out in America: The Origins of Homelessness* (Chicago: University of Chicago Press, 1991), 191.

[8] Levitan and Wieler, "Poverty in New York City, 1966–99"; Bureau of Labor Statistics, United States Department of Labor, "Local Area Unemployment Statistics: New York City, NY", December 4, 2008, http://data.bls.gov. The unemployment rate for New York City reached 10 percent in July 1982 and hit that rate again in February 1983.

[9] Joshua Benjamin Freeman, *Working-Class New York: Life and Labor Since World War II* (New York: New Press, 2000), 301.

[10] Jesse Hoffnung-Garskof, *A Tale of Two Cities: Santo Domingo and New York After 1950* (Princeton: Princeton University Press, 2010), 201.

[11] Michel Marriott, "After 3 Years, Crack Plague In New York Only Gets Worse," *New York Times,* February 20, 1989, sec. NY / Region, http://www.nytimes.com/1989/02/20/nyregion/after-3-years-crack-plague-in-new-york-only-gets-worse.html?scp=1&sq=&st=nyt; Timothy Egan, "Crack's Legacy: A Special Report; In States' Anti-Drug Fight, A Renewal for Treatment," *New York Times,* June 10, 1999, sec. U.S., http://www.nytimes.com/1999/06/10/us/crack-s-legacy-special-report-states-anti-drug-fight-renewal-for-treatment.html?scp=1&sq=&st=nyt.

[12] Francis X. Clines, "Welfare Shelter Called a Success," *New York Times,* December 7, 1972; Murray Schumach, "Welfare Cases in Hotels Called a Modern Horror," *New York Times,* November 23, 1970; Ralph da Costa Nunez and Oliver Cannell, *Homeless Families in New York City: The Public Policies of Four Mayors, 1978–2009* (New York: Institute for Children, Poverty, and Homelessness, 2010).

[13] New York City Mayor's Office of Operations, *Mayor's Management Report,* September 17, 1984; Nunez and Cannell, *Homeless Families in New York City;* Victor Bach and Renee Steinhagen, *Alternatives to the Welfare Hotel: Using Emergency Assistance to Provide Decent Transitional Shelter for Homeless Families* (New York: Community Service Society of New York, 1987); Jonathan Kozol, *Rachel and Her Children: Homeless Families in America* (New York: Crown Publishers, 1988).

[14] New York City Mayor's Advisory Task Force on the Homeless, *Toward a Comprehensive Policy on Homelessness,* 1987; Robin Herman, "City Temporarily Sheltering over 700 Homeless Families," *New York Times,* March 5, 1982, sec. NY / Region, http://www.nytimes.com/1982/03/05/nyregion/city-temporarily-sheltering-over-700-homeless-families.html?scp=1&sq=City+Temporarily+Sheltering+over+700&st=nyt; Joel Blau, *The Visible Poor: Homelessness in the United States* (New York: Oxford University Press, 1993), 159–60.

[15] Sam Roberts, "A Once Homeless Woman Advances, but Her Suit Does Not," *New York Times,* October 5, 1992; Dennis Hevesi, "Yvonne McCain, Plaintiff in Suit on Shelter for Homeless Families, Dies at 63," *New York Times,* November 2, 2011.

[16] Hevesi, "Yvonne McCain, Plaintiff in Suit on Shelter for Homeless Families, Dies at 63."

[17] New York City Mayor's Office of Operations, *Mayor's Management Report,* September 17, 1983; Nunez and Cannell, *Homeless Families in New York City,* 13; United Press International, "New York City Sued on Homeless," *New York Times,* July 27, 1983, sec. NY / Region, http://www.nytimes.com/1983/07/27/nyregion/the-region-new-york-city-sued-on-homeless.html?scp=1&sq=New+York+City+Sued+on+Homeless&st=nyt.

[18] Leslie Kaufman and David W. Chen, "City Reaches Deal on Shelter for Homeless," *New York Times,* September 18, 2008, sec. NY / Region, http://www.nytimes.com/2008/09/18/nyregion/18homeless.html?scp=4&sq=mccain%20v.%20Koch&st=cse.

[19] Kozol, *Rachel and Her Children,* 54–57.

[20] Ibid., 147–51.

[21] Ibid., 39–48, 113–22, 102–12.

[22] *McCain v. Koch,* 117; Susan V. Demers, "The Failures of Litigation as a Tool for the Development of Social Policy," *Fordham Urban Law Journal* 22, no. 4 (Summer 1995): 1022–26.

[23] Manhattan Borough President's Task Force on Housing for Homeless Families, *A Shelter Is Not a Home* (New York: Task Force, 1987); Soffer, *Ed Koch and the Rebuilding of New York City,* 276–77.

[24] "122 Welfare Hotel Families Ordered Moved," *New York Times,* September 16, 1989, sec. NY / Region, http://www.nytimes.com/1989/09/16/nyregion/122-welfare-hotel-families-ordered-moved.html.

[25] Kozol, *Rachel and Her Children*; Citizens' Committee for Children of New York, *Children in Storage: Families in New York City's Barracks-style Shelters.* (New York, 1988).

[26] Nunez and Cannell, *Homeless Families in New York City,* 15–16.

[27] Soffer, *Ed Koch and the Rebuilding of New York City,* 290–91; Alex Schwartz, "New York City and Subsidized Housing: Impacts and Lessons of the City's $5 Billion Capital Budget Housing Plan," *Journal of Planning Literature* 14, no. 4 (May 1, 2000); New York City Mayor's Office of Operations, *Mayor's Management Report,* September 17, 1986.

[28] George James, "Budget Agreement Postpones Showdown on Koch Shelter Plan," *New York Times,* June 18, 1987, sec. NY / Region, http://www.nytimes.com/1987/06/18/nyregion/budget-agreement-postpones-showdown-on-koch-shelter-plan.html?scp=2&sq=Budget+agreement+Koch&st=nyt; Alan Finder, "Board Approves Plan for Shelters," *New York Times,* August 20, 1987, sec. NY / Region, http://www.nytimes.com/1987/08/20/nyregion/board-approves-plan-for-shelters.html?scp=2&sq=Board+approved+plan+for+Shelters&st=nyt; Bach and Steinhagen, Alternatives to the Welfare Hotel.

[29] Manhattan Borough President's Task Force on Housing for Homeless Families, *A Shelter Is Not a Home;* Soffer, *Ed Koch and the Rebuilding of New York City,* 295.

[30] Fernando Ferrer, Howard Golden, and Claire Shulman, "No Way to Treat the Homeless," *New York Times,* October 8, 1987, sec. Opinion, http://www.nytimes.com/1987/10/08/opinion/no-way-to-treat-the-homeless.html?scp=1&sq=No+Way+to+Treat+the+Homeless&st=nyt.

[31] New York City Mayor's Office of Operations, *Mayor's Management Report,* 1990.

[32] Ibid.; New York City Human Resources Administration, *New York City Revised and Updated Plan to Housing and Assisting Homeless Single Adults and Families,* March 1993; Alan Finder, "Should the Poor Get the Housing That Koch Built?," *New York Times,* March 18, 1990, sec. Week in Review, http://www.nytimes.com/1990/03/18/weekinreview/the-region-should-the-poor-get-the-housing-that-koch-built.html?scp=2&sq=Should+the+poor+get+the+housing&st=nyt.

33 New York City Mayor's Office of Operations, *Mayor's Management Report,* 1993; Michael Cragg and Brendan O'Flaherty, "Do Homeless Shelter Conditions Determine Shelter Population? The Case of the Dinkins Deluge," *Journal of Urban Economics* 46, no. 3 (November 1, 1999): 411–13.

34 Adrian Nicole LeBlanc, *Random Family: Love, Drugs, Trouble, and Coming of Age in the Bronx* (New York: Scribner, 2003), 143–210.

35 Chris Hedges, "Hard Times Challenge Goals of Liberal Wave at City Hall," *New York Times,* December 26, 1990, sec. NY / Region, http://www.nytimes.com/1990/12/26/nyregion/hard-times-challenge-goals-of-liberal-wave-at-city-hall.html?scp=1&sq=Hard+Times+Challenge+Goals&st=nyt.

36 New York City Mayor's Office of Operations, *Mayor's Management Report;* J. Phillip Thompson, "The Failure of Liberal Homeless Policy in the Koch and Dinkins Administration," *Political Science Quarterly* 111, no. 4 (1997): 651–55; Thomas Morgan, "Shift in View on Housing All the Homeless," *New York Times,* September 27, 1991, sec. NY / Region, http://www.nytimes.com/1991/09/27/nyregion/shift-in-view-on-housing-all-the-homeless.html?scp=1&sq=Shift+in+View+on+Housing&st=nyt.

37 New York City Commission on the Homeless, *The Way Home: A New Direction in Social Policy.* (New York: Commission on the Homeless, 1992), 13–17.

38 Ibid., 13–17.

39 For more on the history of the Manhattan Institute see Alice O'Connor, "The Privatized City," *Journal of Urban History* 34, no. 2 (January 1, 2008): 333–53.

40 Charles A. Murray, *Losing Ground : American Social Policy, 1950–1980* (New York: Basic Books, 1984), 154–62.

41 Ibid., 219.

42 Alice O'Connor, *Poverty Knowledge: Social Science, Social Policy, and the Poor in Twentieth-Century U.S. History* (Princeton: Princeton University Press, 2002), 248.

43 O'Connor, "The Privatized City."

44 O'Connor, *Poverty Knowledge,* 252–53.

45 Ibid., 255.

46 Tax Policy Center, Urban Institute and Brookings Institution, "TPC Tax Topics | EITC", 2010, http://www.taxpolicycenter.org/taxtopics/encyclopedia/EITC.cfm; Ron Haskins, *Work over Welfare: The Inside Story of the 1996 Welfare Reform Law* (Washington, DC: Brookings Institution Press, 2006), 14–15.

47 O'Connor, *Poverty Knowledge,* 285.

48 Rachel Dunifon, *Welfare Reform and Intergenerational Mobility* (Washington, DC: Pew Charitable Trusts, 2010), 12–13.

49 Katherine Newman, "Hard Times on 125th Street : Harlem's Poor Confront Welfare Reform," *American Anthropologist: Journal of the American Anthropological Association* 103, no. 3 (September 2001): 762-78; see also Kathryn Edin and Laura Lein, "Work, Welfare, and Single Mothers' Economic Survival Strategies," *American Sociological Review* 62, no. 2 (April 1, 1997): 253–66.

50 Barry Bearak and Ian Fisher, "The Republican Candidate; A Mercurial Mayor's Confident Journey," *New York Times,* October 19, 1997, sec. NY / Region, http://www.nytimes.com/1997/10/19/nyregion/race-for-city-hall-republican-candidate-mercurial-mayor-s-confident-journey.html; Catherine S. Manegold, "Man in the News; A Road of Many Turns, an End Triumphant: Rudolph William Giuliani," *New York Times,* November 3, 1993, sec. NY / Region, http://www.nytimes.com/1993/11/03/nyregion/1993-elections-man-road-many-turns-end-triumphant-rudolph-william-giuliani.html.

51 Dan Barry, "The Giuliani Years: The Overview; A Man Who Became More Than a Mayor," *New York Times,* December 31, 2001, sec. NY / Region, http://www.nytimes.com/2001/12/31/nyregion/the-giuliani-years-the-overview-a-man-who-became-more-than-a-mayor.html.

52 Ibid.

53 Nunez and Cannell, *Homeless Families in New York City,* 24.

54 Kimberly J. McLarin, "Welfare Fingerprinting Finds Most People Are Telling Truth," *New York Times,* September 29, 1995, sec. NY / Region, http://www.nytimes.com/1995/09/29/nyregion/welfare-fingerprint-ing-finds-most-people-are-telling-truth.html?scp=2&sq=Welfare+fingerprinting&st=nyt; Kimberly J. McLarin, "City Sued Over Program To Curb Welfare Fraud," *New York Times,* December 30, 1995, sec. NY / Region, http://www.nytimes.com/1995/12/30/nyregion/city-sued-over-program-to-curb-welfare-fraud.html?scp=1&sq=City+Sued+over+program+to+curb+Welfare+fraud&st=nyt.

55 Irene Lurie, "Temporary Assistance for Needy Families: A Green Light for the States," *Publius* 27, no. 2 (April 1, 1997): 73–87; Dunifon, *Welfare Reform and Intergenerational Mobility,* 12–13; Raymond Hernandez, "Rules on Welfare for New York Miss Goals for Change," *New York Times,* September 22, 1997, sec. NY / Region, http://www.nytimes.com/1997/09/22/nyregion/rules-on-welfare-for-new-york-miss-goals-for-change.html?scp=1&sq=Rules+on+Welfare+for+New+York+Miss&st=nyt.

56 Jason Deparle, "What Welfare-to-Work Really Means," *New York Times Magazine,* December 20, 1998, http://www.nytimes.com/1998/12/20/magazine/what-welfare-to-work-really-means.html?scp=1&sq=What%20welfare-to-work%20really%20means&st=cse.

57 Ibid.

58 Ibid.

59 Ibid.

60 Ibid.

61 Newman, "Hard Times on 125th Street," 769.

62 Deparle, "What Welfare-to-Work Really Means."

63 "The New Slavery? Workfare in New York," *The Economist (US),* October 5, 1996; "Workfairness Marchers Demand 'Real Jobs, Not Workfare Slavery,'" *New York Beacon,* September 2, 1998.

64 Sam Roberts, "Burden of Proof Is Shifted To Applicants for Shelter," *New York Times,* January 4, 1995, sec. NY / Region, http://www.nytimes.com/1995/01/04/nyregion/burden-of-proof-is-shifted-to-applicants-for-shelter.html?scp=2&sq=Burden+of+proof+is+shifted&st=nyt; Clifford J. Levy, "Mayor Tightens Screening of People Seeking Shelter," *New York Times,* August 27, 1996, sec. NY / Region, http://www.nytimes.com/1996/08/27/nyregion/mayor-tightens-screening-of-people-seeking-shelter.html?scp=1&sq=Mayor+Tightens+screening&st=nyt; Citizens Budget Commission (New York), *The State of Municipal Services in the 1990s: Social Services in New York City* (New York: Citizens Budget Commission, 1997); Nina Bernstein, "Homeless Shelters in New York Fill to Highest Level Since 80's," *New York Times,* February 8, 2001, sec. NY / Region, http://www.nytimes.com/2001/02/08/nyregion/homeless-shelters-in-new-york-fill-to-highest-level-since-80-s.html?scp=1&sq=Homeless+Shelters+in+New+York&st=nyt; New York City Mayor's Office of Operations, *Mayor's Management Report,* 1994; New York City Mayor's Office of Operations, *Mayor's Management Report,* 1997; New York City Mayor's Office of Operations, *Mayor's Management Report,* 1998.

65 Lynnell Hancock, *Hands to Work: Three Women Navigate the New World of Welfare Deadlines and Work Rules* (New York: Harper Perennial, 2003), 23–33.

66 Dean E. Murphy, "Man in the News; Finding a New Mission; Michael Rubens Bloomberg," *New York Times,* November 7, 2001, sec. NY / Region, http://www.nytimes.com/2001/11/07/nyregion/man-in-the-news-finding-a-new-mission-michael-rubens-bloomberg.html?ref=michaelrbloomberg.

67 Jennifer Steinhauer, "Mayor's Welfare Plan Embraces Job Training," *New York Times,* May 16, 2002, sec. NY / Region, http://www.nytimes.com/2002/05/16/nyregion/mayor-s-welfare-plan-embraces-job-training.html?scp=1&sq=Mayor%27s+Welfare+Plan&st=nyt.

68 New York City Commission for Economic Opportunity, *Increasing Opportunity and Reducing Poverty in New York City,* September 2006, 11.

69 Julie Bosman, "City Will Stop Paying the Poor for Good Behavior," *New York Times,* March 30, 2010, sec. NY / Region, http://www.nytimes.com/2010/03/31/nyregion/31cash.html?scp=1&sq=Opportunity%20NYC&st=cse; James Riccio et al., *Toward Reduced Poverty Across Generations: Early Findings from New York City's Conditional Cash Transfer Program* (New York: MDRC, March 2010); Michael B. Katz, *Why Don't American Cities Burn?* (Philadelphia: University of Pennsylvania Press, 2011).

70 Dennis Culhane and Randall Kuhn, "Patterns and Determinants of Public Shelter Utilization Among Homeless Adults in New York City and Philadelphia," *Journal of Policy Analysis and Management* 17, no. 1 (1998): 23–73; Randall Kuhn and Dennis Culhane, "Applying Cluster Analysis to Test a Typology of Homelessness by Pattern of Shelter Utilization: Results from the Analysis of Administrative Data," *American Journal of Community Psychology* 26, no. 2 (1998): 207–32.

71 Mary Anne Schretzman, *Making Homelessness History: Innovative Strategies to Reduce Homelessness in NYC* (New York City Department of Homeless Services, January 2006).

72 Susan Rosegrant, *Linda Gibbs and the Department of Homeless Services: Overhauling New York City's Approach to Shelter* (Cambridge: John F. Kennedy School of Government, Harvard University, 2007).

73 New York City Office of the Comptroller, A*udit Report on Department of Homeless Services Controls Over Payments to Hotel and Scatter Site Housing Operators July 1, 2001–June 30, 2002,* October 1, 2003; New York City Department of Homeless Services, *Critical Activities Report,* FY 2004; Nunez and Cannell, *Homeless Families in New York City,* 29.

74 New York City Department of Homeless Services, "Mayor Michael R. Bloomberg Announces New Measures to Move More Homeless From Streets Into More Stable Conditions and Provide Enhanced Services to Families Moving Out of Homelessness in Keynote Address to Washington Conference," July 17, 2006, http://www.nyc.gov/html/dhs/html/press/pr071706.shtml; Mosi Secret, "A New First Stop for Homeless Families," *New York Times,* City Room, May 3, 2011, http://cityroom.blogs.nytimes.com/2011/05/03/a-new-first-stop-for-homeless-families/.

75 Rosegrant, *Linda Gibbs and the Department of Homeless Services.*

76 Homeless Services United, *False Start—Fresh Promise: Homeless Service Providers Advocate Reform of New York City's Housing Stability Plus Program,* 2006; New York City Independent Budget Office, *Fiscal Brief: Evaluating the Fiscal Impact of the Housing Stability Plus Program,* March 2005; Coalition for the Homeless, *Homeless Families at Risk: Hazardous Conditions in the Housing Stability Plus Program,* February 2007, 12; New York City Department of Homeless Services, *Critical Activities Report.*

77 Institute for Children and Poverty, *To Whose Advantage Is Work Advantage? New York City's Newest Rental Subsidy for Homeless Families,* Fall 2009; Marybeth Shinn, "Predictors of Homelessness Among Families in New York City: From Shelter Request to Housing Stability," *American Journal of Public Health* 88 (1998): 1651-57; Colin Asher, "Mayor Bloomberg's Silver Bullet Misses the Target," *Uncensored* 2, no. 2 (Summer 2011) 18–24.

78 New York City Department of Homeless Services, *Critical Activities Report;* Asher, "Mayor Bloomberg's Silver Bullet Misses the Target."

79 Sandra K. Danziger, "The Decline of Cash Welfare and Implications for Social Policy and Poverty," *Annual*

Review of Sociology 36 (June 2010): 523–45.

[80] Julien O. Teitler, Nancy E. Reichman, and Lenna Nepomnyaschy, "Sources of Support, Child Care, and Hardship Among Unwed Mothers, 1999–2001," *Social Service Review* 78, no. 1 (March 1, 2004): 125–48; U.S. Census Bureau, "S1702 Poverty Status in the Past 12 Months of Families, 2010 American Community Survey 1-Year Estimates," *American Fact Finder,* December 13, 2011, factfinder2.census.gov.

[81] Danziger, "The Decline of Cash Welfare and Implications for Social Policy and Poverty," 528.

[82] Rebecca Blank, Brian Kovak, *The Growing Problem of Disconnected Single Mothers* (Ann Arbor: National Poverty Center, 2008); Rebecca M. Blank, "Evaluating Welfare Reform in the United States," *National Bureau of Economic Research Working Paper Series* No. 8983 (June 2002), http://www.nber.org/papers/w8983; Rebecca M. Blank, "Improving the Safety Net for Single Mothers Who Face Serious Barriers to Work," *The Future of Children* 17, no. 2 (October 1, 2007): 183–97.

Epilogue

[1] Cindy Rodriguez, "WNYC News–NYC's Poverty Rate Goes Up for 3rd Straight Year," *WNYC*, September 20, 2012, http://www.wnyc.org/articles/wnyc-news/2012/sep/20/new-york-city-poverty-rate-third-year-row/?utm_source=sharedUrl&utm_media=metatag&utm_campaign=sharedUrl; U.S. Census Bureau, *Income, Poverty, and Health Insurance Coverage in the United States: 2011,* Current Population Reports (Washington, DC, 2012).

[2] Patrick McGeehan, "City's Unemployment Rate Reaches 10 Percent," City Room, July 19, 2012, http://cityroom.blogs.nytimes.com/2012/07/19/citys-unemployment-rate-reaches-10-percent/; Bureau of Labor Statistics, United States Department of Labor, "Alternative Measures of Labor Underutilization for States," April 27, 2012, http://www.bls.gov/lau/stalt.htm.

[3] "By-Laws and Regulations of the Society for the Relief of Poor Widows with Small Children", 1813, Misc. Microfilm 48, New-York Historical Society.

[4] Paul Boyer, *Urban Masses and Moral Order in America, 1820–1920* (Cambridge: Harvard University Press, 1992), 150–55.

[5] Charity Organization Society of the City of New York, *Second Annual Report (1884)* (New York, 1884); Charity Organization Society, "Casework Files," Community Service Society Papers, Columbia University Rare Book and Manuscript Library.

Bibliography

Archival and Oral History Collections

Almshouse Records. New York City Municipal Archive.

American Life Histories: Manuscripts from the Federal Writers Projects, 1936–1940. Library of Congress. http://memory.loc.gov/ammem/wpaintro/wpahome.html.

Association for the Benefit of Colored Orphans. Records. MS 24. New-York Historical Society.

Children's Aid Society. Records. MS 111. New-York Historical Society.

Community Service Society of New York. Records. Columbia University Rare Book and Manuscript Library.

Giuliani, Rudolph W. Archives. New York City Department of Records.

Hebrew Orphan Asylum of the City of New York. Records. American Jewish Historical Society, New York, NY.

Lower East Side Tenement Museum. Oral History Collection.

Meeting Minutes of the Justices, Church Wardens, and Vestrymen of the City of New York, 1694–1747. Manuscripts and Archives Division. New York Public Library. Astor, Lenox, and Tilden Foundations.

New York Almshouse and Bridewell Commissioners Records, 1791–1855. Manuscripts and Archives Division. New York Public Library Astor, Lenox, and Tilden Foundations.

Roman Catholic Orphan Asylum of Brooklyn. Records. Archive of the Roman Catholic Diocese of Brooklyn.

Society for the Reformation of Juvenile Delinquents. Documents. MS 2425. New-York Historical Society.

Society for the Relief of Poor Widows with Small Children. MS 2426. New-York Historical Society.

Stanford, John. Papers, 1794–1830. MS 2448. New-York Historical Society.

Published Sources

Abelson, Elaine S. "The Times That Tried Only Men's Souls: Women, Work, and Public Policy in the Great Depression." In *Women on Their Own: Interdisciplinary Perspectives on Being Single,* edited by Rudolph M. Bell and Virginia Yans-McLaughlin. New Brunswick, NJ: Rutgers University Press, 2008.

———. "'Women Who Have No Men to Work for Them': Gender and Homelessness in the Great Depression, 1930–1934." *Feminist Studies* 29, no. 1 (Spring 2003): 105–127.

Anbinder, Tyler. *Five Points: The 19th-Century New York City Neighborhood That Invented Tap Dance, Stole Elections, and Became the World's Most Notorious Slum.* New York: Free Press, 2001.

Ashby, LeRoy. *Endangered Children: Dependency, Neglect, and Abuse in American History.* New York: Twayne, 1997.

———. Saving the Waifs: Reformers and Dependent Children, 1890-1917. Philadelphia: Temple University Press, 1984.

Asher, Colin. "Mayor Bloomberg's Silver Bullet Misses the Target." *UNCENSORED* 2, no. 2 (Summer 2011): 18–24.

Auletta, Ken. *The Streets Were Paved with Gold.* New York: Random House, 1979.

Axtell, James. *The Invasion Within: The Contest of Cultures in Colonial North America.* New York: Oxford University Press, 1986.

Bach, Victor, and Renee Steinhagen. *Alternatives to the Welfare Hotel : Using Emergency Assistance to Provide Decent Transitional Shelter for Homeless Families.* New York: Community Service Society of New York, 1987.

Barry, Dan. "The Giuliani Years: The Overview; A Man Who Became More Than a Mayor." *New York Times,* December 31, 2001, sec. NY / Region.

Bearak, Barry, and Ian Fisher. "The Republican Candidate; A Mercurial Mayor's Confident Journey." *New York Times,* October 19, 1997, sec. NY / Region.

Beck, Bertram M. "Organizing Community Action." *Proceedings of the Academy of Political Science* 29, no. 4 (January 1, 1969): 162–178.

Benson, Allan L. "The New Idea in the Building of Cities." *New York Times,* February 21, 1909.

Bernstein, Nina. "Homeless Shelters in New York Fill to Highest Level Since 80's." *New York Times,* February 8, 2001, sec. NY / Region.

Bethune, Joanna. *The Life of Mrs. Isabella Graham.* New York: John S. Taylor, 1839.

Bird, Caroline. *The Invisible Scar.* New York: D. McKay Co., 1966.

Blackmar, Betsy. "Re-walking the 'Walking City': Housing and Property Relations in New York City, 1780-1840." *Radical History Review* 1979, no. 21 (October 1, 1979): 131–148.

Blackmar, Elizabeth. *Manhattan for Rent, 1785–1850.* Ithaca: Cornell University Press, 1989.

Blank, Rebecca, and Brian Kovak. *The Growing Problem of Disconnected Single Mothers.* Ann Arbor: National Poverty Center, 2008.

Blank, Rebecca M. "Evaluating Welfare Reform in the United States." *National Bureau of Economic Research Working Paper Series* No. 8983 (June 2002).

———. "Improving the Safety Net for Single Mothers Who Face Serious Barriers to Work." *The Future of Children* 17, no. 2 (October 1, 2007): 183–197.

Blau, Joel. *The Visible Poor: Homelessness in the United States.* New York: Oxford University Press, 1993.

Bloom, Nicholas Dagen. *Public Housing That Worked: New York in the Twentieth Century.* Philadelphia: University of Pennsylvania Press, 2009.

Bogen, Hyman. *The Luckiest Orphans: A History of the Hebrew Orphan Asylum of New York.* Urbana: University of Illinois Press, 1992.

Bosman, Julie. "City Will Stop Paying the Poor for Good Behavior." *New York Times,* March 30, 2010, sec. NY/ Region.

Boyer, Paul. *Urban Masses and Moral Order in America, 1820–1920.* Cambridge: Harvard University Press, 1992.

Brace, Charles Loring. *The Dangerous Classes of New York, and Twenty Years' Work Among Them.* New York: Wynkoop & Hallenbeck, 1872. Reprint, Adamant Media Corporation, 2001.

Brandt, Lilian. *An Impressionistic View of the Winter of 1930–31 in New York City, Based on Statements from Some 900 Social Workers and Public-Health Nurses.* New York: Welfare Council of New York City, 1932.

Bremer, William W. *Depression Winters: New York Social Workers and the New Deal.* Philadelphia: Temple University Press, 1984.

Bremner, Robert Hamlett. *From the Depths; the Discovery of Poverty in the United States.* New York: New York University Press, 1956.

Bureau of Labor Statistics, United States Department of Labor. *100 Years of U.S. Consumer Spending: Data for the Nation, New York City, and Boston.* May 2006. http://www.bls.gov/opub/uscs/.

———. "Alternative Measures of Labor Underutilization for States," April 27, 2012. http://www.bls.gov/lau/stalt.htm.

———. "Local Area Unemployment Statistics: New York City, NY", December 4, 2008. http://data.bls.gov.

Burrows, Edwin G., and Mike Wallace. *Gotham: A History of New York City to 1898.* New York: Oxford University Press, 2000.

Cahan, Abraham. *Yekl: A Tale of the New York Ghetto.* New York: D. Appleton, 1896.

Cannato, Vincent. *The Ungovernable City: John Lindsay and His Struggle to Save New York.* New York: Basic Books, 2002.

Caro, Robert A. *The Power Broker: Robert Moses and the Fall of New York.* New York: Vintage, 1975.

Charity Organization Society of the City of New York. *Annual Reports.*

Child, Lydia Maria. *Letters from New-York.* London: Richard Bentley, 1843.

Children's Aid Society. *Annual Reports.* New York.

Citizens' Association of New York. Council of Hygiene and Public Health. *Report of the Council of Hygiene and Public Health of the Citizens' Association of New York Upon the Sanitary Condition of the City.* D. Appleton, 1865.

Citizens Budget Commission (New York). *The State of Municipal Services in the 1990s : Social Services in New York City.* New York: Citizens Budget Commission, 1997.

Citizens' Committee for Children of New York. *Children in Storage: Families in New York City's Barracks-style Shelters.* New York, 1988.

Claghorn, Kate Holladay. "Immigration in Its Relation to Pauperism." *Annals of the American Academy of Political and Social Science* 24 (July 1904): 187–205.

Clines, Francis X. "Welfare Shelter Called a Success." *New York Times,* December 7, 1972.

Coalition for the Homeless (New York, NY). *Homeless Families at Risk: Hazardous Conditions in the Housing Stability Plus Program,* February 2007.

Cohen, Robert, ed. *Dear Mrs. Roosevelt: Letters from Children of the Great Depression.* Chapel Hill: University of North Carolina Press, 2002.

Colored Orphan Asylum. *Annual Reports.* New York.

Conference of Charities. *Proceedings of the Sixth Annual Conference of Charities Held at Chicago, June, 1879.* Boston, 1879.

Connolly, Harold X. *A Ghetto Grows in Brooklyn.* New York: New York University Press, 1977.

Cott, Nancy F. *The Bonds of Womanhood: "Woman's Sphere" in New England, 1780–1835.* 2nd ed. with a new preface. New Haven: Yale University Press, 1997.

Cragg, Michael, and Brendan O'Flaherty. "Do Homeless Shelter Conditions Determine Shelter Population? The Case of the Dinkins Deluge." *Journal of Urban Economics* 46, no. 3 (November 1, 1999): 377.

Cray, Robert E. *Paupers and Poor Relief in New York City and Its Rural Environs, 1700–1830.* Philadelphia: Temple University Press, 1988.

Cromley, Elizabeth C. *Alone Together: A History of New York's Early Apartments.* Ithaca: Cornell University Press, 1990.

Crouse, Joan M. *The Homeless Transient in the Great Depression: New York State, 1929–1941.* Albany: State University of New York Press, 1986.

Culhane, Dennis, and Randall Kuhn. "Patterns and Determinants of Public Shelter Utilization Among Homeless Adults in New York City and Philadelphia." *Journal of Policy Analysis and Management* 17, no. 1 (1998): 23.

Daniels, Roger. *Coming to America: A History of Immigration and Ethnicity in American Life.* 2nd ed., 1st Perennial ed. New York: Perennial, 2002.

Danziger, Sandra K. "The Decline of Cash Welfare and Implications for Social Policy and Poverty." *Annual Review of Sociology* 36 (June 2010): 523–45.

Davies, J. Clarence. *Neighborhood Groups and Urban Renewal.* New York: Columbia University Press, 1966.

Davis, Allen Freeman. *Spearheads for Reform: The Social Settlements and the Progressive Movement, 1890–1914.* New York: Oxford University Press, 1967.

Degler, Carl N. *At Odds: Women and the Family in America from the Revolution to the Present.* New York: Oxford University Press, 1980.

Demers, Susan V. "The Failures of Litigation as a Tool for the Development of Social Policy." *Fordham Urban Law Journal* 22, no. 4 (Summer 1995): 1022–26.

Deparle, Jason. "What Welfare-to-Work Really Means." *New York Times Magazine,* December 20, 1998.

Dunifon, Rachel. *Welfare Reform and Intergenerational Mobility.* Washington, DC: Pew Charitable Trusts, 2010.

Edin, Kathryn, and Laura Lein. "Work, Welfare, and Single Mothers' Economic Survival Strategies." *American Sociological Review* 62, no. 2 (April 1, 1997): 253–66.

Egan, Jennifer. "To Be Young and Homeless." *New York Times Magazine,* March 24, 2002.

Egan, Timothy. "Crack's Legacy: A Special Report; In States' Anti-Drug Fight, A Renewal for Treatment." *New York Times,* June 10, 1999, sec. U.S.

Ely, Ezra Stiles. *Visits of Mercy; or The Journals of the Rev. Ezra Stiles Ely, D.D.: Written While He Was Stated Preacher to the Hospital and Alms-house, in the City of New York.* 2 vols. Philadelphia: Samuel F. Bradford, 1829.

Ernst, Robert. *Immigrant Life in New York City, 1825–1863.* Port Washington, NY: I.J. Friedman, 1965.

Esping-Andersen, Gøsta. *The Three Worlds of Welfare Capitalism.* Princeton: Princeton University Press, 1990.

Ewen, Elizabeth. *Immigrant Women in the Land of Dollars: Life and Culture on the Lower East Side, 1890–1925.* New York: Monthly Review Press, 1985.

Ferrer, Fernando, Howard Golden, and Claire Shulman. "No Way to Treat the Homeless." *New York Times,* October 8, 1987, sec. Opinion.

Finder, Alan. "Board Approves Plan For Shelters." *New York Times,* August 20, 1987, sec. NY / Region.

———. "Should the Poor Get the Housing That Koch Built?" *New York Times,* March 18, 1990, sec. Week in Review.

Fitch, Robert. *The Assassination of New York.* Brooklyn: Verso, 1996.

Fitzgerald, Maureen. *Habits of Compassion: Irish Catholic Nuns and the Origins of New York's Welfare System, 1830–1920.* Urbana: University of Illinois Press, 2006.

Freeman, Joshua Benjamin. *Working-Class New York: Life and Labor Since World War II.* New York: New Press, 2000.

Friedman, Josh, and Frank Emerson. "Ghetto Portrait: A Family in Brownsville, Article I: Check Day." *New York Post,* August 13, 1973.

———. "Ghetto Portrait: A Family in Brownsville, Article V: Just a Place With a Roof." *New York Post,* August 17, 1973.

Gabaccia, Donna R. *From Sicily to Elizabeth Street: Housing and Social Change Among Italian Immigrants, 1880–1930.* Albany: State University of New York Press, 1984.

———. "Inventing 'Little Italy'." *The Journal of the Gilded Age and Progressive Era* 6 (November 8, 2010): 7–41.

Gell, Frank. *The Black Badge: Confessions of a Caseworker.* New York: Harper & Row, 1969.

Gilfoyle, Timothy J. *City of Eros: New York City, Prostitution, and the Commercialization of Sex, 1790–1920.* New York: W.W. Norton, 1992.

Gilje, Paul A., and Howard B. Rock. "'Sweep O! Sweep O!': African-American Chimney Sweeps and Citizenship in the New Nation." *The William and Mary Quarterly* 51, no. 3. Third Series (July 1994): 507–38.

Godkin, E.L. "The Future of Great Cities." *The Nation,* February 22, 1866.

Gonzalez, Evelyn Diaz. *The Bronx.* New York: Columbia University Press, 2004.

Goodman, Cary. *Choosing Sides: Playground and Street Life on the Lower East Side.* New York: Schocken Books, 1979.

Gordon, Linda. *Pitied but Not Entitled: Single Mothers and the History of Welfare.* Cambridge: Harvard University Press, 1998.

Graham, Isabella, Joanna Bethune, and Divie Bethune. *The Power of Faith.* New York: American Tract Society, 1843.

Graham, James J. *The Enemies of the Poor.* New York: Random House, 1970.

Gray, Brenda Clegg. "Black Female Domestics During the Great Depression in New York City, 1930–1940." PhD diss., University of Michigan, 1983.

Greenberg, Cheryl Lynn. *"Or Does It Explode?": Black Harlem in the Great Depression.* New York: Oxford University Press, 1991.

Halliday, Samuel B. *The Lost and Found, or, Life Among the Poor.* New York: Blakeman & Mason, 1859.

Hancock, Lynnell. *Hands to Work: Three Women Navigate the New World of Welfare Deadlines and Work Rules.* New York: Harper Perennial, 2003.

Harris, Leslie M. *In the Shadow of Slavery: African Americans in New York City, 1626–1863.* Chicago: University of Chicago Press, 2003.

Harris, Thomas Lake. *Juvenile Depravity and Crime in Our City: A Sermon.* New York: C.B. Norton, 1850.

Haskins, Ron. *Work over Welfare: The Inside Story of the 1996 Welfare Reform Law.* Washington, DC: Brookings Institution Press, 2006.

Hawes, Joseph M. *Children in Urban Society: Juvenile Delinquency in Nineteenth-Century America.* New York: Oxford University Press, 1971.

Hebrew Benevolent Society and Orphan Asylum of the City of New York. *Annual Reports.*

Hedges, Chris. "Hard Times Challenge Goals of Liberal Wave at City Hall." *New York Times,* December 26, 1990, sec. NY / Region.

Herman, Robin. "City Temporarily Sheltering Over 700 Homeless Families." *New York Times,* March 5, 1982, sec. NY / Region.

Hernandez, Raymond. "Rules on Welfare For New York Miss Goals for Change." *New York Times,* September 22, 1997, sec. NY / Region.

Hevesi, Dennis. "Yvonne McCain, Plaintiff in Suit on Shelter for Homeless Families, Dies at 63." *New York Times,* November 2, 2011.

Hirsch, Adam J. *The Rise of the Penitentiary: Prisons and Punishment in Early America.* New Haven: Yale University Press, 1992.

Hoffmann, Charles. The Depression of the Nineties: An Economic History. Westport, CT: Greenwood, 1970.

Hoffnung-Garskof, Jesse. *A Tale of Two Cities: Santo Domingo and New York After 1950.* Princeton: Princeton University Press, 2010.

Holt, Marilyn Irvin. *The Orphan Trains: Placing Out in America.* Lincoln, NE: Bison Books, 1994.

Homeless Services United (New York, NY). *False Start—Fresh Promise: Homeless Service Providers Advocate Reform of New York City's Housing Stability Plus Program,* 2006.

Howard, Ella. *Skid Row: Homelessness on the Bowery in the Twentieth Century.* PhD diss., Boston University, 2007.

Howe, Irving. *World of Our Fathers.* New York: Simon and Schuster, 1976.

Hoyt, Charles S. *Pauperism: Extract from the 10th Annual Report of the State Board of Charities of the State of New York Relating to the Causes of Pauperism.* New York State Board of Charities, 1877.

Hunter, Robert. *Poverty.* New York: Macmillan, 1904.

Institute for Children and Poverty. *To Whose Advantage Is Work Advantage? New York City's Newest Rental Subsidy for Homeless Families,* Fall 2009.

Jackson, Anthony. *A Place Called Home: A History of Low-Cost Housing in Manhattan.* Cambridge: MIT Press, 1976.

Jackson, Kenneth T., ed. *The Encyclopedia of New York City.* New Haven: Yale University Press, 1995.

Jacoby, George Paul. *Catholic Child Care in Nineteenth Century New York.* New York: Arno Press, 1974.

James, George. "Budget Agreement Postpones Showdown on Koch Shelter Plan." *New York Times,* June 18, 1987, sec. NY / Region.

Jonnes, Jill. *South Bronx Rising: The Rise, Fall, and Resurrection of an American City.* 2nd ed. New York: Fordham University Press, 2002.

Kalm, Peter. *Travels into North America.* Translated by John Reinhold Forster. Vol. I. 2 vols. Second ed. London: T. Lowndes, 1773. www.americanjourneys.org/aj-117a/.

Kammen, Michael. *Colonial New York : A History*. New York: Oxford University Press, 1996.

Kaplan, Barry Jerome. "Reformers and Charity: The Abolition of Public Outdoor Relief in New York City, 1870–1898." *Social Services Review* 52 (1978): 202–14.

Katz, Michael B. *In the Shadow of the Poorhouse: Social History of Welfare in America,* rev. ed. New York: Basic Books, 1987.

———. *Poverty and Policy in American History*. New York: Academic Press, 1983.

———, ed. *The"Underclass" Debate*. Princeton: Princeton University Press, 1992.

———. *The Undeserving Poor: From the War on Poverty to the War on Welfare*. New York: Pantheon Books, 1989.

———. *Why Don't American Cities Burn?* Philadelphia: University of Pennsylvania Press, 2011.

Kaufman, Leslie, and David W. Chen. "City Reaches Deal on Shelter for Homeless." *New York Times,* September 18, 2008, sec. New York Region.

Kelley, Florence. "The Settlements: Their Lost Opportunity." Charities and the Commons 16 (1906): 79–81.

Kennedy, David M. *Freedom from Fear: The American People in Depression and War, 1929–1945*. New York: Oxford University Press, 1999.

Kessner, Thomas. *Fiorello H. La Guardia and the Making of Modern New York*. New York: McGraw-Hill, 1989.

———. *The Golden Door: Italian and Jewish Immigrant Mobility in New York City, 1880–1915*. New York: Oxford University Press, 1977.

Kisseloff, Jeff. *You Must Remember This: An Oral History of Manhattan from the 1890s to World War II*. San Diego: Harcourt Brace Jovanovich, 1989.

Knittle, Walter Allen. *Early Eighteenth Century Palatine Emigration*. Baltimore: Genealogical Publishing Company, 1965.

Koch, Ed. "Text of Address Delivered by Koch at His Inauguration as Mayor of New York City." *New York Times,* January 2, 1978.

Kornbluh, Felicia. *The Battle for Welfare Rights: Politics and Poverty in Modern America*. Philadelphia: University of Pennsylvania Press, 2007.

Kozol, Jonathan. *Rachel and Her Children: Homeless Families in America*. New York: Crown, 1988.

Kraft, Herbert C. *The Lenape: Archaeology, History, and Ethnography*. Newark: New Jersey Historical Society, 1987.

Kuhn, Randall, and Dennis P. Culhane. "Applying Cluster Analysis to Test a Typology of Homelessness by Pattern of Shelter Utilization: Results from the Analysis of Administrative Data." *American Journal of Community Psychology* 26, no. 2 (1998): 207–32.

Kusmer, Kenneth L. *Down & Out, on the Road: The Homeless in American History*. New York: Oxford University Press, 2002.

Lachman, Seymour P., and Robert Polner. *The Man Who Saved New York: Hugh Carey and the Great Fiscal Crisis of 1975*. Albany: State University of New York Press, 2010.

Landesman, Alter F. *Brownsville: The Birth, Development, and Passing of a Jewish Community in New York*. New York: Bloch, 1969.

LeBlanc, Adrian Nicole. *Random Family: Love, Drugs, Trouble, and Coming of Age in the Bronx*. New York: Scribner, 2003.

"Leonard, Moses Gage", Biographical Dictionary of the United States Congress. http://bioguide.congress.gov.

Letchworth, William Pryor. Homes of Homeless Children. New York: Arno Press, 1974. First Published 1903.

Levitan, Mark K., and Susan S. Wieler. "Poverty in New York City, 1966–99: The Influence of Demographic Change, Income Growth, and Income Inequality." *Federal Reserve Bank of New York Economic Policy Review* 14, no. 1 (July 2008): 13–30.

Levy, Clifford J. "Mayor Tightens Screening of People Seeking Shelter." *New York Times,* August 27, 1996, sec. NY / Region.

Lockwood, Charles. *Manhattan Moves Uptown: An Illustrated History*. Boston: Houghton Mifflin, 1976.

Low, Seth. "Out-Door Relief in the United States." In *Proceedings of the Eighth Annual Conference of Charities and Correction (1881)*. Boston: Conference of Charities and Correction, 1881.

Lowell, Josephine Shaw. *Public Relief and Private Charity*. New York and London: G. P. Putnam's Sons, 1884.

Lubove, Roy. *The Progressives and the Slums: Tenement House Reform in New York City, 1890–1917*. Pittsburgh: University of Pittsburgh Press, 1962.

Lui, Adonica Yen-Mui. "Party Machines, State Structure, and Social Policies: The Abolition of Public Outdoor Relief in New York City, 1874–1898." PhD diss., Harvard University, 1993.

Lurie, Irene. "Temporary Assistance for Needy Families: A Green Light for the States." *Publius* 27, no. 2 (April 1, 1997): 73–87.

Mahler, Jonathan. *Ladies and Gentlemen, the Bronx Is Burning: 1977, Baseball, Politics, and the Battle for the Soul of a City.* New York: Macmillan, 2006.

Manegold, Catherine S. "Man in the News; A Road of Many Turns, an End Triumphant: Rudolph William Giuliani." *New York Times,* November 3, 1993, sec. NY / Region.

Manhattan Borough President's Task Force on Housing for Homeless Families. *A Shelter Is Not a Home.* New York NY: Task Force, 1987.

Marriott, Michel. "After 3 Years, Crack Plague In New York Only Gets Worse." *New York Times,* February 20, 1989, sec. NY / Region.

Mary S. Benson. "Graham, Isabella Marshall." *Notable American Women, A Biographical Dictionary: 1607–1950,* 1971. Biography Reference Center.

May, Vanessa. *Unprotected Labor: Household Workers, Politics, and Middle-Class Reform in New York, 1870–1940.* Chapel Hill: The University of North Carolina Press, 2011.

McCain v. Koch, 117 AD 2d 198 (Appellate Div., 1st Dept. 1986).

McGeehan, Patrick. "City's Unemployment Rate Reaches 10 Percent." *City Room,* July 19, 2012. http://cityroom.blogs.nytimes.com/2012/07/19/citys-unemployment-rate-reaches-10-percent/.

Mclarin, Kimberly J. "City Sued Over Program to Curb Welfare Fraud." *New York Times,* December 30, 1995, sec. NY / Region.

———. "Welfare Fingerprinting Finds Most People Are Telling Truth." *New York Times,* September 29, 1995, sec. NY / Region.

Miller, Julie. *Abandoned: Foundlings in Nineteenth-Century New York City.* New York: New York University Press, 2008.

Mintz, Steven. *Huck's Raft: A History of American Childhood.* Cambridge: Belknap Press of Harvard University Press, 2004.

Minutes of the Common Council of the City of New York, 1675–1776. 8 vols. New York: Dodd, Mead, 1905.

Minutes of the Common Council of the City of New York, 1784–1831. 21 vols. New York: M. B. Brown, 1917.

Mohl, Raymond A. *Poverty in New York, 1783–1825.* New York: Oxford University Press, 1971.

Morgan, Thomas. "Shift in View on Housing All the Homeless." *New York Times,* September 27, 1991, sec. NY / Region.

Morris, Andrew J. F. *The Limits of Voluntarism: Charity and Welfare from the New Deal Through the Great Society.* New York: Cambridge University Press, 2009.

Muncy, Robyn. *Creating a Female Dominion in American Reform, 1890–1935.* New York: Oxford University Press, 1994.

Murphy, Dean E. "Man in the News; Finding a New Mission; Michael Rubens Bloomberg." *New York Times,* November 7, 2001, sec. NY / Region.

Murray, Charles A. *Losing Ground: American Social Policy, 1950–1980.* New York: Basic Books, 1984.

Nadel, Stanley. *Little Germany: Ethnicity, Religion, and Class in New York City, 1845–80.* Urbana: University of Illinois Press, 1990.

Nasaw, David. *Children of the City: At Work and at Play.* Garden City, NY: Anchor Press/Doubleday, 1985.

National Bureau of Economic Research. "Business Cycle Expansions and Contractions," October 22, 2009. http://www.nber.org/cycles.html.

New York Board of Alderman. *Semi-Annual Report of the Chief of Police.* New York, 1850.

New York Catholic Protectory. *Annual Reports.* West Chester, NY.

New York City Commission for Economic Opportunity. *Increasing Opportunity and Reducing Poverty in New York City,* September 2006.

New York City Commission on the Homeless. *The Way Home: A New Direction in Social Policy, 1992.*

New York City Department of Homeless Services. *Critical Activities Reports.*

———. "Mayor Michael R. Bloomberg Announces New Measures to Move More Homeless From Streets Into More Stable Conditions and Provide Enhanced Services to Families Moving Out of Homelessness in Keynote Address to Washington Conference", July 17, 2006. http://www.nyc.gov/html/dhs/html/press/pr071706.shtml.

New York City Human Resources Administration. *New York City Revised and Updated Plan for Housing and Assisting Homeless Single Adults and Families,* March 1993.

New York City Independent Budget Office. *Fiscal Brief: Evaluating the Fiscal Impact of the Housing Stability Plus Program,* March 2005.

New York City Mayor's Advisory Task Force on the Homeless. *Toward a Comprehensive Policy on Homelessness,* 1987.

New York City Mayor's Office of Operations. *Mayor's Management Reports.*

New York City Office of the Comptroller. Audit Report on Department of Homeless Services Controls Over Payments to Hotel and Scatter Site Housing Operators July 1, 2001–June 30, 2002, October 1, 2003.

New York Commissioners of the Almshouse, Bridewell, and Penitentiary. *Annual Reports.*

Newman, Katherine S. "Hard Times on 125th Street: Harlem's Poor Confront Welfare Reform." *American Anthropologist : Journal of the American Anthropological Association* 103, no. 3 (September 2001): 762–78.

Norton, Mary Beth. "The Evolution of White Women's Experience in Early America." *The American Historical Review* 89, no. 3 (June 1984): 593–619.

Nunez, Ralph da Costa. *The New Poverty: Homeless Families in America.* New York: Insight Books, 1996.

Nunez, Ralph da Costa, and Oliver Cannell. *Homeless Families in New York City: The Public Policies of Four Mayors, 1978–2009.* New York: Institute for Children, Poverty, and Homelessness, 2010.

O'Connor, Alice. *Poverty Knowledge: Social Science, Social Policy, and the Poor in Twentieth-Century U.S. History.* Princeton: Princeton University Press, 2002.

———. "The Privatized City." *Journal of Urban History* 34, no. 2 (January 1, 2008): 333–53.

O'Connor, Stephen. *Orphan Trains: The Story of Charles Loring Brace and the Children He Saved and Failed.* Boston: Houghton Mifflin Harcourt, 2001.

Orphan Asylum Society. *The Constitution and Laws of the Orphan Asylum Society of the City of New-York.* New York: David Longworth, 1808.

———. *Annual Reports.* New York.

Osofsky, Gilbert. *Harlem: The Making of a Ghetto; Negro New York, 1890–1930.* 2nd ed. New York: Harper & Row, 1971.

Ovington, Mary White. *Half a Man: The Status of the Negro in New York.* New York: Longmans, Green, 1911.

Oxford English Dictionary Online. Oxford University Press, 2009.

Patterson, James T. *Americas Struggle Against Poverty, 1900–1994.* Cambridge: Harvard University Press, 2000.

Pickett, Robert S. *House of Refuge; Origins of Juvenile Reform in New York State, 1815–1857.* Syracuse: Syracuse University Press, 1969.

Plunz, Richard. *A History of Housing in New York City: Dwelling Type and Social Change in the American Metropolis.* New York: Columbia University Press, 1990.

Pozzetta, George E. "The Italians of New York City, 1890–1914." PhD diss., University of North Carolina, 1971.

Pritchett, Wendell E. *Brownsville, Brooklyn: Blacks, Jews, and the Changing Face of the Ghetto.* Chicago: University of Chicago Press, 2002.

Radford, Gail. *Modern Housing for America: Policy Struggles in the New Deal Era.* Chicago: University of Chicago Press, 1996.

Rainwater, Lee. *The Moynihan Report and the Politics of Controversy: a Trans-action Social Science and Public Policy Report.* Cambridge: MIT Press, 1967.

Recchiuti, John Louis. *Civic Engagement: Social Science and Progressive-Era Reform in New York City.* Philadelphia: University of Pennsylvania Press, 2007.

Riccio, James, Nadine Dechausay, David Greenberg, Cynthia Miller, Zawadi Rucks, and Nandita Verma. *Toward Reduced Poverty Across Generations: Early Findings from New York City's Conditional Cash Transfer Program.* New York: MDRC, March 2010.

Richmond, John Francis. *New York and Its Institutions, 1609–1872. A Library of Information, Pertaining to the Great Metropolis, Past and Present.* New York: E. B. Treat, 1872.

Riis, Jacob A. *How the Other Half Lives: Studies Among the Tenements of New York.* New York: Charles Scribner's Sons, 1890. Reprint, Cambridge: Belknap Press of Harvard University Press, 2010.

———. *The Children of the Poor.* New York: Charles Scribner's Sons, 1908. Reprint, New York: Arno Press, 1971.

Riordon, William L., and Terrence J. McDonald. *Plunkitt of Tammany Hall: A Series of Very Plain Talks on Very Practical Politics.* Boston: Bedford Books of St. Martin's Press, 1994.

Rischin, Moses. *The Promised City; New York's Jews, 1870–1914.* Cambridge: Harvard University Press, 1962.

Roberts, Sam. "A Once Homeless Woman Advances, but Her Suit Does Not." *New York Times,* October 5, 1992.

———. *America's Mayor: John V. Lindsay and the Reinvention of New York.* New York: Columbia University Press, 2010.

———. "Burden of Proof Is Shifted To Applicants for Shelter." *New York Times,* January 4, 1995, sec. NY / Region.

Romasco, Albert U. *The Poverty of Abundance: Hoover, the Nation, the Depression.* New York: Oxford University Press, 1965.

Rosegrant, Susan. *Linda Gibbs and the Department of Homeless Services: Overhauling New York City's Approach to Shelter.* Cambridge: John F. Kennedy School of Government, 2007.

Rosenberg, Carroll Smith. Religion and the Rise of the American City. Ithaca: Cornell University Press, 1972.

Rosenwaike, Ira. Population History of New York City. Syracuse: Syracuse University Press, 1972.

Ross, Steven J. "'Objects of Charity': Poor Relief, Poverty, and the Rise of the Almshouse in Early Eighteenth-Century New York City." In Authority and Resistance in Early New York, edited by Conrad Edick Wright and William Pencak. New York: New-York Historical Society, 1988.

Rossi, Peter H. Down and Out in America: The Origins of Homelessness. University of Chicago Press, 1991.

Rothbard, Murray Newton. America's Great Depression. Auburn, AL: Ludwig von Mises Institute, 2000.

Rothman, David J. The Discovery of the Asylum: Social Order and Disorder in the New Republic. Glenview, IL: Scott, Foresman, 1971.

Ryan, Mary P. Cradle of the Middle Class: The Family in Oneida County, New York, 1790–1865. Cambridge, UK: Cambridge University Press, 1981.

———. The Empire of the Mother: American Writing About Domesticity, 1830 to 1860. New York: Institute for Research in History and the Haworth Press, 1982.

———. Women in Public Between Banners and Ballots, 1825–1880. Baltimore: Johns Hopkins University Press, 1992.

Salmon, Marylynn. Women and the Law of Property in Early America. Chapel Hill: The University of North Carolina Press, 1989.

Sanchez, José Ramón. "Housing Puerto Ricans in New York City, 1945 to 1984: A Study in Class Powerlessness." PhD diss., New York University, 1990.

Sánchez Korrol, Virginia. From Colonia to Community: The History of Puerto Ricans in New York City. Berkeley: University of California Press, 1994.

Scherzer, Kenneth. The Unbounded Community: Neighborhood Life and Social Structure in New York City, 1830–1875. Durham, NC: Duke University Press, 1992.

Schneider, David M. The History of Public Welfare in New York State, 1609–1866. Chicago: University of Chicago Press, 1938.

Schneider, David M., and Albert Deutsch. The History of Public Welfare in New York State, 1867–1940. Montclair, NJ: Patterson Smith, 1969.

Schretzman, Mary Anne. Making Homelessness History: Innovative Strategies to Reduce Homelessness in NYC. New York City Department of Homeless Services, January 2006.

Schumach, Murray. "Welfare Cases in Hotels Called a Modern Horror." New York Times, November 23, 1970.

Schwartz, Alex. "New York City and Subsidized Housing: Impacts and Lessons of the City's $5 Billion Capital Budget Housing Plan." Housing Policy Debates 10, no. 4 (January 1999): 839–77.

Schwartz, Joel. The New York Approach: Robert Moses, Urban Liberals, and Redevelopment of the Inner City. Columbus: Ohio State University Press, 1993.

Secret, Mosi. "A New First Stop for Homeless Families." City Room, May 3, 2011. http://cityroom.blogs.nytimes.com/2011/05/03/a-new-first-stop-for-homeless-families/.

Sexton, Patricia Cayo. Spanish Harlem: An Anatomy of Poverty. New York: Harper & Row, 1965.

Shaw, Albert, and William Thomas Stead. "Relief for the Unemployed." The Review of Reviews, 1894.

Sheehan, Susan. A Welfare Mother. Boston: Houghton Mifflin, 1976.

Shefter, Martin. Political Crisis, Fiscal Crisis: The Collapse and Revival of New York City. Morningside ed. New York: Columbia University Press, 1992.

Shinn, Marybeth, et al. "Predictors of Homelessness Among Families in New York City: From Shelter Request to Housing Stability." American Journal of Public Health 88 (1998): 1651–57.

Shoemaker, Nancy. A Strange Likeness: Becoming Red and White in Eighteenth-Century North America. New York: Oxford University Press, 2006.

Simkhovitch, Mary K. Neighborhood: My Story of Greenwich House. New York: Norton, 1938.

Skocpol, Theda. Protecting Soldiers and Mothers: The Political Origins of Social Policy in United States. Cambridge: Belknap Press of Harvard University Press, 1995.

Society for the Prevention of Pauperism in the City of New York. Annual Reports of the Managers. New York.

Soffer, Jonathan M. Ed Koch and the Rebuilding of New York City. New York: Columbia University Press, 2010.

Spann, Edward K. The New Metropolis: New York City, 1840–1857. New York: Columbia University Press, 1981.

Stansell, Christine. City of Women: Sex and Class in New York, 1789–1860. Urbana: University of Illinois Press, 1987.

Steinhauer, Jennifer. "Mayor's Welfare Plan Embraces Job Training." New York Times, May 16, 2002, sec. NY / Region.

Stern, Sol. "The Screws Are on the Welfare System Down and Out in New York; Relief in the Raw State Investigator Waiting for help Boss of the 'Whiz Kids.'" *New York Times,* October 22, 1972.

Tavernise, Sabrina. "Percentage of Americans Living in Poverty Rises to Highest Level Since 1993." *New York Times,* September 13, 2011, sec. U.S.

Tax Policy Center, Urban Institute and Brookings Institution. "TPC Tax Topics | EITC", 2010. http://www.taxpolicycenter.org/taxtopics/encyclopedia/EITC.cfm.

Teitler, Julien O., Nancy E. Reichman, and Lenna Nepomnyaschy. "Sources of Support, Child Care, and Hardship Among Unwed Mothers, 1999–2001." *Social Service Review* 78, no. 1 (March 1, 2004): 125–148.

Terkel, Studs. *Hard Times; an Oral History of the Great Depression.* New York: Pantheon Books, 1970.

"The New Slavery? Workfare in New York." *The Economist (US),* October 5, 1996.

Bayor, Ronald H. and Timothy Meagher, eds. *The New York Irish.* Baltimore: Johns Hopkins University Press, 1996.

Thomas, Lorrin. *Puerto Rican Citizen: History and Political Identity in Twentieth-Century New York City.* Chicago: University of Chicago Press, 2010.

Thomas, Piri. *Down These Mean Streets.* New York: Knopf, 1967.

Thompson, J. Phillip. "The Failure of Liberal Homeless Policy in the Koch and Dinkins Administration." *Political Science Quarterly* 111, no. 4 (1997): 639.

U.S. Census Bureau. "S1702 Poverty Status in the Past 12 Months of Families, 2010 American Community Survey 1-Year Estimates." *American Fact Finder,* December 13, 2011. factfinder2.census.gov.

United Press International. "New York City Sued on Homeless." *New York Times,* July 27, 1983, sec. NY / Region.

United States Work Projects Administration. *Urban Workers on Relief.* New York: Da Capo Press, 1971.

Wald, Lillian D. *The House on Henry Street.* New York: Henry Holt, 1915. Reprint, New Brunswick, NJ: Transaction Publishers, 1991.

Wall, Diana diZerega. *The Archaeology of Gender: Separating the Spheres in Urban America.* New York: Plenum Press, 1994.

Waugh, Joan. *Unsentimental Reformer: The Life of Josephine Shaw Lowell.* Cambridge: Harvard University Press, 1997.

Welter, Barbara. "The Cult of True Womanhood, 1820–1860." *American Quarterly* 18 (1966): 151–174.

White, Shane. *Somewhat More Independent: The End of Slavery in New York City, 1770–1810.* Athens: University of Georgia Press, 1991.

Wiberley, Stephen Edward, Jr. "Four Cities: Public Poor Relief in Urban America, 1700–1775." PhD diss., Yale University, 1975.

Wilentz, Sean. *Chants Democratic: New York City and the Rise of the American Working Class, 1788–1850.* New York: Oxford University Press, 1986.

Wilson, William Julius. *The Truly Disadvantaged: The Inner City, the Underclass, and Public Policy.* University of Chicago Press, 1990.

"Workfairness Marchers Demand 'Real Jobs, Not Workfare Slavery.'" New York Beacon, September 2, 1998.

Wulf, Karin. *Not All Wives: Women of Colonial Philadelphia.* Ithaca: Cornell University Press, 2000.

Yezierska, Anzia. *Bread Givers: A Novel.* Garden City, NY: Doubleday, 1925. Rev. ed. New York: Persea Books, 1999.

Zipp, Samuel. *Manhattan Projects: The Rise and Fall of Urban Renewal in Cold War New York.* New York: Oxford University Press, 2010.

Index

Maps, illustrations, and photographs are indicated by bolded page numbers.

Acknowledgements

This book is the result of almost three years of creative thinking and lively discussion with past and present staff of the Institute for Children, Poverty, and Homelessness and of Homes for the Homeless, one of the nation's largest transitional-housing providers for families. In addition, an invaluable group of research assistants — Sara Johnsen, Rebecca Amato, Oliver Cannell, and Sam Reider — tirelessly pored over many volumes, researching and locating all of the images and providing helpful feedback on the writing. Special thanks go to Rebecca for checking and fixing all of the citations. Cliff Thompson edited the entire manuscript several times, correcting errors and improving the prose.

We are grateful to the New-York Historical Society, the Lower East Side Tenement Museum, the New York Public Library, the American Jewish Historical Society, the New York City Municipal Archives, and City Hall Library for assistance with research and for permission to publish material from their collections. A special mention goes to Eric Wakin and the rest of the staff at the Columbia University Rare Book and Manuscript Library for unparalleled attention to our manuscript and image research and for enthusiastic support of the project. Thanks also to the Community Service Society for their interest in this project and for permission to use their records and images.

Finally, we should acknowledge the many struggling families from the past and present whose lives are represented in these pages. We realize that this book provides only the slightest recognition of the difficulties they faced. It is our hope that *The Poor Among Us* not only will provide a fresh historical perspective to help those with power and authority seize the kinds of opportunities missed in the past, but will also engender the resolve to address the root causes of present-day poverty and family homelessness.